AF538520

FROM ACORN TO OAK TREE

A Personal History
of the Establishment
and
First Quarter Century Development
of the
South American Missions

•

By
Frederick Salem Williams
and
Frederick G. Williams

•

Published by
Et Cetera, Et Cetera Graphics
3026 Brea Boulevard • Fullerton, California 92635

ISBN 0-944329-00-4
Library of Congress Catalog Number 87-82300
Printed in the United States of America

TABLE OF CONTENTS

PART IV: APPENDICIES

PREFACE

THE SOUTH AMERICAN continent covers twelve percent of the earth's surface and contains six percent of its inhabitants, or approximately 260 million people as of 1986. Her people represent nearly every race and language, but the major populations are of European, Amerindian and African descent. Of the literally hundreds of languages, dialects and creoles spoken, the two most widely used European languages are Portuguese and Spanish (English, French and Dutch are also official languages), with large populations of Italian, German, Arabic and Japanese speakers spread throughout the twelve independent nations and one colony. Of the many native languages spoken, the most common are of the Guaraní-Tupí group, located mainly in the Amazon basin, and the Quechua-Aymará group from the Andean highlands.

South America is full of contrasts. It has the world's largest rain forest, the Amazon, and its driest desert, the Atacama. The highest mountain in the the Western hemisphere, Mt. Aconcagua, rising to 22,834 feet, is located here. It also contains the world's largest river, the Amazon, which discharges into the Atlantic fourteen times the volume of water the Mississippi River does.

South America was the seat of highly developed Indian nations, including the Chimu, Tiahuanaco, Chibcha and Inca empires. For more than a decade it was also the capital of the Portuguese monarchy and for a half century Rio de Janeiro was the capital of the Brazilian empire. Lima, Peru, was also the site of the richest of the Spanish viceroyalties.

Many changes, political as well as social have occurred in South America since 1925. Perhaps the most significant event was World War II, which fostered industrialization and a rapid shift away from an agrarian economy toward an industrial base. Rural migration to the cities created staggering problems, swelling urban populations to several millions. Telecommunications, and air travel, now span the continent. Throughout South America there continue to exist deep and persistent political and social problems, exacerbated by serious financial challenges. Despite these problems, however, the continent has continued its phenomenal growth.

Sixty years ago there were no Mormons in South America. As of April 1986, there were some 790,000 members of The Church of Jesus Christ of Latter-day Saints organized into more than 170 stakes and thirty missions. In addition, there are six temples operating or in various stages of construction in Brazil, Argentina, Colombia, Peru, Chile and Ecuador—half the continent's countries. The first native Latin American to be called as a General Authority was Angel Abrea, from Argentina. The second was Hélio da Rocha Camargo, from Brazil. Both were called to the First Quorum of the Seventy.

This phenomenal growth was prophesied by the founder of the first South American mission, Elder Melvin J. Ballard of the Quorum of the Twelve Apostles. After serving for nine months with his companion, Rey L. Pratt of the Council of Seventy, and before his return to the United States, he said:

> *The work will go forth slowly for a time just as the oak grows slowly from an acorn. It will not shoot up in a day as does the sunflower that grows quickly and then dies. Thousands will join here. It will be divided into more than one mission and will be one of the strongest in the Church. The work here is the smallest that it will ever be. The day will come when the Lamanites here in South America will get the chance. The South American Mission will become a power in the Church.*[1]

The period of slow growth was a period of sinking roots, an exciting epoch filled with challenges, disappointments and successes equal to and perhaps surpassing that connected with the establishment of the Church in any land or region. In our chronicle of the events of this period, we have attempted to view them through subjective eyes, rather than through official pronouncements, public postures and documents, although these also form a part of our narrative. We have tried to make the personal reflective of a general trend, but always couched in a broader context of world events. Things done some fifty years ago may seem primitive by today's standards. These were never-to-be-repeated adventures with different cultures, peoples, and languages.

During the first quarter century, only one General Authority of the Church visited the area. No other official Church representative came to South America. The mission presidents who served there were, therefore, much more independent than they are today, and had to rely much more on their own judgments and on the Spirit for direction. South America was a long way from Church headquarters and communication was poor at best.

My son and I have worked together to compile this history. I have provided the basic narrative by recounting stories and experiences which he then edited, checked for historical accuracy and often rewrote or expanded in several places with information taken from my papers and correspondence, from the files at the Church Historical Department, and from other sources.

In 1964 I began writing "The History of My Life," whose format will encompass a total of eight volumes. Five have been written, three of which form the basis of this book. In the late 1960's, we decided to publish a history of all the South American missions from 1925 to 1975. We wrote a prospectus and sent it to all the former mission presidents and important individuals whose lives enriched the story. Although dozens of individuals wrote us letters, only two provided narratives: President Howells on Brazil, (see Appendix C), and President Young, who wrote and published his own history on Argentina, which he then graciously presented to us. We gathered documents, compiled statistics, and began in-depth studies of the countries involved. But without the input of the other contributors, our ambitious plans were frustrated.

PREFACE

What we have in this book is neither the full story nor simply my own biography. We have tried to give some cohesion to the chronicle by using my own experiences as the narrative vehicle. Gaps in my life are partly filled by the brief notes called "Interregna" which come at the close of the first two parts. Since each mission had similar components, and to avoid repetition, we have chosen to focus on different aspects whenever possible. For example, we did not stress music in Argentina, although it was present. We did not stress sports in Uruguay, although a sports program existed in that mission. We did not recount the proselyting techniques used in each mission, but tried to be both selective and representative. The format for the arrangement of the chapters in each section is the same: a chapter entitled "Prelude" covers the period immediately preceding my arrival in that mission field, followed by a chapter on the country itself, one or two chapters that focus on an unusual or significant event or situation, a chapter or two dealing primarily with the missionary efforts, and two chapters dealing with the members and mission activities.

From the beginning of this project, the Church Historical Department has graciously offered us its facilities and services, including a grant to my son during the summer of 1973 to research its archives. We are personally grateful to Dr. Leonard J. Arrington, then Church Historian, and his associates for their interest and support. We also wish to single out Sara M. Stohl for special recognition and express to her our deep-felt gratitude for her unselfish work; first, for typing the entire manuscript, and then serving as overall editor. Without her untiring efforts this project would not have become a reality.

Of paramount importance were the generous grants received from Gerald R. McQuarry of Downey, California, and Junius E. Driggs of Mesa, Arizona, which made possible the publication of this work. Other contributors include Wilford M. Farnsworth, Los Angeles, Franklin D. Richards, Jr., Salt Lake City, Keith J. and Argina W. Morris of Mesa, Arizona. We also owe a debt of gratitude to R. Hector Grillone and his son Virgil N. Grillone of Et Cetera Graphics for their support and professional craftsmanship, and to Thomas C. Clark and James B. Welch of Santa Barbara, California, who carefully read the typescript in the final stages and made valuable suggestions.

Finally, we especially wish to acknowledge the efforts of the men and women who were called to labor in South America. Searching through the General Church Directories and Church Almanacs, we find that of the 800 plus missionaries who served in the four missions during the first quarter century, dozens were subsequently called to serve as bishops, stake presidents or members of stake presidencies, and patriarchs. Forty-four have been called to serve as mission presidents, twenty-one have been called as regional representatives, two as temple presidents: Harold Brown, Mexico City Temple, and Samuel Borén, Lima Temple. Seven have been called as General Authorities: James E. Faust (Brazil) of the Council of the Twelve Apostles, William Grant Bangerter (Brazil), Robert E. Wells (Argentina), Gardner H. Russell (Argentina), Richard G. Scott (Uruguay), Teddy E. Brewerton (Uruguay), and Lynn A. Sorenson (Brazil), all of the First Quorum of the Seventy.

For their hospitality, friendship and faith, we dedicate this book to the members, past and present, of the Church in South America.

Frederick Salem Williams
Frederick G. Williams
Downey, California
August, 1987

NOTES

1. The quotation was written down by Elder Sharp on the day it was given. See "James Vernon Sharp interview, The Church of Jesus Christ of Latter-day Saints Oral History Program," p. 10, Church Historical Department.

PART I

THE SOUTH AMERICAN MISSION (1925-1929)

INTRODUCTION TO PART ONE

"Here we are on the deep, bound for Chili *[sic]*, S.A., self, Phebe and R. Allen." *Thus begins Parley P. Pratt's letter to his family, dated on board the* Henry Kelsey, *September 15, 1851. A few months before, Apostle Pratt had been called as President of the Pacific Mission, an immense field of labor which included, as he explained,* "all the islands and coasts of the Pacific," *with unofficial headquarters in San Francisco. An account of President Pratt's trip to the Pacific coast of South America with his wife and Elder Rufus C. Allen, their brief residency in Valparaiso, Chile, their lengthy stop-over in Perú on the return voyage, and his observations are carefully chronicled in his* Autobiography.

[On the people:]

The chillians *[sic]* are a mixed race of Spanish and Indian blood. . .whilst a few are white and even fair and beautiful. In general they are ignorant and devoted Catholics. Probably more than one half of them can neither read nor write. Their knowledge of arts and industry is extremely limited. In manners they are simple, frank, and extremely sociable and apparently affectionate, but subject to a small low meanness in their dealings, and to trifling thefts. There are, however, many honorable exceptions to those faults or evil habits.

[On religious practices:]

On inquiry, we were informed that this kind of worship prevailed throughout Spanish America and various other countries, and that it is called by the dignified name of Christianity, and that it is very ancient...Priestcraft reigns triumphant in all these countries.

[On government:]

Revolutions have been in progress more or less in nearly all Spanish America during the past year.

[On his lack of skill in Spanish:]

The civil wars, and my own pecuniary circumstances, but more particularly the want of language, prevented my travelling much in the country. . . .

We cannot say with certainty whether Elder Pratt's reports doomed further missionary activities in South America; the fact remains, however, that it would be some seventy-five years before another mission was attempted.

The South American Mission began very auspiciously with the presence of three General Authorities in Argentina in 1925 (one of whom was P. P. Pratt's grandson), but it soon suffered from a kind of benign neglect. The promise to Father Lehi's descendents found in the Book of Mormon notwithstanding, South America was given little attention. Four years after its establishment, I constituted one third of the missionary force on the entire continent: two elders in Argentina, one in Brazil. Yet, Assistant Church Historian Andrew Jensen had traveled there in the interest of Church history in 1923, and the Improvement Era *dutifully published articles on the progress of the little branches from time to time.*

Although it began as a mission to the German immigrants, first in Argentina and then in Brazil, the work soon commenced among the Spanish-speaking people, many of whom were immigrants from Spain and Italy. In the first ten years of its existence, the South American Mission saw 56 missionaries baptize 265 members. From this humble beginning—the acorn that was prophesied would grow slowly—came a mighty oak that continues to spread its branches throughout the land.

CHAPTER I

PRELUDE: PREPARATION OF AN 18-YEAR OLD

EARLY IN THE FALL of 1926, Elder Melvin J. Ballard spoke at the Phoenix Ward; he had just returned after opening the South American Mission and he told us of his wonderful experiences there. He recounted the trip he and his fellow General Authority, Rey L. Pratt, had taken on their way home, going by train from Buenos Aires to La Paz, crossing Lake Titicaca by boat, then continuing by train to Cuzco.

He told of the grandeur of Machu Picchu and the ruins of Sacsayhuaman fortress above Cuzco, and of their trip from that old Incan capital by train to Arequipa and then to the seaport of Mollendo. He told how they boarded their ship by means of a basket from a lighter. When their ship stopped at Lima's port, Callao, they went to the capital city to visit the museums where they saw sheets of gold cut into the size of plates. From Callao, they sailed north through the Panama Canal and finally disembarked in New York.

His story enthralled me. After the meeting, I talked with Brother Ballard and expressed a desire to serve a mission in South America. It was the first time I had ever really wanted to be a missionary. My family had urged me many times to consider a mission, but this was the first time I had seriously thought about such a possibility.

My bishop, James R. Price, interviewed me shortly thereafter. My call came early in December; Bishop Price was now stake president and his brother, George F. Price, was the new bishop. My friend, Paul Davis, had been interviewed at the same time and also received a call to that mission.

I had been instructed to report to the Mission Home in Salt Lake City on January 17, 1927. During that busy December, I bought a wardrobe trunk, shoes, socks, shirts, razor blades and countless other things, not knowing whether they would be available in far-off Argentina. A friend, Eli Swain, fitted me for a mail order suit. I also bought a new overcoat.

The ward members decided they would raise the money to send Paul and me to South America. They raised enough for the third class fare from New York to Buenos Aires: $125.00. I don't recall the cost of the rail fare from Phoenix to Salt Lake City and from there to New York City. As it turned out, we received a letter from Salt Lake City just before we left Phoenix stating that missionaries should no longer travel third class, so we needed more funds in a hurry. We raised money by sponsoring dances. The bishop arranged for all the young girls to line up and kiss us at the last dance, which became our farewell. We had a wonderful time.

Most of the ward members were present at the Union Station in Phoenix for our departure. It was a tremendous send off that January 15, 1927, and Paul and I were ready to begin the greatest adventure of our lives. We again kissed the girls goodbye, and just as the train started to move, my sister Beth said, "Fred, kiss Mother, kiss Mother, Fred." I was busy at the time receiving an orange from a young lady, but I finally got all the family kissed and the train pulled out.

Paul and I sat very quietly after the train started rolling, each busy with his own thoughts, trying to comprehend what lay ahead. We were both appreciative of what the ward had done for us, and we were especially grateful to our families. My brother Orin bought a trunk and the additional clothes that I had been unable to buy. My eldest brother Orlando sent me an Elgin pocket watch (which I still have) and a suitcase. My mail order suit arrived the day before I left. The suit material was beautiful, but it was about two sizes too large. However, it was too late to send it back.

The young do not think too deeply or very long on coming events, so we began to enjoy our train ride. We crossed into California and then Nevada before entering Salt Lake City on a cold January 17th morning at five. The climate was much colder than we were accustomed to in Phoenix. The snow didn't impress us as much as it chilled us. Salt Lake City looked ugly and dingy near the station. The snow was black from the coal soot belching from the chimneys.

Paul and I reported to the LDS Mission Home, 26 North State Street, at nine in the morning. We were still tired from our long train ride, but felt refreshed after a hot bath at the home of my sister, Naoma W. Seaich.

We met the directors of the home, Brother and Sister LeRoy C. Snow, who welcomed us together with more than two hundred other young people from every walk of life who had come to Salt Lake City in response to a call to represent their Church throughout the world. He didn't say it, but I'm sure Brother Snow on more than one occasion must have thought: "Lord save Thy Church! It must be true since it progresses in spite of the missionaries."

What a group to work with! Students, school dropouts, farmers, salesmen, carpenters, jacks-of-all trades; boys and girls in their teens, middle-aged men and women, senior citizens: we were all there. Poor Brother Snow. He had just two weeks to make church representatives of us before sending us into the world like sheep thrown to the wolves.

The missionaries assigned to Stateside missions were given rooms in the Mission Home. Those assigned to foreign missions (a small minority) took over the Whitehall Hotel on State Street.

I don't know why we were so favored as to be put on our own in a hotel away from the supervision of the mission president. Consider for a moment those who were to go to South America: Douglas B. Merrel, from Graham County, Arizona, a married man with four children; his first separation from his wife. Elder Merrel was well educated and proficient in Spanish, but he was the most homesick person I had ever seen. His roommate, Fred J. Heinz, fresh from his father's potato farm near Rexburg, Idaho, was seeing the big city of Salt Lake City for the first time. Half his words were German; we soon learned a lot of cuss words.

My companion was my friend, Paul Davis. He had quit school a couple of years before and had worked at odd jobs since. He knew a lot of Tex-Mex and understood some Spanish.

My background hadn't exactly prepared me for sainthood. I had always been active in the Church, but my friends were mostly nonmembers until I moved to Phoenix. By the time I was seventeen, I was an accomplished pool player and had no trouble beating all my Mormon companions. I had participated in many nonmember activities that aren't especially recommended in the MIA Activity Manual. I was just eighteen and ready to meet the world on this cold January morning in Salt Lake City. My diary contains a few meager notes about my activities in Salt Lake City. Not too many entries deal with spiritual matters:

. . . Nearly had a gang fight in the hotel defending Arizona in its comparisons with Utah and Idaho. . . . Took pictures on Temple grounds and went through the museum. . . ground covered with snow. . . . Were shown through the temple and went clear to top floor. Went on sightseeing tour of Capitol and visited the governor's room. . . . Heard organ recital in Tabernacle. Edward P. Kimball was at the organ. . . . Went to Naoma's for supper, then went to the Blue Bird (a dance hall). . . . Saturday night we went to the Orpheum Theater. . . . Visited the Relief Society. In the evening we had a program. Paul and I played our harmonicas and sang some songs in Spanish. . . . Played basketball in the gym. Our hotel group beat room "D" by big scores. . . .

There was, of course, much more than just these activities. Twice we went to the Salt Lake temple, and these were enjoyable and instructive occasions. We received instruction from the General Authorities and from civic leaders. So many people tried to polish the rough stone of our character and give it a little luster.

Evan Stephens, then an elderly man, tried to impart to us some of his great musical talent. He tried to make music directors out of us. He tried to teach us to sing. He said the most important thing was to start on the right pitch, and that we should all have a pitch pipe. Many times later, I wished I had taken his advice when leading a song without accompaniment; I had to stop and start several times until I got the right pitch.

Brother Stephens was a short man, bowed under the weight of years. He used a small portable pump organ to accompany us when we sang. He would say, "Now let's sing 'School Thy Feelings, Oh, My Brother.'" He would then take his pitch pipe from his pocket and sound it. "Did you hear that? That is the proper pitch for this song." Then, seated at the organ he would begin to play a prelude. Suddenly, he would think of something, some direction concerning how the song should be sung, some emphasis to be given certain parts. He would stand up, the better to be able to talk to us, but kept one foot on the pedal and both hands on the manuals. He never missed a note. The instructions completed, we eventually got to sing the song, although usually we were interrupted many times before its completion. We weren't the Tabernacle Choir, but we enjoyed this great and good man.

Setting apart blessing. On Tuesday, January 25, 1927, I was set apart as a missionary of The Church of Jesus Christ of Latter-day Saints by Elder Melvin J. Ballard, a member of the Council of the Twelve, to serve in the South American Mission. My sister Naoma took the blessing down in shorthand:

Brother Frederick S. Williams, in the authority of the holy priesthood, I lay my hands upon your head and set you apart as a missionary to go to the South American mission even as you have been called, to labor as a minister of Christ, in these the last days. I give unto you the power of the priesthood and bless you as a witness for God. Heed the whisperings of the still small voice and teach the gospel to those with whom you are in contact every day that the kingdom of heaven may be established again upon the earth. And as you go forth acknowledging your Heavenly Father, things shall be made known to you for the advancement of His holy cause; he shall enlighten your undertanding, that the things of God shall be made known to you. You shall grow in comprehension

> *and knowledge and shall be able to preach the Gospel in the Spanish language, for that language you shall be able to learn quickly. Listen always to the whisperings of that still small voice and the spirit of the Lord shall be upon you to take you to the homes of the honest in heart and the words to say to them shall be given unto you by the Spirit that it will convince them that it is the truth. You will be as an example before all men. Be prayerful, be diligent in the Lord's work in that land and you shall be successful and you will be the means of bringing souls from darkness into the fold of Christ.*
>
> *I bless you that you may have a safe journey to go in peace and return in safety and go protected from hardships and all harm, having the spirit of the Lord over you at all times to protect you. The Lord has an important work for you to perform; therefore, go speedily to the field and you shall be blessed with great success. The power of God shall attend you lest at any time you shall be defiled before the children of men. I seal you up and set you forth in the power of the Holy priesthood in me vested and in the name of Jesus Christ. Amen.*

Before leaving the Mission Home on Friday, January 28, we went to the Church Office Building to shake hands with those General Authorities present. As we went down the line, each was asked to give his name, his home and the mission to which he had been called. As I shook hands with Anthony W. Ivins, the Second Counselor in the First Presidency, I told him my name was Frederick S. Williams, one of the first times I had used my full name since the third grade when my teacher told me it was too long. "Was your father's name Frederick G. Williams?" he asked. I told him yes, I was his son. "How nice it is to meet you," he replied. "Your father was my personal friend. We labored together in the Colonies of Mexico. He was a father you could be proud of, a very good man." I was embarrassed at the length of time he spent with me, but at the same time I was proud to have heard these words from such a man as President Ivins.

Later that evening, Paul and I dined at the home of the parents of James Vernon Sharp, who at that time was serving in the South American Mission. The Sharps were most hospitable and we enjoyed the evening. As we left, Brother Sharp presented each of us with two silver dollars.

Salt Lake City to Mission Field. Friday, February 4, 1927: We left Salt Lake City on the Union Pacific railroad at nine that evening. Besides Elders Merrel, Heinz, Davis and me, there were several others who would travel to Europe from New York. We all traveled in the chair car and slept whenever we could. The mountains, covered with a mantle of snow, looked very cold from our warm car. Saturday morning's light showed us some of Wyoming and Colorado. As we rode eastward we realized that we were retracing the steps of the Mormon pioneers. Sunday, we arrived in Chicago and hired a car to tour that city quickly, the largest I had ever seen, but it was too cold to enjoy.

We changed trains and continued to Buffalo, New York. There, at 7:00 a.m. on Monday, we again changed trains for Niagara Falls, which we toured by car. We saw the Falls from both the United States and Canadian sides. They were frozen over, so we were able to go over and under them. We could hear the roar of the water flowing under its ice cap. This was a most impressive experience.

We also toured the factory where Shredded Wheat cereal is made, and we were treated to a breakfast of cereal with cream and strawberries.

On Wednesday, February 9, we arrived in New York City, which impressed me as large, dirty, cold and crowded. Perhaps I got off to a poor start. When our train arrived at the station we were met by a proper New Yorker, a representative from our hotel, dressed very stylishly and wearing a bowler hat. He carried a cane, although he was just a few years older than we and in apparent good health. We tried to make friends with him but he soon made us feel that he was doing us illiterate Westerners a great favor and that talking to us wasn't part of his job. Other New Yorkers behaved the same. Even the restaurant waiters wouldn't accept our silver dollars, believing they were not legal tender.

After checking in at the Cornish Arms Hotel, we went to the Argentine Consulate and secured our visas, then picked up our steamship tickets. The following day we toured New York City and then took a small ferry to the Statue of Liberty. I climbed up to the head and looked out of the windows in the band that encircles her forehead. She didn't seem to mind my being there at all. What a fantastic view for a boy who had never seen the ocean before. I could see the entire city as well as the harbor and docks where ships from exotic places were being loaded and unloaded.

S.S. Western World. We left New York City on Saturday, February 12, 1927, Lincoln's birthday. When we left the hotel, it was snowing. After a short taxi ride we went aboard the Munson Line ship, S.S. *Western World,* and were shown to our second class staterooms. Paul and I shared a stateroom and our two companions had another. We quickly stowed our gear and began to explore the first ship I had ever been on. We were served a wonderful lunch and were all pleased to learn that we could order anything we wanted and eat all we desired. This was living.

By 2:00 p.m. the ship was ready to sail. People crowded the dock to see their loved ones and friends depart. The orchestra played and people threw serpentine and confetti. We didn't know a soul, but joined in the festivities anyway. We were in a wonderland of our own; we went all around the ship and decided that life would be wonderful aboard such a floating hotel. Reality soon intruded, however, when a steward told us that since we were second class passengers we shouldn't ever go into the area reserved for first class passengers. That meant that the best parts of the ship were now off limits to us.

As the young often do, after we recovered our hurt pride, we decided that it still wasn't such a bad setup. The S.S. *Western World* had been designed to accommodate two classes; first class and tourist. Popular demand required that a second class be created; so several first class staterooms were remodeled, i.e., divided, for second class accommodations. The second class dining room had been part of the first class dining area, and was separated only by a thin partition; we could hear the orchestra as well as the first class passengers. We had a nice lounge of our own, a piano, phonograph and library. Our food was the same as that served to first class passengers, and our quarters were identical, too; the only real difference between first class and second class passengers on the *Western World* was that we didn't have to pay as much.

At sea one day tends to flow into another. The passengers follow the same routine each day, arising when they desire (only if they desire breakfast, otherwise, if they are not hungry, they can sleep until noon). The most strenuous activities included games, reading, dozing, taking refreshments, looking at the ocean and sleeping again.

By February 15 it was very warm, as our ship was heading almost due south. However, the heat was a welcome relief after the blizzard that was raging in New York when we sailed. On Saturday, February 19, it rained almost all day, and the rain refreshed us after the heat. The ocean behaved itself, so none of us became seasick.

Intitiation at the Equator. On Saturday night at ten o'clock, we crossed the Equator; my first time. When the foghorn was sounded to advise us of the crossing we all ran out on deck to look for the line, but didn't see it; perhaps it was too dark. On Monday the first class passengers were initiated into the Realm of King Neptune. Dressed in strange costumes, all were tried before the king and cast into the swimming pool after being covered with egg whites and other substances. That night we sighted lights off the coast of Brazil.

On Tuesday, February 22, we saw the coast of Brazil—our first land sighting since leaving New York eleven days before. The Brazilian coast was beautiful; white sandy beaches shaded by palm trees against a backdrop of green jungle. We could see coastal steamers as well as small sailboats. That night we were served a special dinner to celebrate our sighting of the coast.

On Wednesday, although the land had disappeared, we knew we were getting closer to our first stop; the crew was making arrangements to unload the cargo at Rio de Janeiro. Thursday was very hot.

Before I describe our arrival in Rio, I should like to introduce some of my fellow passengers and members of the crew.

Two days out of New York the second class section received a new passenger moved from third class. He was an American educator, the head of a small university in Brazil, who said he preferred to travel third class because he could devote more time to his studies there. However, the president of the Munson Line discovered that he was on board and radioed the ship's captain that his quarters should be changed to first class. At first, the professor (whose name I wish I'd written down) declined this gesture, but finally agreed to move up to second class. We talked a great deal during our voyage. He didn't know too much about our church (frankly, I didn't know much more), but we did talk. He taught us some games and made our life on board much more interesting. I remember particularly one thing he said: "Have you ever read Gray's 'Elegy Written in a Country Churchyard'?" I replied that I had read it in high school. He then asked: "What, then, is the L-E-G of a dog?"

The ship's doctor was an extremely nasty man. He didn't like missionaries in general, and especially disliked Mormon missionaries. Every time he saw us, he tried to belittle us. He was usually drunk and always obnoxious. However, other members of the crew were as friendly as regulations would permit them to be.

A very congenial Argentine businessman on his way home to Buenos Aires from New York City, sat at our table for meals. His English wasn't good, but it was much better than my Spanish. I marveled at his dexterity with knife and fork, and admired his continental style of eating, the first time I had seen anyone use his utensils in that fashion. After one meal, he amazed me with his ability to peel an orange with his knife and fork without once touching it with his hands. I tried to emulate him but ended up with an orange that could only be eaten on deck under cover of darkness.

Rio de Janeiro. On Friday, February 25, I got up well before dawn to see the fabulously beautiful Rio harbor. The harbor lights formed a seven-mile long string of luminous pearls that silhouetted the mountains in the background. The rising sun showed Rio in all its glory—the most beautiful harbor in the world.

We docked at eight that morning, and later went ashore—the first time in 13 days—and walked for miles. I quote from my diary:

> *The people seem to be enjoying life in general. We walked through the residential district. The houses are built on the hills in terraces. Every spot is covered with some kind of vegetation, even the sides of the mountains. The streets are narrow and winding. Most of the people wear a sort of wooden shoe, with a cloth upper. They put their toes in this, and the heel is bare, and I thought they were going to lose them every time they took a step. Some balance boxes on their heads and juggle the shoes wonderfully. Considering everything, I like Rio better than New York. There are parks every few blocks where you can sit in the shade and cool off and enjoy the different kinds of trees and flowers. The people will not accept an American quarter, or any of our money, so we were broke until we could find a bank and change dollars into their money.*

Avenida Rio Branco was most impressive—wide and full of traffic. The wide sidewalks on the main streets were made up of rows of rare colored stones in wavy patterns which seemed to shimmer in the bright sunlight. We saw many men seated at cafés and bars, but no women; this was a man's world.

We ate our first lunch in Brazil at a restaurant. Elder Merrel, the only one of us who was fluent in Spanish, ordered for us all from the menu. I don't remember what we ate but it was good. However, we experienced culture shock when we saw that the men's restroom was in full public view. We decided to wait until we returned to the ship to freshen up.

After lunch, we rode a cable car to the top of the famed *Pão de Açucar,* the sheer Sugar Loaf Mountain that reaches from sea level to 1,155 feet, and thrilled to the view of the magnificent harbor from that elevation. We were happy, tired and awed by Rio when we sailed at six o'clock, just as the sun was setting behind the hills.

At seven the following morning we entered Santos harbor. The green hills on either side of the narrow harbor entrance were a rare treat for a native Arizonan accustomed to barren hills and deserts.

We disembarked and toured Santos by open street car. The city near the docks was very dirty, but the main residential areas were clean and lovely. We climbed all 788 steps up Monte Serrat Hill, where we could see the city in every direction. Our view included a harbor packed with ships and a beautiful beach. I wrote in my diary:

> *Rather than return down the steps we went down the back side of the hill, following a trail. The green trees and bushes were so dense that in some places we had to break our way through. There were many banana trees and much bamboo.*

In the afternoon, we visited the beach we had seen from the hilltop. The water was so warm and inviting that we went swimming and stayed in all afternoon. It was my first swim in the ocean.

Sunday morning the dock hands started loading bananas on the deck of our ship from barges pulled alongside. By noon the entire aft deck was covered with a six-foot deep layer of bananas. We bought pineapples and other tropical fruits from vendors who came alongside in small boats and ate so much that we were not hungry at meal time. Instead, we stayed on deck and watched Santos harbor gradually diminishing as we made our way to the open sea.

The bananas that covered the decks were too green to eat. We kept pinching them, but to no avail. Then the second engineer told us to bring a stock of bananas to the engine room. In a few hours they were ripe. We carried them up on deck, placed them conveniently near our deck chairs, propped our feet on the railing, and ate to our hearts' content. However, we soon noticed that the more we ate the less delicious they tasted. It was some years before I really regained my taste for bananas.

Montevideo. On Tuesday, March 1, 1927, we arrived in Montevideo, Uruguay, sailing past the hill with the fortress that had given this city its name. When the area was first sighted by a Portuguese navigator, he is said to have shouted from the crow's nest: *"Monte eu vejo,"* "I see a mountain!" But the Latin form has prevailed: "monte video."

From my diary:

> *This is a pretty city all laid out on the American plan, so to speak. But it makes me feel funny to have to give $1.04 American for each Uruguayan peso. This country has the highest value for its currency in the New World.*

Carnival was in full swing, and the entire population of the city was literally dancing in the streets. People were dressed in every imaginable costume. In addition to those dancing in the streets, crowds of people watched from specially constructed balconies on either side. We could not resist joining in the festivities. Steel frameworks had been erected at regular intervals along the major streets; from them were suspended figures of fantasy, outlined and illuminated with electric lights, which helped to create a happy mood for all. This was Mardi Gras in all its glory. It was my first carnival and I enjoyed it. I thought Montevideo was a beautiful city and that I would like to live there.

Arrival at Buenos Aires. On March 2, 1927, we arrived in Buenos Aires; my home for the next two years. The first people we met were Elders Waldo I. Stoddard, Heber M. Clegg, and Jewel C. Jensen. The street car fare from the port to the mission home on Rivadavia Street was four American cents.

I met the mission president, Reinhold Stoof, his wife, Ella, and the other missionaries already serving: Lewis E. Christian, I. Russell Spencer, and J. Vernon Sharp. The entire missionary force until our arrival consisted of six missionaries, eight counting the mission president and his wife. Our arrival increased the missionary force by forty percent.

We stayed at the mission home a day or two and then moved into our own quarters a half block away. The following day we picked up our trunks from the customs house and registered at the American consulate.

Since first hearing Elder Ballard speak at the old Phoenix Ward, I had looked forward to visiting the place where the South American Mission had been dedicated. My missionary companions were as interested as I, and after satisfying the residency requirements for Argentina and obtaining adequate living quarters, we urged the longer-term missionaries to take us there.

Parque Tres de Febrero at that time was only partially improved. The north portion was still a wilderness of willow trees, underbrush and tangled vines. As we traveled toward the park, I thought of the three men chosen to open the mission and how they must have had feelings similar to mine. I was a stranger in a strange land who had followed their path from Salt Lake City to Buenos Aires, and now I was on my way to the spot where they had turned the key for the preaching of the gospel on the South American Continent, an action that had made it possible for me to serve in that distant land. In my mind, I relived the hours when my own ship had entered Buenos Aires, the rigors of going through customs for the first time, and then the joy of seeing people of my own faith as I left the port area. The three Brethren had had the same experiences only sixteen months before.

CHAPTER II

ARGENTINA: AN OVERVIEW

ABOUT ONE-THIRD the size of the Continental United States, Argentina is well suited for human occupancy, particularly in the pampa area, that vast fertile plain about the size of Texas which stretches out in a huge semicircle from Buenos Aires. Argentina's wealth lies in its agriculture, especially wheat, cattle, sheep and hogs that thrive on the great interior *estancias*.

Argentines are the most homogeneous of all Latin Americans. Although there are Indians in the northern provinces near Bolivia and Paraguay, Argentina's population is predominantly of European stock, principally from Italy and Spain, but with representation from Germany, France, Russia, England, and even Wales.[1]

At the peak of the world's transatlantic migration, from 1821 to 1932, six countries absorbed ninety percent of the total; the United States was first and Argentina second.[2] Most of the immigrants to Argentina were from the poorer classes of society, and they flocked to Buenos Aires, swelling the population from 230,000 in 1869 to 2,035,000 in 1914. Fully forty-nine percent of the inhabitants of Buenos Aires in 1914 were foreign-born.[3]

An important dichotomy marking the first century of Argentine independence was the struggle between the *porteños* (sophisticates of Buenos Aires) and the *provincianos* (inhabitants of the rural interior pampa). Often the legendary *gaucho* (glamorous, but still uncouth) won the advantage for the federalists, as the *provincianos* called their political party; the *porteños* were the *unitarios*.[4]

Following the tumultuous years after independence was declared in 1810, and the years of chaos under the dictatorship of the *provinciano*, Juan Manuel de Rosas, from 1829 to 1853, Argentina became united by the constitution of 1853 and the presidents who followed. The period between 1860 and 1930 was one of progress and relative stability. Two great presidents, Mitre and Sarmiento, established the basis for a great nation. Bartolomé Mitre served from 1862 to 1868. He was succeeded by Domingo Faustino Sarmiento, the noted educator and diplomat sometimes referred to as the Abraham Lincoln of South America.

When I arrived in Buenos Aires in early 1927, the country was still coasting on the momentum created by those two great men, but with a significant change. The previous governments had been in the hands of a small, conservative minority, which derived its wealth and power from the huge interior *estancias*; with the coming of the great waves of Italian and Spanish immigrants a new class was formed.

This tremendous influx of foreigners, most of whom came to the city to become the labor force and entrepreneurs, became the basis for the growing middle class society. When this group organized itself politically it became the voice of the people opposing the wealthy landowners on the one hand and the city sophisticates on the other.

At the head of this middle class party (organized in 1892) was Hipólito Irigoyen, a radical who conformed more or less to the picture of the typical leader of the Latin American radical-liberal movements that flourished at this time, especially in Uruguay, Chile and Mexico:[5]

> *His platform included electoral reform, rights of petition and speech, constitutional liberties, and representative government.*

However, other liberal aims were not included:

> *Economic reforms such as land division, collective bargaining, and social legislation were barely considered.*[6]

Irigoyen became president in 1916 and his election marked the first time in Argentine history that the common people could vote. The law of 1912, which he helped pass, provided for universal and compulsory male suffrage. After its enactment Irigoyen's election was assured. The people demonstrated their elation by unhitching the horses from his carriage and pulling it through the streets of Buenos Aires to his inaugural ceremony.

The radicals held power from 1916 to 1930: first Irigoyen, then Marcelo T. Alvear, each for the constitutional term of six years; then Irigoyen again, for a term cut short after two years by revolution.

Alvear was president when I arrived in 1927; he was the grandson of one of the great generals of Argentina's war of independence from Spain. I saw him from a distance during one of the national holidays; he impressed me as being very dignified.

Irigoyen's second term was a disaster; it was even more arbitrary, chaotic, wasteful and corrupt than his first. A year after I left Buenos Aires, he was overthrown by the military; the beginning of a series of military juntas that have plagued Argentina until the present. The rejoicing at Irigoyen's election in 1916 was nearly as great as that shown in 1930 when he was ousted:

> *In the interval the Radicals had fulfilled so little of the promise of 1916 that their record could have been summed up as a failure even if their fall had not been so ignominious and definitive.*[7]

One of the main reasons for Irigoyen's ouster was his inability to cope with the worldwide depression which followed the stock market crash of 1929. That Irigoyen was seventy-six and senile when elected to his second term didn't help matters either. When the Depression hit, the populace blamed the government and rebelled.

In general the Argentines have traditionally been friendly toward the United States and its citizens. President Sarmiento had implemented many of our public school practices in his own country and had always written and spoken in admiration of the United States. During this time of turmoil, however, many tried to blame the United States for the ills suffered by Argentina.

As I recall, the monetary exchange rate was stable while I was on my mission; about two Argentine pesos and forty centavos for one U.S. dollar. When I returned as mission president in 1938, it was about 4.30 Argentine pesos for one U.S. dollar.

I cannot overstress the impact of the immigrants on Buenos Aires. I remember seeing the specially built ships which brought thousands each year and the *Hotel de Imigrantes* run by the Argentine government, roughly the equivalent of Ellis Island, which housed all immigrants when they first arrived. There they were fed and housed and given a medical checkup, all free. Until their papers were in order, they were not allowed to leave the hotel compound.

With so many foreigners making up the humbler, lower and middle classes, the class which we missionaries most successfully proselyted, it is understandable that well over half of the initial members of the Church were foreign-born. Church records show that from 1925, when the mission was opened, until 1929, the end of my mission, sixty baptisms were performed in Argentina. Of these persons, twenty-three were born in Argentina while thirty-seven were foreign-born.[8]

COUNTRY OF ORIGIN OF CONVERT BAPTISMS
1925 — 1929

Year	Germany	Italy	Spain	Ireland	Yugoslavia	Portugal	Argentina	Total
1925	6	-	-	-	-	-	-	6
1926	-	3	1	-	-	-	1	5
1927	2	-	3	-	-	-	8	13
1928	6	3	6	1	1	1	10	28
1929	2	1	1	-	-	-	4	8
Totals	16	7	11	1	1	1	23	60

NOTES

Chapter II

1. See my column in the California *Intermountain News* entitled "Americalogical Corner," where I published a series of nine articles on the Welsh colonies in Argentina; January 4, May 10, July 5, August 3, September 13, October 11, October 18, November 1 and December 13, 1973. The Welsh settled primarily in the South in the province of Chubut.

2. See Arthur P. Whitaker, *Argentina* (Englewood Cliffs, New Jersey: Prentice Hall, Inc., 1964), pp. 53, 54.

3. *Ibid*, pp. 56, 57.

4. Cf. James L. Busey, *Latin America, Political Institutions and Process* (New York: Random House, 1964), pp. 127, 128.

5. Martin C. Needler states, "Irigoyen in Argentina, Alessandri in Chile, were surely cut from the same cloth as Clemenceau, Lloyd George, and Woodrow Wilson. Batlle y Ordoñez (in Uruguay) deviated from the general pattern somewhat in lacking the dictatorial personality and in being prepared to go further to the left in his social policies." See *Latin American Politics in Perspective* (Princeton, New Jersey: D. Van Nostrand Company, Inc., 1963), p. 27.

6. Lewis Hanke, *South America* (Princeton, New Jersey: D. Van Nostrand Company, Inc., 1959), p. 66.

7. Whitaker, *Argentina*, p.65.

8. Records of the South American Mission, Church Historical Department. Since the initial six members baptized in 1925 entered the Church before the official opening of the Mission, their names do not apear on the Mission records. I have assumed that all six were born in Germany.

Not included in these figures are the five members baptized in Joinville, Brazil, in 1929, all members of the Sell family, originally from Germany.

CHAPTER III

THE ORIGINS OF THE SOUTH AMERICAN MISSION

Three Elders went sailing
Off into the South,
They were Melvin and Rulon and Rey,
To preach to the people
The Gospel's glad sound,
But not knowing how long they would stay.[1]

The early morning mist still shrouded Darsena Norte as the S.S. *Voltaire* slowly entered the port of Buenos Aires on Sunday, December 6, 1925. This late fall day was an historic one for the three emissaries who were eager to reach their destination to begin the Lord's work there.

Elders Melvin J. Ballard, Rulon S. Wells, and Rey L. Pratt were on a mission that would eventually affect the lives of hundreds of thousands of people in every country on the South American Continent, and they were anxious to begin their ministry. Elder Ballard had just turned fifty-two; Brother Pratt was fifty-eight and Brother Wells was nearly seventy-two.

There had been a farewell banquet in their honor by the General Boards of the MIA in the Beehive House on October 28, 1925.[2] Among the 140 people present were President Heber J. Grant and his Counselor, Anthony W. Ivins, as well as many members of the Council of the Twelve.

Elder Orson F. Whitney first gave a humorous, then a serious speech. Ruth May Fox composed an original poem in their honor, read by Preston Nibley. In response, Elder Ballard expressed his determination to do his best to further the cause of the Lord in that new land, but hoped that his associates would not feel disappointed in the results, nor expect too much. ". . .Everything that is in me, with God's help, I will give to this new mission, but I know that I cannot succeed without God's help. I go, and I will stay as long as the brethren want me to stay."[3]

President Pratt was not at the reception, as he was still in Mexico, but Rulon S. Wells, also a member of the First Quorum of Seventy, responded with these words: ". . .We are not going on a pleasure trip. May we have the help of the Lord in establishing this work in that land. I go with that feeling and knowledge."[4]

President Heber J. Grant said that the Brethren were not overestimating what the elders would do. "They are sent with a belief that it is a duty we owe to the whole world to preach the gospel to all nations whatever the results might be . . . 'I have listened to the remarks of the brethren with interest. I shall be satisfied if we only make a humble start in that southern land. We, each and every one of us, have a knowledge of the truths of the gospel. We are ready to go to the ends of the earth, and go willingly, to bear our message. We are rewarded by our work when we do it.' "[5]

As their ship docked the Brethren looked expectantly for some sign of recognition from the few people at dock side. A large crowd of people jostled for vantage points along the steel fencing surrounding the port facilities. All were excited. Each one waved, hoping to attract the attention of friends or loved ones on board, but the distance was too great to make recognition possible.

After the port formalities were completed, the first class passengers disembarked. As they prepared to leave the ship, their last connection with their North American homeland, what nostalgic thoughts must have passed through their minds. But now the time had come for action. With the aid of Elder Pratt's fluent Spanish, the Brethren cleared Immigration and customs easily. They collected their luggage and made their way to where new friends waited for them.

German Saints in Argentina. Wilhelm Friedrichs, Emil Hoppe, and their families had been converted to the gospel in Germany. During their two years' residence in Argentina they had missed its activities and tried very hard to interest their friends in the gospel.

The Church Historical Department has a file containing early correspondence between Wilhelm Friedrichs and Church leaders in Salt Lake City and Germany. The file is not complete, and it is probable that most, if not all, are English translations of the German originals. From the correspondence we can surmise that the Friedrichs and Hoppes had emigrated together from Germany about 1923. Their membership records had been in the Cologne Conference of the Church. Along with a letter dated March 24, 1924, from Conference President Clyde H. Wilcox, the families were sent Certificates of Identification to serve in lieu of membership certificates which, the letter instructed, should be requested directly from the Presiding Bishopric's Office in Salt Lake City.

The Presiding Bishop, Charles W. Nibley, spoke German; he and Brother Friedrichs began to exchange letters. Even though he had not been called to serve as a missionary, Brother Friedrichs' letters are filled with reports of his missionary activities. On May 2, 1924, he explained that most of his contacting efforts were through newspapers or through his work, with some tracting on the side:

> *About the things which concern the mission here, it is going very hard because one cannot go from house to house, but can only work through newspapers and at the work places, because one must not go in the houses, but must remain standing on the street and make a noise with his hands, and then if somebody comes out and accepts a tract, it is well, but in most cases they will not accept.*

In another letter, he reported on the newspaper articles he had published in the German newspaper, possibly the *Argentinisches Tageblatt,* and of the meetings held during the month of April at which investigators were present:

> *With joy I inform you that on the 6th of April, the Church was given public mention here. I had an article in the German newspaper about "The Apostacy and Restoration of the Gospel of Jesus Christ." There were two friends present*

at our meeting. The next Sunday, April 15th, I made no announcement, but one woman was present. On Sunday, April 20th, I had an article about the "Appearance of Angels in the 19th Century." Four men were there, and I sold one "Voice of Warning" and gave away eight tracts. That is a report about the lectures. On the 27th of April, I had a public meeting for the Church and there were no friends present, but members came, and I had much joy in having a meeting. The spirit of the Lord was with us in rich abundance.

In a subsequent letter he speaks of converting part of his home to a room for Church meetings, and that in the absence of an organ, his son accompanied the hymns on a mandolin. He also reported that he had joined forces with Brother Hoppe who lived two hours away by street car:

In our dwelling here, we have arranged a meeting room, but it is not perfect. We have no organ, but when we have been here another three months, I will buy one. We now help ourselves with a mandolin, which my son plays. . . .

We have now joined with Brother Hoppe, so that on Thursday evenings, at 7 o'clock, we have Bible Class at his dwelling. He lives outside of the City, and I must ride two hours with the street cars in order to get to him, but I will gladly do that if only somebody comes in order to hear the Gospel.

On September 10, 1924, in addition to reporting his missionary activities to Bishop Nibley, he asked for a loan from the Church so that he might build his own home, which would also be used as a meeting place for the Church. The loan was granted. On December 15, 1924, he reported that some friends had expressed a desire to be baptized and had already begun to pay tithing. On April 15, 1925, he summarized the work in the following manner:

The Branch here is in a good condition. The friends admonish the Saints to remain steadfast in the faith. The friends pay tithing, which seems hard to do for the members, but it ought to urge the members in the fulfillment of their duties.

We have held Sunday School and Meetings each Sunday from January 1st to April 1st. In our Sunday School we have been studying the "Articles of Faith," now we are taking up "Church History." We have prospects of gaining new friends. We always have friends with us, but whether they will join the Church, I can't say.

Anna Kullick, and Ernst Biebersdorf and Mrs. Biebersdorf have requested to be baptized. Mr. Kullick also attends meetings now. At first he was against us, but since his wife attends to her duties he comes to our meetings and I believe that when missionaries come he will consent to baptism, and possible [sic] his children. Mrs. Kullick has a strong faith in the Gospel.

In a letter dated June 29, 1925, Brother Friedrichs explained that the investigators as well as the members were keeping the Word of Wisdom, and that to aid in the missionary effort he had written and printed several copies of a short tract. He also explained that meetings were being held in three different locations: Dock Sud, Liniers, and Lanús all suburbs of Buenos Aires. Then, believing his previous letter had gone astray, he renewed his request that the Church send missionaries to Argentina:

> *Last year I forwarded you newspapers and a map of Buenos Aires, also a letter in which I made reference to a possible land purchase by the Church. Have you received them? Please let me know. Also when we might expect some missionaries. Our house is open to them just like it was in Germany. It is possible that more saints will come here from Germany. Brother Uebel would like to come with his family. This would mean a choir leader for us. If we could only help them, but—I hope to find a German who can speak Spanish so that we can labor among the Spaniards and hold meetings with them.*

On May 28, 1925, after the death of Charles W. Penrose, Bishop Nibley became Second Counselor to President Heber J. Grant, and Sylvester Q. Cannon was appointed Presiding Bishop. In a letter dated June 24, 1925, Bishop Cannon advised Brother Friedrichs of the change and explained what had been done about his original request for missionaries for Argentina:

> *We have taken up with the Presidency the matter of sending missionaries to the Argentine, but so far nothing definite has been decided. However, we are making inquiry with regard to suitable men who can speak the German and Spanish languages. I shall be glad to learn from you, at your convenience, about how many Germans are located in Buenos Aires, and whether there are other German colonies throughout that country.*

Brother Friedrichs' service to the Church was invaluable. His proselyting activities included newspaper articles, writing, printing, and distributing tracts, delivering lectures and conducting various religious services. Largely because of his interest and efforts the South American Mission was ultimately established. When missionaries arrived they found six people ready for baptism; it would be some time before that feat would be duplicated.

Sadly, Brother Friedrichs did not continue with the faith of his initial convictions. Although he was not cut off from the Church, his ardor for the gospel cooled in later years, initially perhaps because he was not made a leader of the mission, a position he may have felt he deserved. He had difficulty paying back the loan on his home, and as late as 1945 still owed the Church money. When President W. Ernest Young presided in Argentina the second time, he attempted unsuccessfully to dissuade Brother Friedrichs from the folly of some of his revelations and doctrines.[6]

Dr. de Jong's search for the right man. From the late Dr. Gerritt de Jong, Jr., Dean Emeritus of the Brigham Young University College of Fine Arts, we learn more about the search for someone in the Church who spoke both German and Spanish. On August 16, 1967, Dr. de Jong sent us the following account:

> *I taught at LDS University in Salt Lake City from 1919 to 1925. In April, 1925 I promised Dr. Franklin S. Harris, president of BYU, to come to Provo in August to organize the College of Fine Arts, and be a professor of modern*

languages there. Not long after this, I received a letter from the Presiding Bishopric, signed by Brother Wells, the counselor to Brother Sylvester Q. Cannon, Presiding Bishop. In it, he said that Brother Cannon wanted to see me about mission matters, and invited me to be there at the Presiding Bishop's office on North Main Street at 9:00 the next morning. You can imagine that I was there promptly. I thought, this is just my luck: now that I have promised to go to BYU as Dean of the College of Fine Arts and a Professor of Modern Languages—now the Church wants to send me to preside over a mission somewhere. I could see the whole thing clearly: Brother Charles Hyde wanted to come home from the Netherlands Mission. Or could it be that they wanted to send me as a replacement for Brother Tadje in the German Mission? Then again I thought, surely I would take the place of Brother Rey L. Pratt, who had been president of the Mexican Mission for lo these many years.

Brother Sylvester Q. Cannon and I were close personal friends, for his brother, Tracy Y. Cannon, and I had had our music studios together at 44 East South Temple in 1914-1915, where Brother Tracy Y. Cannon had been stake chorister and I stake organist of the Pioneer Stake. Brother Sylvester Q. Cannon had been a member of the stake presidency.

Bishop Cannon asked me who there was in the Church who could speak both German and Spanish fluently, that could be sent to South America to begin mission work there. He knew that I, as a teacher of modern languages and faithful worker in the Church, would know personnel of that kind. After thinking a long time, I told him that I could give him quite a list of outstanding church members who spoke German and French fluently, and also a goodly number that could speak French and Spanish fluently, but I could think of only two persons in this group who spoke German and Spanish fluently: Professor G. Oscar Russell, and myself. After Brother Cannon had thought about it for a while, he decided that Brother Russell did not have the right kind of personality to do this sort of job. Then, turning to me, he said, "We cannot send you, you are needed right here." You can imagine that that relieved my feelings considerably. Not that I didn't want to go on a mission, but it would certainly be a great upset of plans for me to go at that time.

After talking back and forth a while, Brother Cannon suggested that probably the proper way to do this would be to send someone from the Quorum of Twelve Apostles, since a representation of the First Presidency, especially in opening a new mission, was properly the concern of the Quorum of the Twelve. But since no member of the Quorum at that time could speak both German and Spanish, Brother Cannon further suggested that two men be sent along with the member of the Quorum of the Twelve, one to speak German and one to speak Spanish.

The wisdom of the First Presidency in choosing its emissaries became apparent. President Pratt spoke excellent Spanish, already useful in dealing with the Argentine customs officials, and President Wells was equally at home in German and could communicate with the waiting Saints and their friends.

First meeting. The Friedrichs and Hoppes and their friends met the elders at the port and then took them on a two-hour ride by street car to the Friedrichs home at 1462 Bariloche Street, where they had lunch. Then the three elders checked into the Grand Hotel and later attended a cottage meeting at the home of Ernst Biebersdorf at 1830 Irala Street in Dock Sud; the first meeting of the new South American Mission. It was held in German and President Wells translated. Nine local people attended the meeting and the gospel seeds began to germinate. That same evening (December 6) Elder Ballard sent the following cablegram to President Grant: "Arrived; all well; pleasant voyage." The following day he received this reply: "Congratulations; holiday greetings; all well."[7]

The Brethren spent only that first night in the Grand Hotel because of its excessive rates (thirty-two pesos per day). They lodged in the Cervantes Hotel located at 1367 Rivadavia Street until December 11, when they moved their living quarters to 1301 Santa Fe Street, Apartment C, in the center of Buenos Aires. It was not pretentious, but was very expensive, $190.00 per month.[8]

On Saturday, December 12, 1925, one week after the arrival of the missionaries, they met with the German members and friends on the bank of the La Plata River, and Elder Melvin J. Ballard baptized Anna Kullick, Ernst Biebersdorf (brother of Anna Kullick), Jacob Kullick (husband of Anna), Maria Biebersdorf (wife of Ernst), Herta Kullick (daughter of Anna and Jacob), and Elisa Plassman (daughter of Elizabeth Friedrichs by a previous marriage). Brother Ballard records that on the next day, Sunday, December 13, all were confirmed members of the Church.

> *At four p.m. in the home of Jacob Kullick, at Lanús, the first Sacrament and confirmation meeting was held. All of the Saints and some friends were present, and the following were confirmed members of the Church: Anna Kullick, by Melvin J. Ballard; Ernst Biebersdorf by Rulon S. Wells; Jacob Kullick by Rey L. Pratt; Maria Biebersdorf by Melvin J. Ballard; Herta Kullick by Rulon S. Wells; Elisa Plassman by Rey L. Pratt. . . .*
>
> *The Sacrament was administered by Elders Rulon S. Wells and Rey L. Pratt; in all this work English, Spanish and German was used.*[9]

On December 16, the Brethren called on Dr. Carlos M. Noel, the Mayor of Buenos Aires, who assured them that there would be no interference with their missionary activities. They had been given a letter of introduction by United States Ambassador P. A. Jay, who had received them the previous day, but was full of prejudices against Mormons. I've often thought what a shame it was that they did not go then to the national government officials and apply for the *Personería Jurídica,* the official document that would have granted the Church the right to proselyte in Argentina.

Dedication of the mission. Early on Christmas morning on a beautifully warm and sunny summer day, Elders Melvin J. Ballard, Rulon S. Wells, and Rey L. Pratt journeyed to Tres de Febrero park near the banks of the La Plata River, to hold a very special meeting. They sought solitude in a grove of willow trees, and at seven a.m. began the dedicatory services for the official opening of a continent to the preaching of the gospel of Him whose birthday the Christian world was celebrating that day. Before the offering of the dedicatory prayer, they sang: "The Morning Breaks," "Hail to the Brightness," and "An Angel from on High."

President Pratt read from the Book of Mormon (1 Nephi 13, 2 Nephi 31 and 3 Nephi 21). President Wells read Genesis 29:22 to 26, and Elder Ballard offered the dedicatory prayer, after which they sang "Praise to the Man." Each of the Brethren spoke briefly concerning their mission and their willingness to do their best to establish the work; they also spoke of their perfect love for one another and for the work of the Lord. They blessed one another, and felt that as the result of the opening of this mission, many Europeans in the land would receive the gospel, but that ultimately the great import of the mission would be to the Indians, the descendants of Father Lehi.[10] The prayer offered that Christmas morning 1925 is:

> *Our Father who art in heaven, hallowed be thy name. In the name of Jesus Christ, thy well-beloved Son, we thy servants approach thee on this beautiful Christmas morning, in this secluded spot, in the city of Buenos Aires, Argentina, South America, in a land far distant from our mountain home, but in a country which thou hast called a part of the land of Zion.*
>
> *We are very thankful for our safe arrival, after a voyage of twenty-one days on the seas, without a moment's sickness. We do acknowledge that thou didst temper the elements for our good, and that thy protecting care has been over us in our travels, both upon the land and the sea. And for health, and strength to labor for thee and thy cause.*
>
> *We are grateful that we have been chosen by thy servant, President Heber J. Grant, to come to this great land of South America, to unlock the door for the preaching of the gospel to all the peoples of the South American nations, to search out the blood of Israel that has been sifted among the Gentile nations, many of whom, influenced by the spirit of gathering, have assembled in this land.*
>
> *Put thy spirit into their hearts, that they may receive us as true messengers sent of God, for their salvation. Help us to labor for them with the same spirit in us he had, who loved men so that he died for them, that we may effectually "call, persuade, and invite" men to come unto Christ. We thank thee for the few who have received us and for those we have had the joy of taking into the waters of baptism in this land. May they be the first fruits of a glorious harvest.*
>
> *We pray that we may have the opportunity to present to the people the message which thou hast sent us to deliver, namely, that angels sent by thee have visited the earth in this dispensation, bringing to men again the everlasting gospel; that John the Baptist did visit the Prophet Joseph Smith, upon whom he conferred the authority to baptize; that Peter, James, and John did ordain him an Apostle of the Lord Jesus Christ, and endow him with the keys of the Holy Priesthood, with authority to baptize with fire and the Holy Ghost and to organize the Church of Jesus Christ again in the earth; and that Moroni, thine ancient prophet of the Americas, did visit Joseph Smith and deliver into his hands the plates containing a history of the early inhabitants of this land; and that by thy power Joseph Smith did translate the characters on the plates from which he obtained the Book of Mormon; and that he was visited by thee and thy Beloved Son, who committed into Joseph's hands a great and new gospel dispensation for all flesh.*

We are thankful that we are the bearers of these glad tidings to the peoples of the South American Nations.

We also pray that we may see the beginning of the fulfillment of promises contained in the Book of Mormon to the Indians of this land, who are descendants of Lehi, millions of whom reside in this country, who have long been downtrodden and borne many afflictions and suffered because of sin and transgression, even as the prophets of the Book of Mormon did foretell. But thou didst inspire those prophets to promise their descendants that thou wouldst bring forth in the latter-day the records of the fathers, and that when these records were presented to their children, they would begin to believe, and when they would do this, thy favor would return unto them. And then thou wouldst remember the promises made to their fathers, that if their descendants would repent and receive the gospel, they would begin to be prospered and blessed on the land and would again become a white and a delightsome people.

Oh, Father, let thy spirit work upon them and manifest the truth of these things unto them, as we and thy servants who shall follow us shall bear witness of thy precious promises unto this branch of the House of Israel.

Father, bless thy Church in all the earth; continue to guide those whom thou hast called to lead it with wisdom and power to direct it forward to fulfill its great mission in the earth.

Sustain thy servants who labor as missionaries in all parts of the world, that they may have the opportunity and power to warn all men that the hour of judgment approaches, and that thou hast offered, through the gospel, a means of escape from the calamities that shall come upon all flesh, unless they repent.

Remember in mercy the "Hope of Israel"—the youth of thy Church who are to bear the responsibilities of the future, that they may keep themselves clean and undefiled from the sins of the world, that they may be found worthy of their inheritance and come to their glorious destiny.

Bless those who are their shepherds, the watchmen upon the towers of Zion, that they may guard well the flock, and be able to feed with the bread of life the sheep and the lambs.

We present for thy kind consideration, the members of our own families, from whom we are separated; who are now, and have in times past sacrificed much, that we may carry the gospel to the children of men. May health and life attend each one, and the good cheer thy Spirit brings, be with them, and above all, keep them from sin, and bless them with faith in thee and thy gospel.

Bless the presidents, governors, and the leading officials of these American countries, that they may kindly receive us and give us permission to open the doors of salvation to the people of these lands. May they be blessed in administering the affairs of their several offices, that great good may come unto the people, that peace may be upon these nations that thou hast made free through thy blessings upon the valiant liberators of these lands, that righteousness may be obtained and full liberty for the preaching of thy gospel prevail.

Stay the power of evil, that it shall not triumph over thy work, but that all thine enemies shall be subdued and thy truth be triumphant.

And now, oh, Father, by authority of the blessing and appointment of thy servant the President of the Church, and by the authority of the holy apostleship which I hold, I do turn the key, unlock, and open the door for the preaching of the gospel in all these South American nations, and do rebuke and command to be stayed every power that would oppose the preaching of the gospel in these lands; and we do bless and dedicate these nations and this land for the preaching of the gospel. And we do all this that salvation may come to all men, and that thy name may be honored and glorified in this part of the land of Zion.

Help us to bring men to thee and thy Son, and speed the day when he shall come to rule as King of kings and Lord of lords, and for all thy blessings which shall bring success to our labors we shall ascribe honor and power, and glory to thee for ever and ever. Amen.[11]

In the course of the day's activities Elder Pratt used his pocket knife to cut the date into the bark of a willow tree to indicate the exact place where the South American Mission was dedicated.

When I visited the tree, sixteen months later in 1927, it still seemed hallowed ground to me. I felt the same spirit when I returned in 1928 and 1929. The spirit was no less strong when I took my wife there in 1938 after we had been called to preside over the Argentine Mission. I had an impulse then to return with a saw and cut off and preserve the still legible carving, but regrettably did nothing about it. On a subsequent visit I found that all the trees had been cleared away; the exact location of the dedication ceremony has been lost forever.

First meeting in Spanish language. The first Spanish language meeting was held in the home of William Friedrichs on December 27, 1925. Six Spanish-speaking visitors were present. The second meeting took place on January 1, 1926, in Rogelia Molares' home on Segundo Patrón Street in Liniers; thirty people attended. Rogelia joined the Church three years later, and was confirmed by me December 8, 1928. While I was Mission President, I performed her marriage ceremony.

The Brethren held regular cottage meetings with the German saints and in the homes of a few Spanish-speaking contacts; but they needed a hall. After several unsuccessful attempts to rent one for the purpose of holding religious services they decided to convert one room of their apartment into a meeting hall; but they attracted no visitors. The area where they lived was the civic and business district of downtown Buenos Aires. I was told that only one person, aside from the German saints and their friends who held one or two meetings there, ever entered the hall. It turned out that he was a bit intoxicated and had gone to the wrong address.

Elder Wells had been ill almost continuously since their arrival, and had begun to vomit and suffer severe dizzy spells. On January 14, 1926 he returned to the United States because of a condition diagnosed as brain hemorrhages. His departure created a communications problem with the German members, most of whom spoke no Spanish. The procedure in the Sunday meetings with the German saints and investigators became very complicated but remained highly spiritual. Elder Ballard would speak in English, Brother Pratt would translate the message into Spanish and Elisa Plassman, a twelve-year old girl, would translate it into German.[12]

Because of the lack of success in the Santa Fe Street area, on February 10, 1926, the Brethren moved to 8968 Calle Rivadavia, then touted as the world's longest street. The move put them much nearer to the members in Liniers; the new location served as the mission headquarters until September 1927.

The new facilities were not pretentious. A hall large enough in which to hold meetings faced the street. The living quarters were attached to the hall at the rear. One room served as the mission office. The kitchen and bathroom were detached from the main building, and behind these was a large garden with some fruit trees.

The Brethren bought and painted cane bottom chairs. They also bought a pedal pump organ and a large leather couch, both second hand. (Incidentally, the organ was still in use in the Liniers chapel when I visited in 1958.) Elder Ballard was an excellent organist and had a highly trained voice. The members who knew him in Argentina still remember him playing and singing "I Know that My Redeemer Lives" and "I'll Go Where You Want Me to Go." The leather couch served its purpose well; it was still the main piece of furniture in the mission home during my tenure from 1938 to 1942.

Proselyting methods. To find adults willing to listen to the message of the restored gospel was very difficult; all seemed indifferent. Each meeting, either in German or in Spanish, attracted only fifteen to thirty people. The Brethren turned to the nation's leading newspapers, hoping to get broader coverage of their work through that medium, but they were disappointed. Although *La Prensa, La Nación and La Critica* usually agreed to print announcements of their meetings, they invariably failed to. Next they decided to have several thousand tracts printed in Spanish that would advertise their meetings and the purpose of their mission in South America.[13] These tracts were distributed to the people living in the vicinity of their hall. They also decided to show colored slides of ancient American ruins and to introduce the Book of Mormon. Their first meeting following the distribution of the tracts was held February 28, 1926; it was a resounding success:

> *Fully 200 people came during the evening, and many stood during the entire services. Brother Pratt gave a short account of the coming forth of Mormonism, and we presented 75 colored slides of ancient American ruins while Brother Pratt spoke of their relationship to the Book of Mormon.*[14]

This procedure, not surprisingly, attracted many children, and at times they were very unruly. Brother Ballard's report tries to maintain an optimistic tone: On Sunday, March 7, "Children were very noisy;" on Sunday, March 14, "There was much better order and interest shown;" on Wednesday, March 31, "The children were paying better attention."[15] So many children came out that an unofficial Primary was formed. Elder Ballard taught them to sing and Elder Pratt taught them a few simple but important principles of the gospel. He told them Bible stories and of the love that Jesus had for little children. He instructed them about prayer and suggested that they pray at home; that it was proper to ask the Lord's blessing upon the food before partaking of it and to thank him for it. The Brethren were taken aback to learn of the children's meager religious background.[16]

Later, as the number of children attending these meetings increased, so did the noise level:

Sunday, May 2 1926: At 6:00 p.m. had one hundred children in our meeting for them in the Hall. They are very hard to control. Have no idea of the sacredness of a meeting. Do not even know what a Bible is or of its existence.

Sunday, May 9, 1926: At 6:00 p.m. we held meeting for the Spanish-speaking children in the Hall, there being more than one hundred present, little better order than last time.

Sunday, May 16, 1926: At 6:00 p.m. we held meeting for Spanishspeaking children with one hundred ten present, better order during the meeting but some disturbance on the outside afterwards.

Saturday, May 22, 1926: We gave our Saturday night's meeting for children a trial, but the film went bad, and then the kids went bad, and pandemonium broke loose. We are getting nowhere with these children in these Hall meetings, and we think we will have to keep them all out that do not come with their parents.[17]

Brother Ballard explains with evident disappointment that the result of two months' hard work distributing tracts, inviting people, and showing slides resulted only in attracting children.

At last we did secure a place and rented all of it, a store and living quarters, and then we began to invite people to come. In the meantime, however, we had gone to our friends who live in the suburbs or outskirts of the city. That wasn't the easiest work to do, because we traveled two hours on the street car, and then walked two miles, not on paved streets, but on lanes, through fields, in mud, in dust, and all character of weather, and then when we did this all we could get to come to our meetings, for nearly two months, were children.

In time the children brought their parents.

We continued with those children, teaching them to sing, teaching them to pray, to repeat the Lord's Prayer, the Articles of Faith, and the Ten Commandments. They carried these prayers and songs into their homes, and then one parent appeared, and another, and another, and finally we organized a group meeting of adults, and continued to teach the children. The children brought their parentsand that we true in several places that had opened for us.[18]

Six-year old boy begins the work. Antonio Gianfelice, a six-year old boy who had seen the slide presentations and listened to the Brethren, asked his father at mealtime why they didn't have a blessing on the food. The father responded by saying he didn't know what he was talking about and asked Antonio where he got that idea. Antonio said he learned it from the *gringos* (Americans); although nothing came of it immediately, it gave his father "food for thought."

One evening while the Brethren were holding a meeting in the Friedrichs' home two Italians, Donato Gianfelice (Antonio's father) and his friend Domingo Quici, were visiting at the home of a third friend who lived across the street. They were told that some foreigners held religious meetings there on a regular basis. When he returned home, Donato told his wife Emilia about the beautiful singing he had heard and the North Americans who held meetings a few blocks from their home.

Emilia was interested. She asked whether women were permitted to attend the meetings. Mrs. Gianfelice was a religious person, as was her husband, but because of the considerable distance to the nearest Catholic church, she had been unable to walk to Mass with her small children; and she missed her church. Donato and his friend attended early Mass daily on their way to work, but she was unable to attend. Her husband told her that he and Domingo Quici would find out whether women could attend.

Elder Rey L. Pratt's talk in the 97th semiannual conference of the Church, October 4, 1926, contains the following recollections:

> *I recall the people that Elder Ballard referred to yesterday Donato Gianfelice and Domingo Quici, when they first came to our gathering, two Italian men came first, out of curiosity, I think. They had been in the United States a little while, many years ago, and they learned that we Americans were holding services in their vicinity. They came to our meetings, but they knew nothing about our religion. They knew nothing about the Bible. They wished to get the scriptures, and we obtained them for these men. After attending our meetings for some time, and hearing us try to teach the children to pray in Sunday school, one of the men came to me and said: "Can you get me a prayer book, so that I can pray, too?" I explained to him, as best I could, that we do not pray out of books, but just like a child would ask its father for what it wants, we ask our heavenly Father for the things that we alone know that we need. "Well," he said, "I have been a member of a church all my life, but I have never been taught to pray that way. I must confess to you that I don't know how to begin. Won't you men do me the favor to come to my house some night when I am home from work and teach me and my family how to pray?" It was one of the greatest opportunities that has ever come to me in my life, my brethren and sisters. I went with him, and we knelt around his family altar, with his wife and children and with the other man (Quici) whose family was left back in Italy, and who is struggling hard to get means to bring them over there. We were able to teach them how to pray, how to ask a blessing upon the food, and to thank God for those commonplace blessings that we always thank him for, and think very little about the great blessing that we have in knowing how to do those things.*[19]

As summer turned into fall, Elder Pratt became ill and had to remain in bed, but he was far from idle. He used the time to translate many of the hymns that now appear in the Spanish hymnbook *Himnos de Sión.*

Brother Ballard was left alone; a lesser man would have thrown up his hands in despair. Without an able-bodied companion, speaking neither German nor Spanish, his mission to open a continent for the preaching of the gospel just begun, what could he do? He prayed and he worked. Elder Ballard later told me that during this time he tracted from early morning until late at night. He distributed more than eleven thousand tracts,[20] giving them to anyone who would accept them, putting them under doors or in mail boxes. He tried to speak English to people on the street, only to receive startled looks since they understood neither his message nor his intentions.

On Sundays, Elder Pratt arose from his bed to conduct meetings while Brother Ballard played the organ; he also served as interpreter for Brother Ballard. Of course in the Spanish meetings he was in his glory. The early investigators and members remember his inspirational talks, his mastery of the Spanish language and the messages he gave. They agreed, however, that he couldn't properly pronounce the double "r"; it was much too soft; a commentary on the difference between the Mexican and Argentine methods of pronouncing Spanish words.

With winter came the dreary, cold rains that converted the dusty unpaved streets of Liniers into quagmires. The rich, alluvial soil became sticky black mud, ever increasing in depth. At first it came only to the tops of their shoes as they crossed the streets, but as the rains continued, the Brethren frequently walked in mud that reached halfway to their knees. I speak from experience: I later waded where they waded, washed my legs and shoes under the same faucets they used, and also unrolled my trouser legs to protect my cold, wet legs from the bitter weather.

In 1929, while I was reporting my mission to Elder Ballard, he remarked, shaking his head, "The most vivid memory I have of Argentina is the mud in Liniers. I couldn't believe it then. I still can't believe it!".

Because he was unused to the penetrating damp and cold and lived in a house without any heat, Elder Ballard made an error that almost cost him his life. All the Brethren's cooking was done on a charcoal brazier, which should be used only in well-ventilated rooms. Cooking in the summer posed no problem since the windows did not even have screens on them. But one cold, rainy night, Elder Ballard carried the brazier into his bedroom to try to warm himself and dry his feet. The room was closed against the wintry night air.

When Elder Pratt returned from an errand he found Brother Ballard unconscious on the floor from carbon monoxide poisoning. Elder Pratt carried him out into the cold air where Brother Ballard revived. Had Elder Pratt arrived much later, Brother Ballard would have been dead.

On June 6, 1926, additional help arrived from Zion in the shape of the new mission president, Reinhold Stoof, his wife Ella, Elders J. Vernon Sharp and Waldo I. Stoddard. These were welcome helpers in the fledgling work. The Stoofs, of course, spoke German and Elder Sharp Spanish.

Soon after President Stoof's arrival the first person of Latin descent was baptized. This took place on June 15, 1926. Ironically, she was the Brethren's only convert baptism. A very outspoken woman, Sister Sifuentes said what she pleased often and loudly. She was kind to the missionaries, however, and often invited them to her humble home to eat with her. This was a weekly event when I arrived nine months later.

Group meetings with German societies. With the arrival of the new mission president and his party, the proselyting effort took on a different complexion. For the first time in months Brother Ballard did not have to tract alone, and he quickly initiated Elders Sharp and Stoddard into this activity. Also, a new dimension was added: the group meeting. The Brethren would arrange for a German meeting to be held either at a member's home (Friedrichs, Hoppe, Kullick, Biebersdorf, etc.) or at a rented hall. Once the meeting place had been secured the entire mission force, often including Sister Stoof, would tract or visit in the neighborhood and invite the German families to attend meetings and activities.

The Brethren also capitalized on President Stoof's professional standing as a teacher. On June 17, 1926, Brother Ballard and President Stoof arranged with the Secretary of the German Teacher's Society for a lecture by President Stoof on "The Mormons and their Country." The lecture, given July 10 at the Society's hall, drew sixty-three enthusiastic listeners who warmly applauded the speaker. Later, the Society's president, Professor Wilfert, arranged for President Stoof to give the same lecture before the Society's Rosario chapter. On July 12, the Director of the German Scientific Society asked Brother Stoof to lecture at the German School at Belgrano for that society. The lecture was presented July 16 before an audience of eighty-nine. President Stoof also lectured on July 22 before a crowd of seventy-three Germans in Dock Sud. Each occasion generated interest in the Church.[21]

Meanwhile the Brethren did not neglect the regular German and Spanish meetings. Each missionary's day began with a Spanish lesson by Brother Pratt. Before long, the new arrivals were fairly well established in their work, and Elders Ballard and Pratt began to plan their return to the United States. They wanted to see the ruins of the ancient Andean civilizations, so with the permission of the First Presidency they arranged to visit the ruins of Tiahuanaco near Lake Titicaca; they then crossed the lake by boat and continued to Cuzco, and Machu Picchu. From there they traveled to Callao and then on to New York.[22]

Prophetic utterance. As many members of the American colony in Argentina celebrated Independence Day on a cold 4th of July Sunday in 1926, they were not aware of a meeting held among four of their countrymen and a group of German Saints. Had they known, they probably could not have cared less; Mormonism was somethig most of them could easily do without.

All present at that meeting wore woolen clothing, extra socks and overcoats against the chill winter air. The speaker, Elder Ballard, spoke slowly in short, English sentences, giving ample time for his thoughts to be translated by President Stoof. Elder Ballard remarked:

> *The work will go forth slowly for a time just as the oak grows slowly from an acorn. It will not shoot up in a day as does the sunflower that grows quickly and thus dies. Thousands will join here. It will be divided into more than one mission and will be one of the strongest in the Church. The work here is the smallest that it will ever be. The day will come when the Lamanites here in South America will get the chance. The South American Mission will become a power in the Church.*[23]

With these words Elder Ballard had prophesied the guidelines for the expansion of the Church on the South American Continent.

President Stoof officially took over the mission on July 15; Elders Ballard and Pratt left Buenos Aires on July 23 and arrived in New York August 31, 1926.

Brother Ballard's impact. Elder Ballard's mission was completed; he had turned the key to open the South American continent for the preaching of the gospel. He was the first General Authority to set foot on the east coast of South America, and the first since President Rey L. Pratt's grandfather, Parley P. Pratt, to visit the continent.[24] He baptized the first six members into the Church, as President Wells said, "since the time of the Nephites." He had established the work. What kind of an impression did he leave? The members and investigators I knew always spoke of him in reverent tones. Many of them would show me their right hands and say, "I shook hands with Apostle Ballard with this hand!"

Perhaps the magnetism and impact of his personality can best be illustrated by an experience told by Carmen Escudero. The occasion was a memorial service for Brother Ballard in the Liniers chapel on August 6, 1939, shortly after his death. Sister Escudero, an early investigator of the Church, attended the meetings held by Elders Ballard and Pratt. However, a number of years passed before her husband would consent to her baptism and that of her daughter Isabel. At my request, she told the following story:

> *While shopping in an open street market one morning in the summer of 1926, I chanced to see Elder Ballard with his shopping bag approaching a fruit stall. I knew that he didn't speak Spanish and was curious to know how he would make out, so I stood back in the crowd to watch.*
>
> *By using the time-proven method of pointing, he secured the desired fruit, held out paper money and waited to see if any change would be forthcoming. He then left to return to his living quarters.*
>
> *I saw the fruit merchant standing with hands on his hips, looking in the direction that Elder Ballard had gone. I approached him, and heard him say more to himself than to anyone in particular, "What a strange man!"*
>
> *"What do you means by 'strange'?," I asked. "Do you mean he is bad?"*
>
> *"To the contrary," he replied. "He didn't say a word, but there was something about his appearance, his face, his eyes, that I have never seen in anyone else. He must be a saint. I feel as though I have seen an angel!" I told him "You have.'*[25]

NOTES

Chapter III

1. The first stanza of "Three Elders Went Sailing," by Rey L. Pratt, as published in his book of verse *Just Thinking*, (Independence: Zion's Printing and Publishing Co., 1928), p. 16-22.

2. The official announcement of the opening of the Mission had been made September 4, 1925, by President Heber J. Grant. See *Liahona* Vol. 23 (Tuesday, September 22, 1925), pp. 128,129.

3. *Improvement Era*, Vol. 29 (December 1925), p. 171.

4. *Ibid.*

5. *Ibid.*

6. See letters in Wilhelm Friedrichs file, Church Historical Department.

7. See letter from Melvin J. Ballard to President Heber J. Grant, December 15, 1925, excerpts of which were published in the *Liahona*, Vol. 23 (Tuesday, January 26, 1926), p. 312.

8. *Ibid.*

9. "History of the South American Mission - 1925" (Melvin J. Ballard), unpublished manuscript, Church Historian's Office, Salt Lake City, Utah.

10. *Ibid.*

11. *Ibid.*

12. Cf. Melvin J. Ballard, *Conference Report*, 97th Semi-annual General Conference of the Church, 3 October 1926, p. 35-36.

13. Brother Ballard also wrote to the missions in Europe asking that members who had emigrated or were planning to emigrate to South America make contact with the fledgling Mission. *Millenial Star*, Vol. 88 (Thursday, March 18, 1926), p. 168.

14. Cf. Ballard, *Conference Report*.

15. See Ballard "History of the South American Mission 1925."

16. See Rey L. Pratt, *Conference Report,* 97th Semi-annual General Conference of the Church, 4 October 1926, p. 98.

17. See Ballard "History."

18. See Ballard *Conference Report,* 3 October 1926, p. 36.

19. Pratt, *Conference Report,* October 4, 1926, pp. 98-99. The Gianfelice family was baptized after the Brethren left, but from the beginning has played, and is still playing, an important part in the Church in Argentina. Little Antonio, one of the children they succeeded in attracting, was called as Bishop of the Liniers Ward when the Buenos Aires Stake was first organized. Later he was sustained as that Stake's first Patriarch; he had previously been a counselor in the Mission Presidency.

20. By adding the numbers of tracts distributed almost on a daily basis, as recorded in the manuscript "History of the South American Mission," we learn that between February 27 and June 3, 1926, the actual number of tracts personally distributed by Apostle Ballard was 11,300.

21. See Ballard "History" under those dates.

22. The actual trip home, or that portion to do with ancient American civilizations, was written up by Apostle Ballard and published together with eighteen photographs as "Ancient Ruins of South America, Some External Evidences Supporting the Story of the Book of Mormon," in *Improvement Era,* Vol. 3 (September 1927), pp. 960-973.

23. The quotation was written down by Elder Sharp on the day it was given. See "James Vernon Sharp interview, The Church of Jesus Christ of Latter-day Saints Oral History Program," p. 10, Church Historical Department.

24. In answer to a call from the First Presidency, Parley P. Pratt became the President of the Pacific Mission of the Church (which nearly included all the islands and coasts bathed by the Pacific Ocean), and in that capacity had sailed to Chile to introduce that country to the Restored Gospel. He and his party arrived November 8, 1851 and remained until March 2, 1852. See *Autobiography of Parley P. Pratt,* edited by his son, Parley P. Pratt, Jr., (Salt Lake City: Deseret Book Company, 3rd. ed. 1938), p. 397.

25. Cf. *Gaucho Gazette,* the Argentine Mission magazine, Vol. I, No. 4, September 1939, p. 2. The *Gaucho Gazette* was published in English and intended for the families and friends of the missionaries.

CHAPTER IV

R. STOOF, THE SECOND PRESIDENT

PRESIDENT STOOF invariably signed his name "R. Stoof." He often said he should have been a famous man because his signature was so short. To me and many others, he was a wonderful and extraordinary man.

Karl Bruno Reinhold Stoof was born on Pfaueninsel (Peacock Island) near Potsdam, Germany, on January 12, 1887. He attended a small school and had only one teacher until he was fourteen. An intelligent boy, he loved books and nature. Each Christmas he wished for a book. He wanted to become a gardener, but his parents insisted he become a teacher.

He traveled an hour and a half each day for three years to attend high school in Potsdam. He later attended a teachers college in the small town of Drossen, and after three years received his teaching credentials, on February 11, 1907. Three weeks later he was teaching ninety-nine children, ages six to fourteen, in a small country town three hours on foot from its nearest neighbor.

During the summer break before his last year of college he found the tract, "A Friendly Discussion," in his parents' home and took it back with him to school. His mother had received it from a man who had visited the island, and who had told her to read it, that it would give her happiness; she never did. The message in the tract interested Reinhold, but he put it aside to concentrate on his studies. During his first year of teaching, he wrote to the address on the back of the tract and received from Berlin "The Voice of Warning," "A Short History of the Church," and a Book of Mormon.

He read and studied all of these, prayed about what he read, and received a testimony of the truthfulness of the gospel. When he was ready, he wrote the mission headquarters and asked for someone to come and baptize him. Until the night of his baptism, he had never attended a Mormon meeting, nor ever met a Mormon, not even a missionary.

Two elders arrived at his village on a hot afternoon. Brother Stoof dismissed his school class and invited the missionaries to his room. He then excused himself and returned a few minutes later with three bottles of cold beer. The missionaries took the occasion to explain the Word of Wisdom, which he readily accepted. They continued to teach him gospel principles until two that morning, when he requested that they baptize him in the river. This they did immediately. It was September 21, 1907.

The elders suggested he keep his membership secret from the townspeople because of the widespread prejudice against the Church. He found a small group of members in a distant town with whom he met as often as possible:

In the spring of 1908 I found at last an opportunity to attend a Church meeting in a little town (Sorau). There were only a few members. A very strange thing happened here to me. I being 21 years at that time, saw a seven year old girl and knew at that very moment that she would become my wife. I kept this secret within my heart, did not reveal it to anyone, otherwise her mother might have advised me to apply ice packs on my head. Nevertheless, the inspiration proved to be true—18 years later that girl became my wife, the mother of seven of my children.[1]

Brother Stoof couldn't refrain from teaching the principles of the gospel to his pupils. They, in turn, shared his teachings with their parents, who were not impressed. He was transferred to another small town where he became involved in politics and crusaded against alcoholism (which he called Germany's enemy number one); here he made enemies. He learned that two missionaries had been banished from a nearby town and he wrote a protest in their defense, stating that he was a member of their faith. Thus his membership in the Church became known and he was given an ultimatum: either renounce Mormonism or be fired. He immediately resigned and went to Switzerland where he found employment in a sanitarium.

His joining the Church and giving up teaching broke his mother's heart. She and the village pastor shared their perplexity. "It is difficult to decide whether your son is a big child, a lunatic or a criminal."[2]

When World War I broke out, he returned to Germany and enlisted in the army. He was wounded during the first ten minutes of his first battle. He wrote concerning his war experiences:

I considered myself in good company with Peter and John who stated before the tribunal that one should rather obey God than man, when I ignored the Kaiser's and his general's command to "kill" and obeyed God's law, "Thou shalt not kill."

During all the war he always shot at a tree or wall, never at a soldier.

Half a year before the armistice, the English took me prisoner and they fell so much in love with me that they kept me a full year after the armistice.[3]

He enjoyed England very much and took the opportunity to learn English. He appreciated the English members of the Church who held Sunday services with him. One of the most humbling experiences of his life, he said, was to kneel, dressed in a German uniform, and bless the sacrament at the side of a man dressed in a British uniform. Their uniforms indicated they were mortal enemies, but over the emblems of the atoning sacrifice of Christ, they were brothers.

When he returned to Germany from England, he was reinstated as a teacher, but before he could begin work, he was called to serve a mission without purse or scrip during the inflationary years of post-War Germany. He was very successful. He trained teachers for the auxiliary organizations of the Church, tracted, visited, preached and translated books and hymns from English to German. Our German hymnal contains several hymns with his translations.

During this trying time, when other people were starving and without work, he never went without a meal; he was always invited to share whatever the people had. When his suits became worn, invariably some widow would say that her husband had been about his size and had left a good suit, and she wouldn't need it and would be pleased to give it to him. The Lord blessed him in his labors and he fulfilled his mission without any money.

One month after he was released he was called again to tour the mission and give illustrated lectures; this assignment lasted three months. He then tried to be reinstated as a teacher, but because he had turned down a teaching assignment to fill a mission for the Church, the government would not rehire him.

American friends helped him emigrate to the United States, where he had difficulty getting work. His first job in Salt Lake City was as an elevator boy. He quit after one hour. He couldn't get the hang of it; people who wanted to go to the main floor somehow landed in the basement. He then worked in a bakery, near the hot ovens; but he couldn't stand the heat. He wrote: "Should I consider that kind of a job as a somewhat preparatory work for some future state of mine after this mortality?" [4]

For three months he worked at the freight depot of the Oregon Short Line Railway. Then he returned to work in the office of the bakery, a job he enjoyed very much; but he was soon called as associate editor for the German weekly newspaper published by the Church, where he worked until April 1926.

In September 1925, Ella Hirte, the girl he had met eighteen years before, arrived in the United States; they were married in the Salt Lake Temple on September 11, 1925.

At the 1926 April conference he was called to be the President of the South American Mission. He was nearly forty, Sister Stoof was twenty-six. They left Salt Lake City May 6 and landed in Buenos Aires June 6, nine months before I arrived. The four week sea voyage was their honeymoon.

President Stoof was an inspired teacher and a talented musician. I sat many nights in the dark listening to him play the organ, first playing known compositions and then improvising beautiful melodies of his own.

His Spanish was meager while I served under him, but I understand he learned it well in later years. Before he gave a talk he would write it out and ask me to translate it into Spanish. I also translated directly for him in many Spanish meetings. He always felt his English was inadequate and would interrupt his thoughts to ask whether he had used the proper word. The most unkind thing he could think of to call a man was "that old guy!"

I have never heard a more forceful speaker in any language. His native language flowed from his lips, and his voice filled the room. His listeners, even those who couldn't understand him sat in awe, touched with the humility and power of the man. We also learned not to sit directly in front of him or any else who preached in guttural German.

President Stoof never lost his love of gardening, and the plants responded to his love and attention. He grew flowers and vegetables at the mission home and took delight in showing his plants and blooms to any guests he could lure into his garden. He liked to gather unusual plants and flowers, and he once showed me a small purple flower so delicate that, if touched, would immediately wilt; a few hours later it recovered. I had never seen this flower before, nor have I seen it since.

He was considerate of all things and people to a degree perhaps beyond reason. He walked miles to save a few cents because he felt the mission could not afford his car fare. He didn't want to offend anyone; however, when he felt that a reprimand was necessary, he would give one.

A lifelong student of the scriptures, President Stoof knew them better than anyone I have ever known. No marked passages appeared in his German Bible; he could open it to almost any verse he wished. We tried repeatedly to stump him in our weekly elders meetings by bringing up questions we thought had no scriptural answers. He could tell us exactly which book, chapter and verse contained the scriptures that dealt with our problems. He never ceased to amaze us. Once during a Spanish meeting, he asked me to find a certain scripture, the location of which he had momentarily forgotten. I happened to know that scripture, and was able to open my Bible and give it to him. Later he paid me the highest compliment I ever received as a student of the Bible. He said I knew it as well as he did. However, I never really came close.

President Stoof was occupied primarily with the German-speaking members and investigators and left the Spanish work to the elders who spoke that language. Since he had no companion, he asked me to go with him many times, as he did some of the other elders. He tried to teach me German and said I had a good accent. I was more interested in Spanish, although I did learn enough German to ask directions and to defend myself at the table when eating with the German people.

Ella Hirte Stoof. My mission mother was born October 1, 1900, in Sorau, a small mountain village in Germany. I'm not sure whether her parents were members of the Church at the time of her birth or were converted later. I am sure that any stranger who attended the small branch of the Church must have caught the attention of even a seven-year old girl. One visitor was a handsome twenty-one year old school teacher, from a nearby village. She didn't know it at the time, but that stranger would play an important part in her later life.

In May 1926, as the wife of the newly-called President of the South American Mission, she traveled to Argentina to start work in a new mission field and a foreign land. Their honeymoon voyage was well chaperoned, as two missionaries, Elders Sharp and Stoddard, went with them from Salt Lake City to Buenos Aires.

I thought very highly of my mission mother, although communication was always a problem. She hadn't learned very much English, having been in the States for less than a year; nor did she learn Spanish during my mission. If her husband wasn't there to interpret, we used a mixture of English, German and universal gestures.

She was a shy, provincial lady, and yet some things I saw her do were rather surprising. Of course, I was not familiar with German customs and attitudes. Several times while I was using the bathroom she would try the bathroom door and, finding it locked, would ask who was there and then engage me in conversation.

On one occasion when I visited the mission home, she excitedly asked me, "Brother Williams, do you know what's going to happen?" I replied that I didn't. "We are going to have a baby!" "That's wonderful," I responded. "When will it be born?" "In about nine months," was her answer .

I wasn't too impressed with Sister Stoof's cooking. I had never eaten German cooking in my life, and frankly, I don't think she was a very good cook. Her specialty was *Kartoffelpuffers* or potato pancakes. I think they were served with every meal I ate at the mission home. They were heavy and thick, and sometimes not completely cooked. I wouldn't have hurt her feelings for the world, but every chance I got I would put them in my pocket when she wasn't looking. Seeing my plate empty, she would promptly insist on giving me more. I hope she never knew what happened to the *Kartoffelpuffers*.[5]

Sister Stoof had a very lovely voice and frequently sang in our meetings. She preferred to sing in German, but she did learn to pronounce Spanish words and sing in that language.

At one Spanish meeting on Tonelero Street on a hot summer night, Sister Stoof held her audience spellbound as she sang one of our hymns. As I stood at the rear of the small chapel with my eyes on her face I was suddenly alerted to a possible tragedy, but could do nothing to avert it. As she opened her mouth wide to sustain a high note, I saw a fly winging its way directly into her open mouth. A startled look came over her face as she clasped her hand over her mouth and rushed to the street before losing the contents of her stomach along with the offending fly. Screens weren't introduced to Argentina until many years later.

I thought the world of this good lady. Her life was not easy. She was a young bride married to an older man, far from her native country, living in a land whose language she did not speak, surrounded by young North Americans whose culture was also foreign to her, and faced with the burden of keeping a house, cooking and cleaning, washing clothes out of doors, and all this with small babies to look after. I sympathized with her plight and did all that I could to help her.

I don't know what Sister Stoof would have done without the love and help of the local German sisters and friends. They came as often as they could to help her and give her companionship. With them she was at home and was ever grateful for their friendship and love.

President and Sister Stoof served for over nine years as Presidents of the South American Mission and were released in 1935. Realizing that jobs would be difficult to find during the Depression in the United States, President Stoof wanted to use part of his return trip ticket money to begin a new life among the German Saints in Southern Brazil. I think he would have been very happy there, and certainly his leadership would have been a great blessing to those people. But it was not to be. His letter of release from the First Presidency, dated May 7, 1935, seemed to indicate a new assignment for him to fill back home.[6] Since he was always willing to do everything asked of him, I don't think President Stoof even made his desires known to the Brethren; he simply took the letter to mean he should return to the States. I've been told that Sister Stoof was not particularly happy with the prospect of living in Brazil, anyway.

Life in the United States was miserable for them, and had it not been for the kindness of the German Saints in Salt Lake City, the Stoofs would have starved. Their deprivation was a tragedy which I feel the Church could have averted if it had known about it sooner. Of course, the Welfare Program was not yet established; nevertheless, the Church could have done more to relieve their condition.

When President Stoof did get a job after several disheartening months of rejections, it was menial. Worse, it required all his evenings and nights; not being able to attend Church at night made him nearly despondent. He says:

> *I returned to Salt Lake City with my wife and six little Argentines. For about seven months after my return I was unemployed and lived like a beggar. Employers shrugged their shoulders when they learned about my age of 49 years. At last I became a night watchman. . . . For six years I worked in that position seven days a week, probably not being able to do efficient work in six days.*[7]

Sister Stoof gave birth to their seventh child not long after they returned from Argentina, but because of their circumstances she was unable to regain her strength. In spite of her weakened condition, she continued to care for her family until her health broke completely and she died at age thirty-six on January 20, 1937, leaving her husband to care for their seven small children.

President Stoof apparently had not made his circumstances known to the Brethren. It was not until August 1937 that Elder John A. Widtsoe learned of the situation and brought the matter before the General Authorities; he acted pursuant to a note President Stoof had written him on August 17. On August 20, Elder Widtsoe answered the note explaining what had been done concerning President Stoof's plea for help:

> *I brought your case up before the Council in the temple meeting yesterday. A committee has been appointed to attempt to secure proper employment for you.*[8]

Elder Widtsoe soon left on a conference tour and was therefore unable to follow up on the committee's activities; apparently no new job was found, since, according to Brother Stoof's history, he continued his frustrating job as night watchman for an another four years.

After a very difficult period the Lord blessed Brother Stoof with a wonderful helpmeet whose identity, like Ella's, was revealed to him by the Spirit:

> *Before I found work after my return from my mission, a little North American boy joined my happy bunch of Argentines, and he was very, very welcome, in spite of my poverty. When he was only 8 months old death claimed the good mother of my children. This was the hardest blow that I suffered in my life. The Lord was merciful unto me. Again he showed me that wonderful woman who agreed to share my lot and to be the mother of my motherless chldren.*[9]

Maria Unterspann was born March 21, 1905, in Koenigsberg, Germany (now part of Russia) and joined the Church on June 3, 1925. She emigrated to the United States in May 1929 and lived for a year in Brooklyn before moving to Salt Lake City where she became a nursing aide for seven years at the LDS Hospital. She had befriended Ella Stoof when she was hospitalized for the birth of her last baby. Maria promised then that she would visit Ella and the children. She was also working at the hospital a few months later when Ella died, and she was impressed that she should make good her previous promise to visit the Stoofs. That started the acquaintanceship which led to their marriage, even though many thought she was crazy to marry a man much older than she, and with seven small children. But the spirit prevailed. They were married in the Salt Lake City Temple October 18, 1937. The money she had saved for a trip back to Germany was the basis for their economic recovery. The nightmare was over. On March 4, 1939, this lovely woman bore her husband his eighth and last child. She loved the others as her own and raised them all to be fine adults.

Eventually President Stoof got a job translating for the Church and worked at the Deseret Book Company. Still later he put his teaching skills to good use when he was hired as a lecturer at the University of Utah, where he taught German and related cultural subjects. This position was immensely satisfying to him. He also served in the German-speaking branch presidency in Salt Lake City, taught Sunday School and lectured in various wards. Before and during the War he wrote letters to the newspapers, to friends and to influential persons against the folly of Hitler's policies and general philosophy. After the War, he was on the German Saints Relief Committee which shipped life-saving supplies to that war-torn country. His and his associates' activities were reported in the *Deseret News*.

With his characteristic use of understatement he closed his autobiography with these words:

> *Now near the end of my mortal existence when I look back over my pretty colorful life, I have to confess with deep sorrow that my book of mortal life is filled with bad ink spots that cannot be erased. I failed in nearly every step. The headline of that book of my mortal life should read: A total failure, and not even a brilliant one.*[10]

Certainly the very opposite was true. President Stoof was a man of keen abilities. He had prepared for a career in education and became a master teacher on three continents; he became perhaps the best-known missionary in Europe. He was a student of the gospel and one who truly earned the title scriptorian. He was not given to complaining. Those who knew him well never heard him speak ill of a single person. His nature was gentle and meek, yet he was fearless in the defense of the gospel and totally committed to the Savior and his representatives on earth. He enjoyed the finer things in life and cultivated the arts. He played the organ beautifully, wrote both humorous and serious poetry in two languages, and loved to read good books. He served as the editor of the Church's German language newspaper, *Der Beobachter* (The Observer), wrote manuals and articles, translated lessons, books and Church hymns into German. He was referred to as a second Karl G. Maeser by President Heber J. Grant.

As President of the South American Mission he continued the work begun by Elder Ballard and opened the work in Brazil. He touched the lives of many individuals, instilling in them the desire to live on a higher plane. He was loved by all who knew him, and his testimony was a power for good to those with whom he came in contact. I owe him a great debt of gratitude; he formed my life's pattern. I deeply loved this great and good man.

Reinhold Stoof died of a heart ailment on Friday, August 17, 1956, at the age of sixty-nine in the LDS Hospital in Salt Lake City.

NOTES

Chapter IV

1. Reinhold Stoof's brief and somewhat facetious account of his life, "Autobiography of a Poor Fish," Church Historical Department.

2. *Ibid.*

3. *Ibid.*

4. *Ibid.*

5. In August 1973, while my son Fred was reading this manuscript to President Stoof's widow, Maria Stoof—his second wife—,she and the other family members laughed at the *Kartoffelpuffers* incident and exlained that early in their marriage, Reinhold taught her to make *Kartoffelpuffers* very, very thin. I guess he hadn't liked them thick either.

6. The Brethren worded the letter in this manner in order to facilitate President Stoof's reentry into the United States. Having been out of the country for nine years, he was having difficulty in securing a visa.

President Stoof had received a previous letter from the First Presidency under the date of February 9, 1935, informing him of the division of the Mission and his release. President Rulon S. Howells was to preside over the Brazilian Mision and W. Ernest Young over the Argentine. More details appeared in the *Deseret News* on the same date.

7. See Stoof autobiography.

8. A copy of this letter is on file in the Stoof collection at the Church Historical Department.

9. See Stoof autobiography

10. See Stoof autobiography.

CHAPTER V

THE LIFE OF A MISSIONARY IN THE LATE 1920's

Rivadavia Street Mission Headquarters. My first home was an apartment, one of many in a large apartment house, on Calle Rivadavia, about a half block from the mission home. Around an open patio were a living room, a bedroom, bathroom, and kitchen. Paul and I shared the maid's room upstairs. This was summertime, so we ate in the open patio and competed with the flies for our food. When it rained we hurried inside. All the floors were tile, so on Saturdays we swamped out, washing down the floors with water, scrubbing them first with a brush and hard soap. Then with a squeegee and more water we cleaned them "good" and finally wiped them dry with a mop.

We four elders lived very simply. Elders Clegg, Jensen, Davis and I shared two double beds. We bought our own sheets, towels and personal belongings. Each had a small table to use as a desk. A homemade clothes closet held our suits. Our wardrobe trunks served as dressers. Our girls' pictures hung on the walls. Nothing else.

Our kitchen was simple and easy to keep clean. A built-in coke-burning cooking area was standard for all houses. There was no oven. We cooked on a Primus stove, a Swedish pressure stove that burned gasoline and could turn into a blowtorch in a moment. Of course, it could accommodate only one pot at a time. We had one fry pan, two kettles, one butcher knife, and a knife, fork, spoon and tin plate each. Newpapers served as tablecloths. Whenever the rare special guest came we would use the cleanest sheet for a tablecloth. Each of us had one cane-bottom chair. The kitchen had a tiled sink and a cold-water faucet. The bathroom contained a lavatory, a chain-flushed stool and a cold-water shower.

Shopping for groceries took getting used to. All staples such as sugar, flour, salt, and beans were sold by metric weight (1 kilo=2.2 pounds), in bulk from large barrels. When we had made our wants known the proper amount was weighed onto a piece of newspaper which was shaped into a package by twisting the ends of the paper until it was tightly wrapped around the contents. Our cupboards were filled with newspaper-wrapped packages.

We bought fresh meat from the meat markets, where half carcasses of beef hung on the walls. We indicated the portions and amounts we wanted, which were then cut off, the bone extracted, and the meat weighed; the finest meat in the world cost about five cents per pound. We enjoyed T-bone steaks at least twice a day. Milk came to the door. We could hear the cry *"Lechero!,"* grab a kettle and go outside. When the milkman and his cows stopped at our apartment he milked the desired amount, then they continued down the street to look for other customers.

We had no refrigeration and it was summer. Just before dinner we would buy a small amount of butter, also a cold siphon of carbonated water and some flavored extract, to make our own soft drinks.

Twice each week we bought fresh potatoes, cheese, olives, lettuce and other vegetables from a traveling street market.

We took turns doing housework. Two cooked for a week while the other two marketed and cleaned house. Then we rotated chores. We were not the best cooks in the world. Once an elder prepared a dish based very loosely on his mother's recipe (he obviously hadn't brought the recipe with him). The elder who was to ask the blessing took one look at the concoction and said, "Lord, please bless this food so it won't hurt us. Amen."

Weekdays we arose early and studied, then breakfasted on *mate* and a few cookies. Then Elder Stoddard gave us a Spanish lesson. We would take a chapter in De Torno's Spanish grammar, learn fifty new vocabulary words, and conjugate a new Spanish verb in all its tenses each day. I could quote the grammar book chapter and verse. After lunch we tracted for two or three hours, then returned and prepared for cottage meetings in the evenings. On Saturdays we cleaned the chapel at the mission home and set up the chairs for the Sunday meetings.

Sundays, we arose early and went to Liniers for Priesthood meeting held in the Friedrichs' home. Next we held Sunday School. At noon we usually ate with the Donato Gianfelice family, after which we returned to our quarters. In the evening we held Sacrament meeting in the chapel.

At times it was difficult to hear the speakers. Large farm wagons drawn by four-horse teams came down the cobbled street, and the horses' iron shoes and the iron-rimmed wheels made a tremendous noise. Then the street cars, some with flat spots on their wheels, would contribute to the cacophony. The chapel, which opened right on the sidewalk, got all the noises, including the calls of the vendors selling everything from feather dusters to bread to newspapers.

I will always remember the sights and smells of Buenos Aires in the summers. I could walk the length of any business block blindfolded and tell what was sold in each shop I passed. The reek of assorted cheeses and the pungent aroma of hot bread filled the air. Young boys delivered baskets of fresh unwrapped bread to the housewives every day. Sometimes dogs would select one or two loaves to lick while the lads' attention was attracted elsewhere. The stench of the open sewers was pervasive: a thick, green scum would form in these sewers and occasionally a beautiful white lily-like flower would raise its head, showing that even from baser things good can come. Several elders found to their chagrin that some of these *zanjas* or ditches were too wide to jump.

Of course, there were cars and trucks in Buenos Aires in 1927, but for each of these there were perhaps fifty horse-drawn vehicles of every description. Large-wheeled wagons pulled by three or four horses handled the heavy hauling, but the vast majority were carts pulled by a single animal. These were the pride and joy of their owners and each tried to make his cart the most attractive. The bodies were brightly painted with floral designs or animals. Even the spokes were gaily decorated. Some had canopies in an astonishing variety of shapes. The harnesses were elaborately decorated with shiny brass. All the thousands of horses I saw in Argentina were well kept; I never saw a poor or bedraggled animal. These carts delivered meat, milk, bread, everything. Each cart was decorated appropriately to match the item delivered.

To protect them from the hot summer sun, the Argentine horses wore hats equipped with holes for their ears. This practice seemed very strange to me. I had been raised around horses and had seen hundreds of teams hitched to wagons, but none had worn a hat.

Many times in Buenos Aires I saw new Packard cars, driven by chauffeurs, desperately trying to move from behind a logjam of carts and wagons in narrow streets.

Taking the advice of our senior companions, each of us purchased a pajama coat made of fine linen. It was too hot to wear our street coats when we went shopping, but we could not go out into the street in shirt sleeves. The common workers wore only their undershirts, and that was acceptable, but shirt sleeves were not. We found that many Argentine men also wore pajama bottoms on the street. We even saw them in the theaters. The practice became so widespread that ultimately the city of Buenos Aires banned the wearing of pajama bottoms in theaters.

After living in Buenos Aires a few months we formed the habit of going to the theater on Saturday nights. We usually went into downtown Buenos Aires to see a good American movie and then enjoy the live stage acts. At that time Buenos Aires was said to be the fourth largest city in the world, and it attracted the greatest entertainers from Europe and the United States. During the hot months, since the theaters had no air conditioning, the central portions of the roofs conveniently rolled back, letting in the cooler night air. On occasion, sudden rain storms came up. Then it was touch and go to replace the roofs before the audiences became drenched. They really worked hard to put the roofs back in place as fast as they could, and great was the noise thereof.

Buenos Aires had one subway line which began at Plaza Mayo and ended at Caballito. It also had a good street car system, but by far the best means of transportation was the bus system. We could go anywhere in the city by bus. It was also very cheap.

We soon became adept at catching buses, which rarely stopped, on the run. We would spread out several yards apart and each would swing on and quickly move up the steps so the next could get a toehold. We had to jump off the same way. Although we faithfully signaled for our stops, the bus drivers never actually stepped on the brakes unless a woman—an old woman with a child in her arms—needed to get off.

Passengers entered the buses from the rear and exited from the front. I can still remember the cries of the ticket sellers, *"Un pasito más adelante, por favor"* (Please step forward). No one ever seemed to move, so far as I could tell. The buses were crammed full, but more passengers always managed to board. It was a real struggle to get off. Sudden stops to avoid hitting other vehicles made the ride interesting. The entire mass of humanity fell forward or backward as a single body, so only those at the extreme rear or front were crushed. Chivalry had no place on the municipal buses: women had to fight for their seats, and men routinely crowded ahead of a woman for a seat.

About once a month we would live it up and treat ourselves to some American ice cream. Only one place in the heart of the city (between Florida and San Martin Streets) sold it. Argentine ice cream was entirely different from what we were used to. It was made with raw eggs and had a very strong taste.

The automat was a favorite place to eat. There we could choose from a wide variety of sandwiches and desserts. My particular passion was a hot sirloin steak sandwich. I had to wait while it was cooked, but it was well worth it. With a glass of cold milk, it made a wonderful lunch, all for less than ten American cents.

We also patronized the *panaderías* and *confiterías.* Although the bakers used no salt and very little baking powder, several items were excellent: *medialunas, empanadas* and other *galletitas* (cookies). Much to our dismay, we discovered that some of the chocolates were filled with liquor, which completely ruined their taste for us.

I loved the local hot chocolate, which we could buy *espeso* (thick) or *liviano* (thin). The thick had to be eaten with a spoon. We became adept at dunking with *vainillitas* or ladyfingers, which readily absorbed any liquid. If we dunked them too long in the chocolate, the submerged part invariably broke off just before we got it to our mouths, falling in our cups and splashing our ties and coats. Dunking is an acquired art.

The Buenos Aires flies were plentiful and chummy. We had no screens and had to fight them for everything we ate. The mosquitoes were large and hungry. Every morning we swatted the blood-heavy mosquitoes that hadn't made it out the windows and had stopped to rest on the walls. We never typed the blood to see to whom it belonged, but each mashed insect made an interesting pattern on the wall. Finally, we purchased mosquito netting and then sweltered under it every night.

Buenos Aires has many magnificent parks. The contiguous Palermo and Parque 3 de Febrero parks were my favorites. There, in the proper season, we could see thousands of roses of every hue artistically planted around small lakes. Animals from every country were exhibited in the world famous zoo. The most interesting were the *vizcachas.* This small native rodent looks like a cross between a giant rabbit and a dog; the body is all rabbit. They hopped around freely among the strollers on the lawns.

We learned to our sorrow that one Argentine native had a way of tormenting the unsuspecting. It was the infamous *bicho colorado,* an almost invisible mite that resided in the grass and shrubs waiting for something to eat. They ate their way into the skin and set the body on fire. We tried many remedies to relieve the itching: dousing the red, swollen places on our skin with alcohol, and rubbing them with harsh laundry soap. Nothing really helped.

The Argentine fleas were friendly, too. We picked them up on the buses, in the movie theaters, and at the homes of friends. How they bit. The best way to catch them was to get them between thumb and finger, and then bathe them in alcohol or mash them between two thumbnails.

Last but not least were the bedbugs. I frequently saw them crawling on the shoulders of a man or woman, or on the dinner table. They slept during the days, but got hungry and went hunting at night. They received regular transfusions from us. We waged periodic campaigns against them and the other vermin, but although we may have won some battles, in the end we lost the war.

First Attempts to Teach the Lamanites. President Stoof was anxious to follow Elder Ballard's suggestion and take the gospel to the Lamanites. Within ten days after my companions and I arrived, on March 10, 1927, Elders Merrel and Christian were on their way to Jujuy, in northern Argentina, accompanied by Elder Sharp who was on the first leg of his return trip home.

Jujuy sits on the banks of the Rıó Grande river in a valley of the Andean foothills at an elevation of 4,167 feet. A few miles south of the Bolivian border, its population of fifty thousand was made up primarily of Indians, with some *mestizos.* This picturesque city was founded in 1593, twenty-seven years before the arrival of the Pilgrims at Plymouth Rock. The elders traveled by train and arrived in Jujuy on March 14. Elder Sharp found living quarters and a room where meetings could be held. But they spent little more than a month in Jujuy:

Elder Sharp left April 25 to go home, and Elders Merrel and Christian returned to Buenos Aires, arriving the 27th.

The Elders worked hard tracting and contacting people with the message of the restored gospel. They held street meetings and at first interested a few people, but these soon lost interest because of outside pressure. When the once friendly children began throwing rocks at them, the missionaries wanted to know why. They were finally told that the new hostility, demonstrated by the rock throwing and the nightly shower of rocks on the roof of their house, were the direct result of the instructions of a Catholic priest who wanted no interference with the nominal members of his parish. Probably for the first time he was now taking a personal interest in these Indian children and their parents. I found the same story throughout Latin America: "If you can't compete, begin to tell lies and poison the minds of people against the truth. Appeal to the traditions and frighten them with fire and brimstone if they foresake what they have been told to believe."

They made no progress, Elder Merrel became ill, and they were threatened with serious stonings, so President Stoof had no choice but to bring the missionaries back to Buenos Aires and leave the preaching of the gospel to the Lamanites for a later date. The day after they returned, Elder Merrel was taken to the British Hospital, seriously ill with typhoid fever.

Knowing that there were many Indians in the Chaco region near Paraguay, President Stoof wanted to find out whether missionaries would have more success among them than they had among the plateau Indians near Bolivia. He also wished to learn the condition of the German colonists there. Elder Waldo Stoddard accompanied him by train on May 11, 1927. They expected to be absent from Buenos Aires for two or three weeks.

Much to our surprise, they returned on May 18, just eight days later. Their report was not encouraging. They had found many Indians living in huts in the semi-jungle area of the Argentine Chaco, twenty miles from Charata. Almost totally illiterate, few possessed even a meager knowledge of Spanish.

They realized, too, the problems involved in teaching these people to live the Word of Wisdom. Almost without exception, the men and women smoked cigars made from the strong tobacco which they cultivated. The brethren first became aware of this as their train approached the last station before the Indian settlements. The Indians on the train smoked cigars and spat freely into the aisle. The dust that blew into the car through the open windows covered everything and everybody, and served as an excellent fixative for the noxious brown juice. Before long, the floor was covered with a dark gooey mess, which adhered to the shoe soles of the passengers and crewmen who walked up and down the aisle. The odor was even more offensive.

Unable to communicate with the Indians, and seeing the primitive conditions under which they lived, President Stoof decided that the "Day of the Lamanites" had not arrived as far as the Chaco Indians were concerned, and decided to have the missionaries devote all their efforts for the time being to the millions of cosmopolitan people of Argentina.

We missionaries were disappointed. We had visions of living among the Indians and teaching them. But in later years, as I visited these and other primitive Indians, I realized how right President Stoof had been. Although it was begun as a German-speaking mission, the South American Mission would grow away from the Germans and more towards the Spanish-speaking Argentines. Yet, even as the dedicatory prayer suggested, the real fulfillment of the prophecy uttered by Elder Ballard would come when the Lamanites in the land accepted the gospel. It is understandable that the Brethren would be interested in contacting the Indians because of the promises to the descendants of Lehi in the Book of Mormon, fresh in the mind of Elder Ballard as a result of his trip through the ruins of ancient American civilizations.

There would be other attempts to teach Indians, but the real proselyting thrust among them would come only after the work was begun in Perú, over thirty years later. Curiously, two of the early missionaries to South America would start the work. When my family and I moved to Perú in 1956, we precipitated missionary work in that land. I was the first Branch President of the Church on the west coast of South America; the Church was officially opened in our home. Three years later J. Vernon Sharp became the first President of the Andes Mission, with headquarters in Lima, Perú.

First Trip to Brazil. On December 14, 1927, President Stoof and Elder Stoddard sailed from Buenos Aires on board the S.S. *Sierra Ventana* for Santos, Brazil. We other elders were envious of Elder Stoddard, but he was the best equipped to go. He was the senior elder, he spoke the best Spanish, and he was now studying German; he was also the only one who could afford the trip. He paid his own expenses on all the trips he made with President Stoof, and some of the President's expenses as well, I'm sure.

President Stoof wanted to visit the large German colonies of Southern Brazil, most of which were in Santa Catarina, located halfway between Buenos Aires and Santos. They sailed to Santos, then traveled to São Paulo where they spent a week gathering information about the German colonies. They also searched for a German member of the Church thought to be living there, but they didn't locate him. They found that many Germans lived in São Paulo, but were scattered in much the same way they were in Buenos Aires. On December 26 they took a small coastal steamer (the *Carl Hoepeke*) from Santos to São Francisco do Sul; the next day they boarded a train for Joinville.

Hundreds of thousands of Germans had immigrated to Brazil beginning in the 1870s, but they came with renewed impetus after the First World War. Many settled in the states of Santa Catarina and Rio Grande do Sul, where they acquired small parcels of jungle land. They cleared trees, planted crops, established small businesses and sawmills, and constructed comfortable frame houses with steep roofs similar to the ones they had known in their homeland, even though there was little danger of a heavy snowfall.

The brethren stayed at *pensões* or boarding houses in Joinville and other villages of German-speaking people and made many contacts. Brother Stoof lectured on the Church before a crowd of 142 persons in Joinville and received favorable comments. They also traveled to Blumenau, another small agricultural community, where they expected to find two Mormons; however, one had died and the other, out of work and discouraged with the death of his friend, had returned to Germany.

The German colonists, having weathered the first few years of back-breaking toil to beat the jungle, now had more time to think of religion. In their few moments of leisure time, they enjoyed the visit of their fellow-countryman and his American companion, welcoming them into their homes when they came to call and to distribute tracts. The brethren were impressed that the time was at hand when these hard-working German people would listen to and accept the message of the Restored Gospel. They sailed for Buenos Aires on January 16, 1928, aboard the ship *España*.[1]

During their absence an article on the Church, probably the first in Spanish in the Mission, appeared in the Argentine newspaper *Crítica* on December 19, 1927. It contained some "lies about the prophet of the Church. Also it was said that the Mormons had a barbarous cult, mixed with pagan customs."[2] At long last the *Crítica* had carried news of the Church; unfortunately, it was anti-Mormon. As Apostle Ballard and President Pratt had tried earlier, the missionaries also tried to publish an article in the same paper to correct the mistakes, but they were not received by the editors.

By 1928 our missionary force was depleted. Elder Ashton had returned almost as soon as he arrived in 1926. Elder Davis returned home voluntarily on September 8, 1927. Elder Jensen was released February 27, 1928, because of ill health, as was Elder Merrel on May 3, 1928. Elder Spencer, after suffering from peritonitis and nearly losing his life, was also released that year.

At this time my mother wrote me that she had heard that some of the General Authorities thought it would be a good idea to close the mission and bring home all the missionaries. I don't know where she heard it, but she felt that the mission should continue. She wrote: "The South American Mission is having a hard time just like the English Mission at first, but truth shall triumph and the Lord's work shall be established, and all the imps of hell will not overthrow it." She wrote weekly during all the years I was in South America and her faith always sustained me.

The nucleus of the Spanish-speaking work was in Liniers. Because nothing spectacular had happened in Villa Ballester, President Stoof resolved to have Elder Christian and me, along with Elders Stoddard and Brundage, move closer to the majority of the members.

Calle República Branch. Elder Stoddard and I found a nice place near Rivadavia Street, at 180 Calle República. The street name was later changed to Calle Río Grande. From my diary:

> *April 9, 1928: We moved from Villa Ballester to Calle República, 180. I rode in with the old "cartero" on his two-wheeled cart. He told me of the old times when they used to freight with large two-wheeled carts to the interior. . . . The old fellow told me a lot of things about the country; that the stone used in paving the streets is quarried by the convicts on an island in Tierra del Fuego. It seems to me that they would have plenty of time to think of their misdeeds while using a hammer on a rock pile.*
>
> *We like our new home fine.*

We were very comfortable there. It had a large front room off the patio near the front gate that served as a chapel—our largest since leaving the original Rivadavia Street address. Two connecting bedrooms opened off the patio, with the kitchen at the back. The bathroom was across the patio from the kitchen. The patio was partially roofed, permitting us to walk during a rainstorm from the chapel to any bedroom or the kitchen without getting wet. Elder Clegg, the mission secretary, lived at the mission home.

We began at República as a four-elder branch: Elders Stoddard, Christian, Brundage, and I. In reality, our home was only a point of departure.

We held weekly meetings in member and investigator homes in different cities in order to take our message to the members and to teach the investigators and friends. We tried to keep up the momentum begun when we all lived in different areas. Our weekly schedule was:

Monday. We recovered from Sunday's activities, called on investigators, and attended an elders meeting with President Stoof at the mission home.

Tuesday. Tracted in the morning and early afternoon, and then held a meeting in the Friedrichs' home in Liniers for the members and investigators who spoke Spanish. This was a preaching service for which we had to prepare talks.

Wednesday. Studied, prepared for, and traveled to Piñeyro for an early afternoon meeting with a few interested persons in a chicken coop we had cleaned and papered with newspaper. Three short benches ran the width of the room and when we rose to speak we stood in front of the only door. No one could leave while we were speaking, and if someone wanted to come in, we had to move to one side.

The Kullicks. Also on Wednesdays we held a meeting in Lanús in the home of the Kullick family, the highlight of the week. This wonderful family, Brother and Sister Kullick and their three children, Fritz, Jacob and Herta, radiated friendship and made us feel at home.

The Wednesday meetings, which lasted about an hour, had an average attendance of fourteen or fifteen. Sister Kullick's brother and his family always attended. Several Argentine families also came, one of which, the Martínez family, we later baptized. After the meeting, Sister Kullick always served a delicious dinner with roast duck or chicken as the main course, and I became acquainted with the wonders of German cooking. Sister Kullick was an exceptional cook: how we did eat.

The Kullicks treated us so well that we tried to reciprocate by inviting them to our *local* for dinner one Saturday evening. Fritz, Jacob and Herta came. We took special care to have everything right. I washed and ironed my best sheet for the tablecloth, and made mashed potatoes, beating them with a fork into a fluffy mist. We fried gigantic steaks and made milk gravy for the potatoes. Fresh creamed peas were the vegetable, along with pickled beets. For dessert we served assorted freshly baked pastries.

Sister Kullick communicated very simply in Spanish—she used only the infinitive of the verbs. For example, to tell us that she had gone to the market to buy food and returned home by bus, she said: *"Yo andar mercado. Yo comprar comida. Yo volver casa ómnibus."* (I to walk market. I to buy food. I to return house bus.)

We held a regular English class for Fritz, Jacob and Herta. The Kullicks were anxious to emigrate to the United States and the young people wanted to be fluent in English.[3]

We had to leave the Kullick home no later than 10:30 p.m. If we made all our bus, train, subway, and streetcar connections, we arrived home at about one a.m.

Thursday. In the mornings we made out our reports, studied, and prepared lessons for the evening cottage meeting with the Alvarez family in Villa Ballester.

Shortly after noon we took a bus to the mission home to pick up mail and discuss business with our president. Then we commuted via bus and train to the Alvarez home—a one and one-half hour trip.

Our meetings in their humble home in the light of a kerosene lantern were always interesting and inspirational. They were avid for the gospel teachings and we could never give them too much. Sometimes our meetings lasted late into the night until one of the smaller children fell asleep. The family insisted on sharing their meager food with us. At times it was only *mate* and cookies, but they insisted they were always blessed to share with the missionaries. It was always well after midnight when we returned home after visiting Villa Ballester.

Friday. We completed more reports, studied, tracted, and visited investigators. In the evening we held an English class with an Argentine dentist who actually preferred to talk about the United States. I don't think he learned very much during the six months we tried to teach him.

Carmen Escudero. At eight o'clock we held a class for an investigator, Carmen de Escudero, and her two nieces, Sofía and Laura Morazo.

A native of Spain, Carmen had attended Church meetings since Elders Ballard and Pratt had opened the South American Mission. She had a testimony of the gospel and wanted to be baptized, but her husband opposed her. She attended all our meetings and even taught a Sunday School class for us.[4]

Sister Escudero's niece Sofía became our organist after Elder Stoddard's release on July 2, 1928. She and Laura wanted to be baptized, but their parents would not give their consent, as they were still in their teens.

Saturday. Our one "free" day. We mopped floors, set up benches in the chapel, hosed down the patio, washed and ironed clothes, pressed suits, prepared lessons, and occasionally got to Buenos Aires to a show, returning late at night. It was always a very busy day.

Sunday. This "day of rest" was the biggest day of the week. We began the day by taking a street car to Liniers and then walking more than twenty blocks to the Gianfelice home. From there, we continued to Bariloche Street, accompanied by Brothers Gianfelice and Quici and Sister Gianfelice's son by a previous marriage, Nicolás Lafratta. We met in "priesthood" meeting with a few other men in the small chapel, where we taught them what we could about their duties. At three p.m., the women and children arrived for Sunday School, which was divided into two classes: adults and children. The children sat on beds in one of the bedrooms for their classes. The adults held class in the chapel.

After Elders Stoddard[5] and Clegg left, the task of directing the congregation in hymn singing fell to me, and it was quite a struggle. I deeply regretted not taking Evan Stephens' advice to each missionary to carry (and know how to use) a pitchpipe.

At Liniers we had no organ and no one who could play. I started each hymn at what I hoped was the appropriate pitch. Unfortunately, it was always too high or too low, and I was never able to change my pitch. Some hymns were so high we all literally squeaked, the rest were so low the women couldn't sing them at all.

I knew nothing about music, couldn't (and can't) read notes, and relied entirely on my rote learning as a child for my knowledge of the hymns—not a firm foundation. Now, I was supposed to teach new hymns to people who were not used to singing anyway. However, it didn't really matter that I couldn't read notes. We had no songbooks, just printed or mimeographed word-sheets. Nine years later, when I returned as mission president, I found that I had taught some of the hymns incorrectly. They were still trying to undo my efforts as a music director.

One of the missionaries took a snapshot of me directing the music at the small chapel on Bariloche Street. I have a confused and hopeless look on my face, an exact reflection of my feelings. But the Argentines are a loving and long-suffering people; I love them for it.

The Spanish-language work was centered at the Calle República branch. President Stoof held the German meetings at the mission home in Villa Devoto.

At four p.m. we held a Sacrament meeting. At six o'clock, we held a preaching service for members and investigators. In addition to this regular Sunday schedule, President Stoof occasionally recruited me as operator of a portable movie projector he frequently used in German branch meetings or cottage meetings.

Work Opened in Brazil. On September 12, 1928, President Stoof together with Elders Heinz and Schindler left Buenos Aires for Brazil. They arrived at São Francisco do Sul on the 16th, but were unable to disembark because of a very bad storm. Elder Heinz continues the narrative:

It was storming that day, the wind was blowing and the waves were so high the small boats couldn't meet us. The Captain of our ship (SS. Madrid) said he would wait until morning, then if the storm didn't let up he would have to go on to Santos. President Stoof said, "If it is the Lord's will that we should open the Mission in Joinville, then the storm will stop, if not then we will go on to São Paulo." By morning the storm had let up enough so we could leave the ship and we went to Joinville.[6]

They went directly to Joinville and immediately prepared to give an illustrated lecture on "Utah and Its People:"

The lecture was given in the evening of the 21st of September in the hall of a moving picture house before more than 400 people. Two days later the elders held a little meeting in the same hall with more than 30 present.[7]

The people had greeted President Stoof and Elder Stoddard so warmly on their first trip that they were anxious to officially open the field of labor with permanently assigned elders. This initial meeting, with over four hundred people present, indicated how right President Stoof's decision had been. They secured a house with room for living quarters and meetings on Rua Duque de Caxias, 54, for one hundred milreis per month. President Stoof instructed the missionaries on future progress and returned to Buenos Aires on September 26.

All was not a bed of roses, however. Coincident with their initial meeting, Adventist preachers began holding anti-Mormon lectures in Joinville. Eventually, however, the people paid less and less attention to the Church's detractors, and persecution ceased, at least for the time being:

On the day of his [President Stoof's] departure, Mr. Kaltenhaeuser, an Adventist preacher, attacked bitterly the Church in one of his lectures using all the old lies. Also a pastor of the Evangelic Lutheran Church, Hans Mueller, published on the 1st of October a mean article against the Church in an evangelic paper of the City of Joinville. The elders sent him a Book of Mormon for his own information. In spite of all the attacks of our enemies, the attendance of the meetings, especially of the Sunday Schools, increased. On the 12th of November the Adventist preacher Kaltenhaeuser resumed his fight against the Church giving an illustrated lecture about "The Mormons and Their Doctrines," but he had no success in as much as the majority of the audience left the hall before he had finished his lecture. The elders felt thankful for the good propaganda our enemies were making for the Church in that City.[8]

Elder Ballard used the *Millenial Star* and the *Liahona* to alert Church members of the opening of the South American Mission, and President Stoof wrote about it in the *Improvement Era*.[9] In addition Elder Schindler wrote a letter about the new mission which was published in the Church magazine, *Der Stern*, in Germany (January 27, 1929, page 27). His letter described Joinville as a city of sixteen thousand, ninety-five percent of whom spoke German. Most of these people, he said, were born in Brazil, but spoke no Portuguese. The letter went on to describe the anti-Mormon activity which, instead of turning the people against the Church, served to pique their interest.

The first baptisms in Brazil occurred on April 14, 1929, one day before Elder Heinz returned home. The circumstances surrounding the baptisms included a special blessing and a healing:

On the 31st of March after the evening services, a woman, Mrs. Bertha Sell, who attended the meeting, dropped down in the garden because of sickness. The elders Emil Schindler and William Fred Heinz administered to her in the presence of several of their friends. The next morning she visited the elders being well and asked for baptism.[10]

All but her husband and eldest daughter joined the Church. Elder Schindler baptized Bertha and Theodore Sell. Elder Heinz baptized Alice, Siegfried and Adel Sell. The confirmation took place in the Sell home.[11]

Rosario de Santa Fé. Elder Heber Clegg and I, after considerable discussion, decided that we needed to become better acquainted with this vast South American Continent. Our knowledge so far was restricted to the environs of Buenos Aires and to one-dimensional line drawings on maps. The Church itself existed only in Buenos Aires and in a minuscule new branch in far-off Brazil. With President Stoof's permission, we traveled to Rosario, Argentina's second largest city, two hundred and fifty miles north of Buenos Aires on the Paraná-Guazú River.

We left Buenos Aires by train on Wednesday, October 24, 1928, and soon found ourselves in rural countryside, passing huge fields of corn and wheat and large pastures full of grazing Herefords. Beyond the farmlands we crossed into the legendary pampas, which extended unbroken to the horizon. The only tree native to these lush, grass-covered plains is the solitary, twisted ombú, actually a weed. It provides limited shade, and its porous wood is useless as fuel. The railway was owned and operated by an English company, which kept its rolling stock in excellent condition. The single exception was the second class toilet facilities, which were (and will remain) beyond description.

We arrived in Rosario late in the evening, booked a double room at the Majestic Hotel for two pesos per night, washed away pounds of pampas dust, ate supper and went gratefully to bed. The next morning we went looking for two members of the Church whose names had been given to us before we left Buenos Aires.

The first was a lovely Swiss lady in her thirties who, with her brother, had been converted to the Church just before their recent emigration. We had dinner with them that evening and enjoyed ourselves very much. During our free time we toured the city, visiting museums, parks, and gardens.

The other member was a German gentleman who lived in Los Delicios, an outlying suburb. The following evening we accompanied him to a tiny house to attend the services of a fundamentalist sect with an equally tiny congregation. The meeting, which lasted an hour and a half, was distinguished by loud shouts of "amen," "hallelujah," and other exhortations, and by the congregation rolling and writhing on the floor. It made us a little uncomfortable, and we were very happy when it ended.

Saturday morning we arranged to return to Buenos Aires by river boat and spent the rest of the day tracting. That evening we returned to the home of the Swiss family for dinner. Sunday morning we toured more of the beautiful city and then boarded our ancient river steamer which was originally sail-rigged. We arrived in Buenos Aires before dawn on Monday morning. This trip gave me some of the most wonderful experiences of my life. The memories have stayed with me to the present, and none of my subsequent trips to Rosario made as deep an impression.

Senior Missionary in Spanish Work. On December 26, 1928, Elders Christian and Clegg, who had completed their two-year missions, boarded ship for New York via Brazil and Europe. I was now the senior Spanish-language missionary in the South American Mission. My companion, Elder Brundage, was the only other missionary in Argentina. Elder Heinz, who had come to South America with me, was the senior German-language missionary and was laboring in Brazil with his companion, Elder Schindler, the only other missionary in that country. Four missionaries in the entire South American Continent: two in Brazil and two in Argentina.

In addition to our busy schedule Elder Brundage and I now inherited all the work of Elders Christian and Clegg. For more than six months we averaged seventeen meetings a week. What did we use for manuals? We had none. We had only our Spanish Bibles, bought from the Methodist bookstore, and a poorly translated Book of Mormon. We used the 1922 Revised Spanish Edition which still had many typographical errors in it. Part of our Spanish study was to look for these misprints. There was no Spanish-language Doctrine and Covenants or Pearl of Great Price. No manuals for Sunday School or priesthood lessons. Fortunately, the people were new to the gospel, so that anything we taught them was welcome. However, because the members were so deeply interested in the gospel and so anxious to learn more, they attended all the meetings they could, which made it impossible to use the same talk in different meetings. We had to come up with a new topic each time.

Many times I found myself on the way to a meeting without the faintest idea for a talk. I would idly turn the pages of the Book of Mormon or the Bible, hoping something would leap from the page and inspire me.

Too often I stood to speak, with a half hour to forty-five minutes before me, without a thought in my head. Without exception, a thought would come in time on which I could develop a sermon. I always gave thanks to the Holy Spirit for fulfilling the promise of the Savior in this regard. I had studied hard to prepare myself, to obtain as much knowledge as I could, and always the Holy Spirit inspired me.

I received a lot of practice in preparing and teaching Sunday School lessons in a very short time. I gave three each Sunday for months. First, I gave a forty-minute lesson to the entire congregation. After separation for classes, I gave a twenty-minute lesson to the adults while Elder Brundage taught the children. Then we would change places: I taught the children and Elder Brundage supervised the adult class while Sister Escudero read from a book purchased at the Methodist bookstore about the life of Paul.

Once while directing Sunday School, Elder James Jensen, who arrived in the mission a bit later, announced the time for classes to separate: *"Los niños se quedarán aquí y los adúlteros irán al otro cuarto."* No one moved. He had simply stated that the children should remain where they were and that the "adulterers" should go to the other room. *"Adultos,"* the word he should have used, came out "adulterers." It could have happened to any of us.

I translated portions of the triple combination into Spanish both for my own use and for Donato Gianfelice, who was avid to learn all he could of the gospel. When they were later translated officially, I asked him to destroy what I had done, since mine was not—nor ever intended to be—official or even correct. I did it hurriedly and only to give him a deeper understanding of the Lord's great goodness in giving us these scriptures.

I became quite facile at orally translating English scriptures into Spanish during talks and lessons, a skill which has served me well in later life, both in and out of the Church. I personally prefer to translate English into Spanish rather than the other way around.

Our hymnals consisted of printed pamphlets containing twenty-five hymns which Elder Rey L. Pratt had translated while he was ill.[12] Of course, they were only the words without the music. A few other hymns translated in the Mexican Mission were also included, one of which was "We Thank Thee O God, for a Prophet." One or two English hymnbooks with words and music were available for the organists. Later a few copies of *Himnos de Sión,* printed in 1927 for the Mexican Mission, were sent to us. The German Saints used hymnbooks printed in Germany. Some of the hymns were translated by President Stoof before he emigrated to the United States.

We had a few Spanish-language tracts, originally for use in the Mexican Mission: "Is Baptism Essential to Salvation?," "A Friendly Discussion," "A Voice of Warning," "El Mormonismo," and "Gospel Restored."[13]

In January 1928, President Stoof and I collaborated on a new tract, *"El Mensaje Alegre"* (The Joyous Message). We wrote it first in English, then I translated it into Spanish and it was printed on one eight by eleven inch sheet folded and printed on four sides.[14] I do not know whether it was ever reprinted. No copies existed when I returned in 1938.

As I mentioned before, Sofía Morazo became our organist in 1928, but only for a few months. Her parents opposed her attending all the meetings, and we were once more without an organist. The Lord must have anticipated our need, for the missionaries soon contacted a family of three generations of women, a grandmother, daughter and two granddaughters: Josefa Hernández de Alonzo Sánchez, Isidora de Ohmar, Dora Castro Sánchez (age ten) and Delia (Lita) Carmen Sánchez (age four).

Dora had taken piano lessons, and I suggested that she learn some of the hymns so that she could play them in Church. She became our organist, but we had to solve a couple of problems. First, she couldn't reach the pedals. If we lowered the chair, by shortening the legs, she couldn't see over the keyboard. However, in the mission field no problems are unsolvable when the need is great. I sat at her side and pumped the pedals for her. We became quite a team, and it didn't matter whether I stood or sat to direct the singing, because the congregation paid only token attention anyway. Like most Mormon congregations, they followed the organist rather than the director, and in any case, they always finished a hymn well before Dora or I did. But we sang with great gusto and enjoyment. I miss this kind of singing in our congregations here in the States.

Thinking that a chair was inadequate for an organist, I made a bench with a hinged top. In the nature of piano and organ benches, it became a receptacle for extra copies of the Book of Mormon, songbooks, the Sacrament cloth, and other incidentals. Dora, the organ purchased by Elder Ballard, and my bench served the mission for years. They were still together when I visited the Liniers Branch in 1958, thirty years later.

NOTES

Chapter V

1. Stoof, "History of the South American Mission."

2. *Ibid.*

3. On May 5, 1930, Brother and Sister Kullick emigrated to the United States. While attending the 1964 New York World's Fair, Bishop Horace Sant of the Lynwood (California) Ward met Jacob Kullick, who told him that I, more than anyone else, was responsible for his coming into the Church years later after his immigration.

4. She was finally baptized March 16, 1930, and on February 14, 1934, became the first president of the newly-organized Buenos Aires Relief Society.

5. Before Elder Stoddard's departure, a photo was taken of all the elders in the South American Mission, which was included in an article on the fledgling work, written by President Stoof and published in the *Improvement Era* (October 1928), pp. 1052-1054.

6. Letter of William Fred Heinz to me, dated October 15, 1973, Rexburg, Idaho.

7. "History of the South American Mission," unpublished typescript written by Reinhold Stoof, Church Historical Department.

8. *Ibid.*

9. Before President Stoof's article, Elder Stoddard had sent two photographs, one of each of the Sunday Schools held in the mission, which were printed along with a short explanation in the *Improvement Era*, Vol. 30, No. 4 (February 1927), p. 360.

10. Stoof, "History."

11. *Ibid.*

12. See Ballard, "History," especially the entries in April 1926.

13. See "Mission Annual Reports" for 1926 under South American Mission, inventory of Books and Tracts, p. 349, Church Historical Department.

14. See "Mission Annual Reports" for 1928, under South American Mission, inventory of Books and Tracts, p. 351, Church Historical Department. There were 15,000 "Mensaje Alegre" tracts listed in the inventory.

CHAPTER VI

EARLY MEMBERS: AN INTERNATIONAL FAMILY

Three Italians: Gianfelice, Quici, Notaro. Three individuals made significant contributions to the establishment of the South American Mission, three Italian men whom I will never forget: Donato Angelo Gianfelice, Domenico (Domingo) Quici, and Luigi (Luis) Notaro. As young men they had worked in the States as section hands on the Pennsylvania Railroad. When they had saved enough money they returned home to Campo Basso, Italy, where they married and eventually emigrated to Argentina. They were all poor: Brothers Gianfelice and Quici worked for the city of Buenos Aires digging trenches for water and gas mains. Luis Notaro worked for the Argentine Southern Railway. He lived at a crossing on Rivadavia Street, and it was his job to let down the barrier to halt street traffic whenever a train approached. He and his wife, Mariantonia, were on twenty-four hour duty.

Luis wore a suit most of the time, and was quite presentable. But Donato and Domingo were archetypal Italian movie villains. They wore *alpargatas*—hemp-soled, canvas slippers, simple trousers and shirts, with *fajas* or sashes around their waists. They also sported long, handlebar mustaches (as did Luis). Their fierce appearance was misleading—no men were more loving or kindly. Their lives were devoted to the gospel.

They had been devout Catholics but one thing had bothered them: they couldn't reconcile their priest's actions with his teachings. He would say, "You do as I tell you, don't do as you see me do." He refused to give them a Bible, saying, "No, it will just get you confused. You come and ask me about any religious problem, and I'll answer it; don't get mixed up with reading the Bible." Despite their priest's behavior and their long working hours, they attended Mass every morning at six o'clock. They also enjoyed wine; they often spent their entire wages on wine and were frequently drunk.

Their introduction to the Church came through Elders Ballard and Pratt, who asked to visit with them in their homes. However, the Gianfelices were hesitant to invite the Americans into their humble one-room shack constructed from wooden packing cases. Elder Pratt assured Donato that if the Gianfelices could live in that home, the elders could certainly visit with them in it. The elders were invited to dinner.

Antonio Gianfelice, their son, had been attending the Brethren's Primary and receiving lessons on prayer. When the elders came for dinner, the Gianfelices asked to be taught to pray. Elder Pratt explained the principle of prayer and asked them to kneel with him, whereupon he lead them in a simple prayer and blessing on the food. This was on Wednesday, June 30, 1926.[1] Domingo Quici, whose wife was still in Italy, ate his meals with the Gianfelices and was present on this occasion.

On August 22, 1926, Emilia and Donato Gianfelice were baptized, as was Domingo Quici and Nicolas Lafratta, Sister Gianfelice's son by a previous marriage. Elders Sharp and

Stoddard continued to meet with the family. Luis Notaro and his wife weren't interested at the time.

I became attached to the Gianfelice family and considered Sister Emilia Gianfelice my second mother. She was starved for more knowledge of the gospel. I started reading to her first from a Spanish Bible and later from an Italian Bible. I read almost the entire New Testament to her in Italian, badly mispronouncing the words and understanding very little of what I read.

They also loved to sing the songs of Zion. Their favorite was "O My Father," and we always sang it together before leaving their home.

Their home was indeed humble. Automobile packing crates and a corrugated iron roof enclosed one large room which held all their worldly possessions, a double bed and a table. The children slept on the dirt floor. The "kitchen" (a brazier or charcoal grill) was outside under a big tree. When it rained, the kitchen moved indoors onto the table. The food was simple, frijoles, pastachuta, etc., but exquisitely flavored. Italian meals prepared by Sister Gianfelice were the best.

Antonio Gianfelice stayed overnight with us once in order to see the Carnival parade to be held in our neighborhood the next day. We took the opportunity to introduce him to the rudiments of personal hygiene, since bathing facilities were nonexistent in his home and he needed a bath very badly. I suggested he take a shower. He declined. I insisted. He declined louder. I took off my clothes and his and took him into the shower to give him a good scrubbing. He had never been properly introduced to a cold shower, and he screamed bloody murder (I wondered what the neighbors were thinking). I finally got him all lathered up; once he got out of the shower, he seemed to enjoy being clean. He thoroughly enjoyed the Carnival the following day.

Sister Gianfelice could not afford to pamper herself. On Sunday, May 29, 1927, a bitter winter morning, she gave birth to their second daughter, Sara. When we arrived at their home the following Tuesday for Mutual, she was out in the frigid weather doing her washing.

Brother Gianfelice's tithing. The winter (June, July and August) of 1928 was one of the wettest on record. Rain fell almost continuously for twenty-one days and the sun disappeared altogether. Buenos Aires is as flat as a table top, and at that time had no storm drains. After a few days, the water became so deep that it was impossible for the street cars to move, and they had to stop operating. Soon all traffic stopped. Often we waded across intersections in water up to our belts; we were always cold and wet.

One Sunday during this period, we had to walk the sixty-five blocks to Liniers and the Gianfelice family walked back to our apartment to spend Sunday evening with us. After all the members had gone home that night, and as we missionaries were slowly gathering enough nerve to go to bed (it was very cold), we heard a knock at the door. We wondered who in the world would be calling on us at that time on a cold and rainy winter night. It was Brother Gianfelice, who had left only an hour or so before. He said: "Will you pray to the Lord to forgive me?" "What have you done?" we asked. He explained: "When I paid my tithing this afternoon, I miscalculated and underpaid the Lord twenty *centavos*," (at that time about a nickel in American money). "I've come to pay that twenty *centavos*." "Why in the world did you walk all those sixty-five blocks in the rain when you knew we would be in your home on Tuesday for Mutual, and you could have paid your tithing at that time?" He said: "I would not have been able to sleep knowing that I had cheated the Lord in my tithing." He paid it and then walked home.

The following week he brought his pay envelope (he was paid in cash) and asked me, "Won't you please take out the tithing so that I won't make a mistake?" I told him: "No, I will not. Tithing is a matter between you and the Lord; *you* are to pay what you owe the Lord."

Brother Notaro and the Word of Wisdom. As I mentioned, Brother Notaro had no desire to investigate the Church, and he and his wife couldn't understand what had happened to their life-long friends when they joined. Because they were on duty for the railroad twenty-four hours a day, the Notaros enjoyed company to while away the time. They had a steady income, and were in better financial condition than either Gianfelice or Quici, so Brother Notaro always purchased the wine when he invited his Italian *compinches* to spend the evening with him. They would drink wine and smoke, sing songs and tell stories until all hours of the morning, which never bothered Luis, because he had to stay up anyway. When Donato and Domingo joined the Church and would no longer join him in these revelries, he couldn't understand how any Italian would turn down free wine and jovial company. But they tried to stay as close to him as they possibly could.

Out of deference to their friendship, the Notaros agreed to accompany the Gianfelices to a baptismal ceremony for the Alvarez family on the shores of the River Plate. It was here that I first met the Notaros. After the baptism, we held a short confirmation service and testimony meeting in the shade of a large tree.

I noticed that something in that service touched the heart of Brother Notaro, and that there were tears in his eyes. Sensing that it was an appropriate moment, I asked him if he would permit us to come to his home and teach him the gospel; he consented. We kept our appointment, but as Harry Brundage and I went in the front door, Mariantonia Notaro went out the back door; she didn't want to meet with the missionaries at all. We gave Luis the lessons weekly thereafter, but Mrs. Notaro always managed to be absent.

After a time, we felt Brother Notaro was ready for baptism, so we secured the mission president's consent and agreed to meet the following Saturday, June 29, 1928. Antonio Gianfelice was also to be baptized that day. We were very surprised when we saw Sister Notaro with white clothes under her arm, insisting that she too be baptized. There wasn't much we could do about it, so we baptized her. We learned later that she had been listening to our lessons through the wall. After their baptism, we were invited to a chicken dinner at their home. While Sister Notaro prepared the food in her little kitchen, my companion and I and Brother Notaro sat talking in the front room. Suddenly Luis excused himself rather abruptly and left the house. After a few minutes he returned, and more to make conversation than anything else, I asked him where he had gone. He said, "I had to go over to the *boliche* to pay my wine bill." He had an account of several years' standing. His bill came to a little over sixty pesos. It was quite a bill, because at that time a liter, which is a quart and a tenth, cost about fifteen Argentine centavos.

Brother Notaro kept in a baking powder can on a shelf high in the corner of the room two of the most evil-smelling pipes it has ever been my misfortune to be in the same room with. After a few weeks, I asked him, "Brother Notaro, why do you keep those smelly pipes up there?" "Hermano Federico, I am over sixty years of age. I have smoked since I was six. It was very, very difficult for me to give up smoking. Sometimes I get an irresistible urge to smoke, and when I can almost no longer resist and feel I have to go against my better judgment and smoke again, I come in and look at those pipes, and then I ask them, 'Who's the boss here! Are you the boss or am I the boss?' I then immediately lose my desire to smoke and can go on about my business." A few weeks later, Sister Notaro gave the pipes honorable burial in the garden.[2]

I cannot say too much about the change the gospel made in the lives of the Notaros, changes that will come in the life of anyone who accepts the gospel wholeheartedly. Mariantonia Notaro, in her fifties, was unable to read or write, but now had the desire to learn so that she could trace her ancestors. She became an avid genealogist. She went to first grade for several months, but was unable to learn. She then hired others to help her in her research, and to do the reading for her. Many years later she returned to the little town in Italy where she was born. Unfortunately she made the mistake of explaining to the parish priests why she wanted the information on her ancestors and they closed the doors on her: she was a Mormon, and they would give her no information.

Brother Notaro felt he had missed much by not joining the Church earlier. Shortly after his baptism he retired from the railroad. To make up for lost time, he asked whether he could accompany us to our meetings. We were happy to have him come along. We held an average of seventeen meetings per week all over metropolitan Buenos Aires. As he was rather short, he had to run to keep up with us, because we missionaries were usually just a little late for our appointments and we'd walk pretty fast. We'd turn around and ask him if we were going too fast, and he'd say, "No, I'm fine, I'll keep up with you." Once we took a shortcut and jumped over an open sewer. He tried to follow us, but didn't quite make it. He had to return home and change his clothes.

We regularly visited a very poor family in Villa Ballester. Whenever we passed a grocery store near their home, Luis went inside to purchase a bag of groceries. He asked us to give it to the family and not say where it had come from. We got credit for it, but I'm sure the Lord has a different type of accounting and will give credit where credit is due.

On November 15, 1931, the Notaros deeded their property to the Church, and the Church purchased the adjacent vacant lot; the property became the site of the Liniers chapel which I dedicated while I was Mission President on April 9, 1939.

Domingo Quici. Brother Quici was unable to read or write when he joined the Church, but he too desired to study the scriptures, so he got little Antonio Gianfelice to teach him to read. He became proficient at it, but he was a bit slow. He became so engrossed in reading that he devoted nearly all his time to it.

Whenever we called on him to pray, Domingo would go on and on as though delivering a sermon. I repeatedly tried to persuade him to shorten his prayers, but to no avail. I called on him to offer the opening prayer one night and again cautioned him on praying too long, but he prayed for at least twenty minutes. I then got up and said, "We are grateful for the prayer, and as you've also given the sermon, it is now time for us to go home, we'll see you all next Sunday," and I dismissed the meeting. The shock seemed to have the desired effect, for Brother Quici shortened his prayers thereafter.

Years later, while Argentine Mission President, I appointed Brother Quici as the janitor of the Liniers chapel, and he carried out this assignment very faithfully for many years. The appointment came in 1938 when he was seventy years old. He took his job so seriously that when he got too old to do the job, he wouldn't accept the release. While President of the Uruguayan Mission (1947 to 1951) I made several trips to Buenos Aires to confer with President Brown. On one of these visits, President Brown told me that he was having trouble with Brother Quici, who was now too old to do the job and he needed to retire, but he wouldn't accept a release.

He would say: "President Williams appointed me and he is the only one who can release me." So in 1948, ten years after I had appointed him to the job, I, as President of the Uruguayan Mission, in a Conference of the Argentine Mission, formally released Brother Domingo Quici from his position as janitor of the Liniers chapel. He was eighty, and still a marvelous individual.

Mustache episode. Toward the close of my mission, we were preparing to celebrate the centennial of the restoration of the Aaronic Priesthood on May 15, 1929. Our preparations included a tableau depicting this event. At this stage of the evolution of the South American Mission, we had no young priesthood holders, no young men at all to speak of, who could take the parts of young Joseph Smith and Oliver Cowdery, so we used the older men to portray these Brethren. I asked Brother Gianfelice whether he would be willing to portray Joseph Smith. He felt very humble about it and even made it a matter of prayer before he accepted.

During the course of one of the rehearsals, I kidded him without really thinking, that he didn't look much like the Prophet Joseph Smith with that big mustache of his. The following Sunday, as was our regular schedule, we stopped at the Gianfelice home on our way to Priesthood meeting. As we sat talking with Sister Gianfelice while waiting for her husband that morning, a complete stranger walked in and extended his hand and said, "Good morning, Hermano Federico." On closer scrutiny I could see that it was Brother Gianfelice minus his mustache. "What in the world happened to you?," I asked. He said, "Hermano Federico, you said I didn't look much like the Prophet Joseph Smith with my mustache, and I want to take his part. If the gospel requires that I shave my mustache, then I'm willing to do it; I'm willing to do anything that the gospel requires." I had no sooner recovered from my shock when another stranger came in; it was Domingo Quici minus his handlebar mustache. "What happened to you?" I asked rather faintly. "Well, if the gospel required that my friend Donato shave his mustache, I'm willing to sacrifice also, but it did take me a little longer to decide to do it, because it was my pride and joy; I've had it for over forty years." Now I was really feeling low. Soon Brother Notaro, the third member of this trinity, appeared clean-shaven. He had the same explanation: "If the gospel requires one to shave, I want to conform." I could have been bought for a wooden nickel and I would have returned some change. Though chagrined, I always felt proud of these humble men who, in their simple faith, would go to any lengths to do what they thought the Lord wanted them to do. I truly loved these good and great men, for the simplicity of their lives and their desire at all times to sacrifice everything for the gospel's sake. They would do anything that the missionaries asked of them, for they believed them to be the representatives of Christ on earth. One had only to ask. It made me realize that I needed to be very careful of what I said, that as a missionary my words were taken very seriously.

After serving as Deacons and Teachers, both Donato Gianfelice and Domingo Quici were ordained Priests on August 12, 1928. Luis Notaro was ordained to that same office on May 18, 1930. As I recall, President Stoof did not ordain anyone to the Melchizedek Priesthood during his presidency.

The Emil Hoppe family. Brother Hoppe was a wonderful and impressive person. He stood over six feet tall and ramrod straight. His wife couldn't have been more than five feet tall. They were a dedicated couple who had joined the Church in Germany before moving to Argentina. He and Brother Friedrichs began the work by asking that missionaries be sent.

Brother Hoppe owned a small launch which he named *Nephi I.* He lent me this boat any time I came to Entre Ríos to visit the missionaries or members. I had the privilege of performing the marriage of his son Augusto to Elses Georges at their home in the Delta.

The Hoppes were always staunch members of the Church and never wavered in their testimonies. We could have used ten thousand members like them.

The Ernst Biebersdorf family. When Elders Ballard, Pratt and Wells arrived in Buenos Aires to begin missionary work on the South American Continent, they were met by two German families who were members of the Church, and several friends they had interested in the gospel. Probably one of those friends was Ernst Biebersdorf. Whether he was at dockside or not, the first meeting with the visiting authorities was held in his home in Dock Sud later that evening. Six days later, Ernst Biebersdorf and his wife Maria were baptized by Elder Ballard, along with four others.

I remember Brother Biebersdorf very well. Quiet and unassuming, he never complained, never said a critical word about anyone. He was always faithful to the Church, and was always found in his place; we could depend on him. He and his wife raised their children in the Church, baptizing them as they reached the age of accountability. Later, as mission president, it was my pleasure to see these children grow into young adulthood. Their daughter Maria married a fine young member Juan Parraga from the La Plata Branch. In July 1941, I set Brother Biebersdorf apart as the President of the Quilmes Branch of the Church.

The Franz family. In April 1928, President Stoof asked me to deliver a letter from Germany addressed to Heinrich Julius Gustav Franz. I eventually found the home, and a young German girl about nine years old answered the door. She couldn't understand my Spanish, so in halting German I told her I had a letter for her father and that President Stoof of the Mission had sent me. Placing the letter into her hand was more understandable, I'm afraid, than my explanation in German. Her name was Gertrude.

Brother Franz was a skilled therapist and worked at a sanatorium near Leipzig, Germany, when the Governor of the Province of Córdoba, Argentina, brought his ailing daughter for treatments; as it turned out, he was successful in restoring the girl's health. The Governor, Dr. Teobaldi, suggested he establish himself in business in Córdoba. The Franz family consisted of Heinrich, his wife Hedwig, two sons, Erich and Walter, and an infant daughter, Gertrude; all but the baby had recently been baptized into the Church. Brother Franz explained to Governor Teobaldi that he had a growing family and was financially unable to move them so far away. The Governor countered by inviting them to return to South America with him and his family on his private yacht. This was in 1921.

They resided in Córdoba for five years; they gave up their German citizenship and became Argentines. Brother Franz made a good living, but it was frustrating for him to live with no contact with members of the Church.

In 1926 the family returned to Germany, but once there they were unable to secure housing as they were now foreigners; they had to reside in hotels. They tried to emigrate to the United States, but Brother Franz was turned down because of a physical impairment: he had a hernia. Unable to enter the States from Germany, they decided to return to Argentina and try from there.

They settled in a suburb of Buenos Aires. It was at that time I became acquainted with the family. In the one year's absence from Spanish-speaking Argentina, Gertrude had completely forgotten how to speak Spanish.

On January 14, 1974, H.J. Gustav Franz died in Salt Lake City at age ninety-four. He left twenty-five grandchildren and fifty-six great grandchildren as his monument; he was a devoted and devout member of the Church.

Sister Eladia Sifuentes. The first Latin convert, Sister Sifuentes turned out to be the first drop-out as well. I suppose that if she had been named Mission President all would have been fine. But when she found out she couldn't run every organization and the lives of the members, she lost her interest in the Church. She had previously been active in some small Protestant church and virtually ran it. She wanted to do the same with ours. I have in my possession a letter President Stoof wrote to her in English, which I translated into Spanish, imploring her to change her mind and to remain faithful to her original testimony. She didn't do anything about it, however.

The González family. This family was baptized March 6, 1927. The father, a well-educated, highly opinionated, loquacious man, never did join the Church, but consented to his wife's and children's baptisms. At first, he delighted in trying to stump the missionaries with questions concerning religion and philosophy, but over the years he gained respect for them. During my mission, this family had been very faithful. The mother, Isabel, was a very quiet woman with few opinions and little opportunity to express those she had. She had learned her place and stayed there in the old Latin tradition. I liked her very much. She was always very happy to have the missionaries visit her home. Aurora, twenty, was their oldest daughter, followed by Delia, eighteen, and Libertad, sixteen, then three sons, Germinal, fourteen, Ideal, twelve, and Tito, ten.

While we were holding a cottage meeting at the González family home, their former minister dropped by. He gave us a rather hard time and challenged us to permit him to speak in our Sunday evening meeting. He said that if our church were true, we shouldn't be afraid to let him speak; also, we could refute what he had to say. I accepted the challenge.

We prayed together and discussed what I should say. We tried to anticipate what the minister would bring up, and I personally worried a lot. I also studied and prayed, asking for help to defend my beliefs in the meeting to the satisfaction of our members and investigators.

The fateful hour came. Word had gotten around and the hall was full. The time to begin the meeting arrived, but no minister. We decided to give him a little more time. Finally, twenty minutes late, I started the meeting, keeping my eye on the door. When the preliminaries were over and our expected visitor failed to arrive, I went ahead and gave the talk I had prepared. Much to the disappointment of some of the investigators, the minister never came. I, of course, was delighted. This little experience had a great effect on the members of the branch. It brought them and the missionaries even closer together. This unity of purpose—almost of mutual defense against outsiders—persisted throughout my missions in Argentina.

Sister Jaraguiones. Soon after the Notaros were baptized and started attending our meetings, a lady by the name of Zefera A. de Jaraguiones became interested in the Church. I was at the door of the *local* talking with the Notaros when she came to her first meeting.

For a moment, I didn't think she would come in. She stared intently at the Notaros. They, in turn, were hostile toward her. "Are they members of this Church?" she asked. When told they were, she started to turn and leave. I suggested that as long as she had come this distance she should attend the meeting. The Notaros had taken their seats. She hesitated for a moment, and then sat down as far away from them as she could.

They had been neighbors for some time. She couldn't control her sons and they constantly climbed over the fence into the Notaros' vegetable garden, and hard feelings had developed. After they had been baptized into the Church they became the best of friends and often laughed at their earlier actions, each one thankful that the gospel had brought them together.

On January 14, 1931, this sister sent a Book of Mormon to the President of Argentina, José F. Uriburu. He acknowledged her gift in a letter dated January 19, 1931.

Joaquín Farimiera. On June 3, 1928, Joaquín Farimiera, a Portuguese, was administered to by Elders Christian and Clegg. He was losing his eyesight and, according to his own report, the doctors could do nothing for him. Not long after the blessing, he recovered his eyesight fully, which we considered a miraculous manifestation of the power of God. He and his wife were baptized on October 17, 1928. Their son, born after I left the mission field, was named after me. Unfortunately, little Federico William Farimiera died when he was only two months old.

While living on Calle República a small neighbor boy of about seven years of age was our constant companion. He came early and stayed late, and became a total nuisance. He attended all our meetings and said that he wanted to be baptized when he reached age eight. We tried to interest his parents, but they didn't want to know anything about the Church. His name was Rogelio Paradizo. While living in Perú, 1956 to 1960, I received a letter from him. He stated that he was now an elder in the Church; that his parents never did consent to his baptism while he was underage, but that when he was legally old enough to do what he wanted, he sought out the Church and asked the missionaries to baptize him.

Mission-wide beach party. In January of 1929, I organized a beach party for the mission. We went early and stayed late that Saturday. Organized games and races were staged for the children and the adults. Everyone brought more food than could possibly be eaten, but we all tried.

It was a magnificent success for everyone except me. I should have stayed home. Later people told me how the southern sun burnes a light skin like mine. When I reached home, blisters covered my neck and shoulders and the tops of my feet. I struggled through Sunday, but was unable to go out of the house all the following week, and slept face-down each night. That was one of the worst weeks I can ever remember.

Joy in serving the Lord. At Calle República I came into my own as a missionary. Here the mantle of authority descended upon me and I developed whatever leadership qualities I possess. While a challenge, it was also a joy to me at all times. I became heir to all the good and faithful work accomplished by the excellent missionaries who had preceded me. I was priviledged to build on the foundations laid by J. Vernon Sharp, Waldo I. Stoddard, Lewis E. Christian, and Heber M. Clegg. I shall always look back with the greatest pleasure and satisfaction in respect to the eighteen months I lived and worked at that address.

Our mission calls were for twenty-four months, and I should have been released in March 1929, but there was no one to take my place. President Stoof requested permission to keep me an additional six months. I was delighted when my parents and the General Authorities gave their consent.

The intense early winter rain, storms and cold were not kind to me that year. Traveling constantly without proper clothing, soaked many times between buses and trains and without a warm overcoat, I caught a cold I could not shake off. President Stoof insisted that I go to the British Hospital for an examination. When the doctors learned that I had suffered from pneumonia the summer before accepting a mission call and that my lungs were somewhat weak, he recommended, much against my desires, that I not spend another three months in the damp and cold. Additional missionaries had now arrived, so the President told me I should make arrangements to return home about the middle of June.

I asked that my release be effective on my twenty-first birthday, June 15. Up to that time I had served longer than any other missionary called to the South American Mission, a total of twenty-seven and one-half months. Only the Mission President and his wife had been there longer.

My farewell was on Sunday, the 16th, and the hall was filled to overflowing. I received many tributes of love and affection—things that I had known all along by the actions of the Saints and friends. We all had a good cry and it was a very emotional meeting. Many signed an autograph book which I treasure highly. Many beautiful statements are therein expressed, some of which were tributes to my mother.

I performed the following ordinances on my mission:

Baptisms

Catalina Jiménez de Alvarez	March 31, 1928
José Alvarez Jiménez	March 31, 1928
María Juana Martínez	December 15, 1928
Aurora Antonia Martínez	December 15, 1928
José Ruiz	January 20, 1929
Dora Rosalía Zanardini	June 3, 1929
Adele Zanardini	June 3, 1929

Confirmations

Catalina Jiménez de Alvarez	March 31, 1928
Luigi Notaro	June 29, 1928
Serafina Rogelia González de San Isidro	December 8, 1928
Teresa Felisa Martínez	December 15, 1928
José Ruiz	January 20, 1929
Leonidas Jaraguiones	January 28, 1928
Dora Rosalía Zanardini	June 3, 1929

Priesthood Ordinations

José Alvarez Olmo, a Deacon	September 9, 1928

Miscellaneous

Blessed Jorge Jaraguiones	February 3, 1929

Positions Filled

Vélez Sarsfield Sunday School Secretary	November 25, 1928
Vélez Sarsfield Sunday School Teacher	November 25, 1928
Liniers Sunday School Superintendent	November 25, 1928
Branch President and Presiding Elder in Spanish Work	December 30, 1928

Date of Release from Mission: June 15, 1929, my 21st birthday.

NOTES

Chapter VI

1. See Ballard "History."

2. There is an interesting testimonial signed by Elder Clive S. Walker, attesting to the faithfulness of Brother Notaro in keeping the Word of Wisdom. It came after a somewhat remarkable medical diagnosis of a serious kidney infection.

"I have been living with the Notaro Family for nearly two years and know that they are good, loyal members of the Church. They have accepted the teachings of the Gospel in humbleness and have done their best to obey them. Especially have they obeyed the "Word of Wisdom" and received the blessings promised. Brother Luigi Notaro left his wine and tobacco and has never used them since the day of his baptism.

About three months ago he became ill and it was necessary to call a doctor. We called Dr. Yodice, who is a friend of theirs and who has known them for some years. After examining him and prescribing treatment he turned to me and said, "How much your religion has done for this man! If it were not for your religion this man would be dead, because he used to drink much wine."

Later it was necessary to consult another doctor. After making his examination he said, "Now don't drink wine, nor smoke, nor drink tea nor coffee."

Brother Notaro replied, "Doctor I have not done any of that for years. We are in the gospel and do not believe in such things. We believe in keeping our bodies clean." See Stoof "History," August 14, 1932.

CHAPTER VII

THE RETURN

AFTER SO MANY years, it is beyond my ability to recall all that transpired after the completion of my mission in Argentina. However, some of my experiences are as vivid as if they had occurred yesterday. Perhaps my feelings are romanticized, since at the time I was young and impressionable and deeply in love with the people, the language and the locales where I had been laboring for more than two years.

On the evening of June 19, 1929, I said good-bye to some forty friends and slowly walked up the gangplank of the Italian steamship *Conte Rosso*, firmly believing I would never see those dear friends again. They bravely waved on that bitterly cold night in Buenos Aires until the ship was lost to view in the stormy night. With tears in my eyes, I made my way to my third-class quarters which I shared with several other passengers.

One of my fellow passengers was a young Argentine traveling to São Paulo to visit his sister. We were the only two who didn't speak Italian, so we became friends. We shared a hotel room in Santos. We ran into our first problem in the hotel dining room. We wanted ham sandwiches. We used all the words we knew in Spanish to signify ham, pork, pig or hog, but to no avail. Our Portuguese-speaking Brazilian waiter didn't have the faintest idea of what we wanted. In desperation, I drew the best pig I was capable of, bisected a hind quarter and sliced a piece of ham from it. The waiter's face lighted up, *"Ah, presunto."* We immediately received our ham sandwiches.

The following morning we took the train to São Paulo. After a few miles the train came to an abrupt stop. We thought nothing of it until we noticed that the engine had been detached and backed up to the end of the train to push the cars forward. A few minutes later, to our mystification, train crewmen locked both doors of our car. Presently, the train started moving forward again. We were being pulled by huge cables up the face of the mountain that creates the great Paulista Plateau. How many hundreds or thousands of feet we climbed I don't remember, but it was a thrilling ride, suspended by straining cables. When our courage permitted, we looked out the window at the steep incline. I was impressed and relieved once we had gained the relative safety of the plateau. Shortly thereafter, we reached São Paulo.

According to the map, it isn't far from São Paulo to Joinville, but apparently our train crew didn't know or didn't care. We took our time. There was only a single track, so periodically we stopped and waited for a northbound train to go by.

After a day and night on the train with my pants corrugated from sitting on the wooden slats of the seat, it was good to get off at the railroad junction on Ponta Grossa for a few hours. Another train bound for Rio Negro and Curitiba was waiting in the station. It took most of the day to reach the first stop where, if I had understood enough Portuguese, I would have spent the night awaiting for my train to Joinville. Instead, I stayed on the train, and unbeknownst to me, was on my merry way to Curitiba. That I was on the wrong train was finally made clear to me by a Portuguese-speaking German. I didn't know what to do. However, I found that I could spend the night at a small railroad junction through which my train would pass the following day.

My train pulled in about five o'clock a.m., dumped my trunk on the platform of a small two-story station house, and left. I looked for a *pensão,* but found that the only other building of this railroad junction was a tool shed belonging to the railroad. I had visions of spending the night on the station platform, but the station master had an extra room on the second floor of his station which he offered to rent to me.

I tried to converse with his seven or eight-year old daughter. We didn't do very well. I asked about dinner and whether we would be eating a little later, *"Comeremos luego?" "Não,"* she answered, *"Depois!"* (Afterwards!) We ate beans and rice "afterwards," about seven-thirty. The Portuguese cognate for the Spanish *"luego,"* is *"logo"* and means "soon," instead of "later."

After dinner, I went for a walk. That night was one I shall always remember. I had never seen a sky so full of stars. The Southern Cross swung at anchor in the southern hemisphere, its four bright stars forming a bright cross to guide ships to harbor south of the Equator.

I felt at peace with God and all of his Creation. I seemed to be in a trance, full of love toward all men. The thought occurred to me that I would be happy if I could spend the rest of my life in such surroundings, that here I would be content to live. Then the sound of a large animal moving in the jungle brought me back to reality, and I thought it high time for me to get back to my room.

The following morning, I continued to Joinville. I had no way to alert Elder Schindler as to my time of arrival, so he was not at the station to meet me.

At Joinville a Negro taxi driver inquired in German if I wanted a taxi and where I was going. I responded in German. Our entire conversation was in that language. Hundreds of thousands of German immigrants lived in Santa Catarina, and more than a million in the state to the south, Rio Grande do Sul. Even the street signs were in German. What had originally been Rua Duque de Caxias 54 was now Nordstrasse 54. It was also where Elder Schindler lived. Later, the Church purchased this home and enlarged it into a small chapel. It thus became the first piece of property owned by The Church of Jesus Christ of Latter-day Saints on the South American Continent. Elder Schindler was happy to see me. I spent a week visiting with him and his friends and members in Joinville.

The night before my departure, Elder Schindler threw a farewell party for me and invited many of his friends, young businessmen about his age. It was enjoyable, but a lot went over my head. They certainly had a good time visiting, laughing and singing. Too bad I didn't understand their jokes. Perhaps I would have laughed, too.

The next morning, some investigators asked if I would look after three young German girls who were going to Santos on the same ship with me. They were about my age and quite attractive. I looked forward to the trip. However, our efforts to become better acquainted were hampered a bit by their parents' accompanying us to São Francisco do Sul.

We sailed from São Francisco do Sul on July 2, 1929, on the German steamship *Carl Hoepeke*. The girls said good-bye to their parents after putting their luggage in their rooms, and we all went on deck to wave farewell and to enjoy the beautiful view of the harbor. Our limited conversation was carried on in German, as the girls spoke very little Portuguese and no Spanish.

Once we were on the high seas the ship began to roll and pitch. One girl excused herself and left. Then the second and the third did the same. By that time I knew that I, too, would be more comfortable in my stateroom. We didn't see each other again until we docked in Santos. I remained prone on my bunk until the ship entered the smooth waters of Santos Bay the following afternoon. Relatives met the girls at the ship's gangplank. We said good-bye and I was left alone.

The S.S. Vandyke. On Monday, July 8, 1929, I sailed for New York. After some three weeks in a country where only Portuguese and German were spoken, it felt good to get on a ship with an English-speaking crew.

On the morning of July 18 we arrived in Bridgetown, the capital of the island of Barbados. The ship anchored some distance from the shore, and within a very few minutes dozens of small boats filled with young people put out from shore and approached the ship. When passengers threw coins into the water they dove and retrieved them a few feet below the water's surface. They carried on a lucrative trade until the passengers were ready to go ashore.

After living a sheltered life in Arizona and Utah all my life, and fresh from the mission field, I was shocked at the language and obscene gestures and invitations I received from both girls and boys. I remember in particular one girl, since her color stood out in such marked contrast to the black people. She couldn't have been more than seventeen or eighteen years of age, and once must have been beautiful. She was old far beyond her years. She, along with several black girls, tried to take me, almost by force, to their rooms after making all kinds of lewd proposals to me. The white girl became abusive and very angry after I turned her down, I literally had to break away from the hold she had on my arm.

Walking out of the center of Barbados into the beautiful countryside, I was enthralled with the tropical scenery. Palm trees swayed in the gentle breeze. Flowers grew in multicolored profusion. Small houses, built on stilts to permit the breeze to blow under them (and to give shade to pigs, dogs and children), were surrounded with flowers, shrubs and tropical trees.

I spent all the loose cash I had for souvenirs on my return to Bridgetown, leaving myself just enough money to hold me over in New York until I could receive some from home.

It was a thrill to me to sail the same waters where the pirate ships of infamous freebooters had plowed the Caribbean for more than two centuries. The Caribbean has seen so much history, so much romance, adventure and suffering. The largely peaceful Indians had been mostly exterminated through the diseases brought by the white man or through overwork on the plantations of the foreign conquerors where they had been pressed into slavery. Only the fierce Carib Indians held their own with the interlopers and refused to bow to them.

As the S.S. *Vandyke* made its steady way toward New York, I had much to think about and plenty of leisure time to do it in. The weather was perfect and the sea was calm, and as one day merged with the next I languidly read, conversed or slept in the unexcelled life of a passenger on an ocean-going ship. The food was good and the meals gave the only meaning to time, as they were served at regular intervals.

The United States. During the last few days of the voyage, rather than wash out my soiled clothing, I cast it overboard, so that on the morning we steamed into New York Harbor, I had on my last change of clothing. I had a nice-looking shirt, although it was ready to come apart due to age and hard use, but it was the best one I owned, and I had saved it especially for my arrival. I put it on, along with my only remaining neck tie, and my one and only suit—a dark one—the trousers of which I had mended repeatedly, and went on deck to see the Statue of Liberty.

Great excitement reigned among the passengers. It was the first time many had seen this great city and most of the third-class passengers, who were immigrants, were so overjoyed that they wept. As we came close to the famous statue, one of my German friends grabbed me in his arms and lifted me off my feet. While I appreciated his exuberance, I didn't relish the sound of my shirt tearing into a thousand pieces. I went below, took off my coat and surveyed the damage. The back of the shirt was shredded, but fortunately the front was intact. However, I couldn't take off my coat, and it was the 24th of July, in hot, humid, steamy New York.

My brother, Orlando, had told me that if I could get to New York, he would send me one hundred dollars by Western Union as soon as I arrived. I immediately wired him, spending my last money on the telegram. I then went to my hotel room and read until late that afternoon when I received the money.

I went to a nearby store and bought a shirt. I returned to the hotel and put it on and was now appropriately dressed to go shopping for a suit. I went to a Brooks Brothers' store for men and bought a gray suit. This, together with a pair of brown shoes, completed my wardrobe. After wearing one suit every day for more than a year, it felt wonderful to have a new one. I didn't even mind the New York summer heat.

After paying my hotel bill, I bought a chair-car railway ticket to Holbrook, Arizona, via Salt Lake City. My sister Naoma met me in Salt Lake City at the same depot where she had bade me good-bye when I left for South America. It was good to see her again. Home cooking tasted like ambrosia after eating in restaurants, ships and foreign countries for two years.

Elder Melvin J. Ballard had sent word to the mission that he wanted to see me on my arrival in Salt Lake City. I called his office and found that he was on vacation, but he had left word that if I called, he would return, as he was very anxious to get a report on the mission. His secretary set up an appointment for the next day.

It was a great thrill to report to Elder Ballard, since he had set me apart in 1927. Having established the South American Mission, he was very anxious to hear all that I could tell him about it and about the first members that he had baptized and known in Buenos Aires. After asking many questions, he began reminiscing about his time in that far-off land.

After asking if I had enjoyed my mission and if I thought the mission had a great future—which I answered in the affirmative—he made this observation just before we parted: "Now, your next mission is to go home and get married. We may want to send you back to South America." I told him I would be happy to go at any time, but didn't realize the import of his words.

While in Salt Lake City I got in touch with my old missionary companion, Heber Clegg. He said it was time I had a date, and arranged a double date for me (with himself and his wife Marge). Della Green was a charming young lady. She even volunteered her family car, a new Reo, for the evening, and suggested that I drive. It was the first time since 1926 that I had been behind the wheel of a car, and it seemed strange, especially since, at that time, all traffic in Buenos Aires moved on the left side of the street.

We went up one of the canyons to the "Old Mill." The walls of an old mill still stood on the sides of the dance floor. The moonlight, the sound of the running stream, together with the magic of soft music, made this a romantic evening, although my dancing was very rusty. I very much enjoyed my first date and dance after my mission.

It was time to start traveling again. Naoma again took me to the railroad station so I could entrain for Holbrook, Arizona, where my family was waiting for me. The train arrived early in the morning, but I had already been awake for hours. I saw familiar faces on the platform, and realized for the first time that my South American adventure was just about over; I had almost returned to my starting point. I was delighted to embrace my family.

Mother, Orin and Lucy had come to Holbrook especially to meet me, so we made plans to go to Phoenix. The Williams and Janson Construction Company had prospered during my mission, but now in July 1929, just before the crash of October, things had gone badly for them, as was the case with so many others. Orin and I looked for a car and finally decided to buy a 1927 Studebaker sedan. The car was in good condition, with one exception. The automatic starter had been broken off the engine block and it was impossible to weld back. We had to crank the car, but fortunately it started easily. We made a down payment on it and set out for Phoenix, where we arrived without incident on Friday, August 2, bringing to a close my South American adventure. I was back where I had started.

Naturally, I was curious about what my old friends, the young people of the ward, were doing. I found that the M-Men and Gleaners were having a swimming party that night at the Glendale public pool, and Orin and I decided to go. I got out of the car and started toward the pool, attracted by the happy voices of young men and women standing at poolside. Suddenly, one young lady looked my way. A puzzled look appeared on her face for a minute and then with a joyous cry—heard by all the swimmers—she exclaimed: "It's Fred!"

In the fleeting seconds before she and the others came to shake my hand, I received the definite impression that Corraine Smith, the girl who had yelled my name, would be my wife.

FIRST INTERREGNUM

IN THE NINE years between the end of my mission (1929) and the call to preside over the Argentine Mission (1938), I married Corraine Smith and settled down in Phoenix, Arizona, where our first two daughters were born. I began to work as a carpenter in my brothers' construction company, but soon obtained employment in the U.S. Federal District Court of the Honorable F.C. Jacobs, first as Spanish interpreter and court crier and, two years later, as Judge Jacobs' personal secretary. It was a wonderful position for a young family man: it sharpened my language and administrative skills, brought me in contact with many interesting people, and paid very well, especially by Depression standards. In 1937, Judge Jacobs retired and I soon found work again with the Williams Construction Company where I helped build, among other things, LDS chapels. My Church callings during that time included Elders Quorum President, M-Men leader, and President of the Seventies.

PART II

THE ARGENTINE MISSION (1925-1929)

INTRODUCTION TO PART TWO

THE NARRATIVE OF our mission in Argentina seems to suggest a natural division of its major components: missionaries and local citizens, and the Church programs where the two came together. Of course, these elements generally reflect the historical elements of any mission at any location, but with no outstanding figures among either the missionaries or members (e.g., Parley P. Pratt, Wilford Woodruff, Orrin Porter Rockwell) and with no spectacular or unique exchanges between the two groups (conversion of one thousand in a week, the Battle of Nauvoo), most mission histories have limited appeal.

However, our Argentine story contains two elements of more than passing interest; in fact, they were unique in contemporary Church history. Individually, we were the common variety of Mormon missionaries, foreigners in the distant country come to proclaim the restored Gospel to a largely Catholic and, I might add, disinterested people. What made the experience remarkable were the conditions under which these two groups met: impending world war. Also, we were not only Mormons in a Catholic land, we were also Americans, and America was an Allied country. Argentina, on the other hand—a mixture of several nationalities, but with a more than generous representation of citizens from Spain, Italy and Germany—despite her official neutral stance, was pro-Axis. World War II was to have a marked influence on our mission. It at once complicated and limited our activities, while deepening our commitment and giving new meaning to our message of peace.

The second unique element in our history was the successful technique of simultaneously introducing the gospel into Argentina, changing the Church's poor image in the press, and actively proselyting among the citizenry through participation in organized national and international sports. We became—on a modest scale—the darlings of the nation. The activities of our missionary sports teams, "Los Mormones," were favorably reported almost daily in the leading newspapers. This extensive press coverage helped overcome immense hurdles of prejudice and thereby firmly established the foundation on which the present strength of Mormonism in Argentina now rests.

We even created our own "Zion's Camp" when we organized the Church Welfare Plan locally. Like the unsuccessful Zion's Camp, the Argentine Welfare Plan did not achieve its expressed goal. It did, however, produce a cohesive, close-knit membership, drawing out its future leaders and giving them valuable experience.

The mission's pioneer members—the foreign-born Germans (Hoppes and Friedrichs) and Italians (Gianfelices and Notaros)—although just as dedicated, were a little older and a little less prepared to meet the leadership challenges of the growing Church. This was to be the period of the Argentine-born, the second generation, and our activities naturally focused on the youth: dances, sports, speech contests, conferences. And as the youth responded, we drew from their ranks the mission leaders: branch presidents, counselors, heads of organizations, and missionaries.

These elements—war, organized sports, the welfare plan, youth programs, in addition to our regular proselyting activities—did not follow sequentially. Rather, all functioned at the same time, progressing and developing in parallels, then crossing and interweaving to influence one another until the fabric of mission membership life was formed.

CHAPTER I

PRELUDE: THE CALL TO BE MISSION PRESIDENT

WHILE COMPLETING construction of the branch chapel in El Paso just before its dedication, I received the following letter from the First Presidency of The Church of Jesus Christ of Latter-day Saints:

Salt Lake City, Utah, July 11, 1938

Elder Frederick Williams
c/o President O. C. Williams
3531 Fort Blvd.
El Paso, Texas

Dear Brother Williams:

The First Presidency and the Council of the Twelve, after due consideration, are desirous of calling you to preside over the Argentine Mission of the Church, succeeding Elder W. Ernest Young, with headquarters in Buenos Aires, Argentina.

We should appreciate hearing from you in the near future as to whether or not your circumstances are such that you could accept such a call, and if so, just when you would be able to arrange your affairs to leave for the mission field.

Please send us also a picture of yourself and a brief sketch of your life that we might use in the local papers when announcing your appointment.

We would of course wish you and Sister Williams to come to this city to be set apart.

We shall be pleased to hear from you at your earliest convenience.

Sincerely your brethren,

THE FIRST PRESIDENCY

(Signed) Heber J. Grant
David O. McKay

Corraine and I were thrilled to receive this call and immediately answered that we would be pleased to accept it, and would be ready to go to Salt Lake City as soon as the chapel was dedicated, about a week after I received the letter.

Thus began the realization of a nine-year-long dream. During my mission in Argentina I became very close to our few members. I knew of their hopes and dreams for the future and their desire to know the gospel and to live its precepts. They desperately needed teachers and leaders. I prayed that my mission might be prolonged so that I could help them. This prayer was granted and my mission was extended three months. I prayed that I might some day return and help them in other ways. Now this call would make it possible for the fulfillment of that prayer.

We finished the chapel on a Friday. Elder Melvin J. Ballard arrived early Saturday morning to preside over the dedicatory services. It was a joy to see him again. The father of the South American Mission, he had not lost his interest in the Lord's work in South America. He congratulated me on the call, and I suspect he was responsible for it.

After the final dedicatory meeting on July 17, 1938, Corraine and I drove Elder Ballard to the railroad station. He talked to us the entire trip about our new assignment, and lamented that he would not be in Salt Lake City for our setting apart; he had an assignment in the Pacific Northwest that would keep him busy for several weeks. He also recalled vivid experiences of his mission to South America. We were both enthralled with this intimate visit and later benefited by the counsel he gave us.

He also told us that if we lived frugally, we would be able to build up a nice nest egg to use on our return. This we could not do, however. We found it impossible to save any money as we had to use not only every penny of our living allowance, but depleted our savings as well. I think conditions had changed since he had been a mission president in the United States. We received only one hundred fifty dollars per month, out of which we paid for our children's schooling, our personal medical care, food, clothing and other living expenses. The Church paid for the rent and utilities on the mission home and transportation. We said good-bye to him as he boarded his train. We continued to correspond with him, but this was the last time we saw Elder Ballard.

The following day, a Monday, we began our long journey to Salt Lake City. These were Depression years and we didn't have any money. We sold our 1936 Dodge car (the first new car we had ever owned) and borrowed some money from my brother, Orlando. Then Corraine and I and our two daughters Barbara and Argina, set out. Barbara was seven years old, Argina three and one-half, Corraine was twenty-nine and I had just turned thirty. We arrived in Salt Lake City Sunday evening, July 24.

Because the 24th of July celebration fell on Monday that year, we prepared to go to the Church Office Building early Tuesday morning. We waited until nine o'clock to give President Grant a chance to get to his office. When we arrived his secretary said we would have to wait a few minutes; he had been in meetings since six that morning.

We sat down to wait and in a few minutes he entered. Of course, he didn't know us, but came over and extended his hand and asked, "What can I do for you good people?" I explained the purpose of this visit, and he said in his sweet way, "My counselors are out of town, but they will return tonight. If it isn't too much of an inconvenience, could you come back tomorrow so that they can help me? If it is inconvenient, I can find some of the members of the Twelve to assist me, but I would prefer to have my counselors with me." We said we would be happy to wait until Wednesday. He then said: "There is something we can do today. Come with me and I'll introduce you to some people who can help you."

Then, as though he were an office boy and not the President of the Church, he took us from office to office, directing people to make the necessary arrangements for our trip. After introducing us to Franklin Murdock, President Grant bade us good-bye and returned to his office.

On Wednesday morning, Corraine and I—accompanied by our mothers—went to President Grant's office. After a few minutes' conversation he called in his counselors, J. Reuben Clark, Jr., and David O. McKay. President Grant explained the purpose of our visit and asked me to take a seat. The three members of the First Presidency placed their hands upon my head and President Grant began the setting apart blessing, then stopped.

"What priesthood do you hold, brother?" he asked.

"I am a Seventy," I answered.

President Grant then ordained me a High Priest and then set me apart to preside over the Argentine Mission.

A BLESSING UPON THE HEAD OF ELDER FREDERICK S. WILLIAMS

By Presidents Heber J. Grant and J. Reuben Clark, Jr., President Grant being voice, setting him apart to preside over the ARGENTINE MISSION.

> *BROTHER FREDERICK S. WILLIAMS: We the servants of the Living God, holding the Holy Priesthood and by the authority of the same, lay our hands upon your head, and we bless you and ordain you an High Priest in the Church of Jesus Christ of Latter-day Saints, and seal upon you all the rights, keys, powers, privileges, and authority pertaining to this high and holy calling in the Melchizedek Priesthood, which Priesthood is after the order of Melchizedek the great High Priest, and after the order of the Son of God. And we also in the name of Jesus Christ set you apart and ordain you to this office. This we do in the name of Jesus Christ. Amen.*
>
> *We now set you apart to preside over the Argentine Mission and we bless you with the spirit of missionary work that has come to you. We bless you with every gift, grace, and authority which is necessary for you to possess in order to faithfully and diligently fulfill the duties and obligations of this important mission.*
>
> *We say unto you, remember at all times that the missionaries under your care are there giving their time and their talents at their own expense, and that of their families and friends, and that they should be treated with great courtesy and respect and with love; and that you should endeavor to get them to be diligent and faithful through your own example of diligence and faithfulness. You should be charitable, and kind, and be in every deed a father to the missionaries that will be under your jurisdiction.*
>
> *We bless you with vigor of body and of mind; we bless you with health and strength of body, that you may go forth in peace and return in safety, and that you may have satisfaction and joy in your labors. There is no work in all the world that is more pleasing and acceptable to our Heavenly Father than laboring to bring souls to a knowledge of the Gospel of the Lord Jesus Christ that has been restored again to the earth through the instrumentality of the Prophet Joseph Smith.*

We bless you, dear brother, for your faithful labors in the past, and pray that every desire of your heart in righteousness, through your faith and faithfulness, shall be given unto you, for we bless you unto this end, and we do it all in the authority of the Priesthood of the Living God, and in the name of the Lord Jesus Christ, our Redeemer and Savior, Amen.

(Signed) *Approved:* Heber J. Grant

Salt Lake City, Utah
July 27, 1938

A BLESSING UPON THE HEAD OF SISTER CORRAINE SMITH WILLIAMS

By Presidents Heber J. Grant, and J. Reuben Clark, Jr., and her husband, Frederick S. Williams, President Clark being voice.

SISTER CORRAINE SMITH WILLIAMS: In the name of the Lord Jesus Christ, and in the authority of the Priesthood which we hold, we lay our hands upon your head to bless you and to set you apart to assist your husband to preside over the Argentine Mission, and we ask our Heavenly Father to bless you in every way in which He sees that a blessing is needed.

We bless you with patience and with charity; we bless you with a love for the missionaries and the people over whom your husband will preside. We bless you that you may come to know and understand the way in which their minds work; that you may have a sympathy for them.

We bless you that you may be able to preside over the Relief Society in the Argentine Mission, and that you may lead those sisters there to do the work which the Lord desires them to do. You will have a great opportunity to do good among this people, and we bless you to that end.

We bless you that you may be a mother to the missionaries who will look upon you as a mother indeed. We bless you with all the motherly instincts that it is necessary for you to have in order that you may do your work satisfactorily.

We bless you with health and with life, and with strength, and we ask our Heavenly Father to have heed to these blessings, and to pour them out bounteously upon you, and He will do so in accordance with your desires and the way in which you may live.

We seal these blessings upon you in the name of the Lord Jesus Christ, and by virtue of the Priesthood which we hold, even so, Amen.

(Signed) *Approved:* J. Reuben Clark, Jr.

Salt Lake City, Utah
July 27, 1938

President Grant's instructions. After the setting apart blessings, we lingered in President Grant's office, expecting detailed instructions concerning our new callings. Finally, President Grant began nudging us towards the door.

"President Grant," I said, "we feel very young and are going a long way away. Don't you have some advice or instructions for us?"

President Grant placed his arm around my shoulder and said, "God bless you." With that benediction we left for our mission half-way around the world. We had expected specific instructions; however, over the years we decided that if God blessed us, what else did we need? This was His work and if we could live to merit His blessings, all would go well.

Our mothers accompanied us back to Arizona; both vied for our attention the entire trip. One would tell us an experience or a story. Immediately, the other would tell a greater story. This continued all the way to Phoenix where we left Corraine's mother. She was dying of cancer and the doctors had given her only a few months to live, so the parting was very sad. Quoting from my wife's History:

> *We had been told Mom couldn't live more than three months. She had passed her three months and she lived a year and three months before passing away. When we had first received the call, I felt I couldn't possibly go and leave Mother knowing she had so short a time. Fred said, "But you have to. This call is to you as much as it is to me." I couldn't feel consoled until I saw Mom again. She was so wonderful, cheerful and optimistic. She felt very blessed at having children worthy of such great honor and gave us nothing but encouragement.*
>
> *I felt that the Lord really blessed us both. I knew I would be with her some day in the eternities and I'm sure she felt the same and so we were sustained in this parting.*
>
> *She smiled just as long as we could see her. She didn't shed a tear. What she did after we were gone, I don't know. But she didn't let me see her cry, and it gave me the strength to leave her.*

In El Paso we repaid Orlando and prepared to board a train for New York City. We gave away our canned goods, washing machine, electric refrigerator and vacuum cleaner; loaned our bedroom set and placed our books in the LDS Institute library at the University of Arizona.

Our train ride from El Paso to New York was interesting but uneventful. We were very comfortable in our own compartment which had the luxury of private bath facilities.

We had a six-hour stopover in St. Louis. After consulting the porter, who swore that all would be well, Corraine and I left the two little girls asleep in his care, and went to a movie in town. However, we kept thinking about the girls and of the possibility that the train might leave without us. Unable to enjoy the film, we left the theater and returned to the train to find the girls sound asleep under the watchful eye of the porter.

In New York we stayed at the McAlpin Hotel and in due time visited the Argentine Consulate. When I presented our passport, I told the Consul I was returning to Argentina. He asked if I had a *carnet de identidad.* I assured him that I did, but that it was in my trunk. "Just be sure you find it before you reach Buenos Aires," he said. "You will need to show it then." He then gave me a permanent visa and wrote at the bottom of the page: *"De regreso—Tiene cédula de Buenos Aires."* (Returning—he has an identification card from Buenos Aires.)

We went immediately to the harbor and boarded the S.S. *Pan American.* After storing our luggage, we returned to the deck to watch the bon voyage festivities. We didn't know a soul and felt a little lonely. We were surprised when a lady came to us and asked where we were from. When we told her we were from Phoenix she said she was a correspondent for the *Arizona Republic*, Arizona's leading newspaper. She took our picture and gave us a short write-up, both of which appeared in that newspaper August 31, 1938.

As the mournful sound of the ship's fog horn shook the vessel, signaling the removal of the gangplank, we felt that our last tie with our homeland had been severed and we were finally on our way.

Barbara and Argina had a ball on board. They made friends with everyone including all the crew members, and those friendships paid off. A steward appeared at regular intervals with ice cream or cookies for them. There were three American Catholic nuns en route to Brazil. They played games with the girls and helped them cut out paper dolls. There was also a South American stowaway being returned home in the brig on our deck. The girls made friends with him and he made them small toys.

Every other night the orchestra played on our deck for all who wanted to dance. Noting that we didn't dance, the nuns asked why. We told them of our calling as mission presidents and that while we loved to dance, we were giving up this recreation during the term of our mission. They then asked us what seemed to them to be a logical question: "Why didn't you ask for a special dispensation like our priests do to gamble, so that you could dance while traveling to your mission?" We told them our Church didn't operate that way.

Corraine has always loved to sing. She had brought with her the ukulele I had given her for her twenty-seventh birthday, and in the evening she would take it on deck and sing to herself and anyone else nearby. Two of the passengers, the young wife of a military officer assigned to the United States Embassy in Rio, and her younger sister-in-law heard Corraine's songs. Both had good voices and soon we had a trio. The officer in charge of entertainment also heard the trio, as did the orchestra members, and they were impressed. Corraine's trio was asked to entertain the first class passengers one evening. We four second class passengers were ushered into the first class dining room and with a lot of fanfare the trio was announced. They received immediate attention from all the passengers, many of whom were fairly intoxicated. The trio presented an excellent program and was well applauded. However, trouble began when drunken men insisted on buying us all drinks. We were happy to escape to the tranquility of the second class deck.

The orchestra members told us the trio presented the best program of the entire voyage. On other evenings several first class passengers came to our deck to compliment the trio and to listen to them sing. The leader of the orchestra was amazed that Corraine hadn't studied music; he marveled at her ability to pick up harmony. He was her *hincha* (or fan) during the rest of the trip.

Two Argentine couples on board kept very much to themselves until they found out that I spoke Spanish. From then on I had to order meals for them, and they spent much time near our deck chairs. The women were in their twenties and the men in their early thirties. The men reeked with highly perfumed, expensive French hair "brillantina," and wherever they went their perfume lingered for days. They had been living in Paris and were returning to Argentina. When asked, they were very vague about their activities, but their jewelry, luggage, and clothes were all very expensive.

Just before dawn on the twelfth day we sailed into the most beautiful harbor in the world, Rio de Janeiro. The "String of Pearls" lit up the circular bay marking the shore of Leblon, Ipanema, Copacabana and Botafogo, surrounding Guanabara Bay. Naturally, we spent the day sightseeing.

That night we sailed to Santos and the next day toured the city by street car. Barbara and Gina went swimming on the same beach I had when I first went to South America. We also climbed to the Montserrat Church on the hill that overlooks Santos Bay. As I had before, the family enjoyed the tropical scenery and the beautiful view.

The weather had been tropical and hot all the way from New York, but it changed the day after we left Santos. Winter was approaching in the southern hemisphere, and the day before reached Montevideo the weather became very cold. Strong tides rocked the boat and wintry winds blew up high waves; our heretofore smooth-sailing ship started behaving like a bucking bronco. The cold and the movement of the ship confined us to our staterooms or the lounges.

On the third day after leaving tropical Santos we put on our warmest clothing and ventured out to see the capital of Uruguay. I might add that our clothes weren't very warm. Winter clothes are simply not available in Salt Lake City or Phoenix in July. Soon we reached Plaza Zaballa and the bronze figure of the founder of Montevideo. After looking at the imposing statue for a few minutes, our nearly four-year-old daughter Argina pointed to it and asked, "Daddy, is that God?"

The cold curtailed our tour and we returned to the ship. This was August, the coldest month of the year, about which the gauchos say: "If you don't die in August you will live another year."

After living in staterooms for three weeks we had the feeling that our languid and lazy life would last forever. When we realized we had to disembark the next morning, we spent a frenzied night putting all our belongings in order. Corraine had a horrible thought. The General Authorities had wanted us to reach Argentina as soon as possible so that President Young could be in Juarez when school started in September. She said: "I wonder if President Young knows we are coming to relieve him and Sister Young." I assured her that the General Authorities would have notified the Youngs well in advance.

Argentina: Cold day—warm reception. Some of the first faces I saw were those of friends to whom I had bidden good-bye nine years before: Donato and Emilia Gianfelice, Domingo Quici, and Brother and Sister Luigi Notaro. My nephew, Orlando Clement Williams, Jr., was also there, as was President W. Ernest Young and mission secretary J. Donal Earl.

In spite of the intense cold (the local papers reported that it was the coldest day of the year) we received a joyous welcome at the harbor and at the mission home on Calle Manzone 268 in Villa Luro. It was August 31, 1938.

Corraine was a little disappointed when she saw the large, and unheated mission home. I was delighted, as I remembered the infinitely poorer quarters my mission presidents had occupied. Quoting from my wife's History, "Our Argentine Mission":

> *When we arrived at the mission home, Sister Young welcomed me with a motherly hug and kiss. By then, I felt I needed a little mothering. My first impression of the Mission Home made my heart sink within me. High ceilings, tile floors, drab colored walls, huge shuttered windows and as cold as an ice box.*
>
> *I didn't know my feelings were showing in my face, but sister Young put an arm around my shoulders and said, "I know it doesn't look good to you now, but wait till you see how some of the members live and it will look a lot better to you." Words of wisdom.*

The mission home was a large building with an entry way opening off the front door. To the right was the mission president's office, to the left the mission office. A wide hallway separated the building into two sections. On the left were three bedrooms; the first two separated by a bathroom. The living room (as cold as a refrigerator during the winter months) was to the right, and beyond it the dining room, which opened off the hallway at the rear. Beyond it was the kitchen which ran the length of the house, with a door opening to the back porch. The huge back yard contained a chicken coop and several fruit trees, among them peach, fig, kumquat and loquat. A two hundred-foot bank of Easter lilies grew against our neighbor's wall.

Corraine's premonition about the Youngs' not knowing we were coming had been almost correct. The Youngs did not know for certain our arrival date. President Young had received a letter from the Church on August 17 saying only that he was to be replaced and it was a letter from my brother Orlando to his missionary son that had alerted him to our coming.

That night Corraine and I accompanied the Youngs to visit a family in Caseros, and she had her first exposure to the humble home of an Argentine member. I was very happy with the way she was received by them and by the way she adapted herself to a new way of life. But it was bitterly cold. Quoting again from her History:

> *Later in the afternoon of our first day in Argentina, we went with President and Sister Young to make some visits. It was even colder in their homes than it had been in the Mission Home. I kept thinking, "Oh, when we get to the Church I can get warm." Even though Fred had told me many times that the buildings in Argentina were not heated, I couldn't seem to realize it until I experienced it.*
>
> *There was a welcoming meeting being held for us that nite at Liniers Chapel. We sat in our coats and raincoats. It was colder in the building than out. I wore a beige and red plaid reversible raincoat, I had the reddest side showing. Elder Sam Skousen told me very kindly that I couldn't wear the red side out and that I would have to turn it inside out. He said it was too bright for the people there. So I complied; I wore the beige side for three years, but then turned the red out and wore it my last year.*

The Youngs had made tentative reservations on a freighter scheduled to sail within the week. In the meantime there was much to be done. All the affairs of the mission had to be transferred, and there were new missionaries and members to meet. On September 5, President Young and I went by train to Rosario. During the trip he briefed me on mission matters, personnel and members. We met with the Rosario, San Nicolas and Pergamino missionaries, spent the night at the *local,* and returned to Buenos Aires the next day.

We held a farewell party for the Youngs the evening of September 7 in the Liniers chapel. Members from all of the local branches crowded into its small facilities to say a sad farewell to the Youngs, whom they loved very much. He was the first president of the Argentine Mission after the division of the South American Mission in 1935 to create the missions in Brazil and Argentina. The next night the missionaries gave the Youngs a party. All the area elders were there to say good-bye to their beloved president.

On September 9, we accompanied the Youngs to La Plata and saw them depart on the S.S. *Toro* for New York. As the ship pulled away we knew that we were now alone and responsible for the Church's members and missionaries' activities throughout the entire Argentine Republic. It was a sobering thought.

Circumstances left no time for preparation and meditation. On returning to the mission home we heard that the wife of an excellent member, Luis Costantini, had died. I was asked to conduct the funeral at their home the following morning. This was a difficult assignment. He was the only member of the Church in his family, and his sons and daughters were very bitter because he had joined. Corraine sang and I spoke to a hostile audience. Corraine recalls:

> *Since there is no embalming, except in the British Mortuary, the corpse has to be buried within twenty-four hours, according to Argentine law. We went to the home where the body had been prepared for burial by having a white dickie placed on the chest. The usual candles and Catholic folderol surrounded the casket.*
>
> *During the funeral proceedings, people came in and started taking down the candles, etc., and getting the casket ready to move. We tried to get them to wait a few minutes until the funeral was over, but to no avail.*

The following Sunday we conducted the funeral services for his son who had died the previous day after a long illness. This, too, was held at the home. The audience seemed as hostile as on the previous occasion.

Our forty-four elders were the best a mission president could hope for. All were good; some were outstanding. We shall be eternally grateful for the mission secretary, J. Donal Earl. He was a little older than some of the others, and a more devoted, loyal or capable man I have never met. Except for a six-month period when I insisted he get branch experience, he was my mission secretary for almost two years.

President and Sister Young. The first time I heard of W. Ernest Young was in 1935 when I read in the Church section of the *Deseret News* that he had been called to succeed Reinhold Stoof as the new mission president in South America. The news item also stated that the mission would be divided into the Argentine and Brazilian Missions, and that Brother Young would be the first president of the Argentine Mission. (Cf. *Deseret News*, February 9, 1935.)

He next came to my attention in May 1938. I was in El Paso, Texas, finishing the new Spanish-American Mission chapel. To avoid sitting around an empty house, I spent many evenings with the missionaries. I also went to Ciudad Juarez just to hear Spanish spoken and to see the people. One evening I was in a park in Juarez when an American sat down beside me. We began talking and I learned that he was from the Mormon Colonies to the southwest. He asked me what my interest was in Ciudad Juarez, and I responded that it was my love of the Spanish and of those who spoke it. When I said I had spent much time in Argentina, he said his brother was president of the Argentine Mission and that he expected him to return shortly. Little did I realize that I would be President Young's replacement within a few months.

My first meeting with President Young was on our ship in Buenos Aires harbor on August 31, 1938. His friendly greeting and manifest sincerity made me like him from the beginning. On reaching the mission home, we found Sister Cecile Young to be just as charming and genuine as her husband.

We lived with the Youngs for ten hectic days while they prepared to leave. When he turned over the mission affairs, he gave me all the information he felt would help an incoming mission president. He expressed hope for the mission's future and that the work would soon open up on more fronts in Argentina and other countries.

He was a kind, compassionate man and unsparing of his own comfort and well-being. He was a truly devoted, dedicated mission president. He and Sister Young made regular visits to many of the homes of the members, and were well loved by all who knew them.

W. Ernest Young had an excellent command of the Spanish language and was an inspirational speaker. Raised in the Mexican Colonies and having worked among the Mexican people for the greater part of his life, he understood the Latin psychology and how to reach people of Latin descent. The affairs of the Argentine Mission were in excellent shape when he transferred them to me.

When next we met, my family and I were living in Montevideo, Uruguay, where I was business manager for the Institute of Inter-American Affairs. President and Sister Young were called to replace President and Sister James L. Barker in Argentina. The Barkers had taken our place two years previously. President Barker had called me as a branch president in Montevideo, and now W. Ernest Young was my mission president.

For approximately two years we had the pleasure of visiting with them at conferences in Buenos Aires, and of entertaining them in our Montevideo home. It was a most pleasant association for us.

Before we left Uruguay in November 1945 to return home, we spent three weeks with the Youngs. All our children contracted chicken pox just when we were to take ship. The captain wouldn't let us board; the ship sailed without us and we had to await another vessel. We will always be grateful to the Youngs for their hospitality in the crowded mission home.

When we were called to open the Uruguayan Mission, President Young was still in Buenos Aires. We arrived there late in August 1947, and again were graciously received by the Youngs. We held several meetings to discuss ways in which the two missions would cooperate. President Young offered us every help and encouragement. He shared the *Mensajero Deseret*, the mission periodical, with us. The cooperation between the two missions continued during my four years in Uruguay.

When we were ready, he came with his mission basketball team and quartet to help us publicize the new mission in Montevideo. He permitted the transfer (with the approval of the First Presidency) of two Spanish-speaking missionaries to assist our new elders who were just learning the language. Later, Argentine members were called to serve as missionaries in Uruguay. (A list of Argentine missionaries appears as Appendix E to this book.)

At the Youngs' invitation, we attended most of the semiannual conferences in Buenos Aires, and they attended many of ours in Montevideo. We had a close and harmonious relationship at all times. It was a joy to work with President and Sister Young.

It wasn't until after my release from the Uruguayan Mission in 1951 that I saw W. Ernest Young and his wife in our own country. We had frequently met during thirteen years in South America, but not once in this country.

In 1973, President Young was kind enough to send me a copy of *The Diary of W. Ernest Young,* which includes a history of his missions in Mexico and Argentina. It is a most interesting account and of great historical significance. I treasure my friendship with him and with his very lovely wife Cecile.

CHAPTER II

THE MISSION HOME: A WOMAN'S VIEW

I WILL BE quoting from my wife's history for much of this chapter. I really was unprepared for what I found in the Argentine Mission. There were four hundred members of the Church; twenty *locals* or branches, one of which was owned by the Church in Liniers. There were twenty Primaries, fourteen Sunday Schools and ten MIA organizations. There were also several regularly scheduled meetings held in private homes, and forty-four missionaries in the field, three of whom were honorably released within six weeks of my coming.[1]

The mission was in excellent condition. The missionaries were devoted, the members happy and enthusiastic. A good spirit was evident wherever I went. President Young had done a tremendous job. The mission was so different from when I had left it nine years before. It was big, it was organized, and the Church was moving forward.

Buenos Aires looked about the same to me, and it was a joy to be back, but it was hard on my wife at first. I continue to copy from her History:

> *Among my first impressions of the great City of Buenos Aires was that everyone wore such somber faces. Walking along the streets, I saw no one ever smile. I thought it must be a very sad nation. The tangos of course, bear this idea out. Nearly every tango is sad. The words tell of some tragedy or other.*
>
> *Another characteristic which impressed me was that most of the shops were men's shops. Men's clothing and fashions were everywhere, while only a few stores with women's apparel were to be seen. I learned in other ways that this was a "man's world." Many times I was the only woman on a bus or colectivo, or even at a banquet. On one occasion the gentleman sitting next to my husband said to him: "If I had known you were going to bring your wife, I'd have brought mine." As a rule, the Argentine men were not chivalrous. I never once remember an Argentine man offering me a seat, even when I was pregnant or carried a baby in my arms. Not having lived in a city in the U.S. where I depended on bus, subway or streetcar for transportation I can't say how the men in this country would react. I only know I was surprised and disappointed in the lack of chivalry in the Argentines.*
>
> *We found food prices much less than they were at home. We bought T-bone steaks for five cents apiece. Whenever we ate out, we found that the entré, regardless of what cut of meat it was, always cost less than the price of the*

dessert. Our favorite dining place was the Cabaña, where they would let you select the steak you wanted and then cook it for you. One evening in the company of Brother and Sister Edgar B. Mitchell, an older missionary couple, we each ordered what they called "baby beef." It was brought on braziers. We ate all we could hold and had to leave one and one third of the steaks, they were so large.

Buenos Aires is a beautiful city. So many people thought we were going to the backwoods to live among primitive people when we were preparing to go. Buenos Aires was a city of nearly four million people. We found a network of subways some of which had beautiful mosaic designs on the terminal walls. I saw nothing to compare to it in New York City. Out in the suburbs one sees a very different picture, however. Humble dwellings and open sewers, a condition I'm afraid I would never get used to. Many of the sidewalks are of tile. After a rain one can walk along and get a good soaking by inadvertently stepping on a loose tile.

Although the Argentines appeared impersonal and detached, Corraine soon learned that they could be very warm and friendly once she got to know them:

Where I found coldness and solemn faces on the sidewalks of the city, I found wonderful warmth and love among the members of the Church. The Argentines are a very loving, lovable people. They are very demonstrative. If they like you there's no doubt about their feelings for you. They literally open their hearts to you, making you feel warm and loved and sustained to do the job you were sent to accomplish. So much so, that at times it leaves one in fear and trembling of not living up to their expectations of you. There is also the danger of beginning to think you really were important. Since we never had a visit from the General Authorities nor any of the general boards of the organizations in over four years there, it became a real worry to have the members look up to you in almost a worshipful way. I hope this will not be misunderstood by some who may read this. In talking to others who have served as mission heads, we have found that they too have shared a similar problem. Probably the fact that we were instrumental in helping to bring the gospel to them gave them this feeling. After all, it was the dearest thing in their lives. I heard my own words, those I had written in articles in the Mensajero Deseret (the Mission publication) being repeated in talks given in the branches. The young girls wanted to dress and to raise their babies like I dressed and raised mine. Many came for advice on courtship and marriage. Since finding and accepting the gospel, they wanted a better home and a better way of life than their parents had had.

Life in the mission home. When we recall impressions received in a foreign country, we understandably bring to mind those things unusual or different from what we are accustomed to. Raised in Arizona, Corraine acutely felt the bitter cold Argentine winters, and the lack of adequate heating in all buildings:

The winters were very cold. It was necessary to wear lots of clothing. I bought woolen underclothes for us all, to be worn over our other underclothing. It was the first time I had had any experience at this since I was a small child in Safford, Arizona, where I slept in an outing flannel gown and a woolen sweater, or bed jacket called a mañanita.

Our only heat in the Mission home was a wood and coal stove in the kitchen. There were some little electric heaters used in the offices and on occasion in the living room. With these the part of your body directly in front would burn while all the rest of you froze. As the Uruguayan Ambassador's wife said once trying to heat her bedroom with an electric heater, "It was only a gesture."

To bathe we heated water in the kitchen and carried it in buckets to the bathroom. In the summer we used a little alcohol burner which would heat the water just above your head and it was always a race to finish your shower before the alcohol ran out.

At one time when we ordered coal for the stove, they delivered 30 percent coal and 70 percent corn on the cob. This seemed awful to actually burn food when you knew people elsewhere in the world were starving. Corn was also used for fuel to run the trains. Well, Argentina had plenty of corn during the War years, but didn't have coal.

The children also found things to complain about, but the complaints were directed at us for not allowing them to follow local customs:

Barbara and Argina loved and enjoyed the Mission home and the yard. We had "nísperos" (kumquats or loquats), tangerines, etc. Two little girls just their ages lived next door, Licia and Elsa. They played together many hours of the day during the summer. Winter was a little different as they didn't attend the same school or church. On hot summer nights I would put Barbara and Argina to bed around eight or eight-thirty. They could hear the children in the neighborhood playing on the sidewalks. Many nights it was midnight and still later before quiet finally reigned. One day Gina said, "I wish I were an Argentine." I asked her why. "Because they get to have tea and stay up till midnight playing." Tea, sandwiches and cookies are usually served in the Argentine household in the afternoon.

The girls went to the American Grammar School, Colegio Ward. It proved to be a very trying, even frustrating experience for Barbara as the students were required to speak Spanish half the day and English the other half. The penalty for forgetting and using the wrong language at the wrong time was a fine.

The school was a private school, of course. However, there were no uniforms required, thank goodness. But they did have to attend on Saturday as well as all during the week.

The children who attended school locally all wore "delantales" or aprons or dusters. This really was a good thing and I used them on Babs and Gina when they returned from school. The weather was so cold and the buildings unheated, they had to have woolen dresses and sweaters which of course aren't easy to clean. The "delantales" were made of cotton material and could be washed easily.

Argentines do their Christmas gift-giving on January 6, Epiphany, the day of the visit of the Three Kings. To avoid a potential problem I asked the girls who they would prefer to bring them their gifts, Santa or the Magi. They talked it over and decided on Santa. I made it clear to them that if Santa came the Magi would not. They said they understood. Christmas came and so did Santa, and I thought things had gone just right. On Epiphany Eve, however, I found that Barbara and Gina had put out their shoes with a note for the Kings and a carrot and cup of water for the camels.

Two children were born to us in the Argentine Mission: Frederick Granger (March 31, 1940) and Nancy Lou (March 23, 1942). Argentine law prevented us from using non-Argentine sounding names, so Fred is Frederick Jorge, and Nancy is Nancy Catalina on their records, while their American names are listed on the records of the U.S. Embassy.

Corraine had great help from a lovely, capable German member girl who lived and worked at the mission home:

The Youngs had a young German girl seventeen or eighteen years old who was working for them when we arrived. We were more than happy to have her continue on with us. She was a member of the Church and was a very capable and willing worker. During the years we came to love her as our own daughter. She would do anything that needed doing: clean the chicken coop, wash the dog, cook, clean house, or care for the babies. She was completely trustworthy and made it possible for me to participate and travel in the Mission more than I could have otherwise. Greta Schimkat spoke not only German, but Spanish, English and a German dialect.

Our daughters learned Spanish quickly, which in the beginning posed a problem for Corraine as she could not be certain of what they were saying when they played in Spanish. Corraine soon learned the language, however, and not only gave numerous talks and counseled members, but wrote lessons and published articles in Spanish:

Barbara and Argina learned Spanish very rapidly. Upon our arrival Gina, who was three and a half years old, asked, "Daddy, are we in Mexico?" Her father, of course, told her we were not, whereupon she asked, "Then what are these Mexicans doing here?" She recognized the sound of the Spanish language if not the accent.

The girls learned Spanish much quicker than I. They would play and use only Spanish. Sometimes I would have Greta interpret what they were saying because I couldn't understand, hence I couldn't correct or check on what they were up to.

I had taken a couple of years of Spanish in high school, but I learned very little. I felt as though I were behind a curtain, not being able to understand the people. However, it paid off in some instances. It was convenient at times when a member started telling me something better left unsaid, to merely state: "No entiendo, hermana" (I can't understand you, Sister).

At first I heard everyone talking about the "culpa." I could understand enough Spanish to realize it was something everyone was interested in and all talked about a great deal, but no one had it. I was really puzzled as to what the "culpa" could be. Imagine my surprise when I learned "culpa" meant blame. No one would admit to having it: "I'm not to blame," "Yo no tengo la culpa."

Besides our family, Corraine also had the extensive missionary family to care for, and she worked very hard for their well-being and comfort:

I was Mission mother to many young men. We had no lady missionaries in the Argentine Mission, with the exception of Sister Mitchell who came with her husband and was his companion throughout their stay.

As I mentioned previously, I had just turned twenty-nine and Fred thirty when our Mission call came. I was trying to feel mature and was beginning to realize some of the responsibility which was going to be mine. Before leaving the States, we stopped over in Chandler, Arizona, to visit with my sister Edna. Rather early the next morning, an Elder Tenny came to the house; he had just returned from the Argentine Mission. Fred talked to him for a while, and then called me to come and meet him. He took a look at me and exclaimed: "Well, it looks like the missionaries are going to have a sweetheart instead of a Mission mother." I was crushed. I'd been trying so hard to be dignified and show that I was old enough to be their Mission mother. It turned out that there were many missionaries my own age, and some even older, but I think I had the respect of them all.

One day one of the Elders said he would like to speak with me. As soon as I could leave the work I was doing, I went with him into the living room where we sat down. His opening remark gave me a jolt. He said, "Sister Williams, it's my understanding that Mission Presidents aren't supposed to have children while they are on their mission. I'd just like to have this explained." He seemed quite wrought up over it. The reason it was so startling to me was that I was about seven months pregnant. I hope I gave him the right answer. I told him we had never been advised not to have children by the Authorities nor had I ever read words of theirs to that effect. I told him Apostle Callas had spent many years in the mission field as President of the Southern States Mission, and that all of his children were born there. If he had been asked not to have them in the Mission field, then he would have no family at all. The Elder seemed satisfied and proved to be a fine missionary.

Periodically we held Mission-wide conferences. The missionaries that came in from distant branches would be assigned to branches in the City of Buenos Aires.

We housed as many as we possibly could at the Mission home. It was always an exciting time. We welcomed those missionary sons we hadn't seen in months.

I spent many hours with Greta's help preparing food. We always invited all of the missionaries for dinner on the day of our Elders' Testimony meetings. These meetings were among some of the most precious experiences I ever hope to have. I often wished there were some way for the parents of those boys to listen in on the wonderful testimonies they bore. It was a sort of barometer for us. By the testimony the Elder bore, we could tell just how he was progressing. Some were new and homesick. Some felt they didn't have a testimony. Some said they only came on a Mission because their parents wanted them to. Still others were so enthused nothing could stop or daunt them. They had a wonderful spirit of missionary work and felt their remaining time all too short.

We watched their progress and worried about them and helped them every way we could. What a joy when they finally made it up the hill to the top where they knew the gospel was true and were so thankful to have a part in teaching it to others. Then, we would mentally check them off of the worry list. I felt that my husband was especially gifted with insight into the problems of the Elders. His understanding and manner of dealing with them was outstanding.

For conference I would also bake pies by the dozens and we would always make big freezers of ice cream. It was a special treat to the Elders as they never had that kind of food except at the Mission home. I also used to invite all the Elders whose birthdays occurred in that month to dinner; this applied only to those who lived in the City. On Christmas Eve, we held a party for all those close enough to attend. I made candy and sent it to the outlying branches and sometimes homemade jams.

Through the help of Roland Kaiser, a brother-in-law of Richard L. Evans who lived there, we were able to buy from Swift Company wholesale goods. We bought big beautiful hams of from ten to fifteen pounds for $2.50 and huge slabs of Swift Premium bacon for fifty cents. We could buy whole lambs for the same price. I often bought the whole tenderloin (filet mignon) or lomo, as we called it, just for a roast. In order to help the missionaries with their diet and economizing, we stocked the basement and let them buy from us at great savings, the same price we paid Swift. The only trouble was that sometimes they didn't have the money and we would let them have it anyway. Then there would be transfers, and no one would feel responsible for past bills. We soon found we were holding the bag in too many instances and had to call a halt. The same happened with dry cleaning. We tried to help by paying for it, but we couldn't seem to collect from them, so we had to stop that also. Some of the lessons we learned the hard way in Argentina helped us in our second mission in Uruguay.

Relief Society and Primary. In addition to the care and welfare of our immediate family and the missionaries, Corraine was also President of the Relief Society and Primary organizations for the entire mission. She published over forty Spanish language articles in the *Mensajero Deseret,* wrote lessons, presided at meetings, gave talks at branch, district and mission conferences, organized choirs, quartets, and trios, sang solos, taught the women to can, sew, and run a home, and set the overall level of religious behavior for the entire female membership. She became their example. Her beautiful singing voice, her young babies, and above all her loving sweet ways endeared her to the Argentine Saints. Our mission was a success in large measure due to the spirit of the Lord she carried with her:

> *I was privileged to be in the Argentine Mission at the time of the Centennial of the Relief Society. We had each branch prepare a special program for the occasion. Then on a district basis, we wrote a special play to celebrate. I worked out a skeleton plot depicting families in several European countries becoming dissatisfied with their lives and having a desire to emigrate to South America. There they found the Church and became members. We had a family from Spain, one from Italy and one from Germany. They became acquainted here, and there was even a marriage of two of the young people. Elders Lawrence Janson and Darrel Taylor wrote the part for the Spanish family, Elder Robert Sorenson the German, and I did the Italian.*
>
> *Since I was in the Mission at the time of the Centennial, my picture appeared in the publication, "A Centennial of Relief Society." This was an honor which came about only because I was there at that time, and not because of any ability or accomplishment on my part.*
>
> *We prepared a wall hanging depicting an Argentine woman offering her hand in sisterhood to a North American woman with appropriate words expressing their love and the common bond of the gospel. I sketched the idea we wanted portrayed and wrote the message. Bendor Olmo, who is now Middleton since her marriage here in the U.S., designed and then embroidered it on a sewing machine. She is an artist. Each time I visit in Salt Lake City I see it hanging there for all to view in the Relief Society Building. My husband sent up some other things which are on display in the Museum of the Bureau of Information on Temple Square.*
>
> *For the dedication of the Liniers Chapel, our one and only Church-owned building, I taught about eighteen young girls trios to be sung for that occasion. I also directed a chorus of the Elders. For many months we had a Mission quartet composed of J. Donal Earl, Rolf Larson, Jim Jesperson and myself.*

NOTES

Chapter II

1. *The Diary of W. Ernest Young*, privately printed by the author, (Provo: Brigham Young University Press, 1973), p. 306.

CHAPTER III

POLITICAL SITUATION: THE WAR AND ITS EFFECTS

SINCE MY DEPARTURE from Argentina nine years before, the military had moved into the political arena to initiate a series of coups and government takeovers led by its generals. When I left in 1929, left-wing Irigoyen was still President. In 1930, this octogenarian was ousted by right-wing Uriburu, who was backed by the military. General Uriburu attempted to establish a fascist dictatorship patterned after Mussolini's in Italy and especially Primo de Rivera's in Spain. But he went too far even for the military, which still held some democratic traditions, and within a year plans were laid for his replacement by General Agustin Justo. The overthrow became unnecessary, however, since Uriburu—mortally ill and unable to fight—permitted Justo's election that same year (1931). Justo was not as far to the right as Uriburu had been, and the military leaders supported him and his brand of conservatism through his six-year term. However, corruption in the government and fraud at the polls plus the Depression precluded his continuing in office.

In 1938, the year we arrived, Roberto M. Ortiz was elected president. He was, in effect, the last chance for a democratic, middle-of-the-road government for Argentina. He was reputed to be a man of complete personal integrity and to have a talent for leadership demonstrated both in public affairs and in his private practice as a lawyer.[1] He did his best to restore integrity to the government and honest secret ballots at the polls.

President Ortiz was pro-democratic and officially neutral regarding the impending war, but certainly benevolent towards the Allies. His government held the friendliest attitude toward inter-American cooperation and the United States of any in the previous decade. Unfortunately, his own class turned against him because of his unpopular stand, and he was hit by crippling diabetes, exhaustion and near blindness, which made it impossible for him to perform the duties of his office. In 1940 he was forced to turn over his power to his Vice President, Ramón Castillo, who became President in June 1942. Castillo and his cronies literally dined Ortiz out of office. Knowing that he suffered from severe diabetes, they made sure that he was at receptions and dinner parties around the clock, until the pace and the food took their toll. Ortiz died shortly after leaving office.

Castillo reversed all President Ortiz' efforts. While the United States moved away from neutrality and into the War on the Allied side, Argentina under Castillo moved in the opposite direction.

> *Argentina now became a hotbed of Axis activities. Axis sympathizers penetrated and at times dominated the government, while Axis propaganda flooded the country and flowed out into the rest of South America by the tons.*[2]

The mood of the country changed almost overnight; we could see it in the newspapers as the hate propaganda began to spread. The Argentine Jewish press was suppressed. Hugo Wast, a well-known anti-Semite, was made Minister of Education and promptly fired all university professors who opposed the military regime. Professor Bernardo Houssay, a Nobel Prize winner, said good-bye to his class in these dramatic words: "This will be my last lecture. The next one will be given by a colonel."[3]

With Wast as Minister of Education, religion, i.e., Catholicism, reentered public school curriculum. Wast generated as much anti-Jewish and anti-United States sentiment as he could. Not until February 1944, when the United States and Britain presented indisputable proof that foreign Axis agents were operating under Argentine diplomatic immunity, did the government begin to have a change of heart. It wasn't until 1945, however, that Argentina finally declared war on the Axis.[4]

> *Its course is understandable, if not praiseworthy. The Axis was at the height of its power; Generalissimo Franco had won the Spanish Civil War with its aid; and the Argentines had heard reports, since confirmed, that the United States did not plan to defend South America south of the northern "bulge" of Brazil, so that Argentina would be left alone to face an attack or reprisals from Hitler. And the Argentine military, whose voice was now loud again in public affairs, fully expected him to win.*[5]

Police raid on the mission home.. One of the most dramatic ways to show the anti-Axis stand taken by President Ortiz was the raid conducted against the mission home by sixteen armed policemen early Saturday morning, April 8, 1939. I have borrowed from my wife's account of the incident and from the report I sent the First Presidency, which begins: "There is a great deal of agitation being stirred up in this country about the so-called Nazi penetration. In fact, we were made partakers of it."[6]

The raid came the morning before our mission-wide, semiannual conference; it was also the morning before the dedication of the first Church-built chapel at Liniers. Earlier in the week, elders had arrived by twos and fours from all over the Republic of Argentina.

> *Of course they were all blond, at least by complexion, and were carrying briefcases. From the Mission Home we directed them to the different branches and kept many of them at the Mission Home itself. We held the first session of our Elders' report and testimony meeting that Friday afternoon in the Liniers Chapel. That nite there was a Priesthood meeting.*[7]

Most of the elders had written to tell me the amounts of money they would require for expenses during the coming weeks. I had withdrawn this sum from their trust account at the bank, and was holding it for them at the mission office; it amounted to several thousand Argentine pesos. Needless to say, I was rather concerned with the large amount of cash and had considered buying a safe where it could be properly protected.

We had gone to bed quite late Friday evening. At half past one on Saturday morning, Corraine and I were awakened by the insistent ringing of the door bell. Having been asleep only a short time, I was not fully conscious of what was happening. While putting on a bathrobe, I heard someone or something at our bedroom window. It was summer—we had no screens—and the window was wide open. As I walked towards it, a man pointed a gun at my face and told me to be quiet. The first thought that entered my mind was that these were robbers and that I was too late in procuring a safe for all the cash. My reaction was to quickly close and lock the window, which was made of glass, and turn on the lights. It was a very foolish thing to have done under the circumstances, but I was more asleep than awake. From my wife's history:

> *I thought Fred must have lost his mind. With the lights on we were in full view of whomever was there with the gun. He called out, "It's robbers, call the police." An Elder from the front hall yelled back, "It is the police." Nothing made sense. We turned off the light. I was hunting for my robe and couldn't find it.*[8]

The elder called us to come and unlock the front door. When I got there I found Elder McBride dressed only in his underwear with his hands high in the air and his body pressed close to the door. He had been awakened by the same bell and had opened a small window in the door to see who it was. A policeman had immediately stuck a gun through the opening and pressed it against his stomach. Although they kept insisting that he open the door, they would not allow him to move and the key was hanging on the wall, back in the hallway.

We were surrounded; policemen were stationed at all the windows and doors. As soon as I unlocked the front door, a detail of six plainclothes officers led by an inspector from the central police station quickly entered and covered us with their guns. The barrel of a pistol was thrust into my back and I was ordered to lead them on a search of the house. Corraine was panicky:

> *They were coming down the hall—where was my robe? I was dancing around frantically in my nite-gown. Just a second before they came in our bedroom, I found my robe on the foot of the bed. I was just too excited to see it before, I guess. They came in and looked under the bed, in the closets. I thought for sure they were after an escaped convict that had come in there. All I could think of to say through my chattering teeth was, "Qué tiene, qué tiene," which only means, "What do you have?" I knew better Spanish than that but that's all that came out in my excitement. They wouldn't say a word. They went on into the children's bedroom and flashed their flashlights in their faces and in the face of Greta, the German girl who worked for us. Fortunately none of them awakened. They then went through every room on the floor with Fred in front of them and a gun in his back.*

With the gun still at my back, we explored all the ground floor rooms and the basement. They wouldn't allow me to talk, but asked me questions from time to time. In the basement they asked to see our printing press; the only thing I could point to that even remotely resembled a printing press was a small hand-operated mimeograph machine. It didn't satisfy them.

Asleep in a rear bedroom were two missionaries and Fermín Barjollo, a local brother. When the light from the police flashlights was shined into their faces, Brother Barjollo awakened and asked in Spanish, "What do you want?" He received a terse reply. "Shut up, you Nazi." "What do you mean, Nazi? You're more Nazi than I, I'm an Argentine."

We then went upstairs where most of the missionaries were sleeping. Corraine could only guess at what was happening:

I stood in the hall shaking like a leaf. They were upstairs for at least an hour. I didn't know what they had done to Fred. I was sick to my soul. I called to the Elder down the hall, but a policeman stood guard over him and wouldn't let him talk to me.

Elder Rolf Larson, returning from a basketball game, was stopped out front. They searched his bag, but only found basketball clothes. They stood him in the hall, too, and wouldn't let him move or speak. I couldn't imagine what was going on. Finally we heard voices upstairs.

Upstairs, the elders were told to get up and to stop playing "possum." As they stumbled out of bed, one of the policemen noticed American passports lying on the table. "What are you doing with these?" It was clear that he wanted an answer. For the first time they permitted me to speak. I told them who we were and our purpose in Argentina. They were surprised by my answer and wanted to check our personal identification. Once they were satisfied that we were North Americans, they became very courteous and apologized for the intrusion. We were then escorted downstairs where the inspector allowed Elder McBride to put on his clothes.

After he realized his mistake, the inspector became worried. He explained to me that a call had been received at the central police station advising them that our home was a Nazi headquarters. They were so sure of the tip that they hadn't bothered to get a search warrant. Apparently someone in the neighborhood, seeing all the young, blond missionaries carrying suitcases into the mission home, and hearing the mimeograph machine run from time to time, had surmised that this was a Nazi cell where party literature was being printed for distribution throughout Argentina and that an important party meeting was being planned for that night.

The inspector asked whether I would be kind enough to sign a paper absolving him of the responsibility of searching our premises without a warrant. He said that if we wanted we could make it very tough on him, and that he and several of the others would probably lose their jobs if we went to the American Embassy and complained. I felt it would be better to sign and have him as a friend than to make trouble and have him as an enemy. He started typing the statement, right there in the mission office, but was too nervous to complete the job. I asked him whether I could type it for him, which I did, and he thanked me. I then signed it and gave him a copy. I began explaining our mission in Argentina, and offered him copies of our tracts and other literature including our monthly magazine, the *Mensajero*, which he readily accepted. Inspector Aguilar, in turn, gave me his card and told me he was our friend, and that we should call upon him if we ever needed assistance. The inspector and his entire detail left the mission home at about three-thirty a.m.

Corraine was most affected by the visit, and didn't sleep the rest of the night. For two hours she had watched policemen going from room to room, looking under beds and in closets, and her husband leading the procession with a gun in his back. No one had been allowed to talk.

Later that day, I learned that we could have avoided the incident if the mission headquarters had been registered with the police. I immediately went to the police registry office and found they kept a large book containing information on every store, school, church and public building in the district. The following week I took steps to have all the meeting houses and the residences of the missionaries throughout the mission registered with the police.

Our new friendship paid off for us at a later date. When the Argentine Government decreed that no meetings could be held in any language except Spanish, I went to Inspector Aguilar at the central police station and explained to him that we had many young North American missionaries and that we desired to hold our missionary meetings in English. He made good his promise of assistance and readily secured a permit for us to hold English language meetings; we had no further problems with the Argentine police during my presidency.

The silver dollar miracle: visas and landing permits. One direct result of the War was that the Catholic authorities made it extremely difficult for our missionaries to obtain Argentine entry permits. For a time it looked as though the work might be seriously jeopardized when even high-level diplomatic attempts from Salt Lake City and Washington, D.C., failed to secure the needed permits. And then suddenly and quite miraculously a simple incident became the catalyst which led to the favorable resolution of the difficulties.

The situation arose with the hostilities in Europe, when thousands and thousands of Europeans with relatives in Argentina attempted to capitalize on their family ties by emigrating. Unscrupulous Argentine Consuls quickly saw an opportunity to get rich quick and began to charge as much as five thousand dollars each for the previously free visas. The would-be emigrants from the war zone had no recourse but to pay the high prices. The Argentine Government's response was to legislate against this vulgar practice by requiring landing permits before visas could be issued. The law went into effect October 1, 1938.[9] The landing permits were obtained in Buenos Aires by relatives or sponsors. As soon as the landing permit was issued, it was cabled or mailed to the appropriate Consulate and only then could the Consul grant a visa, free of charge. This restriction on visa issuance curtailed the Consuls' mercenary tendencies. However, it also gave tremendous power to the authorities in Buenos Aires and increased the red tape and formalities we were required to follow to obtain the permits.

The first missionaries for whom I secured landing permits were John H. Meyers and Byron W. Wheeler. Visas had been applied for, but the new government regulation was now in effect. As soon as I received word that the elders were coming, I went to the Department of Immigration to secure the landing permits. That office opened at one o'clock, and I thought that by going at ten o'clock I would allow enough time easily to be at the head of the line. When I arrived, however, a string of people stretched three city blocks. I got in line and began the long wait.

By seven that evening I had traveled the three blocks and moved up the stairs and down the hall on the second floor. There were only about eight people ahead of me, but it was touch and go as to who could hold out the longest. The man at the head of the line finally gave up (I guess he needed a bathroom more than the rest of us) and had just got down the stairs when a secretary stepped out and called his name. There was a momentary silence, and then, reacting a bit faster than the others, I spoke up and was promptly ushered in. As I was being introduced (as the absent gentleman), I interrupted saying, "I'm sorry, but my name is President Williams, Mr. Minister, and I have a letter of introduction from your friend the Consul General of the United States, Consul Davis." The officials were sufficiently distracted to forget that I wasn't the man whose name had been called, and the minister attended to my needs. He granted the landing permits and I immediately cabled them to New Orleans. It was Friday, October 28, 1938. The elders left New Orleans the next morning and arrived in Buenos Aires Thursday, November 17, 1938.

Although the landing permits for Elders Meyers and Wheeler were granted, I was told that the Church would have to show proof of our permit to conduct religious services in the country. The Argentine Mission History records this incident:

During the year a new law went into effect requiring a landing permit for everyone coming into the country. Upon making application for two permits for missionaries, they were held in abeyance pending an investigation of the Mission—as to its political status and teachings. The Mission President, Frederick S. Williams, was cited to appear before the Police Department and show documentary proof of our permit to conduct religious services in this country. We have no such document, but the appearance was made, and a satisfactory showing made (it is hoped) to satisfy them. Since then we have been visited several times by investigators at the office who promised to visit each Branch and to contact members. The investigation is still being carried on, and no permits have been granted as yet, although 7 missionaries have arrived through the courtesy of the Argentine Consul in New Orleans.[10]

During the investigation the missionaries who entered the country came on preferential visas granted by the Argentine Consul at New Orleans. On February 15, 1939, we received word that the investigation was completed and we had been granted the right to apply for landing permits and to bring missionaries into the country:

We were notified by the Emigration Authorities that the Mission investigation had been successfully terminated, and that we could secure landing permits for our missionaries. The last 9 Elders have entered the country through the courtesy of the Argentine Consul in New Orleans, who granted them a preferential visa.[11]

I received a letter dated February 28, 1939, from Elder Ballard expressing his satisfaction with the government's decision. He also said he felt it was unfortunate that he had not secured that permission in writing when the mission was first established:

I appreciated your letter of February 17th and have read it with great interest. I also rejoice that you have succeeded in establishing the right of our missionaries to come to that country. It is rather unfortunate that when Brother Pratt and I called upon the Mayor of that City we did not get a letter from him, but we were welcomed by him and assured that there would be no objection to our doing missionary work in that city. We failed, however, to get a letter and had only his verbal statement. It is good to have contacts with the officials so that they will know exactly what you are doing.[12]

Even though we had been granted the right to bring missionaries into Argentina, we continued to have difficulties securing the landing permits. Of the approximately eighty missionaries called to Argentina during the next year, only nineteen actually made it to their assigned field, and most of these came on temporary tourist visas.

The problems came to a head with a group of five missionaries: Elders Brown, Madsen, Tolman, Pugmire and Huish. I received notice of their intended assignment in June 1939. On June 28 I wrote Harold G. Reynolds, the Mission Secretary in Salt Lake City, that I thought we would have no problems securing permits. However, I suggested that, should they not be issued, the elders could do as the Seventh-Day Adventist missionaries did, and come on tourist visas, which could be changed to permanent visas at a later time:

We were very happy to receive word of the assignment of Elders Pugmire, Tolman, Madsen, Brown and Huish to this mission. Applications for landing permits have been duly filed. I just returned from the Immigration Office. The permits for Elders Pugmire and Tolman will be ready at the first of the week, and the other three a short time later. They will be either mailed to the Consul in New Orleans or cabled. Have the Elders go to New Orleans and inquire for them from the Argentine Consul. If by chance they haven't arrived they can secure a tourist visa which entitles them to stay for three months and it can be extended three more. It is a simple matter to have them changed after they arrive here for a three year stay. I don't believe this will be necessary, as I have every assurance that they will be granted in time, and have an appointment with the Director of Immigration for Friday of this week to help things along. But in this country one never knows what to expect and we must be prepared for anything.

The Seventh-Day Adventist Church has been bringing in all of their missionaries by the tourist method and having them changed here. I have talked with several of them and also with other Americans who have done the same thing. The two Elders from Brazil came on tourist visas, and had no difficulty whatsoever in extending them. Please don't send these Elders elsewhere. We need them too badly.[13]

The missionaries routinely traveled to Argentina on Delta Line ships from New Orleans. A Delta Line representative coordinated the paperwork involved in securing the needed visas. When we failed to obtain landing permits and, therefore, the permanent visas for these five missionaries, we tried to obtain tourist visas for them in the hope that they would receive longer-term visas once they had arrived in Argentina. The Delta Line representative, H.J. Rovira, asked the Consul in New Orleans whether he thought this might be possible. The Consul could see no reason why this method of entering Argentina would present any problems and stated that the stringent regulations were directed principally against Jewish emigrants:

We also confirm our exchange of telegrams today concerning the securing of tourist visas for those Elders going to Buenos Aires, since the Argentine Government has declined to issue landing permits.

We contacted the Consulate in this respect and have been advised by him that they can see no difficulty in these Elders being allowed to stay in the country. It is entirely in sympathy with the problem as it concerns the Mormon Church in particular. It seems that the method of securing the landing permits is particular [sic] directed against Jewish immigration.[14]

Unfortunately, four days later, July 17, 1939, Rovira informed Mission Secretary Reynolds by telegram that the Consul was now unable even to issue tourist visas to our five elders. He suggested in the following telegram that the Church authorities contact the New York Consul General directly since it was he, apparently, who had denied the visas:

Argentine consulate now advises unable issue missionaries tourist visas due receipt letter from consulate general New York advising missionaries require landing permits cannot therefore issue tourist visas without consent New York Consulate Stop Suggest you communicate explaning circumstances and requesting them authorize New Orleans Consulate issue visas Stop We also communicating but your request will bear more weight.[15]

On July 18, Secretary Reynolds telegraphed Rovira to say that J. Reuben Clark, Jr., of the First Presidency, a former Ambassador to Mexico, had contacted the Argentine Consul General in New York and Senator William H. King in Washington, D.C., regarding the matter. If these efforts proved fruitless, the elders were to be transferred to the Brazilian Mission:

President J. Reuben Clark, former Ambassador to Mexico, has wired Argentine Consulate New York also Senator William H. King, Washington with reference to the issuing of visas, for missionaries proceeding Argentine Delsud July.

If favorable action not taken these missionaries will disembark Santos. We presume Brazilian Consul will grant visas. We have usual permits from Brazil certified by American Vice-Consul. We will insert missionary names.[16].

The Consul Genral wrote President Clark disclaiming the power to authorize the Consul of New Orleans to issue the visas and stating that the permits were issued exclusively from Buenos Aires:

We have your letter of July 17, and we are sorry that we cannot issue any instructions to the Consulate in New Orleans authorizing them to issue landing permits for your missionaries.

We understand your situation but unhappily, we cannot do anything because the Immigration Department (Direccion General de Inmigracion) in Buenos Aires takes care of these cases exclusively.[17]

Senator's report. Senator King wrote to the First Presidency July 20, 1939. Assistant Secretary of State Welles had written to the Argentine Ambassador, who had contacted Senator King, assuring him that there should be no reason for the denial of the landing permits, but that he was powerless to do anything since the Commission in Buenos Aires had full control of these matters. Senator King felt the Ambassador was friendly toward the Church, which should help reverse the action of the Buenos Aires Commission:

Upon receipt of your telegraph of the 17th instant concerning the difficulties encountered in obtaining the necessary visas and landing permits for a number of Elders assigned to do missionary work in Argentina, I conferred with the State Department and requested that the government interest itself in obtaining a removal of the obstacles which have been encountered.

Assistant Secretary of State Welles immediately conferred with the Ambassador of Argentina and indicated that so far as he was advised there were no valid reasons why the necessary visas and permits should not be issued. I also conferred with the Ambassador, with whom I am well acquainted, and he manifested a very friendly attitude. He stated that he would immediately confer with the Consul General in New York City and obtain full information as to the reasons why the Elders were not permitted to obtain the necessary visas and permits.

This afternoon the Ambassador advised me that upon investigation he had discovered that the Consul General of Argentina at New Orleans, upon request being made for visas and landing permits, had referred the matter to a Commission at Buenos Aires which has been set up by the government of Argentina to deal with immigration and other cognate matters. The Commission apparently without thorough investigation acted unfavorably upon the applications for visas and landing permits. Undoubtedly the Consul at New Orleans, rather than make a decision, referred the matter to the Commission at Buenos Aires. This Commission, as I understand from the Ambassador, has the final say in immigration matters. The Consul at New Orleans did not confer with the Ambassador, but, as stated, referred the applications to the Commission.

The Ambassador stated to me, and also to our State Department, that he had no authority in the matter and that any reversal of the action of the Commission can only be made by the Commission itself. He evinced a very friendly spirit and stated that he would be glad to do whatever he can in a proper way to secure a reversal of the action of the Commission. The Ambassador suggested that the best course to pursue is for me to address a letter to the Department of State calling attention to the missionary activities of the Church, facts concerning the Church generally, and reasons why our missionaries are being sent to Argentina. He then suggested that the State Department then communicate with him calling attention to my letter, and request that he, the Ambassador, take the matter up with his government with a view to obtaining a favorable decision from the Argentine Commission as to the issuance of the visas.

I shall immediately write a letter to Secretary Hull, and I have the assurance that he will promptly communicate with the Ambassador, and bring his attention to my letter and will express the hope that the matter might be adjusted in a friendly and proper manner. I regret that there may be a delay of several weeks before final action is taken. I cannot help but believe, however, in view of the interest of the State Department, and what I believe to be the very friendly attitude of the Ambassador, that the outcome will be favorable.

The Ambassador, when I mentioned President Clark's name, stated that he knew him and entertained for him a very high regard. I stated that President Clark was one of the leading officials of the Church, and I have no doubt that that fact will be taken into account by the Ambassador and the Argentine Government in taking final action upon this matter.[18]

Senator King's report to the First Presidency was sent to Mr. Rovira, who was skeptical, particularly with regard to the stated attitude of the authorities toward the Mormon missionaries. He also suggested to Mission Secretary Reynolds a new procedure for obtaining the needed visas:

We have your letter of the 19th instant.

The five missionaries in the "Delsud" July 22nd originally booked for Buenos Aires had to go to Brazil instead, and all details were taken care of. Possibly it can be arranged that they can continue to Buenos Aires from Santos in the same sailing, and to the end that this may be accomplished and future missionaries may not experience the same difficulties, we suggest that you have your people in this country—Senator King in particular—communicate with the Argentine Embassy in Washington with a view to having the missionaries classified under Decrees 8972 Article 5D, and 3411, Article 5. These decrees allow Argentine Consulates to grant visas based on their personal judgment as to financial condition of the passenger and his good character. **Confidentially, we have learned from a friend in the consulate that despite the manifest friendliness of the consul to missionaries, he actually bears them a "grudge" and is not sincere in his efforts to help. Naturally, this opinion must be kept in confidence for obvious reasons.** (Emphasis mine.)

We feel that if the question of applying decrees described is followed to the conclusion no trouble may be expected in the future. In the case of the missionaries already en route to Santos, however, an additional appeal should be made to grant them the visas at Santos, or at least enable them to secure tourist visas so they may at least enter the country and proceed in line with Elder Williams' suggestions. If this can be accomplished, we have merely to authorize our Santos Office to grant them passage from that port to Buenos Aires. Until this is cleared up it is just as well we hold the passage money here.[19]

The First Presidency wrote a confidential letter to Senator King on July 27, advising him of Rovira's suspicions. The full diplomatic route had been followed: the Church had petitioned the Consul in New Orleans, the Consul General in New York City, and the Ambassador in Washington, D.C., to obtain the five permits. Each official indicated he had no authority to issue landing permits, and that that power resided solely with the Commission in Buenos Aires.

The five elders ultimately served missions in Argentina; they arrived August 17, 1939, two months after the difficulties began. The U.S. Ambassador to Argentina sent word to Washington of their safe arrival in Buenos Aires via Brazil on tourist visas, and of my hope, as mission president, that they could secure extensions. The State Department forwarded this information to the First Presidency through Senator King's secretary, James B. Murray, in a telegram dated August 25, 1939:

Further reference missionaries entering Argentine Republic following paraphrase of telegram from American Embassy Buenos Aires to Secretary of State Quote With reference to your telegraph of Augest Twelfth. Temporary visitors visas valid for three months, granted in Brazilian port, were issued

> *to the group of Elders of the Church of Latter Say (sic) Saints, and they were admitted without question. The head of the Mission here states that he feels they will have no difficulty in securing extensions of three months on expiration and that after that period if permanent entry cannot be obtained, they will be sent by their mission to Chile for two and a half years to complete required missionary service. The mission here in the meantime states that it hopes for a favorable decision in the case which is up for reconsideration (refusal based on fact that Church is not one recognized by government here). The case is being followed by the Consulate General, end quote.*[20]

I outlined some of the particulars surrounding the difficulties in a September 2, 1939, letter to the First Presidency. The U.S. State Department had cabled our Embassy in Argentina inquiring why the landing permits were denied. The reasons were few and vague. All the immigration officials could say was "the Church was unknown," and when we brought proof that we were known, they said it is because the Church had not been "officialized" in Argentina. The Embassy filed a complaint with the Foreign Office and the U.S. Consul General did everything in his power to secure the permits, even sending an aide to personally interview the Argentine Director of Immigration. After explaining these details, I added in the letter that the real problem seemed to stem from the activities of the Catholic Church:

> *Nearly everyone with whom I have talked says it isn't the government that is denying the permits but the Catholic Church. It is putting pressure on all Protestant churches here in every way possible. The trouble is, as one of the minor officials of the Immigration Department told me, there is a committee of three people who has the power to grant or to deny all applications for permits and, as the official told me, "it grants the ones it is told to grant," and I suppose it denies those it is told to deny.*[21]

The next group of nine missionaries arrived in Argentina on August 27, 1939. The rest of the year we received only nine more elders, although over sixty were called to Argentina. We still could not get landing permits or even tourist visas for them. After a time we received word from Salt Lake City that missionaries intended for us had been reassigned to other missions in the States, Mexico, Canada or Brazil. It was a very frustrating situation: we needed the missionaries and they were available, but they couldn't enter the country. Of the nine who did enter Argentina during this period, all but one (Jay A. Quealy, Jr.) entered on tourist visas. He knew the Argentine Consul in San Francisco and through this friend obtained a permanent visa. Ironically, he became extremely ill in Argentina and had to be transferred home two months after he arrived.[22]

As suggestions for solving the immigration difficulties, I wrote to the First Presidency (1) that we try to get the visas through the San Francisco Consul (Elder Quealy's friend), (2) that the Argentine Mission open the work in Uruguay, or (3) that I be given power of attorney to establish the Church legally in Argentina, for without legal standing it was improbable that we be granted landing visas:[23]

In pursuance to your cablegram of September 28th, which was sent in answer to my letter of September 2, 1939, I immediately placed the matter before the attorney that has been handling our affairs here. Before acting on the matter, however, he went on a three months' vacation and has just recently returned and given me the necessary information as to what he would need to secure official recognition before the Argentine Government.

The following documents are needed:

1. *Power of Attorney, containing as its principal clauses the draft Power of Attorney as enclosed—the subordinate clauses being similar to the Power now in my possession;*

2. *Articles of Incorporation of the Corporation of the Presiding Bishop of The Church of Jesus Christ of Latter-Day Saints;*

3. *An extract of the Law of the State of Utah relative to Churches and Religious Societies.*

I have a copy of the documents referred to above under paragraphs (2) and (3), but as it is necessary to have all the above duly legalized by an Argentine Consul in the United States, it would expedite matters if copies were sent from Salt Lake City together with the Power of Attorney. This legalization could be done through the courtesy of the Eastern States' Mission Office, and sent to me by Air Mail. They very kindly attended to the legalization of the present Power of Attorney that I have. Such documents, under Argentine law, are absolutely worthless in this country without their being certified by consular officials in the country of origin.

Apparently no progress is being made here by the American Embassy or Consulate regarding the landing permits, and until we have official recognition I doubt if anything can be done. The government has granted landing permits for part of the Elders who are here on tourist visas, after we filed a petition for a re-consideration of their case, but they haven't acted on the petitions of the other missionaries. The one of longest standing is dated October 18, 1939, and it is still pending. This and other circumstances make us believe that it is the desire of one or a number of individuals to retard their approval, and until we get official status no pressure can be brought to bear upon the higher officials.

Elder Quealy secured a full time visa from the Argentine Consul in San Francisco, who happens to be his personal friend, and after learning of the difficulties encountered by the other Elders in getting visas to Argentina, he returned and talked to the San Francisco Consul who told him that it must be the Catholic Church who was bringing pressure to bear on the consul in New Orleans, as he had received no word from the Argentine Government that would prohibit him from issuing full time visas to missionaries, and that he could and would grant them if the missionaries would present themselves there.

If it were permissible, I would like to make the suggestion that from two to four missionaries be sent on each Delta Line boat that leaves from New Orleans every three weeks, and that they stop off in San Francisco to secure their visas. I don't believe the railway fare would be excessive, and would certainly be more economical than having to secure both Brazilian and Argentine visas, together with the attendant costs in Brazil. If a smaller group were sent they would be less conspicuous, and if sent regularly they would be a sizable force in a year's time. If this could be done until our official status be secured we will be able to carry on in fine shape.

The American Embassy assures us we will have no trouble in keeping the missionaries that we have, even though the government refuses to grant them permanent visas, as they have no facilities or money to deport anyone, and no check is made as to the whereabouts of people entering the country, nor are they required to register upon arrival. The Embassy reported a certain individual who was destitute and had overstayed his stay authorized by his tourist visa by two years, and in hopes of having him sent back to the United States, the Embassy had him taken to the immigration authorities. They were told that the man had come here by his own free will and choice and that it would be his responsibility to get back to the States in the best manner possible; they had not the time, facilities or money to send him; as long as he was a law abiding citizen he could stay until he could get back. However, we still have hopes and every assurance that permanent visas will be forthcoming for all of them sooner or later.

Now that there are many missionaries to place would it be possible to send some to Montevideo, Uruguay? As you know Uruguay is one of the most progressive countries in South America, with a population of over two million, and has one of the best and healthiest climates in the world. Montevideo has a population of three-quarters of a million people, and is just over night from Buenos Aires by river steamers that cross in both directions nightly. It would be much closer to Buenos Aires than are a number of our own Branches, and could easily be supervised from here. If missionaries could be sent directly there from the States, I could send several from here who speak the language to start the work and teach the new ones the Spanish language.

Special short time permits can be secured to go and come between Uruguay and Argentina and all the Elders laboring there would be able to come to Buenos Aires for our semi-annual conferences cheaper than do many of our own missionaries, as the steamship company gives us all a 25% missionary discount on all boats.

This seems to me to be a wonderful opportunity to use more Elders in the Spanish work, and a chance to carry the Gospel to a new country that is so close to this mission at a very little expense. We realize that we have much work to do in the Argentine Mission, but if the missionaries can't be sent here at the present this would be a fine opportunity to advantageously use a goodly number of new missionaries. I have several very capable missionaries at the present time who could go there and direct the work, and I could spend a few days each month with them.

If this were your wish I could inquire as to passport requirements at the Uruguayan Embassy here in Buenos Aires, and send them to you at once.[24]

In the hope that it would get better results, the Church switched its business to the Argentine Consul in San Francisco who had issued Elder Quealy's permanent visa. However, we ran into difficulties with him as well. They began when he questioned an apparent discrepancy regarding Elder Ruel J. Gunnell's occupation:

We are returning the passport of Mr. Ruel J. Gunnell. In your letter to us, you claim he is a missionary, while in his passport the U.S. Government gives his occupation as "farmer." Also, we would like to know the reason why you have been sending so many missionaries to Argentina.[25]

In reply to his inquiry, President Clark explained on behalf of the First Presidency:

This will acknowledge the receipt of this day of your letter of April 5, 1940, informing us that you are returning the passport of Mr. Ruel J. Gunnell whom we appointed as a missionary to the Argentine Republic. You call our attention to the fact that in his passport the United States Government gives his occupation as "farmer."

The facts are that Mr. Gunnell is a farmer who was called by the Church to contribute two and a half years of his time and means as a missionary of the Church. There are approximately two thousand such young and middle-aged men preaching the gospel throughout the various countries of the world.

In your letter you say specifically that you would like to know why we have been sending so many missionaries to Argentina. There are only two reasons for this increased number; one being the request of the Mission for increased help in Church work, and the other the expressed desire of the missionaries to go to South America.

You and your Government may rest assured that both in sending missionaries and in their Church work in your Republic, the General Authorities of the Church will fully conform to all regulations and rules of your Government.

The work of our missionaries in your country has absolutely no political purpose or significance. Our missionaries are studiously instructed to refrain from any and all political activities or comment; we are not seeking to colonize in your country. The sole purpose of the work of the missionaries is to bring to your people a message of truth and right living in accordance with the highest Christian standards.[26]

Juan M. Gutiérrez, the acting Argentine Consul in San Francisco, wrote to the First Presidency on April 18, 1940, indicating that the Argentine State Department would not allow him to issue anything but a tourist visa.

> *I beg to acknowledge receipt of your letter of April 17 enclosing passport of Mr. Gunnell. I deeply regret that by instructions of our Department of State, we can no longer issue visas except as tourist, which are valid for only a stay of six months in Argentina.*
>
> *Therefore I could only issue to Mr. Gunnell a "Tourist Visa" for that, it will be necessary [for] you [to] send to this consulate a tourist declaration in duplicate, as per instruction printed in a leaflet which I enclose.*
>
> *I have no doubt that Mr. Gunnell, on his arrival in Argentina, could make through the representatives of your Church in Argentina, an application to the Department of Immigration, for a permanent stay and that the Immigration Department will grant same. Also you can instruct your representatives in Argentina, to apply to the Immigration Department for a Permiso de Desembarco (Landing Permit) which they must send to use and will allow us to issue Mr. Gunnell a permanent visa.*
>
> *I believe that the best procedure will be to let Mr. Gunnell travel under a Tourist Visa. He will have to risk the chance of the Department of Immigration denying a stay longer than six months, but I feel quite certain that being a member of your Church, with own means of support, his petition won't be denied.*[27]

The leaflet read:

> *Effective May 1st, 1940, the Consulate of Argentina will not require Police and Medical Certificates, but instead after answering all the questions in formal declaration add the following:*
>
> *"I swear, under oath that I am travelling to Argentina as a tourist and will not remain there for longer than ninety days. To the best of my knowledge I do not have any infectious or contagious disease, or trachoma.*
>
> *(Signed) __________________________"*

Elder Gunnell arrived in Argentina May 31, 1940, on a tourist visa. When we tried to bring in other missionaries by this same method the San Francisco Consul refused on grounds that our missionaries were not bona fide tourists. In a letter dated June 17, 1940, to the new Salt Lake City Mission Secretary, Franklin Murdock, the San Francisco Consul stated:

> *In reply to your letter of June 17th, I am sorry to communicate to you that according to the laws of the Immigration Department of Argentina, I can't issue visas in the six passports you sent to this office.*
>
> *Some time ago, in the case of your Mr. Ruel G. Gunnell, I told you then, that we can only issue tourist visas. I made then, an exception, but I can't continue doing so. If I will grant tourist visas to this [sic] six gentlemen, knowingly I will be disregarding the instructions and laws of my Government. This [sic] men can't be classified as "Bona Fide Tourists" since they go with the intention of remaining over a period of two or three years.*

So here we were; unable to secure the landing permits from the Department of Immigration, and the Argentine Consuls in the United States refusing even to issue tourist visas. I continued to apply for these documents, but to no avail and "our" missionaries were transferred to other fields. I went to the ministry offices so many times that the employees began to recognize me. During a conversation with one official who seemed friendlier than most I began playing with a silver dollar which I usually kept in my pocket. When he saw it he asked, "What is that you have in your hand?" I told him it was an American silver dollar and asked whether he had ever seen one. He said no, but would like to look at it, so I showed it to him. He showed such interest in the dollar that I offered it to him. He thanked me profusely for the unusual gift. We talked a few more minutes and then he confided: "Would you really like to know what your problem is in securing the permits?" I said yes. He said: "It's the Catholic Church. Your applications, the ones you have been presenting to this Ministry for these past several months, are over there in that basket," and pointed to a table. "The Catholic Church has enough influence that it can put pressure on the department heads here so that nothing is done; the applications are not processed, they just sit, right over there." I asked what I could do to get the applications processed. He answered: "I don't know, but I'll see what I can do to help you."

To my great surprise, ten days later I received a postcard from the Department of Immigration stating that I should come to its offices on a particular day; there was some information that would interest me. I arrived at the appointed time and was pleased to learn that landing permits had been granted the eleven missionaries waiting in New York. I immediately cabled the permits to the Argentine Consulate in New York; the elders in due course arrived September 10, 1940. Thereafter, each request for landing permits was processed without delay. In my letter of October 17, 1940 to the First Presidency I wrote:

> *It has been gratifying to have procured the landing permits for the new missionaries during the past few months, although I can't explain why they have been granted. I have done the same as I did during the past year and a half, presenting the same kind of a letter from the American Consul General with the application. Before they were denied; but now they are granted. Perhaps they got tired of seeing me around there so much and felt this the easiest way to get rid of me. I am grateful to my Father in Heaven for having touched their hearts.*[28]

I received a delegation of administrative personnel from several churches one day: Baptists, Methodists, Seventh-Day Adventists, and others. They asked me how I was able to secure entry documents for my missionaries when they were not. I answered truthfully, "I don't know, I just ask for them." They answered, "But we ask for them, too." I showed them a completed application and they all copied it word for word. They were pleased with my cooperation, but I don't know whether it helped them.

The missionaries who arrived September 10 were Phil Davis, William Ellsworth, Clarence Geslison, Bruce Radcliffe, Junius Reed, Gardner Russell, George Sowards, Melvin Adams, James Barker, Stanley Moore and George R. Smith. While awaiting permission to enter Argentina they had been sent to the Eastern States Mission where the mission president kept them busy in and around New York City and then sent them to the Hill Cumorah to help prepare for the annual pageant.

The elders, while happy to visit Hill Cumorah, were not thrilled to work there. George Reynolds Smith, son of Joseph Fielding Smith, regularly wrote to express the group's discontent and desire to get to Argentina. His father's replies were full of encouragement and requests for patience.

Conditions at the Hill were primitive in those days, and the missionaries objected to cleaning the latrines. George Reynolds again wrote his father to complain that he had not been called to clean latrines and wanted another assignment. His father's reply telegram was pointed: "You should be proud to clean the latrines at the Hill Cumorah. Get to work."

As might be expected, these elders had lost much of the missionary spirit and began to horse around, but after a few weeks had a change of heart. They mutually concluded that they should be humble and do whatever the Lord wanted them to do: if he wanted them to labor in and around the Hill Cumorah, they would be willing to do so. Then they knelt in prayer. The following morning they received a telegram informing them that their visas had been approved; they were finally on their way to Argentina. The speedy answer to their prayers was a testimony to them all.

NOTES

Chapter III

1. Arthur P. Whitaker, *Argentina* (Englewood Cliffs, New Jersey: Prentice-Hall, Inc., 1964), p. 100.

2. John Crow, *The Epic of Latin America* (Garden City, New York: Doubleday & Company, 1971), p. 783. For additional reading see Allan Chase, *Falange, The Axis Secret Army in the Americas,* (G.P. Putnam' Sons: New York, 1943), and Sax Bradford, *The Battle for Buenos Aires,* (Harcourt, Brace & Co.: New York, 1943).

3. *Ibid.*

4. Whitaker, *op. cit.*, p. 101. It is reputed that just a matter of weeks before the end of the War, a lecture was presented at the War College at Buenos Aires in which it was "proven" how the Axis could not possibly lose.

5. *Ibid.*

6. The report is contained in a letter to the First Presidency dated September 2, 1939, a copy of which is in my files.

7. Corraine Williams History, "The Night We were Raided," unpublished.

8. *Ibid.*

9. See "Argentine Mission History," report for 1938 dated December 31, Church Historical Department.

10. *Ibid.*

11. *Ibid.*

12. Letter from Melvin J. Ballard in my files.

13. Letter on file at the Church Historical Department, Argentine Mission, CR 301/17 Box 4 Folder 1. We had a few missionaries work for six months in Argentina among the German Saints who had completed their regular two and one-half year missions. The work in Brazil at that time was carried on exclusively in German.

14. *Ibid.*.

15. *Ibid.*

16. *Ibid.*

17. Letter date July 19, 1939, *ibid.*

18. *Ibid.*

19. Letter date July 24, 1939, *ibid.*

20. *Ibid.*

21. Letter in my personal file.

22. Elder Quealy arrived December 17, 1939, and departed February 16, 1940. The ship he arrived on had been in the midst of the sea battle involving the *Graf Spee*. Elder Quealy later became Stake President in Hawaii, Los Angeles Temple Mission President, and Taiwan Mission President.

23. Cf. the telegram quoted above from Senator King's Acting Secretary, James B. Murray, to the First Presidency dated August 25, 1939, in which he quoted the U.S. Ambassador to Argentina as stating that the refusal to grant permanent visas to Mormon missionaries was based on the fact that the Church was not one recognized by the Government of Argentina.

24 Letter to First Presidency dated January 8, 1940, copy of which is in my files.

25. Letter from Argentine Consulate in San Francisco to Mission Secretary Reynolds dated April 5, 1940, *ibid.*

26. Letter dated April 9, 1940, *ibid.*

27. *Ibid.*

28. Letter in my personal file.

CHAPTER IV

THE BATTLE OF MONTEVIDEO AND THE SCUTTLED *GRAF SPEE*

TENSION MOUNTED in the neutral city of Buenos Aires in the early days of December 1939. Because of war-time restrictions on news, the man on the street didn't know exactly what was happening, but it was widely rumored that there was an impending naval battle off the coast of Uruguay.

The daily English newspapers, the *Buenos Aires Herald* and the *Standard,* printed what little was known about a powerful German warship in the vicinity being pursued by British naval vessels. Other Argentine dailies' reports were just as vague, but each echoed the rumor that a naval battle was in the offing. News flashes from the local radio stations repeated and amplified the rumors, each colored according to the newscaster's point of view and imagination.

Then a call broadcast over the radio for all available doctors and nurses to immediately contact the British Embassy heightened the tension. When we heard that the British Hospital of Buenos Aires had stripped its medical staff to a minimum and that many of its regular patients had been transferred to other hospitals, we knew that disaster had struck. The battle actually occurred December 13, 1939. Again, rumor had sent all the doctors and nurses to the Falkland Islands (known in Argentina as the Islas Malvinas) to care for the British survivors of the battle about which we were not supposed to know.

The ban on news was finally lifted when the powerful German battleship, the *Admiral Graf Spee,* put into neutral Montevideo harbor for repairs. We also learned that the British light cruisers *Ajax* (which a few days before had sunk the German ship *Olinda* off the Uruguayan coast), *Exeter* and *Achilles,* were en route to the Falklands with their battle casualties.

Eyewitness report. Jay A. Quealy, a missionary in transit, gave us our first "eyewitness" news of the battle in an article published in the December 1939 *The Gaucho Gazette,* an English language publication of the Argentine Mission:

> *I have been asked by President Williams to write a short article on what I saw of the naval battle off Montevideo, between the Admiral Graf Spee, Ajax, Exeter and Achilles.*
>
> *I was aboard the S.S. Delnorte bound south from Santos, Brazil to Montevideo, Uruguay. Shortly after eleven a.m. our radio shack picked up a flash that "there was a naval battle raging off the coast of Uruguay at the mouth of the Río de la Plata." This was all the radio operator could pick up. Word went over the ship in "grape vine" style, as no one is usually told anything that is received*

on board ship, but within an hour all was known. In forty-five minutes we had received a warning from the Uruguayan government saying that we should not try to enter the port of Montevideo as the ships were engaged in battle twenty miles north of that city. By that time it was just about noon and we were due to dock at seven p.m. The good ship Delnorte was making 12 knots which put us about 105 miles from Montevideo and 80 to 85 miles from the scene of the battle then raging.

We all heard the steady drone of the ship's turbines slow down to about half speed, but we proceeded right on our course. We were all rather excited but there wasn't anyone on board who showed the slightest bit of fear. When one gets into a position of that kind it seems mighty good to feel that security of the "stars and stripes" flying overhead, not to mention the six flags painted on the top deck and sides of the ship...

We heard two, four, and finally eight bells and then we heard the drone of the turbines stop completely. We were stopped in the south Atlantic. Everyone was dead still, then came through the still air the sharp clanking of the anchor chain paying out its links to the falling anchor. We all were listening with all our might and scanning the fast-darkening horizon for the battleships. Then came an even more piercing noise; it was the report of a cannon somewhere off our port side. As the sky grew darker we saw bursts of light from the cannons in the not too far distance, I would judge ten to fifteen miles away. We could see only one boat's guns. The other was undoubtedly on the opposite side. About 11 p.m. we "upped" anchor and resumed our course. We arrived in the harbor of Montevideo at 2:30 a.m. As we dropped anchor again we could make out the outline of a big battleship against the background of city lights.

I don't think anyone went to bed that night. The dawn brought one of the most pitiful, helpless sights I have ever witnessed. There, riding at anchor, was what we later learned to be the Graf Spee, with a large hole in her bow, and, upon looking at her more closely through field glasses, we could see many more hits on her superstructure. The sea plane was completely blown off and all that remained of the forward part of the funnel and signaling tower were two searchlights. I counted 47 hits on her at different points. However, she had the Nazi flag flying high, and as we went past her on our way to the dock, Captain Smith of the Delnorte gave orders to dip our flag to her. This is a custom of the sea. It is always the thing done by merchant vessels when they pass any vessel or part of the navy of a country with whom they are not at war...

We watched them remove the dead and wounded, and saw the funeral procession proceed up the main street of Montevideo.

The rest of the day they worked to patch up the damage, and to take on oil and foodstuffs.

I interrupt Jay's narrative to return to rumors—many of which were deliberately spread in the ongoing battle of psychological warfare.

It had been widely published that although the three light cruisers had been hit, they were still battle-worthy and were anchored off shore to await the sailing of the *Graf Spee,* which under international agreement could only remain in a neutral port for seventy-two hours. Periodic reports were given over the radio on the approaching of the French battleship *Richelieu*—then the world's largest, which was to join the three cruisers and several British warships that supposedly were waiting just over the horizon for the *Graf Spee*. These reports made a definite psychological imprint on the eleven hundred crew members (for the most part, members of Hitler's "Youth Corps") of the German battleship.

The German Embassies in both Buenos Aires and Montevideo were busy circulating rumors of their own: the three British cruisers had been sunk, and the *Graf Spee* was nearly ready to break out of Montevideo and return to the high seas. On the, quiet, the German Embassy in Montevideo was doing all it could to get an extension of the seventy-two hour limit to allow time for major repairs. The English, on the other hand, were busy putting pressure on the Uruguayan Government not to grant additional time.

I later met some of the people who had been involved in that battle of nerves and wits. The man who bore the brunt of the diplomatic assaults was Dr. Alberto Guani, the Uruguayan foreign minister later elected vice president to Dr. Juan José de Amézaga. He told me in 1944 that the last twenty-four hours of the *Graf Spee*'s stay in Montevideo were perhaps the most hectic of his life. Both sides offered bribes and threatened dire punishment if he declined. The pressure was so great that he felt he might break under it, and was relieved when his friend, the British Ambassador, Sir Middleton-Drake, offered to take him for a short drive to help him relax.

Both Dr. Guani and Sir Middleton-Drake were fond of poetry. The Ambassador told Dr. Guani hat he had just received a book Dr. Guani had long desired to own, and he offered to read him poetry while they drove in the park.

After a few minutes of friendly conversation the Ambassador began reading poetry in a soft, soothing voice. It wasn't long before the foreign minister was asleep—since he had had very little during the preceding forty-eight hours. The car left the park and took the road toward Rocha on he east coast of Uruguay. Still the foreign minister slept. When he finally awakened they were a long way from Montevideo. The Ambassador expressed his "regrets" that it had become so late and immediately instructed the driver to return to the city. Before they could reach Montevideo, however, the seventy-two hours had elapsed and Guani, even had he wanted to, was unable to extend the permit.

Seated in the waiting room of the foreign office during this time were the German and Italian Ambassadors, little dreaming that the man they were desperate to see was riding with the British Ambassador, listening to poetry and sleeping soundly.

All of Montevideo was excited by the events that war had placed in its midst. International newspaper correspondents from Buenos Aires came to observe and report the happenings. Buenos Aires radio carried nothing but the drama occurring 108 miles away across the River Plate. Fortunately, it was the closest World War II came to the American Continent.

Thousands of residents of Montevideo went to the *cerro* or hill that gave the city its name and which lies at the outer entrance of the harbor. There, they had grandstand seats.

When the six o'clock deadline had passed, the first ship to leave the harbor was the German supply ship S.S. *Tacoma*. It sailed out of the harbor and dropped anchor. Then the *Graf Spee* moved out.

Just beyond the three-mile zone the ship came to a stop and its entire crew marshalled on deck. Captain Hans Langsdorff told them what they were up against. They didn't have full power. Several battleships were rumored to be waiting just beyond the horizon. He didn't believe the rumors, the ships were days away and they could fight their way out in any event. He desired to fight at all costs, and he wanted volunteers to fight with him to the finish. Then he asked for volunteers. To his dismay, fewer than twenty of the original eleven hundred men stepped forward. He is reported to have said: "If that is the kind of navy Hitler has, I don't want any part of it."

He signaled for the *Tacoma* to approach the ship and take on all the personnel except a demolition team. That team prepared explosives to sink their own ship and opened the sea cocks, and then joined the others on the supply ship. The *Tacoma* then sailed for Buenos Aires; the *Graf Spee* sat alone. Jay Quealy describes what happened next:

> *...We saw a terrific burst of smoke and steel go up in the air. I counted six seconds before we heard the report of the same explosion. It was with such force that it shook the entire city of Montevideo. It was then seven thirty-five a.m. Each few seconds brought another report. We sailed for B.A. at 11:30 p.m. and as we passed the burning wreck, about one mile off the starboard side, we still heard small explosions and could see the outline of the superstructure which was standing above the water line. The first officer showed me on his chart that the German ship was sunk in about 22 feet of water...*

Capitan Langsdorff made arrangements in Buenos Aires to intern his crew for the duration of the War, and then, two days later, depressed over what had occurred, shot himself in the head with his own gun in a Buenos Aires hotel room.[1]

The Argentine Government felt that the Nazis would win the War and settled on a monthly stipend of 250 Argentine pesos for each crew member. At that time that was a good salary; many wage earners were raising families on less. The crew were scattered throughout Argentina and Uruguay, most of the boys living four to eight to an apartment. Their only restrictions were that they couldn't leave their assigned cities and couldn't accept jobs. Some of them lived a carefree existence for many years. Our missionaries contacted many of them, but they were interested only in friendship and not in hearing the gospel.

Some of the sailors, tired of living a useless life, made their way back to Germany. Others married Argentine girls and then found that they had to go to work, since by doing so they had forfeited their monthly stipend. Some are still living in Argentina with their families.

We never learned how many English sailors had been killed in the battle. The *Graf Spee* had sunk nine British cargo vessels in the South Atlantic during the previous three months, and had captured three hundred British seamen who were transferred to the *Altmark* bound for Germany as prisoners of war.[2]

Ironically, during the last two years of the War, steel plate was taken from the *Graf Spee* to repair Allied merchant vessels damaged by German cannons. However, after six divers lost their lives cutting the steel plate, the government ordered the wreck to be left alone. The changing currents in that particular location made it very hazardous to try to remove more.

NOTES

Chapter IV

1. See William L. Shirer, *The Rise and Fall of the Third Reich,* (Simon and Schuster: New York, 1960), pp. 669-670.

2. *Ibid.* p. 679.

CHAPTER V

AXIS VERSUS ALLIES: DIVIDED LOYALTIES POSE POTENTIAL PROBLEMS

THE OUTBREAK of hostilities was recorded in the Argentine Mission History with the following entry, dated September 1, 1939:

> *Great Britain and France declared war on Germany because of her recent invasion of Poland. Being a great exporting and importing nation, Argentina will suffer the effects of the war.*[1]

With the War we faced a potential problem caused by the divided national loyalties of the local Saints. Our numbers were Italian, German, Spanish, English and American; our five hundred mission members represented twenty-five different nationalities.

I taught the members and missionaries that since we were in Argentina we should adopt its position of neutrality; that we were members of the Church first and citizens of our respective countries second; that we were all brothers and sisters regardless of our political loyalties, and that we should not attempt to impose our views and opinions on anyone else. In general, the members and missionaries abided by this admonition, and we were blessed with harmony and cooperation.

The only problem was getting the missionaries to remember to be careful of what they did and said. The Mission History reflected our concern:

> *President Williams felt it necessary to instruct the missionaries not to talk politics in their visits and meetings. Due to conditions which have arisen as a result of the War the missionaries have been told to put their cameras away for a few months and to speak English only when necessary and not in a loud voice. Many take us for Germans, and the feelings against the Nazis and the activities of the "Fifth Column" are running quite high in Argentina at the present time.*[2]

During the first part of October 1940, the government passed a decree which seriously affected our work. We appealed to our friend Inspector Aguilar of the central police station, and reported the matter to the First Presidency:

> *A Presidential Decree issued last week may prohibit us from tracting. It is directed at foreign political societies, and is rather comprehensive in its coverage. Any tract before it can be distributed must be approved by the police. I have already taken a copy of ours to our erstwhile friend, the police inspector who*

raided us over a year ago, to have him help us. He is doing all he can for us, and I am quite sure we will get the necessary approval, unless there be a little church influence exerted on the side. The decree was also a dissertation upon the "rights of holding meetings." It held that the right of public meetings as set forth in the constitution of Argentina could and should be circumscribed or even abated under certain conditions of political unrest, and that only those organizations who had registered with the government as provided by the decree of the 15th of May of 1939, would be granted permission to hold meetings. The mission was registered in accordance with that decree, so I don't believe there will be any trouble.[3]

The Mission History entry for October 30, 1940:

Once again it was necessary to warn all missionaries and members and those who attend our meetings to refrain from talking about politics and the war in our locals. Many times we have had visitors who come with the intention of spying on us to try to find evidence that we missionaries are political agitators in this country. War and politics are the subject of too many conversations nowadays, and one has to be careful.

When someone not of our acquaintance would enter one of our meetings in which English was being used, we would immediately switch to Spanish with not so much as a pause or a misspoken word to betray the transfer.

Unfortunately, war news began to absorb more of the time and attention of the missionaries; this was particularly true following Pearl Harbor. Quoting from the Mission President's report for 1941:

The fact that the United States is at war with Japan, Germany and Italy has a tendency to distract the missionaries from their duties, and they spend too much time listening to the radio. The state of siege proclaimed throughout the Argentine Republic is aimed at political parties, and if we are careful [it] will have no effect on our work. Several decrees have been made during the year with respect to holding public meetings, but permission has been granted to us each time to continue.[4]

By mid-1942, our missionaries were being stopped and questioned by the police so often that I prepared answers for them:

Due to the fact that the missionaries in the different cities have been called in and questioned by the police the following information had been sent to the branches by President Williams. These questions may be asked and the answers are also here.

1. *By what authority does the Church function in the Argentine, and*
2. *Did you register in accordance with the decree of the Executive Power of May 1939?*

Answer to No. 1: We are laboring here as a cultural and religious organization and are protected by the laws of the country, having been duly admitted by said laws.

Answer to No. 2: Yes. The mission complied with the decree, by submitting all the necessary information to the Minister of the Interior on August 9, 1939, and a receipt for the same is—Expediente No. 30390 Letra M. Año 1939, Mesa de Entradas. Any information can be given from the office.[5]

Scurrilous Attack. What was labeled as "one of the most scurrilous attacks ever made on the Church in South America" appeared in the newspaper *La Crítica* April 29, 1942. It centered on a complaint received by Judge Dr. Clodomiro Cordero of the Juvenile Court of an alleged Polygamy Club in Buenos Aires, run by the Mormons. I contacted Judge Cordero and he issued a statement that the accusations were untrue. Armed with this statement, I visited the *Noticias Gráficas* offices which published a denial of the charges. The United Press also sent a denial bulletin to both the *La Crítica* and *La Razón* newspapers; the latter published the retraction, but not the former. It did send a reporter to interview me for a new story, stating that it didn't want to admit that it had made a mistake.[6]

German Branch. One of my earliest concerns as mission president was the German Branch, many of whose members I had known on my mission. Since then, some of the stronger families had moved to the Delta Islands, and there were no German-speaking elders left in the mission. The last, August George Martin Ostendorf, had been released on February 22, 1938.[7] Since then an English- and Spanish-speaking elder had been assigned to oversee their activities and help where he could. Actually, he was more of a referee. I instructed him that he should not interfere with their discussions until the participants entered into a heated argument, at which point he was to dismiss the meeting. They were always arguing about something—I've never seen a group more disposed toward verbal assault on one another.

With the permission of the First Presidency on October 10, 1938, I snared a Brazilian missionary, Elder Marion Eugene Tippetts, at the end of his two and a half years among the Brazilian Germans. The German members were delighted with him and, with Elder Tippetts as interpreter, I was able to straighten out several matters. He also helped start a German section in the mission monthly publication *El Mensajero*. It was appropriately entitled "*Nuestro Hermano Alemán*" ("Our German Brother").

One other Brazilian missionary helped our mission, Donald Anderson Knight, who arrived January 18, 1939. He worked principally among the Germans living in the Delta. Both elders served with us six months.

The South American Mission had been opened as a German mission, and our German Saints felt particularly proud that Reinhold Stoof, the first president, had been one of them. Some of these members had lived in Argentina for twenty years and still spoke no Spanish. They felt slighted when, for eight months before Elder Tippetts' arrival, there had been no German-speaking elders to help them. President Young's journal records that when Elder Ostendorf was released, he told the German members they would have to take more responsibility:

Sunday the 20th [of February 1938] we attended several meetings. At the White Branch at 3 p.m. we met with the German members and told them of the release of Elder August G.M. Ostendorf. They would have to take more responsibility now with his departure after he had served them so well. Brothers Sholtz, Hoffman, Stefancijosa, and Erich Fischer were ordained teachers.[8]

Now at last, with Elder Tippetts they had an elder with whom they could communicate, and with his help, the German Branch in Buenos Aires began to function again. Those adults comprising its membership included:

Members	**Office/Date of Ordination**
Maria and Ernst Biebersdorf	(Elder, 4-2-33)
Wilhelm Krauss	(Elder, 4-11-36)
Elise and Wilhelm Gabriel	(Elder, 4-14-40)
Maria and Luis Stefancijosa	(Elder, 10-8-40)
Ernst Schimkat, daughter Margaret	(Priest, 3-31-36)
Helene and Wilhelm Hofmann	(Priest, 6-4-39)
Erick Fisher, and mother Berta	(Teacher, 2-20-38)
Rosalia and Auguste Liebenberger	(Teacher, 4-26-40)
Hans Finger	(Deacon, 6-4-39)
Andreus Trummer	
Katharina Georges	
Ernestina Wesenberg	
Eufrida Seibt and daughter Annelese	
Maria Heupp	

There were also a number of children.

Also on the rolls, although now living on the Delta Islands of the Paraná River, were:

Mathilde and Emil Hoppe	(Elder, 2-20-36)
Minna and Wilhelm Friedrichs	(Priest, 12-13-25)
August Budde	(Priest, 10-9-38)
Kurt Walter Sholz and wife	(Priest, 6-4-39)
Elizabeth and Carlos Berger	
Carl Peters (a nonmember)	

Here, too, were a number of children, some of whom held positions of responsibility.

Brother Sholz traveled from the Delta, where he grew and harvested trees, to Buenos Aires every six months. His first tithe was so large that the missionary who received his offering exclaimed that tithing was only ten percent, not ninety percent. Brother Sholz had paid only ten percent, but his tenth was more that what many of the members earned in a full year. He had perhaps the best leadership capabilities of all the German members.

After January 4, 1938, the German Branch met weekly at the home of Sister Eufrida Seibt. The branch was presided over by a missionary, but nearly all the German members (including those who later moved to the Delta Islands) had held leadership positions in the auxiliary organizations. These positions were quite frequently rotated, usually after someone's feelings had been hurt. Sister Elise Gabriel made the best Relief Society President because she knew how to get along with everyone.

Each Sunday the members gathered for a combination Sunday School and Sacrament meeting which lasted from two to three hours with a brief intermission. Many members had to travel great distances and several hours to attend. Brother Wilhelm Gabriel was the organist, but one could never tell from his introduction which hymn he was playing.

Just before the government decree of June 1940 which prohibited meetings in any language other than Spanish, I received the distinct impression that I should dissolve the German Branch. After one of their regular meetings had ended, I arose and addressed the congregation in Spanish, using a translator. I explained that under existing conditions—little success among the German residents, growing resentment against the Axis powers—I thought it would be much better if the branch were dissolved and each member attend meetings in his branch of residence (the members were scattered all over metropolitan Buenos Aires). They sustained me in the dissolution, many with tears in their eyes. During the following days, however, they had second thoughts and were now rather unhappy about it. A delegation which included Brothers Sholz, Gabriel, Biebersdorf and Krauss met with me at the Liniers chapel and with impassioned pleas asked that the branch be reorganized. I told them I couldn't reorganize it in the same way; now they must carry out the program among themselves, for the missionaries previously assigned to them were needed elsewhere (I could have added in more productive fields of labor); furthermore, it was dangerous for our American elders to be seen working in the German communities. I said: "Now, you brothers will have to do it all yourselves; you are going to have to do this, and you, Brother so-and-so, are going to have to do that." They looked at each other without saying a word, so I reiterated that I felt it would be better if they attended their residence branches, that they should give the Argentine Saints the benefit of their strengths and testimonies. By the end of the meeting they agreed.

The very next morning the newspapers published the government decree prohibiting meetings except in Spanish. That ended the matter right there. It would have been rather difficult now, even had we wanted to carry on with the branch. The Argentine Mission History entry for June 19, 1940, reads:

> *Effective today, the missionary work has been disorganized and discontinued among the German people. This has been due to new laws established in Argentina which prohibit to some extent, meetings in the German language. It has been hard for the Elders to tract and carry on their regular duties due to so much hatred against the German race. Of course visits and contacts are still made with our German members and friends, but no active work will be carried on by the Elders. German members and friends will attend Spanish meetings in the future. The Elders will work in the Spanish work also; Elder L. Stanford McCullough going to Liniers, and Billy Huish staying in Urquiza, but switching to Spanish.*

One result of the dissolution was that in later years the German members thanked me for doing it; they were so much happier working in the regular (Spanish) branches. They had fought constantly among themselves, but they were happy in the other branches. They frequently told me, "You should have done it years ago." Their initial resistance was only temporary; they thought they were being picked on. They soon took their places in the other branches, assumed leadership positions in the organizations and were very happy. Incidentally, it also saved them a lot of travel time.

We also continued to visit our German members in the Delta, but did no proselyting. Earlier President Young had written an article that described their attempts to tract by boat and using a special slide projector with a generator to help teach the Gospel. Inasmuch as there was no electricity in the Delta, the projector was quite a hit. He described the region:

> *This delta region is made up of many islands that are from a few inches [to] several feet above the level of the river. Until recently this region was considered a rendezvous of bandits and hunters. The land was covered with a semi-tropical underwood and grass. Today it is the most profitable timber belt of Argentina. The wild forest is being replaced with many groves of poplars and Italian blackwillows ... These islands are being colonized, principally, by German, Swiss, Danish, and other European peoples during recent years.*[9]

The Buenos Aires German members did not seem to go in for displaying signs of Nazism. In contrast, many of the nonmember German families in the Delta openly displayed swastikas, German flags and photographs of Hitler in and around their homes. Our occasional visits to their homes were a little unnerving.

As I have said before, the Friedrichs and the Hoppes had been instrumental in establishing the Church in South America. Brother Hoppe remained steadfast, but Brother Friedrichs seemed always to be out of harmony.[10]

When we returned to Argentina as Mission Presidents, he was mixed up with a nonmember named Carl Peters. Together they had devised a plan for a New Zion, a communal order complete with commandments. He had written a ten-page letter to President Heber J. Grant containing a detailed colonization plan and describing revelations he had received.[11] Of his visit with Brother Friedrichs at his home in Parque Luján, Tigre (in the Delta), President Young recorded:

> *Thursday, August 4, [1938] I took Elders Willard Skousen and new Elder Verden Bettilyon to Tigre, where we walked to Brother Wilhelm Friedrichs' home along the canal. Here we found him filled with ideas of a New Zion, and with a Mr. Peters, a nonmember, they have concocted an idea of redeeming Zion now and inviting the world to participate. Brother Friedrichs told me that it was not against the Church, but that he would work independently of it and not against the Church. I warned him that he was headed out of the Church and that his idea is not in harmony with the mission nor the Church.*[12]

Unlike her husband, Sister Minna Friedrichs remained steadfast. Still faithful at eighty-one in 1971, she sent me a letter containing her life history which gives new insights into the establishment of the South American Mission:

> *To all my loved ones that want to read my life's story: This is the story of how we came to Argentina. I am sure it was to be, that the Lord wanted us to come to South America.*
>
> *After the first World War no one had any money. My husband remembered he had an uncle in the United States and decided to write and ask him to send*

us money for the trip...Three weeks later a letter was received from him and he promised to help us. That made us very happy. Since my husband's handwriting was poor, I wrote the letters for him. When I answered to thank him for his kind offer, I inquired if there were any Mormons where he lived. His answer came back fast. He wrote, "The Mormons all live in Utah and nobody likes them. They are hated everywhere."

In my next letter I told him that the Church of Jesus Christ is the only church in the world that can solve its problems, and I told him to look into it.

For about a year we received no correspondence from him. He wouldn't write to us, and we lost all hope.

Brother Hoppe sold all of his possessions and purchased steamship tickets for himself and my husband and they were scheduled to sail for Buenos Aires from Hamburg. Two days after they left for Hamburg the mailman delivered a letter from the United States that contained paid tickets for us to go there. I asked two missionaires to go to the port city to see if they could reach my husband and Brother Hoppe before they sailed, but they had already departed. I cried and prayed for weeks on end.

The missionaries told me that only savages lived in Argentina and that they still ate humans. They said the people lived in metal containers underground.

One morning I prayed real hard. A voice said to me loud and clear: "I have his life in my hands, so don't worry." From that moment on I thanked God for my blessings and felt reassured.

One month later I received a letter from my husband and he told me that he was working and that soon he could pay back Brother Hoppe and send for me. Some nine months after my husband's departure I sailed over the great ocean to rejoin him. The first thing I did was to bury my newly born child.

I met many German families. The Biebersdorfs and Kullicks wanted to be baptized. I wrote the letters my husband sent to Salt Lake City asking that missionaries be sent so that the gospel could be taught to the people of Argentina. Soon our prayers were answered and Elders Melvin J. Ballard, Rulon S. Wells and Rey L. Pratt arrived. Brother Wells spoke German and Brother Pratt Spanish. That was the beginning of the South American Mission.

We were so grateful to the Lord for all the hardships we went through, so that the gospel could be taught in this land. Soon Brother Stoof came and organized the mission. I had three more children and Sister Stoof had six. They headed the mission for nine years. President Stoof loved the people of Argentina and the gospel of Jesus Christ. I have never met a person like him. He truly was a servant of the Lord Jesus Christ. Knowing that he has gone from the earth, I have shed many tears, but they were tears of joy for having known this good man.

I am 81 years old 1971 and I only have one regret, and that is that I never learned Spanish or English. I am so grateful to my Father in Heaven and I send all my love. Amen. Minna Friedrichs.

Most of our members were not politically oriented—at least we knew of no involvement. Brother Wilhelm Krauss may have been the exception. I don't know if he was a card-carrying Nazi party member, but he was a strong sympathizer and he did all that he could for Germany's cause. It was his prerogative: Argentina was a neutral country. I should hasten to add that he was a faithful, dedicated member of the Church, albeit somewhat overzealous. He used to stamp all his mail with a rubber stamp which read: "Read the Book of Mormon." He had one stamp in German and one in Spanish.[13]

Brother Krauss was ordained an elder April 11, 1936. He never married. He worked as a waiter at the Alvear Palace Hotel, *the* hotel of Buenos Aires, and his job brought him in contact with many people. During March 1942 he arranged for us to meet "someone who is interested in the Church and would like to make a large financial contribution to it." This someone turned out to be a very talented and glamorous lady in her late thirties.

Because it was our business to meet people who were interested in the Church, we accepted her invitation. The date was set and Corraine and I traveled to one of the swankiest residential areas in Buenos Aires.

She lived at 1276 Junín Street in a very large home much like a fortress with a big fence around it. We couldn't help but notice a giant shortwave radio antenna on the roof. We rang the bell and a butler came to unlock the front gate; he then unlocked the front door and ushered us in. We then were invited to sit in the beautiful and luxuriously furnished living room. It contained a grand piano and, in the middle of the room, an easel with a nearly finished portrait perched on it.

Very shortly Elsa Barretto de Vega Ocampo, a gracious, beautiful young woman, entered the room and greeted us. I can't recall whether she spoke to us in English or in Spanish, but we soon could tell that she was highly educated. She invited Corraine upstairs with her to leave her coat. "Upstairs" was reached via a private elevator, and our hostess unlocked and then relocked each door they passed through. Apparently she trusted no one. The servants didn't go anywhere in the house unless she accompanied them with her keys.

We ate a delicious formal dinner, after which she began to ask questions about the Church—very superficial questions, I might add. Next, she asked who we knew in the American Embassy. I told her I knew some people casually. She asked me if I could set up an appointment for her to meet Consul General Davis. I tried to be noncommittal, but told her I'd call him. She began asking more questions about the Church and I explained that we had an upcoming mission-wide conference she could attend, and she wrote down the pertinent information and asked whether we needed money for it. We thanked her kindly but declined any offer of money.

For a few moments she entertained us by playing the piano; she was very accomplished. Next, she discoursed on flowers, particularly the pollinating process. I don't know who she was trying to impress, going into details, making sexual innuendoes, and the like. The evening ended with a brief explanation of the techniques she employed in the painting she was finishing.

As promised, I called Consul General Monnett Bain Davis.[14] He said, "Do you know who she is? I said, "No, not really." "She's alleged to be the head of the entire Nazi spy organization down here; purportedly an illegitimate daughter of King Alfonso of Spain. She is indeed very talented, very cultured, very shrewd. She has been trying to meet with me for a long time, but when I see her coming in the front door, I go out the back." He advised us to be very careful in our dealings with her.[15]

The only other contact we had with her was during the evening session of the April 1942 mission conference when she and three other persons made a grand entrance into the Liniers chapel after the session had begun. They were in formal attire including fur coats which contrasted sharply with the modest dress of our Saints. They sat right on the first row. It was obvious that she had never had any interest in the Church.

After my release as mission president, I went to Washington, D.C. to look for employment. I visited Heber M. Clegg, my former missionary companion who had, subsequent to his mission, taken a job with the FBI. In the course of our conversation I mentioned the dinner with this intriguing lady. As I said her name, he interrupted me and said, "She lives on Junín Street 1276. We know all about her."

During my visit with Heber, his superior said, "We would like to recruit you to go back down there; we will get you a job and let you do undercover work." He asked if it would be proper for me to return as an assistant mission president of the Church. Both Heber and I laughed and I explained that that wouldn't be possible. He offered me a very good salary. I never entertained the proposition seriously, however. Because I had held a relatively important position in the church, if something were to happen and my activities were discovered, all my work as Mission President would have been under suspicion.

Returning missionaries recruited in the war effort. A few of our returned ex-missionaries, however, were recruited in the United States by the FBI. Other missionaries returning home via Panama were met at that airport by U.S. Government and industry officials who offered them high-paying jobs. There was a manpower shortage in Panama and, as an invasion of Japanese troops was expected, there was a frantic effort to fortify the Canal, and much help was needed.

It was difficult for our elders to resist work offers in Panama. They had been living on thirty dollars a month for two and a half years, and were now being offered five dollars and six dollars an hour, plus overtime. The Brethren became concerned that these former missionaries would go to work in Panama, thereby avoiding their responsibilities; as missionaries, they had been granted draft-free status and could not be called up until they returned to American soil. I received some strongly worded letters from Salt Lake City, but there was little I could actually do. I gave the elders instructions as the Brethren requested, but they were free agents; I couldn't chain them to the plane.

We were released in August 1942, and when I arrived in Panama one of our former missionaries took me to see the commanding general of the Panama Zone. He was very blunt. He said, "President Williams, I am surprised at your Church and that your officials are unhappy about these boys being down here. They are doing a vital service. We recruited them. We need a lot more of them down here where they can be of far greater service than as fighting men. Would you please let your authorities know that, because your boys feel guilty about being here, but we need them."

When I explained all this to Presidents Grant and McKay they felt better about the situation. The Brethren were understandably sensitive to the possible criticism against the Church.

We wondered about the future of the mission. We knew that missionaries had been pulled out of Europe and assigned to other areas, but could only speculate about our fate. As it turned out, my administration saw the last American missionaries called to South America until after the War. No missionaries were sent to Brazil after July 9, or arrived in Argentina after October 30, 1941. It was only a matter of time before all would return home, leaving the missions without elders. Both President James L. Barker, who was called to preside after us in Argentina, and President William Seegmiller who replaced Rulon S. Howells in the Brazilian Mission, had to operate their missions without missionaries.

The mission presidents who succeeded them, Harold M. Rex in Brazil and W. Ernest Young in Argentina, began their missions with no missionaries. The War interrupted regular missionary service to South America for more than four and a half years.[16]

We were faced with a gradually dwindling missionary force, but we got some idea of what it would be like to have them all recalled at once. We received a letter from the First Presidency, March 15, 1942, followed by one from Mission Secretary Murdock, informing us that all our missionaries were to be transferred (flying via Pan American) to other missions in Mexico and the United States. This news hit us pretty hard. When I announced in our April Mission Conference that it looked like we were all going to be sent home, the atmosphere became funereal. The elders and members expressed deep regret, and many tears were shed at the thought that the elders might not be able to fulfill their missions in Argentina.

I wrote to Salt Lake City for particulars and received a second letter from the First Presidency stating that the recall of the missionaries was not being considered at that time. We were relieved and also perplexed; something had been mixed up somewhere. In any case, we were very grateful for the change of policy.

I quote a portion of my April 25, 1942, reply to the First Presidency's initial letter:

> *Your letter of March 25, 1942, regarding the withdrawal of missionaries from the Argentine Mission left us all rather stunned and in somewhat of a quandary. I wasn't quite sure if you meant all of the missionaries, or only those whose names you had already requested, and who were to be released during 1942. But when I received a letter from Brother Murdock stating that many of our missionaries would be assigned to the Spanish American Mission, I concluded that all of the missionaries would be sent home, as surely only the newer missionaries would be reassigned.*
>
> *When I announced at our general mission-wide conference that I believed it possible that within a few months the missionaries would be sent home it really made the mission heartsick. Missionaries as well as members cried openly, and we rededicated our efforts to fully carry out our duties as long as we are permitted to stay.*

In this same letter I stated that I had just called some sixty-two local missionaries to serve part-time missions. I also tried to make a case for a mission president to remain in Argentina:

> *The question most frequently asked is, will the Church leave a mission President in Argentina? I have answered that I thought they would, and that is my prayer and request. This as you know is a new mission. True, we have members who have been in the Church for fifteen years, but they are old men and women with no leadership qualifications. The majority of them are of Italian extraction and speak very poor Spanish. They are loyal, true members, but they cannot lead or*

direct. Our only hope in this direction lies among the young generation, but it is not yet ready. Given another five or ten years, things would be different.

I felt that approximately ten branches could carry on the work under local leaders if they had the supervision of a mission president; six branches were being directed by local leadership at that time, but they needed supervision. Next I tried to allay any apprehension the Brethren may have had concerning the safety of a mission president remaining behind:

Under present conditions, or even future ones, I can't feel that he would be any better off anywhere else. The conditions here would have to change very radically if he and his family were to be in any danger. And under the conditions of war, who can say just where the most danger lies? And although there might be some danger, perhaps the good that one might do would make it worth while. After all a soldier is called upon to take risks and hardships, and a soldier of the Lord surely is engaged in a more worth while activity and can do more good than one with a gun. I feel that any risk that a mission president might be called to take in this southern Zion would be worthwhile, even though it might mean staying for the duration.

Finally I expressed my love and concern:

The people of this mission and the mission itself are very dear to my heart. I have seen it grow from its infancy (I arrived here as a missionary 15 months after its dedication) to reach adolescence, with all the possibilities and promises of becoming one of the greatest missions in the Church. To see it left without a mission president would be a great blow to all of us who have had a part in its development.[17]

NOTES

Chapter V

1. Church Historical Department.

2. Entry dated June 12, 1940.

3. Letter dated October 17, 1940, a copy of which is in my files.

4. Mission President's Report dated December 31, 1941, included in the "Argentine Mission History."

5. "Argentine Mission History," June 16, 1942.

6. "Argentine Mission History," May 2, 1942.

7. Elder Ostendorf was the first missionary called to the new Argentine Mission after the South American Mission had been divided. He arrived in Argentina July 24, 1935, after visiting his parents in Germany. He did an outstanding job among the German-speaking people of Argentina.

8. Young, *The Diary of W. Ernest Young*, p. 275, entry dated February 20, 1938. Some who attended the branch were not Germans. The Liebenbergers were Hungarian, the Stefancijosas were Yugoslavian and the Fingers were Swiss.

9. *Deseret News*, April 2, 1937. The article includes a photograph of Elder Ostendorf and his machine.

10. In a letter to the Presiding Bishopric dated June 30, 1932, President Stoof, after despairing from ever collecting on the loan the Church made to Brother Friedrichs in 1925, reported that what money he did have was used to buy a "money" printing machine. Letter on file in the Church Historical Department.

11. Young, *Diary*, p. 289.

12. *Ibid.* p. 298.

13. President Young reports that he even stamped Argentine currency and was warned to stop. Young, *Diary*, p. 298. During President Barker's administration, a brief note appears in the Mission History that implies another member had some Nazi leanings: "Brother Max Alfred Seibt seems to be influenced by Nazi propaganda, but still claims a strong testimony of the gospel." Argentine Mission History, April 13, 1944.

14. Consul Davis died December 26, 1953, while U.S. Ambassador Extraordinary and Plenipotentiary to Israel. See *Who Was Who in America,* Vol. III, 1951-1960.

15. There are a number of books which deal with the Axis influence in Argentina, each clearly pointing to the coordination between Nazi German, Falangist Spanish and Fascist Italian operations. Spanish agents often took their instructions directly from the Nazis; the Spanish could appeal to racial, religious and traditional ties with the Argentines: the approach was through culture. On March 27, 1942, Argentine National Deputy Juan Antonion Solari warned: "We must not lose sight of the fact that Nazi Germany is attempting to hide its infiltration into our country by making use of others. Falangism is actually the mask of Nazism and in many cases acts for it." Quoted in Sax Bradford, *The Battle for Buenos Aires,* (Harcourt, Brace & Co.: New York, 1943), p. 154.

"With usurious interest, Franco is paying his debt to Hitler in South America. He has provided Nazi Germany with a shipping service that passes the British blockade. Every two weeks his combined freight and passenger liners clear Buenos Aires for Spanish ports laden with correspondence, drugs, strategic materials, food, en route to Germany in the end . . ."

"Falangist Spain has provided more than an easy communication and freight system for Nazi Germany, it has provided a supplementary commercial and political espionage service, through the Spanish diplomatic and consular establishments." Sax Bradford, *Ibid.*, p. 97.

Other books of interest include: Allan Chase, *Falange, The Axis Secret Army in the Americas,* (G.P. Putnam's Sons: New York, 1943). Ray Josephs, *Argentine Diary, The Inside Story of the Coming of Fascism,* (Random House: New York, 1944).

16. The first missionaries to Argentina after the War were the Vances, a husband and wife team, and their children, who arrived December 31, 1945; the first single missionary came April 5, 1946. The first to leave for Brazil were likewise husband and wife, the Mertlichs, who departed Salt Lake City November 8, 1945; the first single missionary bound for Brazil departed Salt Lake City March 23, 1946. See Appendix E for list of missionaries who served in Argenina and Brazil.

17. Letter to the First Presidency dated April 24, 1942, a copy of which is in my files.

CHAPTER VI

PROSELYTING THROUGH ORGANIZED SPORTS: MEDIA PROVIDES EXPOSURE

An athletic and cultural event—San Nicolás. As the train approached San Nicolás, Argentina, on October 29, 1938, we didn't know what to expect. Elder L. Pierce Brady had sent us clippings from the local newspapers of the publicity items he had published; frankly, we didn't know just how to interpret them, since participation in organized sports to achieve publicity was a radical departure from any previous mission activities in Argentina.

Publicity. October 21, *El Norte—*

By arrangement with Mr. L. Pierce Brady, a young North American missionary living among us, "The Hill Billy Boys," an interesting orchestral group made up of ten young men coming from less populated parts of the United States where the typical music of the cowboys is played with rare and melodious sounding instruments, will entertain in this city on Saturday the 29th.

. . . The same representative and the active sub-commission of basketball of the Belgrano Club have arranged after much effort to have the team of North American missionaries play a game in which the new style toward which the basketball of the country is evolving will be displayed.[1]

October 27, *El Tribuno* (with first page photograph)—

Mr. Frederick S. Williams will visit San Nicolás.

Frederick S. Williams is president of the Argentine Mission of the Church of Jesus Christ of Latter-day Saints and it is under his direction that the North American missionaries of sports and music come to San Nicolas, represented by the basketball team Los Mormones and the orchestral group "The Hill Billy Boys."

The arrangement could not be more pleasing for it contributes to a better understanding between our Americas and puts in practice the good neighbor doctrine. Surely this is the best way to bring to pass our desires to unite all America. . .[2]

> October 29, *El Tribuno—*
>
> *Tonight in the Belgrano Club the team of North American basketball players that make up the team of "Los Mormones" will meet a team from the unit "Roja." Also of special interest is the training system that the team uses. In addition to the fact that the "Mormons" do not approve of the use of alcohol nor tobacco, these players abstain even from using tea or coffee, with the object of getting in better physical condition.*
>
> *Many of them have played in the international league called "M-Men," fostered by their organization in North America, besides having played on various school teams of the western states.*[3]

With this build-up we didn't know what to expect.

A large crowd greeted our arriving train, and we were happy to see our missionaries standing at its head. Elder Brady introduced us to the mayor of San Nicolás, Dr. José Leo Morteo, who greeted us warmly on behalf of his city. Then Mr. Cayetano Cavalli, a bank manager and president of the Belgrano Sports Club, welcomed us and introduced us to a delegation of club members.

An automobile calvacade transported our rather large group of missionaries, who had caused quite a stir among the train passengers who marveled at so many young, blond foreigners traveling together. We visited the river area and then toured the city. After the tour, we attended an *asado* or Argentine barbecue in our honor at the Belgrano Club.

A long table was piled high with fruit, soft drinks (for our benefit), bread and salads. My wife Corraine was conspicuously the only woman present. True to the Argentine tradition, the men had left their wives at home while they came alone to enjoy the social occasion.

Several lambs—barbecued on a steel pit in the shape of a cross over corncob coals—were soon *"a punto"* (ready) and then cut up. We ate this delicious, tender, golden brown meat, seasoned with a garlic and onion sauce, until we could hold no more.

Dr. Morteo and the club president were very gracious hosts. Also present was Carlos del Forno, LLD, noted Argentine attorney and Rotary Club President. They were interested in our work in Argentina. The Mayor was also concerned for the safety of the missionaries. The police chief had told him that the missionaries were visiting some of the people who lived along the bank of the Paraná River. He wanted us to know that most of the people who lived there were cutthroats, robbers, former convicts and poachers, a loosely knit group that sought refuge at the river edge so that at the approach of the police they could cross the river and disappear into the sparsely settled province of Entre Rios. He didn't think it was safe for the missionaries to visit them. The Mayor said that if a lone policeman were to go there he would be killed, and that when the police did raid the area, they went in large numbers.

After the barbecue, we were again escorted on a brief tour and afterwards taken to our church headquarters in time to make final preparations for the public concert. The *local* was just a half-block from the central square, Plaza Mitre, and we were rather impressed to see a huge banner stretched across the entire street at the entrance to the square entrance emblazoned in Spanish "WELCOME MORMONS." Many smaller signs were posted around the town advertising the concert and the basketball game.

One newspaper account of the concert read:

> October 30, *El Norte—*
>
> *The Hill Billy Boys performed in Mitre Park. A very large crowd was present applauding the original interpretations of these boys who showed great ability in playing their rare instruments.*[4]

Several thousand people crowded around the bandstand in the center of the Plaza to hear the program, which was also carried by loudspeakers throughout the neighborhood. One of the "rare" instruments was a bazooka made by Elder Don Hyrum Smith. The crowd was enthralled with the singular sound this homely instrument produced.

It was a noisy, hilarious program until my wife Corraine began to sing her first solo. She immediately received the crowd's hushed approval as she sang "Que lejos estroy del suelo donde he nacido" (How far I am from the land where I was born). That she sang it and "La Virgencita" in Spanish came as a happy surprise and they applauded loudly.

After the program we adjourned to the Belgrano Sports Club to play basketball. Quoting from the newspaper account:

> October 31, *El Tribuno—*
>
> *In a stupendous display of energy "The Mormons" beat the Belgrano Club basketball team. The score was 26 to 13. Very few times has such brilliant basketball ever been played in this city. . .*
>
> *It began Saturday at 10:00 p.m. in the Belgrano Sports Club before a very large crowd which instantly applauded the good plays made by both teams. . . A few moments after "The Mormons" came in, applauded by the crowd, they astonished the onlookers with the speed at which they took their warming up preliminaries. . . One might say that even before the match began it was certain that the Yankees would present a polished demonstration of their playing abilities, which in fact happened. In this respect, suffice it to say that never has such a good brand of basketball been seen here, except for the time when we were visited a few years ago by "Huracán" of Rosario. . .*
>
> *The match was refereed by the coach of the North American team, Mr. Williams, his actions being completely impartial.*[5]

I'd asked the missionaries to keep their score down. Not being in good physical shape, they were happy with the frequent substitutions I made, but felt that my "impartiality" militated against them.

After the game, we were the guests at a reception at the Belgrano Sports Club. We were asked to sign the guest book, and when I wrote a short thank you note in Spanish, the president was astonished that I knew how to write in that language. He said, among other things, "Mr. Williams, you may not know this, but we feel that you are the best ambassadors your country has ever had. We know that the United States has an ambassador in Buenos Aires and that there are many members of the diplomatic corps in Argentina, because occasionally we read about them when they attend official functions of the government, but we never see them personally. You and your missionaries have met with the people to show us how North Americans really are. You little realize how much your government owes your church."

October 29, *El Tribuno*—

> *Tomorrow, Sunday, at 8 p.m. a conference of a cultural character will be held in Conference Hall at 534 Nación Street, under the direction of Mr. L. Pierce Brady, president of the San Nicolás Branch of the Argentine Mission. Present at this meeting will be several members of the orchestral and sports groups, who are our guests . . . the meeting should be very well attended. . .*[6]

New proselyting approach. A large crowd attended our Sunday meeting, and some of the people began taking the missionary lessons. Others responded warmly whenever the missionaries called on them later in tracting, or on the street. The people knew who the Mormons were; they weren't afraid of us, and many were genuinely interested in hearing about our beliefs. The concert and basketball game had broken down barriers of prejudice and ignorance and had speeded up exposure. For months the missionaries continued to reap positive dividends. The favorable results and the possibilities of using this same approach elsewhere were not lost on us; from then on, we used the Argentine news media to introduce our sports teams and musical groups, which in turn introduced the gospel to Argentina, preparing the way for our missionaries to enter hundreds of Argentine homes to preach the gospel of Christ; homes which had previously been closed to us. What a blessing this was.

Missionaries in sports before 1938. Mormon missionaries have participated in organized sports in Argentina almost since the establishment of the South American Mission. During my first mission, we elders got some exercise and very welcome hot showers at the Buenos Aires YMCA. We also enjoyed shooting baskets and playing ball with the local club members. On one of these occasions the coach of the Olimpia Basket-Ball Club—a first division team in Argentina's top basketball league—spotted us playing and decided to recruit us for his team.

Waldo I. Stoddard, who came to the South American Mission with President Stoof, had led the Oregon State University championship team just before receiving his mission call. Elder Heber M. Clegg was also an excellent ball player. I did all right.[7]

On February 23, 1928, we received a letter from coach Enrique P. Rumbo of the Olimpia Basket-Ball Club inviting us to try out for the Olimpia team. Stoddard, Clegg and I made the team and played first string for the Club, which nearly took the league championship that year, due in large measure to our efforts. A popular slogan used by the press was a play on the coach's name *"Con Rumbo al Campeonato"* (Enroute to the Championship).

The next time the mission saw players like Stoddard was during W. Ernest Young's presidency. The mission history is silent, but President Young recorded a brief note in his *Diary:*

> *The Elders in Quilmes are playing some [basketball] games with not too much winning, but they succeed in making friends which is our objective in taking part in athletics.*[8]

The missionaries under President Young had also played softball among themselves and in friendly games against company teams from Goodyear and Swift.[9] The Youngs were released in September 1938. Individual missionaries had played basketball for various teams until we organized the "Los Mormones" team and officially entered the Argentine National Federation Basketball League, November 1, 1938. The previous season, Elders Rolf L. Larson and Dale A. Bergeson had played for Club Atlético of Lanús. Both elders were invited to play on the Buenos Aires All-Star team in the National Championship, but because they failed to meet residency requirements they were unable to accept.

Why organized sports. Our decision to enter organized sports competition was based on several factors. There was my own inclination towards sports; I was young, just turned thirty, and had enjoyed participating in sports all my life.[10] We also had a number of exceptionally gifted athletes among the missionaries, who played basketball or baseball whenever they could. But the most important factor was the positive result of the San Nicolás trip.

Before we could interest the people in our message, we had to change the image of the Church in Argentina and we realized that organized sports was one of the best means of achieving our goal. The Argentines are very sports-minded and the many daily newspapers had and still have tremendous sports sections.

Sports gave us an opportunity to present a favorable image of the Church. We wanted to be identified as healthy, clean-living sportsmen rather than as polygamists or any of the other imaginative personae attributed to us. In those days, whenever people first heard the word "Mormon," they sought their priests for information, or looked us up in their old encyclopedias (published in Spain under the auspices of the Catholic Church): "A small sect living out on the desert in the western part of the United States where they practice polygamy"—as if we were still practicing it. They invariably asked: "How many wives did Brigham Young have?" or "How many wives do you want to take from Argentina?" I remember a classic comeback to that inquiry given by Elder Guestlesson. Two Anglo-Argentine girls sneeringly asked: "How many wives do you have?" Never breaking stride, with a smile he answered: "Only seven, but I'm young yet."

Softball League teams. As many as seven different clubs and schools fielded softball teams during the four years we were involved. The final standings of the 1938-1939 softball season were:[11]

Team	Won	Lost
Los Mormones	*6*	*1*
Goodyear	*5*	*2*
Boca Juniors	*4*	*2*
Union Deportiva Argentina	*2*	*4*
Deportivo Central Argentino	*2*	*4*
Cambridge	*2*	*4*
Young American	*1*	*5*

El Mundo of January 20, 1939, made the news of our championship its second headline; beneath FRANCE WON'T CHANGE HER POLITICS came MORMONS ARE SOFTBALL CHAMPIONS. Inside was a synopsis of the game:

> *It is not very common to see in a spirited game of ball of the type which was played yesterday in Hurlingham, such amiable and sportsman-like contact. Some 70 fans of "Los Mormones," whose headquarters are in Quilmes, accompanied the team to Hurlingham where they became a vociferous stimulus to the players, demonstrating a frankly optimistic spirit.*

For four consecutive years the results were always the same: "Mormons Win League Championship."

At the beginning of the 1940-1941 season, the league's third year, *The Standard* joined the newspapers covering softball by printing a lengthy article:

> *Softball which has spread across the United States like a prairie fire during the last few years, so much so that it has superseded Baseball in popularity, has come to Argentina, and this summer seven or eight teams will participate in the competition organized by the newly formed Softball League. . .*
>
> *Mr. S. [sic] Williams, President of the new League and also President of the Mormons Club, was present and gave an interesting talk, in which, after reviewing the prospects for the coming season, he referred to the international league which organizes annual championship [sic]. This year's event is being held in Cuba. Mr. Williams said that he hoped that Argentina will be able to progress sufficiently to take part in these international events.*[12]

The final league standing for the 1941-1942 season, our last year in competition, was:

Team	**Won**	**Lost**
Mormons	*5*	*1*
Ateneo de la Juventud	*4*	*2*
American Grammar and High School	*3*	*3*
YMCA	*0*	*6*

The Mormon line-up was:

W. Wale	*Pitcher*
E. Jones	*Center Field*
F. Williams	*Second Base*
P. Davis	*Left Field*
D. Hughes	*Catcher*
K. Schwendiman	*First Base*
R. McKay	*Third Base*
S. Forrest	*Right Field*

In addition to the regular season, we were occasionally invited to play teams from U.S. military or passenger ships. One such game we won thirteen to ten; I did some of the pitching.

My January 14, 1942, report to the First Presidency stated:

> *On December 20th we were invited to play a baseball game with Grafa Club and have the orchestra play for a dance for our members and the members of their club. The baseball game was well attended and some two thousand people crowded the outdoor dance hall they had improvised by putting canvas over basketball courts. We were very well received and much good was accomplished. I gave out fifty-two Articles of Faith cards, and among all of the missionaries present we estimate there must have been at least one hundred and fifty Gospel conversations. Pictures and a nice article were printed in their magazine. Two members of their club have since been out to meetings.*[13]

The Club's magazine included five pictures; in one "Vice-president of the Liga Argentina de Base Ball, Don Federico Williams" is seen presenting Mr. U.H. Santalla, the President of Grafa Club, with the winner's cup donated by the Delta Line.[14]

On January 26, 1942, a few days after our fourth softball championship, we played a team from the USS *Savannah*. This was one of those occasions when I pitched, and we were lucky to beat them two to one in seven innings. Articles and photographs appeared in both the *Herald* and *Standard* the following day:

> *Neither team scored in the first five innings of the game which resolved itself into a pitching duel between Malin of the Savannah and Williams of the Mormons. Malin drew the advantage when the Marines "landed" their first run, and apparently had everything well "in hand." An explosive surge in the final inning, however, brought the Mormons two runs and victory.*

The *Standard* amplified the nature of the surge:

> *The Mormons, who had last bats, did not manage to retaliate in the sixth, and there were already two out in the last inning, with two strikes and two balls on S. Forrest; so the game was practically in the bag for the Marines.*
>
> *But then came the fatal error, when with two men on base Dettenback—in his anxiety to end the game—made a bad throw to first base after picking up Forrest's grounder, and Gulley, having to reach out for the peg dropped the ball, thus allowing the batter safe at first, while Russell and Brown were crossing the plate safely for a victory which seemed almost miraculous.*
>
> *An unusual number of popflies and good fielding on both teams made the game go very fast, and relieved the strain on the pitchers, both of whom were steady and had good control.*

Service teams only played against other Americans; they didn't want to get involved with the local people and risk a political incident.

Liga Argentina de baseball and the Bill Terry trophy. Baseball had an even larger following than softball. Our games were given extensive news coverage. People told us, "If it weren't for the Mormons, baseball would be dead in Argentina." It revived because of new faces, and we became the favorite team for many previously nonaligned Argentines.

About two weeks after we clinched the national championship, I was asked to field a team for a special exhibition game of baseball against the recently crowned Atlantic fleet champions, the marines of the USS *Quincy*. In the accompanying letter, Mr. Cesar S. Vasquez, Director General of Physical Education in the Ministry of Public Instruction, explained that all the high school students of the capital would be invited to the game, "since that sport [baseball] has preference in our school physical education program."[15]

The Mission History entry for May 8, 1939:

> *The baseball team of Mormon missionaries lost a baseball game to a team of sailors from the U.S. Cruiser "Quincy" 4-2 before a crowd of 2,000. It was a special invitation game that was heavily publicized by local newspapers and magazines including "The Buenos Aires Herald" and "El Mundo." Photos of both teams appeared.*

The crowd was actually closer to five thousand, the largest group I've ever played before. Our lineup was: Vance, pitcher; McBride, catcher; Jesperson, first base; Williams, second base; Allen, shortstop; Bergeson, third base; Hatch, left field; Dana, center field; Willis, right field.[16]

On April 25, 1939, we won the national championship; on the first of May both our baseball and basketball teams played in exhibition against Club Gimnasia Chacabuco of Buenos Aires; on the eighth we played the *Quincy* team at the request of the Ministry; on the twelfth the Baseball League of Rosario paid the team's entire expenses to that city to play exhibition games against their locals; on the nineteenth we traveled to Pergamino as guests of the Club Gimnasia y Esgrima de Pergamino; on the twentieth we played in San Nicolás against Club Belgrano.[17]

Our best hitter was Elder Phil Davis, featured in the Buenos Aires *Herald:*

> *"Music hath charms. . ." and though there was but little music last Saturday afternoon at the Ateneo field, the baton-wielding hands of Phil Davis, Mormons' centre field, had plenty of charm in establishing a new game batting record in local baseball by smashing out six consecutive safeties, including a home run and a double, in as many trips to home plate.*
>
> *This feat was accomplished by Davis under the handicap of having his right hand in a cast, the result of having suffered a broken bone in that hand.*

The article speaks of his missionary calling and the Mormon team:

> *Phil is one of a number of sports-loving young Americans who work for a period of two and a half [years] with the Mormon organization whose playing and fine sporting example has been one of the causes of the recent revival of*

interest in local baseball. During their three years of competition in the Liga Argentina de Baseball, the Mormons have twice won the championship failing to tie for first place last season by one game, and thus forfeiting their claim to the permanent possession of the Bill Terry championship cup, which must be won for three consecutive seasons.[18]

The baseball league was never very large, only four to five teams each season. The 1939 final standings were

Team	Won	Lost
Mormons	*5*	*1*
Boca Juniors	*4*	*2*
Asociacion Jovenes Nipones	*1*	*4*
Gimnasia Chacabuco	*1*	*4*

What received the most publicity was the annual foreigner versus Argentina baseball classic, a traditional competition begun in 1941. These were all-star teams with usually four to five Mormons on the "foreign" team. I was captain-player for the foreigners two consecutive years. The Consejo Nacional de Educación Física (Ministry of Education) donated a large loving cup some twenty-four inches high and fourteen across. Days before the game, all the newspapers devoted entire front pages to the teams. The foreigners won the first year but lost the second.[19]

As a result of the nationwide publicity, we constantly received invitations to play against other teams in the interior cities. The most successful tour was sponsored by the Asociación Rosarina de Baseball (Rosario Baseball Association) on May 12 and 13, 1939. Our greatest benefit from that trip was the conversion of Raul Rovira. Raul was the secretary of the Rosario baseball league. Elder Harold Brown, who was then President of the branch at Rosario, spent an entire afternoon (during an *asado* in our honor) speaking with him about the Church. He converted almost immediately, attended meetings the following Sunday and hasn't missed much since. He has held almost every position in the Church in Argentina. He was certainly a tremendous acquisition, one that came to us as a result of our athletic activities.[20]

Each baseball season ended with a big celebratory banquet. When we left in 1942, a special banquet was held in my honor. Our mission band, the "Hill Billy Boys," provided the entertainment.

Mission Band. The "Hill Billy Boys" band usually played for our Church dances as well, which were quite frequent, especially during carnival time. Several missionaries played in the band over the years,[21] but it became a really good orchestra when Elder Gerald McQuarry came. He had led a dance band in the Compton area of Los Angeles, and he had all the orchestrations, which he had shipped to Argentina. For a while, with good musicians, we had a fine group. Elder Grant Thomas was an excellent pianist, and Elder Phil Davis was an outstanding clarinetist. We had three saxophones, three trumpets, two trombones and drums. Phil Davis was also a fine arranger; he had done some arrangements for Glen Miller, and had put himself through school at the University of Southern California playing clarinet.

There is an interesting follow-up to that last banquet. About a year later, while working in Venezuela, I was at a reception hosted by the Minister of Labor. I sat next to the Papal Nuncio, a consummate drinker. Each time a waiter passed with a tray of drinks, he didn't look up, just reached out and took one. I held a soft drink in my hand all night. Toward the end of the evening a young man came up and said, "You're Mr. Williams, aren't you?" I said: "Yes." He said: "You don't know who I am, but I have been watching you all evening." I said: "Is that so?" He said: "I was studying in Buenos Aires and a friend of mine invited me to your farewell held at the Gimnasia y Esgrima Club. I asked him who all those young, blond North Americans were, drinking Orange Crush, and he said, 'Well, they are missionaries,' 'Missionaries!' 'Yes, Mormon missionaries; they're the ones who have been playing ball here.' I said: 'How come they are drinking Orange Crush?' He said: 'They don't drink; they don't drink any alcoholic beverages.'" He then said to me, "So, I have been watching you all evening. I know you were not here with the mission now; I don't know of any Mormons here in Venezuela at all, and I just wondered if now that you were away from the others if you would drink some alcoholic beverages."

When we first organized, I asked the missionaries to select a coach for each team. Some of them had played college ball and were very knowledgeable, more so than I. They agreed, however, that I should be coach and manager to avoid any possible difficulties. I've been asked if I found myself making transfers in and out of the capital branches according to a missionary's athletic ability. The answer is "no." I was tempted on occasion, but I didn't. In fact, I sent some of my best players into the interior, because they were primarily good missionaries. In addition, because the seasons were short, only a month or so, they never interfered with our regular proselyting activities.

On Pearl Harbor Day, December 7, 1941, I wrote the First Presidency:

> *The six appearances of the base ball and basket ball teams [for the past months] were before some thirty-five hundred people, and the attendant write-ups were published in five newspapers with a circulation of nearly two million copies on Sunday, as well as in one widely-circulating sports magazine which carried our pictures.*
>
> *We play under the name of "The Mormons" and are nationally known. We have countless friends through our sports and they have done a great deal to overcome prejudice.*

Basketball and Club Atlético Los Mormones. Even though we received much favorable publicity as a result of our involvement in softball and baseball, basketball brought us even more. The Lord blessed us with missionaries whose great athletic abilities made them the premiere basketball stars of the nation. As a result, the Church was in the public eye constantly. Elders Rolf Larson and Dale Bergeson were the key members of the Argentine all-star team chosen for the South American Basketball championship. Publicity about them and about the Church flooded Argentina. When we learned that Bergeson could not participate—he could not meet some residency requirements—Larson became a sensation. It was wonderful. We could not have asked for a better vehicle for breaking down prejudice against the Church. Our basketball glory lasted only one season; after that our stars were released with predictable results. The establishment of the Club, however, had a lasting effect.

All of Argentina's athletics are handled through sports clubs. To participate in organized sports, we needed our own facilities. We found three available vacant lots four blocks from the Liniers chapel, and I made a down payment on two of the lots. I'm sorry we didn't on the third lot; as it turned out we needed the room.

We made the purchase in the name of the Church, but did not use Church funds to pay for it. Labor and materials were donated, and mortgage payments came from membership dues. Many missionaries contributed substantially to the financing and construction. I even asked the First Presidency, through Elder Ballard, for a contribution. He reported:

> *I went with some of the returned missionaries and made a plea to the Presidency for $1,000.00 to help you create that Athletic Court. I don't know what has come of it but I believe that favorable action will be taken.*[22]

The Presidency approved an appropriation of four hundred dollars, notifying us of the same on March 15, 1939.[23]

We drew up plans for the facilities and a basketball court, and missionaries and members donated their labor. Domingo Quici and other brick layers put up the building in short order. The plumbing was also donated. Soon we were able to begin clearing the rest of the land for the court. Nearly all basketball courts in Argentina were outside courts at that time; one exception was the new Ateneo de la Juventud. We built railings to keep people off the playing court, and put up bleachers.

Federico Forrest had plans for making cement basketball standards, which were not used very much then. We put them in, and then held our breaths during the inspection by the Basketball Federation; they were approved.

For our dedication and inaugural we held a nonconference match with Ateneo de la Juventud on May 25, 1940. It was a particularly cold and miserable day for playing, but Ateneo took it very good-naturedly, because they won thirty-two to twenty-four.[24] Afterward, we held a dance at the Liniers chapel. The mission history reads:

> *May 25, 1940. Today is national independence day and also proved to be an important day in the history of the Mission. Our Club, Los Mormones, located on Calle Carué 1132, was inaugurated under the direction of President Frederick S. Williams. It consists of a very fine out-door basketball court and dressing room. A volleyball game and two basketball games were played and a special ceremony conducted to dedicate the Club.*
>
> *This is quite a step in the Mission, because most of the athletic and social activities in the country are carried on by means of clubs. To provide the same for our members and friends a club was almost a necessity. The missionaries have been very instrumental in founding the Club. They worked on the construction of the club and were liberal with donations.*

The initials of our club, Club Atlético Los Mormones, spelled the word "calm" on the backs of our uniforms with "Mormons" on the front. It was a nice thing to have calm on our shirts, because it was easy to get excited about the games, and especially about the calls made by the referees. As a general rule, Argentines do not like to lose. It doesn't matter how they win, but they must win; second place means nothing.

The Club, formally organized December 23, 1938, sponsored events in sports, drama, speech and music.[25] A monthly column in the *Mensajero* detailed events and expenses of the Club.

We also organized a softball team made up principally of members, a Mormon girls volleyball team,[26] and a member basketball team.[27] We also organized our own Mormon leagues and tournaments; Liniers was usually the victor.[28]

Over the four years we got reams of publicity from the three sports we entered. Members and friends enjoyed seeing us play. People we didn't even know would follow our team. We broke down prejudice, spread good will, made the Church's name synonymous with good sportsmanship and clean living, attracted investigators and friends (many of whom joined the Church), and had a lot of enjoyment doing it. Unfortunately, the War stopped the influx of missionaries, which meant we could not continue fielding teams, and more important, without the missionaries we could not take advantage of the goodwill climate for proselyting.

NOTES

Chapter VI

1. The newspaper coverage was reprinted in the November 1938 *Mensajero Deseret,* p. 21. In addition, the trip was written up in English in the *Gaucho Gazette* and in the April 1939 *Improvement Era* where it appeared with pictures in an article entitled "The Hospitable Argentine," pp. 220, 221, 237, co-authored by Elder Brady and me.

2. *Ibid.*

3. *Ibid.*

4. *Ibid.*

5. *Ibid.*

6. *Ibid.*

7. Elders Stoddard and Clegg also played tennis on their missions for the Vélez-Sarsfield Tennis Club and did very well in national competition.

8. The entry appears March 26, 1938. *The Diary of W. Ernest Young,* 1973, p. 279.

9. Cf. *Diary,* pp. 202, 241, 264.

10. The following is taken from a taped interview with Frederick S. Williams conducted by his son, May 5, 1974:

FSW: I have always been an avid sports fan, not an outstanding athlete perhaps, but, I've always enjoyed participating. When I was in the eighth grade in Holbrook (Arizona) I was playing on the high school basketball and baseball teams; also on the football team. At Phoenix Union High School I started on the third football team and worked up to the second team my freshman year. As a sophomore I was playing first string on the varsity football team and second string on the varsity basketball team. The school had an enrollment of five thousand; it was larger than the University of Arizona at that particular time.

After my mission I was also very active in sports. We had an M-Men team from the Phoenix Ward and we played basketball; we also played a little baseball, but not too much. When I became secretary to the Judge of the Federal Court, Judge F.C. Jacobs, I used to go to the YMCA for exercise, which was located right next door to the Federal Building. I guess I impressed them, because they elected me President of their baseball league and also of their basketball league. It was about that time that Corraine and I spearheaded the organization of the Phoenix Ex-Missionary Club which was intended to give activity to the Elders as they returned from their mission assignments. We met once a month; we had our own charter and our own organization. We had monthly activities; we sponsored dances, outings, banquets, and fielded basketball and basesball teams in the YMCA League I was president of.

FGW: Did you play on it?

FSW: Oh, yes, I played first or second base and guard on the basketball team.

FGW: How many teams were in this YMCA League?

FSW: It was a church league and there must have been eight or ten. We won the league championship in basketball one year; I still have the cup. We did well in hardball too. I remember that my Church job at that time was president of the Mutual, and our Bishop, John H. Udall, asked me to go up to Conference with him. When we left to go up we were in first place in baseball. When we came back a week later, we had been dropped from the League. The team members got to squabbling among themselves and had decided not to play any more. I finally got them back in again, but it was a constant problem to get everybody there on time and to keep track of the equipment. Corraine used to despair when we opened the closet door and the baseball bats would fall out. It was the only place in or small apartment where I could keep the equipment.

FGW: What did your duties consist of as president of the league?

FSW: My duties consisted of presiding over the meetings, making up the schedules, securing the facilities, motivating the members to pay their dues, organizing the annual banquet and different things like that.

FGW: This kind of experience certainly must have prepared you then to be president of the Argentine baseball leagues.

FSW: Yes, in some respects it helped.

11. See *El Mundo,* January 20, 1939.

12. *The Standard,* Thursday, October 17, 1940.

13. A copy of the letter is in my files.

14. See *Grafa Club* Publication Vol. 2, No. 14 (December 1941), pp. 10, 11; 26, 27.

15. Letter to the Argentine Baseball League President, Juan Carlos Noodt (mistakenly spelled Loodt) dated April 27, 1939, in my files. I also have the translated letter of Captain John F. Robinson of the *Quincy* addressed to Honorable Jorge Coll, the Minister of Justice and Public Instruction, requesting the game.

16. *El Mundo,* May 9, 1939.

17. *El Mensajero,* June 1939, p. 30.

18. Buenos Aires *Herald,* March 14, 1942. For other players and photo see July 1940 *Mensajero,* cover and p. 139.

19. See particularly the *Standard,* March 1, 1942, for numerous large photographs, but also the *Herald* and *El Mundo* of the same date.

20. For coverage on both the baseball and basketball exhibition games held in Rosario see particularly the *Democracia,* May 12 and 13, 1939.

21. See *Mensajero,* November 1940, cover and p. 220, for photo and history.

22. Letter dated February 28, 1939 in my files.

23. The lots were purchased March 31, 1939. See Argentine Mission History.

24. See *Mensajero,* June 1940, p. 117, and November 1940, p. 220.

25. Fifteen days before we arrived in Argentina, President Young had established an MIA Club; it was shortlived. However, many of the same people were involved in the organization of the Club Atlético Los Mormones.

26. *Mensajero,* December 1940, p. 243.

27. *Mensajero,* August 1941, p. 251; also June 1942, p. 187.

28. The basketball tournament winner received the Bergeson trophy, see *Mensajero,* August 1940, p 157; September 1940, p. 177; also May 1941, p. 155.

CHAPTER VII

MISSION ACTIVITIES AND PROGRAMS: REACHING OUT

OCTOBER 7 to 9, 1938, we met with all the missionaries from the capital for the first time. Friday, the elders held a meeting to receive instructions, bear their testimonies, and express their love for the gospel. Corraine speedily found a way to their hearts by feeding them all the food they could eat, topped off with homemade pies. She always had excellent rapport with the missionaries and, in many cases, handled their personal problems with compassion and understanding. Saturday evening of the conference nearly five hundred people attended the road shows; a loving cup was awarded.[1]

The new chapel in Liniers was under construction at the corner of Cañada de Gómez and Tonelero, but since only its walls were up we could not use the facilities, and had to settle for the cramped old meeting hall in the front of the Notaro home. Sunday, some two hundred people crowded into the hall to attend the sessions.

I learned that missionaries do not, as a general rule, comply with the limits given for their talks. Time had been carefully allotted for each speaker; but long after the concluding session should have ended I had not yet had a chance to address the congregation. When the last elder finally found the word he had been looking for all evening and pronounced "Amen," I was ready to close the meeting. Corraine, who was seated at my side on the stand, persuaded me not to. This was my first conference and she felt the people would be disappointed if I didn't speak. I explained the dilemma to the congregation by saying that the time was up, but if they wished to remain, I would speak. They stayed.

I had planned to speak for just a few minutes, and accordingly put away my notes for a longer talk. The Lord blessed me with his spirit, and before I said my "Amen," I had spoken forty-five minutes. I have never felt the Lord's spirit in more abundance than on that occasion. There was absolute silence as I talked. No one shifted or squirmed on the crowded benches. No one dozed or looked at his watch. Afterwards, both the missionaries and members said it was the most spiritual talk they had heard and were sorry I hadn't continued longer. It is a wonderful feeling to repeat the words the Holy Ghost prompts one to say.

Dedication of first chapel in South America. On January 1, 1929, Elder Harry Brundage and I were guests of the Luigi Notaros for New Year's dinner in their new home on Tonelero Street, near the corner of Cañada de Gómez in Liniers. Luigi had just retired from the railroad and they had moved into their new quarters; there was no furniture. Sister Notaro cooked dinner on a Primus stove brought from their former home, and we ate seated on the floor.

Two years later on July 28, 1931, the Notaros transferred this same property to the Church with the understanding that they could remain in the house as long as they both lived. Their small one-story house sat back away from the street, so the Church erected the first Liniers chapel in front, at sidewalk level. Construction began September 8, 1931, and President Stoof offered the dedicatory prayer November 15. This chapel served not only the needs of the Liniers branch, but was the building Presidents Stoof, Young and I (for a time) used for all our mission conferences.

We soon realized that the Liniers chapel could not meet the Saints' needs and we made plans for a larger meeting house to be constructed. In March 1936, President Young purchased the lot between the Notaro property and Cañada de Gómez Street. President Stoof had begun negotiating for the property in 1931.[2] Final payment was made August 19, 1936; the total price was $3,672.51.

When I arrived in the mission, the chapel was still under construction. Progress was very slow, but eventually we got the roof on and finished a second story apartment for the Notaros to replace their home, which was to be converted into classrooms.

The original plans for the chapel interior called for a small raised platform centered at the end farthest from the entrance, with choir benches arranged at each side of the platform. Since this was to be our only chapel—comprising only one large room—I felt we could better utilize the space by changing it slightly so it could accommodate all our activities, cultural and spiritual.

I asked the contractor, Philip H. Massey, a North American, to bid on the changes: elimination of the choir benches, extension of the platform the width of the building to serve as a stage and, in the center of the stage, a baptismal font. Theretofore, it had been necessary to go to the river or to Melo to perform our baptisms. Both areas were open air, subject to weather, and in the winter, bitter cold.

The First Presidency accepted the changes and authorized the few hundred dollars for the modifications. The original estimate for the chapel had been eight thousand dollars.[3] We even installed our own heating system: to warm the water of the font we circulated the water through the coils of the fuel oil stove.

This was something new in South America: a large chapel built and owned by the Church. Neither the Brazilian meeting house in Joinville or the first Liniers chapel could compare in magnitude or impact. Thirteen years after the organization of the South American Mission, we had a chapel almost large enough to seat all the baptized members in Argentina; it was a place of our own where we could be proud to bring our friends and investigators. A photo of the chapel under construction and a lengthy article appeared in the Church section of the *Deseret News*, November 26, 1938.

The dedicatory service was held in conjunction with the April Conference of the Argentine Mission. Songs were translated into Spanish for the occasion. Scheduled to perform were the mission choir directed by Elder Ernest J. Wilkins, a girls' triple trio and a twelve-voice missionary chorus, both organized and directed by Corraine. Among the speakers were Donato Gianfelice and Roland G. Kaiser.

It was my privilege to direct the dedicatory service and to offer the dedicatory prayer. I had requested that a General Authority come, pointing out that this was a very special occasion, and that a General Authority had not visited South America since the mission's organization. In a letter dated February 28, 1939, Elder Ballard expressed hope that "someone, if not myself, may have the privilege of visiting those missions in South America soon. I rejoice in the near completion of a meeting house. It would be a very happy occasion for me if I had the privilege of coming there to dedicate it, if not when it is finished at some time in the future."[4] On April 12, 1939, he wrote:

I was happy to hear from you in your letter of March 22nd wherein you tell of the success that has attended you in that you were able to complete a chapel. I note also that you planned to dedicate it on April 9 unless you heard from me before that time.

Of course there was no possibility of me or anyone else coming just at this time so I suppose you went forward with the dedication and that by now you are enjoying the first Church building erected in that country.[5]

Three days before the services, I started composing the dedicatory prayer. The night before the dedication, I showed the prayer to Brother Fermín Barjollo, our faithful member from Rosario. He corrected only one sentence. I had planned to ask the Lord to bless all those who had contributed toward the building, adding *"que nunca les falten las necesidades de la vida"* (that they may never lack the necessities of life). The expression works in English, but in Spanish, he pointed out, the meaning becomes a request for more necessities or cares, and the members already had enough of those. He suggested I say "que nunca les falten las cosas necesarias para la vida" (that they may never lack those things that are necessary to sustain life).

The three-day conference proceedings were summarized and published in English in the Mission's *Gaucho Gazette* (June 1939), and in Spanish in the *Mensajero* (May 1939). The Sunday morning session was also reported in the *Herald* and *El Mundo*, and also in the *Improvement Era* (August 1939). Quoting from *El Mensajero*:

Sunday, April 9, 1939, was for the Argentine Mission a most important day. We celebrated two great events: the resurrection of our Lord and the dedication of the new chapel—the first to be constructed for the Church in South America. This was the culmination of a dream and the result of a great deal of work. For thirteen long years the members had waited and longed for the construction of a chapel.

The weather was ideal. Never was there a more beautiful day seen than the 9th of April. It was one of those rare autumn days which was neither hot nor cold. The sun shone in all its splendor in a cloudless sky; it was a day that made everyone feel that it was good to be alive. It seemed as though God had reserved this day for the dedication of his house.

The dedicatory service had been announced for ten o'clock. At nine o'clock the people began arriving. They came with their arms full of flowers, beautiful flowers of every kind and color. They came with flowers they had picked themselves, picked with hearts full of love for their neighbors and with gratitude to their God, ready to make an offering of love with an appropriate sacrifice for such an occasion. God created the flowers to beautify the earth and the lives of men. It is impossible to contemplate their beauty without thinking of their Creator who in His wisdom created them. All the flower vases were filled, and still they came. At last they were stacked loosely on the floor of the stage.

At ten minutes before ten o'clock with the stage filled with people and flowers, two photographers came to take pictures. One was from the newspaper "El Mundo" and the other from the English language daily Buenos Aires "Herald." They took pictures of the congregation, the baptismal font, the stage and the exterior of the building.

At ten o'clock the service began with the chapel filled with people. There was not seating for all of them and many remained standing around the walls during the entire two-hour service. It was truly an inspiring sight from the stand to see so many smiling faces, and one could feel the influence of God's Spirit which had been solicited by the silent and secret prayers of the more than three hundred people that filled the chapel. After the first hymn had been sung by the congregation, the invocation was offered by Brother Luigi Notaro who had done so much for the Church in Argentina.

I read a special salutary message from President Grant, written for the occasion.

The full program, published in the *Gaucho Gazette*, was:

Song-	*Congregation, "Redeemer of Israel"*
Prayer-	*Luigi Notaro (original owner of part of the property on which the chapel is built and who donated this property to the Church)*
Song-	*"For the Strength of the Hills," Missionary Chorus, under the direction of Sister Williams, consisting of: Elders Max L. Willis, Rolf L. Larson and Dale A. Bergeson, first tenors; Ernest J. Wilkins, Ben R. Allen and Karl Fenn, second tenors; J. Avril Jesperson, Jesse B. Smith and O. Clement Williams, baritones; and Oren E. Moffett, I. Dwight Dana and J. Donal Earl, basses.*
Talk-	*J. Donal Earl—History of the Construction of the Chapel*
Song-	*"Our Prophet Dear," Ladies Chorus directed by Sister Williams, consisting of: Armida Ercolini, Angélica Romero and Alicia Roza, sopranos; Teresa Brandi, Yolanda Duarte and María Montot, second sopranos; and Dora Castro, Delia Sánchez and Evira Duarte, altos.*
Talk-	*Roland G. Kaiser—Practical Mormonism*
Song-	*"The Prayer Perfect," Mission quartet, composed of: Sister Corraine S. Williams, soprano; J. Avril Jesperson, baritone; Rolf L. Larson, tenor; and J. Donal Earl, bass.*
Talk-	*Donato A. Gianfelice—Early History of the Mission*

Song-	*"Dedication Song," special words written for the occasion by President Frederick S. Williams and set to the music of "Out of the Dust," sung by the Missionary Chorus, directed by Sister Williams.*
Talk and Dedicatory Prayer-	*President Frederick S. Williams. Before offering the Dedicatory Prayer President Williams spoke at length on the Resurrection of our Savior and its importance to us as members of this Church.*
Closing Song-	*Congregation, "The Spirit of God Like a Fire is Burning"*
Closing Prayer-	*Sister Josefa Hernández de Alonzo Sánchez.*

The afternoon and evening sessions on Sunday were devoted to a comprehensive presentation of the history of the Church, from its restoration to the present.[6]

The only hitch in the entire three-day conference came just before the Sunday morning session began. I suddenly could not find the dedication prayer. I looked through books, in drawers, everywhere. I felt helpless, and I prayed silently that I could find it, or if not, that I could remember what to say. The time to leave for the chapel had come, and still no prayer. My last act was to pull out the desk table—and there was the prayer.

The excitement, high during the entire conference, now became electric. We felt like the Kirtland Saints must have felt at the dedication of the Kirtland Temple—the first building; humbled and exhilarated.

Dedicatory Prayer, Liniers Chapel

O God, Father of us all, we give thee infinite thanks for the great privilege we have of gathering for the purpose of dedicating this chapel. We bow before thee today in the name of Jesus Christ, thy son, with hearts filled with love for the many blessings we receive from thee, day by day; for the lives thou hast given us, for the privilege of living in these the latter days when the gospel of thy beloved son has been restored in its fullness; to be able to live in a nation that extends to all the freedom to believe in thee. We thank thee for the privilege we have to live in a period when thy promises to the Lamanites and the House of Israel begin to be fulfilled, and for the opportunity we have to begin this work of bringing souls to thee; and also for the honor we enjoy of being called thy servants and sons and daughters.

We thank thee for this chapel. We ask thee to bless all those who had a part in its construction. Pour out thy blessings on all those who contributed towards the building. Bless them that they may never lack those things necessary to sustain life. Increase thy favor towards them that they may prosper and know that it is good to offer their means and time to thee.

Bless this chapel that everyone who comes here to listen to thy words may feel the influence of thy Holy Spirit in such a manner that they will have the desire to search further and come unto thee; that they may know that the events of the restoration of the gospel are true and that thy son has established his Church on the earth once again.

We give thanks for thy son, Jesus Christ; for his life and labors, and his sacrifices, and for having given his life in order to bring about the resurrection. We thank thee for the Prophet Joseph Smith, for his life of sacrifices, for his testimony and faithfulness to the principles of justice. Thanks we give for the constancy of his mission and for having sealed his testimony with his life.

We thank thee for our progenitors who have sacrificed their all for the gospel. We thank thee for thy Prophet Heber J. Grant, the Twelve Apostles and the other authorities of thy Church. We are grateful that thy prophet Heber J. Grant sent Apostle Ballard and Presidents Wells and Pratt here to open this mission—that through their labors the mission was established. We are also grateful for the work of President Stoof and of President Young, together with the labors of the sixty-seven missionaries who have served in the mission and returned to their homes. Their work has been profitable. Many people have heeded their words and have taken upon themselves the sacred ordinance of baptism, according to thy commandment. Now Father, accept the work of the fifty missionaries who now work in this land. Protect them, and guide them to the homes of the honest in heart. Bless their labors so that thousands of good people may accept of their offering. Pour out thy blessings upon their families who have sacrificed to send them here with the message of salvation.

Upon the heads of thy members in this mission we ask thy blessings. They have accepted thy message. Thy Spirit has touched and changed their lives. Be with them always. Help them day by day with temporal as well as spiritual blessings, so that they may always have the assurance that thou doth reign in the Heavens and thou art mindful of us and our works.

Bless the officials of the branches of the mission so that they may always minister unto the needs of the members. Bless all those who preach and teach in this chapel that they may always speak with clarity and teach the beautiful truths of the restored gospel in all the organizations of the Church, to the young and the old, and that it always be done under the inspiration of the Holy Ghost.

Bless the sorrowful who come to this chapel that they may be consoled. Bless those that come joyfully to participate in the activities of the Church, that whether at a dance, drama, or in any other capacity, they will know that thy spirit is here. Bless the youth of this mission that their testimonies may be strengthened, that they may prepare themselves for the great responsibility of spreading thy word in South America; that by means of their participation in the activities of the Church they may develop physically, mentally and spiritually. Keep them clean from sin and corruption. Inspire them that they may use their talents to glorify thy Holy Name and that they may grow to be strong, honorable men and women, with clean bodies and spirits dedicated to thee.

We give thee thanks for the leaders of the Church with President Grant at the head. Give him a long life and continue to bless him in the future as thou hast in the past. We are grateful that he loved us enough to send the funds for the construction of this chapel and to continue the missionary work. Help us that we may build many more chapels in the Argentine Mission.

Oh Father, guide many people with thy spirit to this chapel that they may come to know thy gospel and enjoy thy blessings.

Now, Holy Father, we offer this house as thine own. We ask thy blessings upon it, and as thy servant, I bless it and dedicate it and set it apart for the glorification of thy name. I bless it in all its individual parts from the roof to its foundation, that each section may stand strong against the power of the elements, and that nothing may disturb them, so that the chapel may bless the lives of many people. Now it is thine, O Father. We give it unto thee with all our love and blessings, humbly asking that thou wilt accept it, and this we do in the blessed name of the Lord Jesus Christ, Amen.

(April 9, 1939)

Frederick S. Williams
President of the Mission

(Offered in Spanish by Frederick Salem Williams, President of the Argentine Mission, Easter Sunday, April 9, 1939. English version translated from "El Mensajero," May 1939, p. 78ff.)

El Mensajero Deseret. I've referred often to *El Mensajero Deseret,* the oldest Spanish-language periodical in the Church. When it was first published by President Young (January 9, 1937), it was called simply *El Mensajero* and printed on the hand mimeograph purchased during President Stoof's administration:

The first issue of "El Mensajero," Spanish monthly mission paper rolled off the mimeograph today. 100 copies were made first, and later 20 more before the stencils were destroyed.[7]

President Young adds in his *Diary,* "On the title page was printed the image of the angel Moroni with his trumpet, a lighted candle, and the three Wise Men on camels."[8] By February circulation had reached 175, at which level it remained for the next several months, reaching two hundred in July. Three hundred copies of the January anniversary issue were printed.

At first, copies were sold to the members and missionaries after Church on Sundays, but soon subscription copies were mailed. During my first two years as president, the magazine was still mimeographed with one or two printed pages (mostly photographs) inserted.

Nevertheless, circulation continued to increase. By the second anniversary (1939) we had three hundred subscribers and were running off 450 copies of the thirty-two page monthly.[9] The Church section of the *Deseret News* for February 4, 1939, gave a short account of our publishing venture.

The *Mensajero* filled a great need in a day when there was very little contact with the headquarters of the Church. The membership was small and scattered, and we needed all the instructional and fellowshipping contact we could get. If I were to state the objectives of the magazine succinctly I would say it was to unify the members of the Church, feed them spiritually and bring to their attention timely talks, articles and books written by the General Authorities of the Church. But we also had fun with it.

Beginning with the fifth year of publication, I decided our magazine was so successful we could justify printing it. I felt that the increased printing costs would be more than offset by new subscriptions plus revenue from advertisements; but more important, I felt that an aesthetically superior magazine would be a much more effective missionary tool. When we went to register the magazine with the government, we found that another publication already bore the name *El Mensajero,* so the word *Deseret* was added to the title. A copy of each issue thereafter was sent to the National Library. I'm proud to state that the printed *Mensajero,* without doubt one of the finest religious magazines published in South America, lived up to expectation and subscriptions rose to over one thousand. When publication ceased in 1955, circulation was around five thousand, well over the combined membership of the Argentine and Uruguayan Missions.[10]

The *Mensajero*—published continuously from January 1937 to April 1955—was the official organ of the Argentine Mission alone until 1948, when it expanded to serve the newly estabished Uruguayan Mission.[11]

The editors of the magazine were:

Argentina		**Uruguay**	
W. Ernest Young	*1937-1938*		
Frederick S. Williams	*1938-1942*		
James L. Barker	*1942-1944*		
W. Ernest Young	*1944-1949*		
		Frederick S. Williams	*1947-1951*
Harold Brown	*1949-1952*		
		Lyman S. Shreeve	*1951-1954*
Lee B. Valentine	*1953-1955*		

We had subscribers in every South American country, many in Central America and some in Spain. It ceased publication in 1955 when the Church-wide Spanish-language *Liahona* began publication.

I must acknowledge the untiring work of Eurídice Turano, who worked on the *Mensajero* from its inception. She proofread, translated, wrote and solicited articles, and prepared copy in her capacity as Associate Editor to Presidents Young, Williams, and Barker for ten years. I cannot say enough regarding her work, for without it the *Mensajero*'s high standard of excellence might not have been achieved or maintained.

The original South American Mission had a short-lived publication entitled *La Estrella del Sur* (The Southern Star), edited by President Stoof, an experienced and capable journalist. It began after I had left Argentina as a missionary, but President Stoof referred to it in a letter to me, asking me to contribute both financially and literarily; I did both. The bimonthly publication consisted of four mimeographed pages:

> *We did not buy a rotation mimeograph. The Underwood Company has stopped making them. The British Supply Company sells them for 559.- pesos. We cannot pay that amount; therefore we bought a flat one for 100.- pesos. We will try to publish our first number of the little magazine on the first of April [1930]. The magazine will be called: "La Estrella del Sur." Each number will contain four large pages. We need many subscribers in order to pay all our expenses for the different kinds of stationery we need. We cannot expect to get enough to pay gradually for the mimeograph. The magazine will be published twice a month. I will try to get the former missionaries of South America interested that they might subscribe at least for the first year. The price would be one American Dollar a year which includes the expense for postage. Can we expect you as one of the subscribers and above all as one who might write something for us? I am sure that your greetings will always be appreciated here.*[12]

President Young also began a second, English language publication, the *Gaucho Gazette*:

> *As the official publication of the Mission, "El Mensajero" is printed entirely in Spanish. It has no value for the parents and friends of Missionaries. Therefore it was decided to print a quarterly publication in English for the benefit of the parents of the missionaries in which would be included the Quarterly comparative reports. The first issue of this new publication, called "the Gaucho Gazette," was finished this week.*[13]

We continued to publish the *Gaucho Gazette*, although it was April 1939 until issue number two came out. It was mimeographed and the same size as the *Mensajero*, but only two volumes were printed, a total of 12 issues. I edited the second and succeeding issues. The *Gazette* contains some valuable historical information not found elsewhere.

Chief Trifón Zanabria and the Toba Indians. I wrote my mother May 26, 1939, concerning my visit with an Indian chief. She promptly showed the letter to President McKay:

> *Night before last I had an Indian chief here to supper. He is from Formosa, the most northerly province of the Argentine. He has been in Buenos Aires for seven months trying to get some help from the Government for his two thousand people. One of our members contacted him several months ago and gave him a Book of Mormon. He can't read nor write, but is a very fine fellow. They neither drink nor smoke in their tribe, as they saw what these vices did to the Christians that lived near them. His father told the tribe that they had to stop these things, so they did. He asked me to send two missionaries there to help*

them. Show them how to farm and learn the language. Teach them to read and write and to teach them the Gospel. They are not Christians. He is very sincere, and I think I will return with him to look it over. If we could convert him we could convert almost the entire tribe. There have been some missionaries among them before, but they stole their land and their cattle. The chief doesn't think that was very Christian of them. He is sending one of his daughters to live with one of our members to learn Spanish and to be educated. He speaks quite fluent Spanish and a lot of the younger people also speak Spanish. This might be our golden opportunity to start work among the Lamanites.[14]

However, on June 12, 1939, *El Mundo* carried news of Chief Zanabria's baptism into the Catholic Church. He had met an extremely wealthy and influential widow, a Mrs. María Adelina Aguilaos de Olmos, who had conceived the plan of sponsoring him and using her influence to get land for this Indian tribe from the Argentine Government, and then converting him and his tribe to Catholicism. Chief Zanabria had told her that none of them had ever been baptized and she thought this was a good opportunity to convert the entire tribe to Catholicism. The chief got his land, according to *El Mundo,* on September 12, 1939, but he wasn't really converted to Catholicism, just as he had not been converted by the Protestant missionaries who had contacted him earlier, and—contrary to his show of interest—was not really interested in our Church; he was a wheeler-dealer, trying to gain concessions for himself and his tribe. The Argentine government had granted them some excellent land. The soil was so good that any number of crops could be produced to feed the tribe.

The last word I had from that region was that Trifón Zanabria had been bitten by a poisonous snake and had died. Unfortunately the chief and his tribe were not the right contacts and did not provide us with our golden opportunity to work among the Lamanites; that was still in the future.

The Church Welfare Plan In Argentina.

A Mission garden project has been started to help combat the unemployment situation among many of our members. If we had canning equipment we could almost entirely solve the food problem of our poor.

These telling words, recorded June 30, 1939, in the Mission History, mark our first attempt to meet a growing problem in Argentina. It became evident that the members would need organized help to get through the difficult period of war-time Argentina. Argentina was a neutral country, but the entire world was embroiled in war. Many people were losing jobs. I decided that if we started working together, we might be able to solve some common problems.

The Church Welfare Program in the United States was still very new and no encouragement had been given for its establishment in the missions; but we knew about it and felt that if it could meet the needs of U.S. members, it could help our Argentine members. The Brethren were not encouraging. "We are not sure it is even wise for you to start a Welfare Program." But we felt we needed to help our members, and so we launched a formally organized Argentine Mission Welfare Program. The first step was to meet with all the Relief Society Presidencies to discuss the Church Welfare Program and what would have to be done if it were started in this Mission.[15]

I headed the program, ably assisted by Brother Edgar B. Mitchell, a retired farmer serving a mission with his wife. Many other missionaries were farmers as well and really gave us the know-how that was needed.

One step followed another very swiftly: we rented a welfare farm on July 31, 1940, in Libertad:

> *The Welfare Program work is progressing. We have rented a sixteen-acre farm located eighteen miles from Buenos Aires, near the city of Libertad. From welfare contributions we are buying animals which include pigs, chickens, rabbits, two horses, ducks, geese, and bee hives. The eggs more than pay for the rent, and with other produce and meat that we can raise and sell, it will be a big help to the mission. We are planning on planting five acres of potatoes and sufficient grain for the animals. The members are rallying to support the plan and are getting ready for spring planting in all of the larger branches of the Mission.*[16]

The Santanas, a member family from Pergamino, lived on the farm. In our mission conferences we began teaching the Welfare Plan: we stressed family conservation, home gardens, and even the cultivation of vacant lots (with the owners' permission). We also stressed that as members we should contribute towards meeting the needs of others by working on the farm and by donating food and clothing. We devoted a monthly column in the *Mensajero* to welfare. The *Gaucho Gazette* also carried a few articles and progress reports. We encouraged the Saints to contribute to the Welfare Plan in a variety of ways, but our efforts were most successful when we held dances or roadshows with donated canned food or clothing as the entrance fee. The first dance was held in Liniers, August 15, 1940:

> *During the day, most of the missionaries in Buenos Aires, together with some of the members and friends went out to the recently acquired farm in Libertad to clean up the place and do any necessary work.*
>
> *In the evening a program and dance was held in the Liniers local for the benefit of the Welfare Plan. Admission fee was foodstuffs, clothing, or something of value for the Plan. The response was good, and an encouraging start has been made in establishing the Welfare work here in South America.*[17]

Almacén Deseret: Mormon co-op. On September 3, 1940, we rented "a large and very nice store near the Liniers chapel for the cooperative store which will be started up among the members and friends. It is located on Calle Cossio, 6901, and will provide rooms for those who work in the store as well as another family."[18] We hired one of the members, Oscar La Vista, to run it. Juan Borén, an accountant, supervised and kept the books. We stocked it with all the merchandise the members usually purchased: noodles, eggs, candy, canned goods, potatoes. In a letter to the First Presidency dated October 17, 1940, I reported:

> *On the 15th of September we opened a cooperative grocery store two blocks from our chapel in Liniers; members, friends, and missionaries contributing the capital at the rate of ten pesos apiece. A certain percentage of its profits go to the Welfare Program of the Mission. The members are cooperating very well*

with this, as well as many of our friends outside of the church, and in one more month [it] should be paying a profit. The members reasoned that they had to buy food somewhere and it would be better to buy it from themselves. It has given employment to two people, and will eventually be able to give help to many others by selling their produce. The store has the name of "Deseret" and is now quite well known. Through it we are selling all the eggs we can produce, as well as other produce. Elder Edgar B. Mitchell, a retired wheat farmer from Logan is at the head of the Welfare Program of the mission and is surely doing a fine job.[19]

We advertised the store in the *Mensajero*; one selling feature was that we delivered. We had a three-wheeled pushcart in which Brother La Vista would deliver as far away as Sáenz Peña. That was about ten miles away, and he nearly died pushing the cart there and back over the cobblestone streets.

We also established "Bishop's storehouses" for the mission:

In the same building as the store we have a small room containing over a thousand cans of foodstuff, cooking oils, soaps, etc., that the Welfare Program is storing. There are also over two hundred pieces of clothing belonging to the Program. Aside from this there are two regional storehouses, one in Rosario and another in La Plata, which have a small stock of food started.[20]

I requested that funds, an estimated six hundred dollars, be sent for the construction of a proper storehouse.

March 4, 1941

The First Presidency
47 East South Temple
Salt Lake City, Utah

The Presiding Bishopric
40 North Main Street
Salt Lake City, Utah

Dear Brethren:

At the time our last budget request was sent, I didn't have time to send any supplemental information regarding the request on the back thereof for additional money for building purposes. I am sending this letter for that purpose.

About the proposed purchase of the farm in Libertad: This consists of six and one-half hectares (about 16 acres) of good land situated at thirty-three kilometers from Buenos Aires, and six blocks from a small town named Libertad. There are excellent transportation facilities connecting Libertad with Buenos Aires, and one can go either by train or by bus in one hour's time. By cutting through back roads our cart and horse can make the trip in three hours when it comes into town to bring produce.

The house that is included with the land isn't by any means a new one, but it is comfortable and dry. It consists of three rooms 12 x 14 feet each; a kitchen 8 x 10 feet; a small room 6 x 8 feet and a roofed-in patio 8 x 10 feet. It is sound, plastered on the inside, but unplastered on the exterior brick surface, as is the custom in the country here. It is worth four hundred dollars, and would cost over a thousand to rebuild at the present cost of materials.

The fencing on the place is worth another two hundred dollars and would cost much more to replace. In Argentina a good fence costs a dollar and twenty-five cents per yard to build. The wire is imported from Europe or North America and the posts from the far northern provinces of the republic. Two small sheds are included and a small chicken run. Outside of this we have now installed on the place nearly five hundred dollars worth of livestock, pig pens, chicken runs, etc., that the members are paying for. We need a few more improvements to properly accommodate our chickens and animals, but won't build them until we can buy the property.

There is a good drilled well by the house, equipped with a Meyers pump. The water is good and plentiful, and the pump is made with a connection for a windmill. We have a windmill available that can be installed, thus making it possible for a modern bathroom, and connecting pipes to all the animals and a small truck garden.

The soil is a rich black loam, and very productive. In spite of being rather heavy we were quite successful in the raising of potatoes for the Welfare Program this year. We have about one-hundred and fifty sacks of sixty kilos each already dug, which we are selling and storing. We planted twenty-two sacks of spuds. We have five hectares of very fine corn, standing nearly nine feet tall. Our problem now is to store it.

We were fortunate in finding this property through a member of the Church, and the price asked by the two old maid sisters is much under what other land in and around Libertad is being sold for.

The purchase of this farm would mean a great deal to this mission—a tangible evidence of the Church's personal interest in the welfare of its members, and something with which to put into action the Welfare Program here. It would create a sense of stability, and the ability to help cope with world conditions as they now exist. In case of necessity, four families of members could be placed on the farm, as it is so arranged that it could be worked as four small farms, or truck gardens, and all could use the horse power that we now have, as it would be ample for all. They could make a good living for themselves, produce food for many others and return a goodly interest to the Church. The raising of chickens in Argentina is a business with a good future, and this farm is ideally situated for the biggest market in the country: five and one-half million people within a radius of fifty miles. The food for chickens costs so little that it becomes almost negligible, and the year round price of eggs is high. I have found eggs imported from Poland selling in the stores of Neuquén, a thousand miles from Buenos Aires. Now that eggs can't be brought from Europe they are being imported from Brazil and Uruguay. We have plans for two thousand chickens on this farm, but we need to buy the property to be able to put in the accommodations. We already have an offer of an incubator free of charge whenever we can use it.

Another thought: This country at the present time is passing through a great political and economical crisis. We have two presidentes—the President of the Nation who is temporarily retired because of ill health, and the Vice President who is in power. The Vice President seems to be in league with the sub rosa politicians of the country, and they are enjoying their opportunities to the utmost, as you probably have read in the papers. All of the local newspapers are up in arms about it—the President in retirement has sent an article to the press denouncing the conditions, and asking the Vice President to do something about it; the majority party in the Chamber of Deputies is opposed to the Vice President and his friends and will not permit any legislation to be discussed in the Chamber until election frauds are straightened out by the Vice President (perpetrated by his political cronies); the majority party in the Senate is loyal to the Vice President, and so it goes. They can't get the budget for this year approved, as the Chamber won't even consider it. Nor will they discuss any proposed legislation to help out the financial condition of the country, nor ratify the 110 million dollar loan from the United States.

This country's finances are based on its export of meat, cereals and other agricultural products. They normally exported around 1-1/2 millions of tons per month, and never over 16-1/2 millions of tons in any year. Argentina now exports about 60,000 tons per week, and the exportation decreases monthly due to the scarcity of ship's bottoms and the blockade. The country has on hand from last year's crop marked for export (according to figures taken from the daily Buenos Aires paper "Diario El Mundo": 4,612,956 tons of wheat; 1,366,562 tons of linseed; and 6,495,708 tons of corn. This doesn't take into consideration the present crop of some ten million tons of corn ripening on the fertile fields of Argentina. Altogether, there will be some twenty million tons available for export in the next few months, and very few purchasers.

All this results in the closing down of industry and the resulting unemployment of workers. It has affected the interior of the country much more than Buenos Aires, but its evil effects can be seen more clearly day by day here. The vast majority of our members are day laborers, and one by one they are losing their jobs. The months ahead will be hard ones, and I feel it our duty to try and get into a position to help them to help themselves. Two thirds of the mission membership reside in and around Buenos Aires where they can work together. We have an ideal situation to work cooperatively, and this farm would give us a rallying point for poultry and truck gardening. Other members in better financial conditions want to buy small places around the farm if we buy it.

Continuing with local conditions: The country's trade balance is fast becoming an unfavorable one. They can sell to England and Spain in Europe, and England can't spare many ships, nor can she pay in cash. Spain can buy very little as it has no resources or money. Argentina, however, is going to give Spain cereals on credit; but this won't help her financial condition. The large wheat and corn growers are facing financial ruin, and were it not for the steps taken by the government in buying up their crops at a minimum price they would let them rot in the fields. Now the government has this large surplus on its hands and is trying to recover some of the money expended by internal sale. A big patriotic campaign is now on; the Minister of Agriculture has even suggested that it makes an ideal fuel (corn) and that in this manner much can be consumed. Large factories are now burning corn to generate steam; railways will soon use it in a 60 to 40 corn to coal in its engines as they did during the last war. Corn is being sold for one dollar (four pesos) per ton, and the government is begging for buyers.

We would like very much to be able to build a corn crib and store fifteen or twenty tons of this good number one corn. At this price we can afford to have many more pigs and chickens that we now have. Also it can be ground into meal and used for food in the Welfare Program. Our only drawback is a place to build the crib. The purchase of this farm would solve our difficulties and give us an ideal location centrally located. The $1500 necessary to purchase it (this includes a guaranteed title) would, in our humble opinion, not only be a splendid investment for the Church, but a very large contributing factor to the feeding of hungry people in the times to come. It would be a place where they can raise their foodstuffs. Times are critical, and there is an urgent need to be prepared. Argentina is not blessed (?) with any New Deal, and the government does not feed its unemployed, but they must rely on private charities. The Associated Press and the representative of Life Magazine have taken recognition of our Welfare Program and have asked for pictures and data. Two men from the Associated Press want to visit the farm this weekend. The Time man wants to write an article and have pictures published in the magazine. We shall see if it is done.

The plans for the Haedo Chapel are not yet complete, nor do I have all of the data on the Rosario Chapel that I mentioned in the request, but will send them as soon as possible.

About the storeroom on the roof of the old chapel: Am enclosing a pencil sketch (to the P.B.O.) taken from the drawing of the builder who designed and built the new Chapel in Liniers. His price is high, however, and a good contractor that was baptized into the Church in January of this year gives me the figure of the equivalent of $650 U.S., if it is built soon, as the price of materials is going up.

The construction of this room would give us a storeroom with inside measurements of about 13'9" x 14'8"; about 184 square feet of floor space 11'4-1/2" high. In this permanent bins and shelves can be built, giving us a proper store house away from the reach of vandals. For $200 more we can completely cover the available floor space of the old Chapel and have another room 10' x 10' in which to put clothing or other articles.

This store house, together with the purchase of the farm where a potato bin or cellar could be built would give us something to work with here, and help us cope with the conditions that are developing. We are proud of our members, who, although poor, try very hard to comply with all the teachings of the Church. They are very good payers of tithing, as the records will bear us out. They rank with the leading missions of the Church in this respect, and it isn't a true picture. For actual money earned and paid as tithing, our tithing figures should be four times as high as they are. They earn pesos and the tithing is computed in dollars, and here a peso is as valuable to them as a dollar home. Many heads of families here only earn from one hundred and twenty pesos to 150. Two hundred pesos is a very, very high salary here. Yet the pesos that they pay as tithing, even when converted into dollars at the rate of 3.30 : $1.00, they rank splendidly with the other missions who pay their tithing in dollars. We humbly suggest and request that they be helped at this time, so they can help themselves later.

May the Lord bless and protect you all, is the prayer of

Your brother in the Gospel
Frederick S. Williams

One part of our plan was to instruct the sisters in home canning. We had to do something with the hundreds of pounds of tomatoes coming in. Domingo Quici donated a great deal of time overseeing this crop. He was quite a horticulturalist. Sisters Williams and Mitchell spent many hours holding classes demonstrating and then actually helping the sisters can their tomatoes:

February 11, 1941: Sister Williams and Mitchell gave a food demonstration to the Relief Society Presidents of the Buenos Aires District today. The theme of the demonstration was the use of tomatoes in cooking. Those present enthusiastically received the new information with a desire to also teach the various members of their groups the results of the demonstrations. Such demonstrations are aids in making the Welfare Plan a success, here in the Mission.[21]

Corraine later recalled:

We had bottles, and we got a capper. I recall having classes at the Mission Home and at Liniers, where we would teach the women different dishes to make use of these tomatoes. One time it was tomato soup and some of them thought we were trying to poison them by mixing milk with tomatoes—it was unheard of; it will curdle.[22]

The possibility arose of colonizing in Chubut (located in the southern part of the country), a newly opened area called Cholila. I wrote to the First Presidency:

I have been wondering what the condition of thousands of European saints would be after this war, and what chance they would have to earn a living in Europe; and the thought has repeatedly occurred to me that perhaps the Church might want to acquire land in this fertile country where they could be colonized; where food could be raised and shipped to Europe. This land is rich and fertile. Much of it has never been cultivated and the rest only superficially. Scientific farming is carried on only in experimental and a few large farms. There are large tracts of mortgaged land constantly being sold by the heirs of large estates who have gambled and dissipated away their inheritance in the casinos of Paris. Due to the war the price of land is decreasing, and many opportunities are offered from time to time. Many of the saints are looking toward the land, and are awaiting the time when they might be together in a colony. The majority of them are day laborers and they realize the precariousness of their position, and would gladly sell or exchange their homes in a Church project.

. . . .

This is a great country occupying 1,078,278 square miles with only a population of 13 million people—many of which are the best blood of Europe who had the desire to build their homes in the promised land. I feel this will become one of the great missions of the Church and is progressing very well in spite of the unsettled conditions that we have had. I have seen it increase one hundred percent in two years: from 317 to over six hundred members. There are in the Church here members from twenty-four nationalities—surely a melting pot if there ever was one.[23]

I had heard through a nonmember that the government had opened the area for colonization and that great advantages were to be given the colonizers. This same nonmember told me about four friends of his who had lived near there for the past three years and had done very well. We decided to investigate.

Brother Eric Fischer, who had offered to drive us, had a 1928 Whippet he call "Isabella," which he had modified by adding a sort of camper. Thank goodness he was a very good mechanic. The mission history records:

President Williams, Edgar Mitchell, John H. Meyers, Berry Banks and Eric Fischer left tonight (April 15, 1941) for a two week trip to the southern part of the country. They went to look over some land in the Province of Chubut for a possible Mormon Colony. They went in an old made-over car which belongs to Brother Fischer and are leaving with threatening weather. They will no doubt need all the luck we can possibly wish them.

Brother Mitchell and I were accompanied on the three thousand mile trip by two senior elders (Elder Banks was also a photographer). We drove through Buenos Aires and along the Andes Mountains to Cholila, rebuilding the car every so often.

When we arrived in Cholila, we quickly found and talked to the man in charge. He told us a little about the valley: there was a lake at one end fed by a river flowing in the middle, and many miles of grazing land on either side up to the mountains. He asked us who we were and we told him. "Oh, you're Mormons. That's very interesting. When the government asked me to set up this colonization project, I studied up on where I might get some ideas and I found many references to the Mormon colonization in the American west. I would be very happy to have you enter into this; we'll give you every inducement we can." He then explained the set-up: colonizing families would be given X number of acres of tillable land, and the rest in grazing land. The terms were generous: nothing down, the first payment in five years, with twenty years to pay off the government loan; the price was very reasonable. In addition, for the first few years the railroad would ship tools and equipment, seeds and food, free of charge; it wanted to promote future business. Each family could live on its own land or several families could together form a town; the requirement to live on the land would be waived as long as the land was being improved. "Within five miles there is a coal mine that is still public property—anyone can go and dig the coal they want." There were forests nearby where timber could be cut for buildings. The river could be dammed for hydroelectric power, and canals could be dug for irrigation. Finally, the colony was only fifteen miles from the railroad head.

In all, it appeared to be an ideal set up. Brother Roland Kaiser, who worked for International Harvester, was very enthusiastic about the project. He said, "I'll tell you what I can do. You come to the showroom floor and pick up a five-ton truck and a pickup and the company will give you twenty years to pay for them; we want this kind of business." Brother Looney was also enthused. A retired farm equipment salesman turned experimental farmer, he quickly offered to live in Cholila and supervise the colonizing project.

I submitted the entire program to the Church in a letter, our only communication in those days. We needed twenty-five thousand dollars in advance for materials and equipment to help get started. The advance would be repaid, something on the order of the Perpetual Emigration Fund.

I've been told that the General Authorities thought about it for quite a long time and discussed it at length. Ultimately, they decided against the investment. I have forgotten the precise reason, but I am sure it had to do with the War, and the still precarious financial situation after the Depression. The members were very disappointed; they thought this would mean a new way of life for them, a chance to build for the future. Elder John A. Widtsoe told me later, "I sure did like it; I voted for it when it came up for a vote in the Quorum." President Clark also said, "That was quite an experiment you had going down there. It would have been very interesting."

In summary, most of our various welfare projects never lived up to their potential. The colonizing venture in Cholila was turned down. The co-op store never did quite operate in the black—we couldn't undersell the local merchants who sold in volume. We could not get clear title to the property for the welfare farm, so we used the fifteen hundred dollars to build the Bishop's storehouse.[24] We distributed supplies to many of the needy, widows and others. It proved to be a blessing. The building was very good, by the way, made of brick. But even the storehouse had its problems. We found it almost impossible to keep canned foods in the humid climate. We instructed our people to keep their vegetable gardens, do their own canning and storage, but always on an individual basis.

Many positive by-products resulted from our effort: it got the members working together, it taught them the value of working with their hands, it taught them the principles of sacrifice and conservation, and it provided many with food and clothing and the opportunity to work. But above all it had a great unifying effect. The members rubbed shoulders with each other, shared experiences and really got to love one another. They soon realized that they could do anything if they worked for it. When it came down to actually working and organizing for effective use of time and manpower, it was plain to see who the mission leaders were. These were the brethren and sisters who would soon have to carry on the entire Church program by themselves when, because of the War, all the missionaries were released and none were called to replace them.

NOTES

Chapter VII

1. See Argentine Mission History for that date.

2. "As soon as we agree with the owner of the adjoining lot to Bro. Notaro's we will buy that lot to erect the hall on it. Brother Notaro's lot is not large enough to have a hall on the remainder of his lot. The First Presidency authorized me to buy the adjoining lot, at the corner of the street, in order to erect the building there. But the owner is not yet reasonable enough. He wants to gain a lot of money. But I have not the right to let him gain the money that belongs to the Lord, in such an easy way. As soon as we can buy the lot we can start the building. I hope that the building in Joinville has already been started. It was one of the main things I had to do in Brazil: to arrange everything for the construction of our meeting house in Joinville." (Letter from Reinhold Stoof dated from Buenos Aires, August 20, 1931, in my files.)

3. Mission History, August 26, 1938.

4. Letter in my files.

5. Letter in my files.

6. For a list of the speakers see *Gaucho Gazette*, June 1939.

7. Mission History.

8. (P. 237.) He also indicates that involved in the creation of the magazine were Elders Lee B. Valentine and Don H. Smith, his daughter Amy, and Sister Eurídice Turano of the Mission Office. More details are given concerning its operation during the early days by President Lee B. Valentine, writing in the editorial to the last issue of the *Mensajero*, April 1955.

9. "We have 3 subscribers in Bolivia, 1 in Brazil, 5 in Chile, 1 in Colombia, 4 in Mexico, 1 in Panama, 1 in Peru, 1 in Puerto Rico, and some fifty throughout five states in Argentina outside of Buenos Aires." My letter to the First Presidency, March 16, 1939.

10. See Paul Roger Hoopes, "An Evaluation of *El Mensajero Deseret*, former organ of the Argentine Mission; And a Review of Directors and Policies," unpublished research paper done for Dr. Milton C. Hollstein, University of Utah, May 27, 1963, on file at the Church Historical Department.

11. The Uruguayan Mission established its own magazine in 1954, entitled *El Deseret Oriental.* Its founder was President Lyman S. Shreeve. It ceased publication when the *Mensajero* did.

12. Letter from Reinhold Stoof dated from Buenos Aires, March 26, 1930.

13. Mission History, July 14, 1938.

14. President McKay wrote: "We are taking the liberty to make a copy of that part which refers to the Indian Tribe in the Province of Formosa. Thank you for your kindness in bringing this letter to our attention. As President Williams says, 'this might be our golden opportunity to start work among the Lamanites'." Letter to Nancy A. Williams, June 21, 1939. My experience with the Indians was published in Spanish in the *Mensajero* as "Con Rumbo al Norte," April-September 1940. It also appeared in English entitled "Formosa" in *ALAS*, March-July 1975. The Mission History also contains a report dated November 30, 1939.

15. Mission History, June 10, 1940.

16. Mission History.

17. Mission History.

18. *Ibid.*

19. Copy of the letter in my files.

20. Letter to First Presidency dated October 17, 1940.

21. Mission History.

22. Corraine S. Williams in Frederick G. Williams interview, April 13, 1974.

23. Letter dated October 17, 1940.

24. October 1, 1941: "Work was started today on the new building for the Church Store on the lot where the club is now located. The building is being built by the help of the missionaries and member donations" (Mission History).

CHAPTER VIII

MEMBERS TAKE OVER LEADERSHIP ROLES

Samuel Borén and the Youth Program. Of my many Argentine acquaintances, few impressed me more than Samuel Borén. Born February 26, 1916, he was twenty-two when I first met him and had been a member just a little less than two years, having been baptized September 12, 1936. His father, Mariano, was the first of their family to be baptized (December 25, 1934).[1] They were followed by Juan (November 1, 1938), another son, and much later the mother, Angela. A third brother, José, as far as I know, never joined the Church.

Sam, as most of the missionaries called him, was at first more interested in them than he was in their message. He enjoyed their company, playing basketball and going with them to the meetings. However, he soon realized that the Church was true and asked to become a member. From young people like Sam we called full-time and local missionaries, and when they returned from their one-year missions, we put some of them into the first branch presidencies.

On March 14, 1939, Sam was called as the Mission M-Men President with Antonio Gianfelice as secretary. Eurídice Turano was the Gleaner President. Sam was jovial, yet serious minded. A good basketball player by Argentine standards of that day, he was also an excellent soccer player and a member of the second division team of one of the best soccer clubs of Buenos Aires. He had been offered a contract to play first division soccer but was in a dilemma. First division soccer was played on Sundays, and he knew that if he accepted the offer he would be unable to meet his religious obligations during the season. When he asked my advice, I said, "That is a decision that only you can make, and I have confidence in you that you will make the correct one." "Thank you, President Williams," he replied. "I will follow my first inclinations and turn down the contract. The Church means more to me than a career as a professional soccer player."

I felt it would be beneficial to Sam, as well as to us, to call him on a mission. I also contemplated calling other Argentines; as it turned out Brother Luis Constantini became the first Argentine missionary (called April 19, 1939). Sam had a conflict. I wrote the First Presidency:

> *We have among us a young man twenty-three years of age, named Samuel Borén, whom we think to be worthy of a mission. He is employed by the government of the Province of Buenos Aires, and works four hours daily in the city of La Plata. His position is a good one with an opportunity to advance within the provincial government in the course of a few years. Due to his job and his financial condition he is unable to fill a long term mission.*

Is it possible to call Brother Borén as a part time missionary for eighteen months? He could work in La Plata, where we have missionaries, and work his four hours a day, either from nine to one, or from two to six, and devote the rest of his time to missionary work. He is always free on Saturdays and Sundays and could devote those days in their entirety to missionary work. Taking into account the fact that the weekends are free, and that he works only four hours on week days, and that there are seventeen national holidays during the year, he could devote practically as much time to missionary work as the regular missionaries, as he isn't obligated to study the Spanish language.

If such an arrangement were acceptable to you, I would humbly recommend he be called as soon as possible, as he would be a welcome addition to our depleted missionary force, and is ready to accept such a call.[2]

The First Presidency approved my suggestion and Samuel Borén was called on a mission, serving from June 1, 1939, to October 7, 1940, or one year and four months. I always checked his monthly missionary reports and was pleased to see that often this "part-time" missionary put in more hours per month than the full-time elders.

One interesting anecdote concerning Sam came while he and his companion were tracting. It was his turn to give the door approach. A young boy answered the bell and came to the gate. Sam presented himself and told them who they were. The boy turned and in a loud voice shouted to his mother: *"¡Mamá, éste habla como nosotros!"* (Mother, this one talks like we do!)

Sam married Clara Lorenzi in Buenos Aires on September 4, 1941; I officiated. When they moved to Arizona in 1952, it was my pleasure to serve as a witness at their sealing in the Mesa Temple.

Their first years in the United States were difficult. Neither spoke English and it was impossible for Sam to work at his profession. He worked on Marion Vance's farm near Tempe for a while. Then I got him a job as a bookkeeper at Dana Brothers Automobile Agency, which he liked better than farming. Former Argentine missionaries Marion Vance, Ben R. Allen, Willard Skousen, Rolf L. Larson and others helped him through the difficult years. They returned to Argentina in 1955, but it was impossible for them to readjust to the country, especially under Perón.

In 1963 Sam was called as Treasurer of the Church Building Committee for South America, and they moved to Montevideo, Uruguay. He did exceptional work and also served as a counselor to President Fyans. They had a harrowing experience en route to Montevideo: their ship sank at night in the dead of winter. They hung on to a floating bench for nearly five hours. Nine people clung to it initially, but one by one lost their grip and slipped under. Only four were left when they were picked up.[3]

After their return in 1963, they moved to California and stayed in our home in Downey until Sam could find an apartment. After a few months they decided to return to Mesa, Arizona. He was better known there and soon secured an excellent position as Director of the Mesa Housing Authority. In 1969 he was called as President of the Mexico Southeast Mission with headquarters at Veracruz. Then he served as Regional Representative [June 29, 1972], with responsibility over Ecuador, Colombia and Venezuela. Clara was called as a member of the Relief Society General Board, as reported in the *Church News*, July 22, 1972. They were the first to preside over the Temple in Lima, Peru, in 1985.

The Argaults. How much time should someone be willing to devote to achieve an ideal, to reach a goal such as being able to live among the Saints in Zion? Are twelve years too many? The Argault family didn't think so. When President Heber J. Grant made his historic trip to Europe in 1937, he visited Paris to meet with the French Saints; the four members of the Argault family made up a considerable percentage of the members in attendance.[4] So impressed were they upon meeting the prophet, they resolved to emigrate to Utah to live among the members of the Church.

The Argaults had been converted in Orleans, France, where the father had owned an electrical shop and the mother a small grocery store. Translating their resolve into deeds, they approached the United States Consulate in Paris to apply for immigrant visas. They were disappointed to learn that the waiting list would take a lifetime to exhaust. They later found that by going to Argentina, in only twelve years they would be able to emigrate to the United States. After more than a year of preparation, Jules Leon Argault, his wife Juana and daughters Renée and Eduarda (or Eddie, as she was called) sailed to Argentina, arriving in Buenos Aires August 31, 1938, the same day my family and I arrived. The family moved to Neuquén; there, they constructed a makeshift house and started preparing their land for cultivation. The girls, fourteen and thirteen, soon learned Spanish.

Knowing that they were having a difficult time, I decided to visit them to see what could be done to help. I took Elder Gerald O. Lynn with me. We stopped for the night and shared a room at a small *pensión* in Centenario.

The following morning Brother Argault came for us in a two-wheeled cart pulled by a black horse. Printed in Spanish in large letters across the back of the cart was the legend, "Service your cows with our beautiful bull." After a short drive we reached their home.

They had transplanted several hundred apple tree seedlings, cleared several acres and were just ready to plow for the first time. Having grown up on a farm and (as a boy) plowed with a team of horses, I volunteered. However, there was only one horse and the plow had only one handle. In addition, the cart horse was reluctant to pull a plowshare through hard, virgin sod. I had never before tried to guide a plow with only one handle and the first furrows were anything but straight. Elder Lynn had the time of his life filming my woes. Eventually the horse and I became accustomed to the task.

We then helped plant a crop of potatoes. Sister Argault was busy in the kitchen and house, so the work fell on the two girls. The father was always helpful with suggestions, but I never saw him lift a finger to help. He was an electrician and didn't want to soil his hands.

My next visit to the Argaults coincided with the potato harvest. The black horse and I did better this time as we plowed up the potatoes, the two girls following behind to gather them up.

For three years the family had virtually no contact with the Church; there were no other members even remotely close to them. But each month I received a letter from the girls, usually containing tithing, which they paid faithfully. I felt that such devotion merited help, so I sent two missionaries to work around Neuquén and to help the family all they could. That was a happy time for the family, but then the missionaries had to leave and were not replaced.

I met Sister Argault and her two daughters again at the April 1944 mission conference in Montevideo. Brother Argault had become so depressed when the Nazis overran France it affected his mind. When he threatened them with a butcher knife, the three women fled into hiding. I helped them find jobs and a small apartment in Montevideo. The girls accepted the first jobs offered them, but then studied hard to improve their skills so they could get better jobs. They attended night classes, saved their small pay checks, and were always active in our branch activities. They mastered English and after many months of difficult work, both became trilingual secretaries, taking shorthand in French, Spanish and English.

Their first apartment was very modest and in a bad neighborhood. As they got better employment they acquired better living quarters, and as always, the first thing they did after receiving their checks was to pay their tithing.

Somehow their father found that they were living in Montevideo and wrote to them. He was sorry for what he had done, and now he needed their help. He had a large apple crop ripening, but couldn't get the necessary help to pick it. If they returned, he would pay them twenty-five thousand pesos, or about six thousand dollars, truly a great sum of money. They declined. They had their sights on higher things. They learned later that their father had returned to France after the War, dying there not too long after.

We left Uruguay at the end of 1945, but returned in September 1947 to open the mission. Sister Argault and Eddie came to the first meeting held in the New Uruguayan Mission in the Florida Hotel, Montevideo. Renée had obtained a job with the United Nations and was working in Montreal, Canada; Eddie was a secretary in the French Embassy in Montevideo. They had calculated that within three months she and her mother would be able to move to Canada, and eventually to the United States. They had saved two thousand dollars for fares and expenses.

Eddie and her mother made reservations on a cargo steamer to sail from Montevideo to Baltimore on January 7, 1948, but the Lord had other plans. I felt inspired to call Eduarda to a year's mission in Uruguay. She wanted to accept the call, but thought she should consult Renée first. She knew the passage money she had saved would be needed for her mission.

Renée told Eddie to accept the call. On January 7, 1948, I set Eddie apart as the first lady missionary of the new Uruguayan Mission. That afternoon her mother, Juana Seguin de Argault, left alone for Baltimore, where she was met by R. Glen Brewer, a former Argentine missionary who had worked and lived with us in Montevideo. She received her patriarchal blessing in New York and then flew to Montreal.

Wonderful things began to happen to the Argaults. Almost immediately Renée received a raise. She saved this additional money and at the end of a year had enough money for Eduarda's plane fare. Eduarda was a very fine missionary; her first companion was my daughter Argina, who worked with her while we awaited the arrival of Elsa Vogler, a young lady who had been called as a missionary from Río Cuarto, Argentina.

Eddie departed for the U.S. on February 8, 1949, after serving thirteen months in the mission. In the meantime, Renée and her mother had emigrated to the States; they were soon reunited.

They had finally made it to Zion through hard work, faith and compliance with the revealed word of the Lord. It was a rough, long, and lonely road, but they achieved their goal in ten years, two years ahead of schedule.

Fermín C. Barjollo. I know of few who contributed more to the Argentine Mission than Fermín C. Barjollo. He was known and loved by almost everyone in Rosario and by many others who had met and heard him at the semiannual conferences in Buenos Aires.

Fermín was a fellow traveler with Elders Christian, Clegg, Jensen, Ashton and Spencer on the ship that arrived in Buenos Aires on December 22, 1926. He was returning to his homeland after working for a number of years in Philadelphia, where he learned to read, write and speak English. He enjoyed the company of these young North Americans, but wasn't impressed with their message or their calling as missionaries. He moved to Rosario and worked for the Central Argentina Railroad. He married a young Argentine girl and established his home. His first contact with Mormonism was completely forgotten.

In June 1937 missionaries tracted his home. He was glad to speak English with them, but really didn't know who they were. Being hospitable by nature, he invited them back. The elders couldn't keep their appointment with him, but left an Articles of Faith card in his mail box with the name of one of the elders and a brief handwritten note on the back. Only then did Fermín connect these young missionaries with those he had accompanied from New York to Buenos Aires eleven years previously. They had also given him Articles of Faith cards.

He soon started attending meetings and studying with the missionaries. He was baptized on November 13, 1937, at age thirty-nine.

Brother Barjollo was a very faithful member. He attended every meeting and took an active part in the proselyting work, going with the missionaries to call on members. He also put his knowledge of English to good use and translated lessons, manuals, and entire books from English to Spanish. His first translation appeared in the September 1937 issue of the *Mensajero*, and very few issues came out thereafter that didn't have one of his translated articles.

He attended every semiannual conference in Buenos Aires while I was mission president, and always stayed with us at the mission home. He was also a frequent speaker.

Sister Barjollo was not religious by nature. I once asked Fermín when he was going to baptize his wife. "President Williams," he answered, "I will baptize her the day after you baptize the Pope in Rome. She is the next on the list after him."

I ordained Fermín Barjollo an Elder and set him apart as President of the Rosario Branch on January 19, 1941, with Raúl Rovira, a Priest, as his first counselor. During the years when there were no missionaries from the States and the branches were left to their own resources, Brother Barjollo, using his railway pass, spent nearly every weekend visiting congregations in Río Cuarto, Córdoba and Santa Fé, where he admonished and guided the members and administered the sacrament for them. He rendered outstanding service and was able to keep many of the members faithful to the Church during those difficult times.

Raúl Rovira. Raúl was baptized February 17, 1940, and I had the privilege of confirming him. He became a pillar in his mission. Born June 12, 1915, he was twenty-five when he joined the Church. Humble, he was a forceful speaker with a great testimony. He has been teacher, branch and district president and has contributed greatly to the welfare of the Argentine Mission. A traveling shoe salesman, he constantly visited branches in nearby towns.

He lived in the United States for a few years, but finally returned to Argentina. He spent a week with us in Lima in 1959, and it was my privilege to take him on a trip to the "Montaña" of Peru. We spent three interesting days together in jungle towns.

Raúl cared for a widowed mother and several sisters, one of whom died of tuberculosis. When penicillin first came to the attention of the world, I was working in Montevideo for the Institute of Inter-American Affairs, in the Health aand Sanitation Division [1941]. Raúl hoped that the miracle drug would cure his sister's malady and asked me to help secure it for her. It was in such short supply that I couldn't get the Uruguayan Government's permission to release any of it for export. Her infection was so far advanced that she died shortly afterwards.

Emilio Vergelli. Córdoba has always been the strongest Catholic province of Argentina. It contains seminaries and universities where priests have been trained for the ministry for nearly three hundred years. That church also exercises great influence on the public schools.

In July 1939 a priest came to an elementary classroom to give religious instructions to the pupils. One little boy asked to be excused. The indignant priest demanded to know why. "Our family is studying Mormonism and my mother will soon be baptized," responded the boy, "and we have our own teacher."

The priest ordered the child to the front of the class; then, taking the boy's ear between his thumb and index finger, forced his face to the floor, and while holding him there, shouted so all of the students could hear, *"¡No hay Mormón que valga!"* (There isn't a Mormon who is worth anything!) Emilio Vergelli was hurt and ashamed to be so shabbily treated by a so-called minister. He ran home crying.

Sister Vergelli immediately told Elder Harold Brown what had happened. Harold, incensed, went with the Vergellis to see the school principal. He had been raised in Mexico and spoke eloquent Spanish, and when angry spoke it very convincingly. He pleaded Emilio's case with such power that the boy was excused from taking Catholic religious training. Emilio was baptized October 1, 1940.

The family subsequently moved to Ramos Mejía, a suburb of Buenos Aires. He was a counselor in the Buenos Aires Stake Presidency and in 1972 became the bishop of his ward.

Roland G. Kaiser. The Kaisers had lived in Argentina for eight years, first in Santa Fé and then in Buenos Aires. Although not a member, he was always very kind to the missionaries and was partial to the Church. Shortly after we arrived, they left for a vacation in the States. While there, Roland visited President J. Reuben Clark, Jr., whom he had known in Montevideo, and requested that he baptize him. President Clark noticed Roland's Masonic ring and asked, "If your Masonic brethren should object to your joining the Mormon Church, what would you do?" Roland told me later he forgot for a moment where he was and who he was with and blurted out, "I'd tell them to go to hell!" President Clark laughed and said, "Yes, I guess you would. Come on, let's go over to the Tabernacle." There he baptized Brother Kaiser a member of the Church. On October 23, 1938, I ordained Roland G. Kaiser an Elder.

Marta Núñez. Marta was one of the happiest members of the Argentine Mission. No one would think she had a care in the world. She was always laughing and joking and was a constant delight.

Marta, born January 15, 1886, was one of many faithful members who never missed a meeting if she could help it. She and her frequently-out-of-work husband, a plasterer, had two children, a son, Fernando, and a daughter, "Martita." Even though things at times became difficult, Marta never complained. She had great faith in her Heavenly Father and loved the Church and all its members. Her loving nature included all mankind; I don't know of anyone she disliked.

Orphaned while young, she had been raised as a "daughter" by a wealthy family and had all of the advantages of wealth. A "brother" and "sister" thought a great deal of her, and her foster mother adored her. Although never legally adopted, she was considered a member of the family.

In her late teens she fell in love with a poor young man. Naturally her mother tried in every way to break up the romance. Marta had given her heart to that young man and wouldn't be dissuaded, even though she was threatened with disinheritance. When the marriage was consummated her mother told her she was no longer welcome in her home.

Marta never became bitter. She remembered all the "family's" birthdays and each year made a courtesy call on her mother. Sometimes she was permitted to see her and other times was not. Once the lady admitted Marta and asked how she was getting along. Marta told her they were struggling, but were very happy. After a short visit she left. Relenting somewhat from her previous attitude, her mother occasionally gave Marta money and on one occasion helped her purchase a modest house, but she still lamented her choice of husband.

The missionaries found and converted Marta, and baptized her January 26, 1935, at age forty-nine. On her next family visit she told her mother about her new religion and the happiness it had brought into her life.

The woman was furious; she was a devout Catholic, close to her church, and an active participant in charitable functions and committees. How could Marta so disgrace her by joining an organization that wasn't even considered a legal church? She must have lost her mind to join such a lowly sect as the Mormons.

Marta explained what she could of the Church and what it meant to her, but in a fit of anger her mother ordered her from the house. Marta's name would never be mentioned again in her presence. She had loved Marta more than her own daughter, but now she was disgraced. Marta thanked her for all she had done and departed. However, she continued to send birthday greetings to all her family, and as her children were born, she sent announcements but never received an acknowledgment. She still sent greetings as though nothing had happened.

Finally, hearing that her "mother" was seriously ill, Marta persuaded the maid to let her see the sick woman, who, sensing the seriousness of her illness, expressed some pleasure at seeing Marta, who left after a short visit. She recovered and after a few months, to Marta's surprise, she received an invitation to visit her old home. After a few minutes, her mother asked how things were going. Marta told her that everything was going well, but on direct questioning admitted that things were rough. Her husband was out of work and she didn't know when he would get another job.

Her mother was pleased. She made Marta an offer: "I can forgive you marrying the man you did, and if you will give up your religion and return to the bosom of the Catholic Church I will make you the following proposition. I'll provide for your future. I'll give you a new modern home. I'll see that your children receive the best education. I'll see that you have enough money to live in luxury even though your husband never works again. I'll give you an automobile and place a chauffeur at your disposal. I am getting old and I want to do this for you before I die. Will you come to your senses and accept my offer?"

Marta graciously thanked her, expressing love for her mother and appreciation for all she had done. But to give up her religion was unthinkable. She would prefer to live in poverty the rest of her life. "But," she said, "I'll always love you and someday you will know why I made this decision." She was again told to leave and never return. Marta continued to send greeting cards to her family, but they were returned.

By the end of my mission Marta's eyesight was failing. When I visited her while we were presiding in the Uruguayan Mission [1947 to 1951], she could see very little, but she hadn't lost any of her happy spirit. She asked me to send her some needles made especially for the blind.

Leaders in the organizations. Certainly one of the biggest thrills a missionary can have, and a sure indication of the strength of the Saints in a given area, is to see the local members in positions of responsibility. I began my presidency of the Argentine Mission at an opportune time; Presidents Stoof and Young had laid a strong foundation on which I was able to build, calling local members to ever more responsible positions of leadership.

Right from the beginning in 1926—when missionaries did everything—it was our goal to replace ourselves with members; first as speakers and teachers, then as counselors and finally as leaders of organizations. Several branches still had missionary leaders when I was called as president.

As soon as members and investigators in an area showed enough interest and had enough strength, a Sacrament meeting or a Sunday School or both would regularly be conducted at the meeting house. Then a Primary might be organized, or a Relief Society, followed by an MIA. Each organization was directed initially by the missionaries, with as much help as possible from the members: as teachers, counselors, secretaries. Some branches had only one, others had all four organizations presided over by members.

Below is a list of the first auxiliary organizations in Argentina under local members. The information comes from the Mission History and the *Mensajero*.

Relief Society. President Stoof organized the first Relief Society on February 14, 1934 in the Buenos Aires[5] Branch; its officers were:

President: *Carmen de Escudero*
1st Counselor: *Josefa de Sánchez*
2nd Counselor: *María de Papp*

Other branch Relief Societies soon followed:

Villa Devoto on September 22, 1935:
President: *Ernestina Wesenberg*
1st Counselor: *Elise Gabriel*
Secretary: *Elsa Gorges*

Liniers on October 8, 1935:
President: *María Magdalena de Cedolín*
1st Counselor: *Emilia de Gianfelice*
2nd Counselor: *Mariantonia de Notaro*

Haedo on October 11, 1935:
President: *María Antonia de Call*
1st Counselor: *Amelia Santana*
2nd Counselor: *María Sciorra*

Sunday School. On January 26, 1930, President Stoof set apart these Sunday School officers to preside over what had been the German Bible class:

Superintendent:	*Ernst Biebersdorf*
1st Assistant:	*Wilhelm Friedrichs*
2nd Assistant:	*Ernst Wesenberg*

President Young organized the first Primary presided over by local members on September 30, 1935, in the Liniers Branch:

President:	*Angela Maricia de Peyrera*
1st Counselor:	*Amy Young*
2nd Counselor:	*Angela Pallota*

The first member MIA presidency was organized by President Young in the Pueyrredón Branch on April 19, 1936:

President:	*Wilhelm Gabriel*
1st Counselor:	*Hans Fischer (then a nonmember)*
2nd Counselor:	*Rosa Gorges*
Secretary:	*Greta Schimkat (then a nonmember)*

Six Branch Presidencies. It was my privilege to organize the first local member branch presidencies in 1941:

Sáenz Peña (January 5, 1941):

President:	*Cirilo Guinaldo (34; ordained an Elder October 6, 1939), member six years*
1st Counselor:	*Basilo Lebrero (46; Teacher January 14, 1940), member two years*
2nd Counselor:	*Francisco Cortese (55; Elder April 13, 1941), member one year*

Rosario Branch (January 19, 1941):

President:	*Fermín Barjollo (52; Elder January 19, 1941), member four years*
1st Counselor:	*Raúl Rovira (26, Priest January 19, 1941), member one year*

Liniers Branch (February 23, 1941):[6]

President:	*Pedro Cedolín (46; Elder April 11, 1937), member eight years*
1st Counselor:	*Donato Gianfelice (62; Elder April 11, 1936), member fifteen years*
2nd Counselor:	*Alfonso Guillamón (27; Elder February 23, 1941), member 6 months*

Relief Society. President Stoof organized the first Relief Society on February 14, 1934 in the Buenos Aires[5] Branch; its officers were:

Haedo Branch (April 13, 1941):[7]

President:	*Santiago Sciorra (57; Elder October 9, 1938), member seven years*
1st Counselor:	*Juan Borén (30; Elder October 8, 1940), member three years*
2nd Counselor:	*Pedro José Alvarez (19; Elder January 19, 1940), member six years*

Quilmes Branch (May 18, 1941):[8]

President:	*Ernst Biebersdorf (50; Elder April 2, 1933), member sixteen years*
1st Counselor:	*Augusto Liebenberger (62; Elder May 18, 1941), member two years*
2nd Counselor:	*Juan Reynolds (59; Elder May 18, 1941), member five years*

La Plata Branch (October 26, 1941):[9]

President:	*Samuel Borén (25; Elder June 1, 1939), member five years*
1st Counselor:	*George R. Smith (a missionary from Utah, 20)*
2nd Counselor:	*Juan C. Párraga (26, Priest October 26, 1941), member three years*

Summing up the mission activities for October 1941, the mission historian, Elder John Wayne Fronk, recorded the following in the Mission History regarding the new member branch presidency in La Plata:

> *A local Branch Presidency was set apart in the La Plata Branch of the La Plata District, making a total of six branches presided over by local brethren. Samuel Boren, the new president, is a returned missionary from the Argentine Mission (a native boy) who is now married and settled in La Plata.*

Priesthood quorums. Opportunity for leadership came at the annual branch and Relief Society conferences; there were talks to give, bazaars to plan, meetings to conduct, etc. In November 1941, the Liniers Branch Priesthood quorums were placed under local presidencies:

> *This is the first time in the history of the mission that this has been done and we are proud to think that the branches of the mission are growing fast enough to be able to make this improvement. We have some very nice members in all the different offices of the Priesthood in this branch.*[10]

The December 1941 issue of the *Mensajero* contained a few more details. All the priesthood quorums were organized with local brethren, but no names were given.

Mission-wide leadership. While I was President, missionaries still presided over various mission organizations (genealogy, music, priesthood and the auxiliaries); my wife was both Mission Relief Society President and Primary President. However, we did have two district organizations under local members. On March 14, 1939, the mission history records:

> *Today the foundation was laid for a mission-wide M-Men and Gleaner Girls organization. The District of Buenos Aires was organized with the following officers:*

	M-Men		**Gleaners**
President:	*Samuel Borén*	*President:*	*Eurídice Turano*
V. President:	*Juan Duarte*	*V. President:*	*Teresa Brandi*
Secretary:	*Antonio Gianfelice*	*Secretary:*	*Armida Ercolini*

Club Atlético Los Mormones also provided our young people with leadership opportunities. When officers were first installed November 1, 1938, most departments were headed by local members, including:

Public Speaking:	*Eurídice Turano*
Drama:	*Pedro Cedolín and Cirilo Guinaldo*
Athletics:	*Samuel Borén*

Mariano Borén and I were counselors:[11]

Full-time missionaries. It was my great privilege to set apart the first full-time Argentine missionaries. Most did a fine job and pushed the work forward. They were:

> **Luis Constantini** *(66; member seven years). Called from Liniers and served from April 19, 1939 to March 25, 1940. On September 17, 1938, Brother Constantini had lost his wife one week after losing his son. He later remarried and he and his second wife served another mission.*
>
> **Samuel Borén** *(23; member three years). Called from Haedo and served from June 10, 1939 to October 7, 1940.*
>
> **Salvador Parisi** *(26; member one year). Called from Pergamino and served from August 31, 1939 to April 9, 1940.*
>
> **Roberto Antoniette** *(22; member four years). Called from Haedo and served from January 18, 1940 to January 31, 1941.*
>
> **Pedro José Alvarez** *(18, member four years). Called from Haedo and served from January 22, 1940 to January 31, 1941. The mission history for January 17, 1940 records:*

Elders Pedro José Alvarez and Roberto Pedro Antoniette were set apart to fill full-time missions here in Argentina. The parents of Elder Alvarez will support him, and sister Rosa de Pecollo of Ciudadela has volunteered to support Elder Antoniette.

Antonio Gianfelice *(21; member fourteen years). Called from Liniers and served from April 14, 1942 to May 15, 1943. It was a thrill to call this young man whom I had known as a very young boy while serving my first mission.*

Oscar La Vista *(26; member three years). Called from La Plata and served from July 17, 1942. He was the same fellow who had worked in our co-op grocery store and pushed the delivery cart clear out to Sáenz Peña (10 miles away).*

I also called local missionaries on a short-term basis:

During the time of the conference a number of members of the different branches were called upon by President Williams to short term local missions, to work in their proper branches. These missionaries are presided over by Elder J. Wayne Fronk, and will serve under his direction.[12]

Other opportunities for service and leadership came during our annual and semiannual mission conferences, where members were called to speak and sing. In addition to three Sunday sessions, roadshows and special auxiliary and departmental meetings were held on Fridays and Saturdays (genealogy, MIA, Sunday School, Relief Society, Primary, music, etc.). Annual mission MIA and Relief Society conferences and an annual mother-daughter banquet also offered leadership opportunities. Of course, each of the ten mission districts also held annual conferences. There was plenty to do, and the members rose to the occasion, particularly the youth. I reported to the First Presidency on October 17, 1940:

There are approximately one hundred of the finest young men and women that I have ever known—young men and women from the age of sixteen to twenty-five. They attend to all their duties and do a great deal of missionary activity on the side. They are now beginning to intermarry and establish Mormon homes. Upon their shoulders I would be happy to stake the future of the Argentine Mission.

We sorely lacked facilities, i.e., chapels, to make all the programs work. I made a plea to the First Presidency at the close of 1941:

Our big need in this mission is either the purchase or the building of chapels and a mission home. We spend some 18,000 pesos per year for rent—or over $5,000—and at the end of the year have nothing but rent receipts to show for it. That much money would buy the land and build two chapels. I believe it would be a good investment for the Church to advance money for at least ten chapels, as the work would progress much faster, the missionaries would have better living conditions, and in ten years they would pay for themselves. As it is now, the money is thrown away. Some buildings suitable for our purposes could be purchased even cheaper than we can build.

We could have used our own printing facilities as well. We never had enough religious and instructional literature for our members, and our standard works editions were not the best.

I also spent (perhaps wasted is a more appropriate term) many hours on trains and buses traveling to the branches. A car would have helped me use my time much more efficiently. I detailed these conditions in my letter to the First Presidency dated September 1, 1941. I also made a strong pitch for a visit from a General Authority. It would not only be a great blessing to the members, but the Brethren would then better understand our needs.

I made what I thought was a strong case:

September 1, 1941

The First Presidency
47 East South Temple
Salt Lake City, Utah

Dear Brethren:

At times I hesitate writing to you as it seems that in each letter I ask for something, and I surely hate to give this impression. However, there are things that I feel that would be for the interest of the Mission, and it is only for that reason that I do send requests from time to time. In this letter I am asking for two favors, the visit of the mission by one of the General Authorities, and a mission car.

President Bowers of the Brazilian Mission and I feel that it would be of immense worth to us if one of the Authorities could come and visit us. Then the Church would know at first hand what our problems are. Then too, the visit would be a great stimulation to the missionaries and to the saints. There are hundreds of saints who are eagerly looking forward to the time when they can meet one of the Authorities. It is true that we have been visited by Brother Ballard, President Clark and Wells, but this was a long time ago. There are less than twenty saints that knew Brother Ballard, and perhaps about fifty that were fortunate enough to hear President Clark. Since then our mission has changed as from day to night. It is now scattered throughout the Argentine Republic, and at that time was centered in Buenos Aires.

Our conditions are varied and our problems many, and they are hard to explain in letters. I have written many such, and then torn them up and thrown them away. We are happy to meet and try and solve any situation that arises, as we know that is why you sent us here, but at times we need tools with which to work. For example our printing problem and the books that we have to work with. We were four months without a single Book of Mormon in Spanish, either for the new missionaries or for the members and investigators. We were finally able to secure some from the Mexican Mission, but they will soon be gone, and we have no hopes for others until the new Spanish Edition is published.

Fifty percent of our missionaries and members have no adequate song book containing our hymns. The Spanish song book has been out of print for some two years and there are no copies to be had. In order to sing at all we had to mimeograph three hundred copies of a few songs, but these are now gone. Others will have to be mimeographed unless we get the new ones.

Every year we spend hundreds of pesos mimeographing lessons for the many organizations for the Church. These lessons are valuable, but cannot be kept in a permanent form. If we could print them in quarterly issues they could be bound and become valuable reference books for the future.

What we need, and I would like to go over it thoroughly with one of the Authorities, is a small printery, so that we could supply the Spanish speaking race with literature and the necessary books for background study. All that we have to work with are six tracts, The Bible, the Book of Mormon (when available), a part of the Doctrine and Covenants (now unavailable), and what doctrinal themes we can put in our small Spanish Magazine "El Mensajero Deseret", small because the printing costs makes it impossible to do more. The great promises of the Book of Mormon are to the peoples of this continent, yet I know of no missions in the world who have less literature to work with.

I was going to save the printery for another letter, but now that I have started I'll include it here. I believe we have a wonderful opportunity to establish it now. We have a very good member who has been in the Church for some ten years who is a printer by trade and has his small shop. He has been doing the work of the mission up until now, but with the increased work that we have and the work of his other clients, he is many months behind, and now refuses to print our tracts. He is now 60 years of age, and does not want to work over ten hours a day as he has been doing to try to keep up. His name is William Gabriel, a good German saint. He has been suggesting for the past few years that the Church establish a printery while he could show someone how to run it. He has all of the necessary machinery with the exception of a larger press. His is small and will print only one page at a time. He has no children interested in the printing business and would be glad to put it at the disposal of the Church. I told him that if the Church took it over they would pay him for his equipment, and he said that in that case we could have it for half its market value, or about one thousand dollars. A good second hand press the size we would need costs about $1500. Brother Gabriel is in no hurry for his part, and would be willing to manage the printery for a percentage of its earnings and teach what he knows to others. He is an expert book binder and a good printer.

When he joined the Church he was employing four men in his business, but didn't want the responsibility of running that large a business, as he wanted time to study about the Church. He is sure that he can get back a share of his former clientele, as he has frequent calls now for jobs. At the present time he has some six hundred books to be bound and a lot of other back orders that he can't fill, and he has every confidence in the world that he can make this a paying business from the start as he will bring his steady customers with him. It would give us the opportunity of employing one or more persons, too, as the business would justify.

There is room on the front of our club lot to build a building suitable for a small printery. The mission membership is small at the present time (approximately 700), but we have the continent before us, and it will be just a matter of time until there will be missions throughout the other South American countries, and they will all need literature.

This is one of the reasons that I feel it would be well if one of the Authorities could come and see what the conditions and needs are.

I realize how busy you all are and that the time involved is great, but if the airlines were used one can be in Buenos Aires from Salt Lake City in less than a week's time. And between the Brazilian and the Argentine Missions I feel a great work could be accomplished by said visit. But I would ask that at least a month be spent in Argentina so that one could become thoroughly conversant with the conditions and the wonderful promises for the future.

There are a number of reasons that I am asking for a mission automobile, and I will try and make them brief:

First would be the time it would save me in traveling. I believe it would give me an additional month every year in time saved. The mission has become somewhat scattered, and for me to visit the outside branches, I have to go from Buenos Aires to each outlying branch and return. There are few connecting lines between the outside branches, as almost all of them are serviced by different railways. Railway service is becoming less dependable due to the fuel shortage, and the inactivity of the railways themselves due to the loss of shipments to other countries of cereals. There are many less trains now than before and several railways have now refused to give us a Missionary Discount during the duration of the War. An automobile would help inasmuch as nearly all the branches could be visited in one tour, permitting me to stay as long as necessary in each branch, but not be subject to a one train a week schedule, as we now have.

On our conference trips we are forced to arrive in some of the towns at dark one night, have a meeting, visit the missionaries and saints, and catch a train at five o'clock the following morning, or stay there for a week. A car, and a good network of roads, would save this.

In order to visit the branches around the suburbs of Buenos Aires at times I have to go on as many as three buses, but if we had a car one could go directly in fifteen or twenty minutes. At times now we are an hour and a half going the same distance, depending upon our luck in getting a bus. For this reason, I have found it almost impossible to get to bed before 12:30 or 1:00 a.m. as I try and visit the missionaries in some of the branches daily.

This would facilitate my visiting the outside elders oftener, and in the long run it would be more economical than train fare for conference trips, as several could go. Whenever Sister Williams accompanies me she has to pay full fare on the train as they give no discount to women missionaries.

Gasoline is cheap and is the same price throught the country. We are acquainted with the Good Year Rubber people here and can get tires at a big discount.

The purchase price of a car is high here, but the upkeep is cheaper than at home. A Ford, Chevrolet, or Plymouth sell for $1500 U.S. here, and we certainly would feel happy and honored with any one of them. It might be that if you dealt directly with one of these companies you could get a discount on it for us, pay for it there, and have them deliver it to us here. It would be a great asset to the missionary work and it would be greatly appreciated if you see fit to answer our plea.

I didn't think this letter would be this long when I started it, and I thank you for your patience for having read it all.

Trusting you will see fit to honor us with the visit of one of the General Authorities, I am

Sincerely your brother,

Frederick S. Williams,
Mission President

P.S. Spring arrives the last part of September, and October and November are the most delightful months in Argentina for a visit.

The reply came quickly.

September 17, 1941

President Frederick S. Williams,
Argentina Mission
Calle Manzoni, 268 Villa Luro
Buenos Aires, Argentina

Dear President Williams:

In your first paragraph of your letter of September 1, 1941, you say you hesitate to write as it seems that in each letter you are making some request. You may rest assured that we understand that when you ask for something that you do so because you are sure it is for the best good of your Mission.

Visit of One of the General Authorities

Your first suggestion is that one of the General Authorities visit you and the Brazilian Mission at the earliest opportunity. We know from the results of other missions that official visits by members of the First Presidency or of the Council of the Twelve to the Missions result in a great deal of good. Direct observation is far more enlightening than information obtained by correspondence, especially is this true when conditions in the Mission are more or less unfamiliar. At present, however, the prospects of such a visit to South America are somewhat remote.

Printing Press

We recognize your difficulty in getting literature printed in the Spanish language. We had hoped that before this another edition of the Book of Mormon printed in Spanish would be published, but the Committee having the matter in hand reports that some of the plates are so faint or defaced that they have to be replaced. This has caused another delay. However, we shall push the matter as rapidly as possible so that your needs in this regard will be supplied. Your suggestion regarding the necessity of printing tracts, song books, and other literature has been referred to the Committee of the Council of the Twelve to investigate and report.

Automobile

From what you say, and judging from reports we have received from other sources, an automobile would be a contributing factor in furthering the work in the Argentine Mission. We are therefore granting your request of a car, possibly a Ford or Chevrolet, and will take steps to supply this need in the very near future.

With prayerful wishes for your continued success, and with greeting and blessings to the Elders and Saints in the Argentine Mission, we remain

Sincerely yours,

H.J. Grant
J. Reuben Clark, Jr.
David O. McKay
The First Presidency

I got the car; one out of three isn't bad.

My Release as Argentine Mission President. We scheduled an elders meeting for August 1, 1942, the day President and Sister Barker arrived in Buenos Aires. After greeting them at the airport with a number of elders from the capital, we asked the Barkers to join us for a testimony meeting:

> *During the Elders Meeting many expressions of thanks and appreciation were made to our departing President and a scene of sadness was prevalent; however, the meeting was extremely spiritual. President Williams made the following observations: "President and Sister Barker will be very capable leaders and will have to support him the best staff of missionaries the Argentine Mission has ever known."*[13]

We hurriedly completed our preparations to leave. A farewell party was held for us at the Liniers chapel August 12, and then on the fifteenth some two hundred members and friends came to the airport to see us off. They waited with us most of the day, since bad weather had grounded most flights. Finally the flight was postponed to the next day because of fog in Córdoba. We finally got airborne August 16, 1942, leap-frogging short distances each day (there were no night flights). Five days later we landed at Brownsville, Texas. The War was in full fury and the U.S. was in it with all her might.

NOTES

Chapter VIII

1. Mariano Borén had attended several different churches, and at the time of his conversion was the leader of a group of believing people dissatisfied with organized religion. Through his example, all but one family from this group followed him into the Church. Cf. Samuel Borén Interview, Church Historical Department, Oral History Project.

2. Copy of the letter to the First Presidency dated April 1, 1939, in my files.

3. See details in Samuel Borén Interview, pp. 26-27. Church Historical Department, Oral History Project.

4. Coverage of the 80-year-old president's European trip, his first since 1906, is found in the August, September and October issues of the *Improvement Era*. President Grant remained in Paris from the 24th to the 26th of June, 1937, "where, on June 24, he addressed the American Club as an invited guest. A brief stay in Paris was devoted to making the acquaintance of members of the Church there and to visiting scenes of war interest, art interest and other general attractions." *Era*, August 1937, p. 467.

5. The first member-presided Relief Society in the Mission was organized in the Joinville, Brazil branch on October 11, 1933:

President: Martha Toni (Merz) Barsch
1st Counselor: Martha Otto
2nd Counselor: Margarete Buchli

6. The Mission History states that the organization in Liniers took place January 23 and further states under the entry for January 31 that three branches had been organized in the Mission. Nevertheless, the March *Mensajero*, under Liniers Branch Activities, states that the organization was on February 23, a Sunday, and that it was held during the final session of the branch conference. This last date seems the more likely, since January 23 fell on a Thursday, and the pattern established in the organization of the other two branch presidencies was to sustain them in their conferences, which were always held on Sunday. As further corroboration, the Mission History does record that on Februry 23, Alfonso Guillamón was ordained to the office of Elder; he was one of the newly sustained counselors in the presidency. The other counselor, Donato Gianfelice, was one of the original members of the Mission.

7. The details on the organizaion of the Haedo Branch presidency appear in the May issue of the *Mensajero*. The article fails to mention a specific date, however, and merely states that it took place "last month." The Mission History is silent, but does indicate that on Sunday, April 13, 1941, a large number of Priesthood ordinations took place in the branch; something which was usually reserved for special occasions such as conferences.

8. Again the Mission History is silent on the organization, but the details were recorded in the July *Mensajero*. The article indicates that the presidency was organized during their branch conference at which time Brothers Liebenberger and Reynolds were both ordained to the office of Elder. The Mission History records the ordinations of these two brothers as occurring on Sunday, May 18, 1941. Brother Biebersdorf had been baptized in the initial group by Apostle Ballard on December 12, 1925.

9. The Mission History is again all but silent, but the details of the organization of this sixth and last branch presidency appear in the December 1941 *Mensajero*. Since the Mission History indicates that on Sunday, October 26, 1941 several ordinations were made to the Priesthood—among them that of Juan Carlos Parraga to the office of Priest—and since it further states, under the entry for October 30, that the La Plata branch was organized with Samuel Borén as president, the date of Sunday the 26th can be considered correct; Parraga was one of the counselors.

10. Mission History, November 27, 1941.

11. See December 1938 *Mensajero* for details.

12. Mission History, April 12, 1942.

13. Agentine Mission History.

SECOND INTERREGNUM

FROM 1942 TO the end of the War in 1945, I worked under the United States State Department. I trained in Washington, D.C., for eight months, then began serving as the Business Manager of the Institute of Inter-American Affairs, Division of Health and Sanitation, first in Venezuela, and then in Uruguay. I was without my family in Washington (they stayed with Corraine's sister, Mona Page, in Arizona), but thankfully they were with me in South America. Among other activities, our Division set up malaria control programs and vaccination drives, and constructed hospitals. While in Uruguay (1943 to 1945), an English-speaking branch of the Church was formed—over which I presided—to serve the needs of the Latter-day Saint personnel stationed there in various war-related capacities. When the War ended, we settled in Los Angeles, California, where I worked for just over a year in my brother-in-law's plastering business, before we were called to open the Uruguayan Mission.

PART III

THE URUGUAYAN MISSION: ORIGIN AND GROWTH (1947-1951)

INTRODUCTION TO PART THREE

PRESIDING OVER the opening of the Uruguayan Mission was pure joy. When we arrived in 1947, the government was strong and confident, the people were happy and enjoyed a relatively high standard of living. Word War II was over and there was a tremendous feeling of rebirth and sure growth. The nation seemed ready for the introduction of the gospel of Jesus Christ. Indeed, an intelligent, high class of people was quickly attracted and joined the Church in ever increasing numbers, making Uruguay, in the opinion of President McKay, the fastest growing mission at its inception in the history of the Church, after Great Britain. Soon the number of convert baptisms in Uruguay far outdistanced those in either Argentina or Brazil, the other two missions in South America, and was greater even than their combined totals.

Uruguay was the fortieth mission of the Church to be organized and the first field of labor opened after the War. I could not help but feel confident about the assignment. I was thirty-nine and my wife Corraine thirty-eight, and this was our second call as mission presidents. Furthermore, we were well acquainted with Uruguay because I had recently labored there on behalf of the United States Government and was known and respected by persons of high standing in government and in other walks of life. The circumstances were better, too; in Argentina we had presided over a mission that in many ways was winding down because of the War. In Uruguay just the opposite dynamics were in operation: it was a period of growth and expansion, and we received large groups of missionaries, sometimes weekly, which posed some grave logistical problems; almost none of them spoke Spanish; what could they do? where would we put them? how would they be trained?

In addition to our youthfulness and inexperience when called to preside in Argentina, we faced problems associated with replacing a successful president in an established mission. In the beginning it was not uncommon to hear "But that's not how President Young did it." Uruguay, on the other hand, was virgin territory, we inherited no old problems, prejudices, grudges or inactive members. The feeling in the nation was different, too. The Argentine government had been profoundly pro-Axis during the War; Uruguay's, fiercely pro-Allies. We were generally regarded as heroes; Hollywood movies made us idols, a thing to emulate.

Where we had used sports to introduce the Church in Argentina, we turned to the arts, particuarly music, in Uruguay. With the help of a number of very talented missionaries, as well as members of my family, we produced a weekly radio program which brought the Church before the citizens of that land and its neighbors. The programs would vary, sometimes featuring the mission choir, at others a quartet or trio. Our live performances were augmented by the services of two fine missionaries. Roy Fitzel was a professional dancer who had been in several movies. Maughan McMurdie was an extraordinarily talented pianist who could also sing, arrange music, and sight-read anything placed in front of him; if there was no sheet music, and if you could whistle the tune, he could play it by ear. Prestigious social clubs paid transportation and lodging expenses for our troupe to perform in concert. We found that with culture there were no hurt feelings—no one lost as in a sporting event—everyone won. Local newspapers gave the Church good publicity, too. In Uruguay there was complete freedom of religion; Catholicism was not the State Church and not all-powerful; rather, it often suffered a good deal of persecution in the Uruguayan press.

The Uruguayan Mission was also easier from an administrative standpoint. The Church authorized mission presidents to call counselors, and it streamlined many reports and consolidated various funds which had theretofore been kept separate. We even had a little more money to spend than we had had ten years before, and we had a much nicer mission home and furnishings. We also received a visit from a General Authority, which lent great support to the mission.

Given Uruguay's modest size (comparable to Kansas) and a consistently large number of missionaries, we were able not only to teach in all parts of that country, but to expand into nearby Paraguay, whose beginnings in the Church are also chronicled herein. This warm and friendly Guaraní Indian nation—which lost more than three-quarters of its men in the war against Brazil, Argentina and Uruguay (1865 to 1870), and which since that devastation has been trying to rejoin the modern world—likewise opened its arms wide to receive the gospel.

Part III also contains an account of the beginnings of the Church in Peru which, as in the case of Paraguay, first came under the jurisdiction of the Uruguayan Mission. Although it was a decade later (1956) and I was not then a mission president but a branch president (I was the manager of an airline headquartered in Lima), we have included that account because our family was closely linked with the introduction of missionary work in that ancient land, once part of the Inca empire. The growth here was likewise phenomenal and led to the establishment of a separate Andes Mission in 1959.

CHAPTER I

PRELUDE: CALLING ATTENTION TO SOUTH AMERICA... WHY DOESN'T THE CHURCH DO MORE THERE?

IN AUGUST OF 1946, Corraine and I accompanied her niece, Louise E. Peacock, and her fiancé, Earl L. Singleton, from California to Utah to witness their marriage in the Salt Lake Temple. While there, I contacted some of my former Argentine missionaries, and we held a small reunion. Present, among others, were Robert Riggs McKay (son of David O. McKay, then the Second Counselor in the First Presidency), Don Hyrum Smith, Kay A. Schwendiman and Keith McCune, who had just recently returned from Panama where he had been serving as President of the English-speaking branch of the Church, formed there among largely military personnel during the War.

After reliving our experiences in South America and reaffirming our commitment to and love for the people, we began wondering why the Church wasn't expanding into new South American countries. At that time only the Argentine and Brazilian missions existed. It seemed to us that Europe and the United States had received far more attention over the past twenty years. After some discussion we came to the conclusion that we should do something about it, for no one was in a better position to bring the matter to the attention of the Brethren. We felt we could point out to them in a forceful yet loving manner the tremendous proselyting opportunities existing to the south.

President George Albert Smith. Don Smith called his uncle, President George Albert Smith, and secured an interview with the Prophet for the following morning. At the appointed hour, Corraine and I and one or two others were ushered into the office and received in a kindly manner. I was chosen as spokesman for the group, and I began by stating that we felt a bit awkward coming to make suggestions to the Presiding Brethren. I said if our concern dealt with any other topic or region we would not have come; but because no General Authorities had ever lived in South America, with the exception of those who opened the work there under Elder Melvin J. Ballard (who died in 1939), we felt perhaps they were not sufficiently acquainted with the conditions.

I pointed out that Elder Ballard had opened the South American Mission in 1925, some twenty-one years before. Since then, the only General Authority to visit had been President J. Reuben Clark, Jr., of the First Presidency; he had been there less than a week to represent the United States Government in Uruguay and had visited with the Saints in Buenos Aires for only a matter of hours.[1]

We briefly recounted the history of the South American Mission and then mentioned other countries where we felt the gospel would be readily accepted. Just returned from an additional three years' residence in South America, first in Venezuela, then in Uruguay as Business Manager of the Health and Sanitation Department of the Institute of Inter-American Affairs (not to mention six years in Argentina, two as a missionary, later as mission president), I felt I was speaking on the subject from a position of strength. I mentioned the ethnic makeup of each South America nation, its languages and its peoples. I also pointed out the degree of religious freedom that existed in each, as well as its level of education.

During the more than one hour that my presentation required, President Smith sat in silence. He neither commented nor asked questions. When I had finished, he excused himself and left the room. Because he had made no observations we felt that we had displeased him and began thinking to ourselves, "Well, it was wonderful being a member of the Church while it lasted."

In a few minutes President Smith returned with his Second Counselor, David O. McKay.[2] After we shook hands with Elder McKay, President Smith said, "I asked David to leave the meeting he was attending and come back with me. Please repeat to him what you have told me, President Williams."

I reviewed the items previously mentioned and added some topics I'd thought of in the meantime. Again, as before, there was complete silence for a few minutes after I had finished. Our hearts fell. Finally, the President turned to his counselor and asked, "David, what do you think of all this?" President McKay in his sweet way said: "I'm impressed with it. I'm happy they came and brought it to our attention; I think we should do something about it." "I do too," said President Smith, "but I wanted to get your reaction." Then he turned to us and in his kindly manner—as though embracing us in his love—said: "Thank you for coming. I too appreciated hearing what you had to say, but I wanted my counselor to hear it also." Then, as though perceiving our anxiety about dictating to the Brethren, said: "President Williams, don't you know that you have just as much responsibility to preach the gospel as we do? If any member of the Church knows something we don't know, it is his responsibility to come and tell us." We began to feel better about our Church membership. He continued: "Now we'd like you to put in writing all that you have told us and make whatever recommendations you feel necessary concerning the opening of new missions in South America. I want to submit this to the Council of the Twelve. Thank you one and all for coming to see us." Of course, we felt we were walking on air as we bade goodbye and left these two great men.

Recommended master-plan for proselyting in South America. Upon returning to South Gate, California, I worked hard preparing a narrative with maps and charts on South America, as the President had requested. In late October 1946, I submitted a twenty-page document to him, containing the following information for each country.[3]

1. History
2. Population
3. Ethnic makeup
4. Educational level
5. Religion(s)
6. Language(s)
7. Type of government
8. Living conditions
9. Principal industries

I also included a list of the countries I thought were ready to receive missionaries and suggested the order in which they should be opened, according to where I thought the most initial progress could be made. As I recall, Uruguay headed the list, followed by Perú, Chile, Paraguay, Ecuador, Colombia and Bolivia. I also respectfully recommended that someone, preferably a General Authority, be called to live in South America to supervise and coordinate the activity of the various missions after they were established. I suggested that that person be at least a member of the First Quorum of Seventy. I sent the document off but never heard of it again.

The President of Uruguay. The following January, President David O. McKay visited our stake, the South Los Angeles Stake, as the speaker at stake conference. I spoke to him after one of the sessions and indicated that a Uruguayan friend of mine, Tomás Berreta, the former Minister of Public Works, had just been elected President of Uruguay, and that according to a Los Angeles newspaper he would extend his pre-inaugural visit of the United States to include a visit to Los Angeles, where a reception would be held in his honor. Because this was the Utah Centennial, I suggested that it might be a nice gesture to invite him to that state. President McKay, the Chairman of the Utah Centennial Commission, asked me to contact Berreta in his name, inviting him to visit Utah as an official guest. The president-elect was due to arrive in the United States the first week in February. I sent him a telegram in care of the Uruguayan Embassy in Washington, D.C., on a Friday. When the expected answer did not arrive, I thought the invitation had been ignored.

The following Monday morning I went to work and found that a telegram with my name on it had been shoved under my office door; I'd forgotten I'd used my work address. The telegram read:

> FEB 8, 1947
>
> FREDERICO S WILLIAMS
> 3309 INDEPENDENCE AVE SOUTHGATE CALIF
> AGRADEZCO ESTIMADO AMIGO SU AMABLE INVITACION VISITAR ESTADO UTAH LAMENTANDO NO PODER ACEPTAR DEBIDO ESTAR TODO EL PROGRAMA MI ESTADIA EN ESTADOS UNIDOS PREPARADO ANTERIORMENTE STOP SALUDOS CORDIALES
>
> TOMAS BERRETA[4]

In English the telegram reads: "Frederick S. Williams. I appreciate, dear friend, your kind invitation to visit the State of Utah. I lament not being able to accept because the entire program of my stay in the United States has been previously prepared. Stop. With kindest regards. Thomas Berreta." I made copies of both telegrams, sent them to President McKay, and went on about my business.

Call to be Mission President. During a telephone strike in April 1947, in which the long distance operators would only process emergency calls, I received the following telegram:

> PLEASE CALL DAVID O MCKAY TOMORROW 900 MST EMERGENCY

It was too soon after the War for us to have our own telephone, so I phoned from the office the next morning; Corraine came with me. After a few moments President McKay's voice came on the line. "Do you remember recommending opening a mission in Uruguay?" he asked. I acknowledged that I did. "How would you like to go down and open it?" I assured him that it would be a pleasure. He asked me, among other things, whether Sister Williams would support me in this call and I indicated that she would, for she was seated by my side, agreeing. He inquired if I could leave immediately, because there was a group of some eighteen missionaries already in Uruguay who were waiting to get visas to enter Argentina; if we could go there now they would be able to remain in Uruguay. I told him that we would do anything he asked, but that it would be much better for my family if the children could finish out the school year, just two months away. I suggested that we arrange to be in Salt Lake City at the time of the Centennial Celebration, July 24. He said that would be fine and that we were to contact Franklin J. Murdock, Mission Secretary, for all our preparations and travel arrangements.

We were delighted to be returning to Uruguay, and more important, to be serving a mission again, for, among other things, the call was an indication to us that our standing before the Lord was acceptable, and this feeling was very sweet. The Church's announcement of the creation of the new mission, together with my photograph and a rather detailed biography, appeared on the front page of the Church section of the *Deseret News*.[5]

Because we were opening a brand new field of labor, we would be required to purchase and furnish a mission home and office. Accordingly, we sent in a list of suggested supplies, including office machinery and kitchen utensils and dishes. We also requested a formica-top table and matching chairs, newly on the market. We had purchased a 1946 Plymouth and asked the First Presidency whether we should take it to Uruguay with us; we knew that this soon after the War it would be next to impossible to purchase a car in Uruguay, and one was so very necessary.[6] They agreed and the Church bought the car, as well as our gas stove.

When school ended we packed, sold our furniture, bought four new tires for our car and prepared to leave. The members of the South Gate Ward gave us a wonderful farewell and, against our expressed desires, insisted on taking up a collection for us. The money raised was invested in sports equipment for the future missionaries.

Our plan was to take a leisurely trip from California to Utah, camping in various national parks as we went; we didn't have to be in Salt Lake City until the Centennial. Our entourage also included Corraine's sister, Mona Page, Mona's son Kay and daughter Mona Lou, and a friend of Mona's, Verda Mausson, driving their own car. In addition, my former secretary in Montevideo, Alice Banks, made the trip with us. Alice had flown to the States to visit with us the month before we returned to Uruguay and planned to return there soon herself to be married.

One of my new tires went flat before we had gone ten miles. The tube had been pinched when the tire was mounted. We fixed it and continued our trip. The first night caught us near Bakersfield. It was dark when we pulled off the road near a shallow river and made camp. We all took a bath in the water, cooked our supper and made ready for bed. Before I turned in, however, I had to soak Freddy's foot in a kettle of hot water with Epsom salts and plain cooking salt to cure an infection he had recently acquired. This was a nightly ritual until the infection cleared up. The morning light showed us that we were camped in an old dump. We were happy to get an early start toward Sequoia National Park.

We camped in Sequoia's beautiful forest for several days, and hated to leave its primeval beauty for further adventures. After spending a couple of days in Yosemite, we drove by Mono Lake and continued north to Lake Tahoe, Carson City, and Reno, Nevada. We passed through Winnemucca on our way to Twin Falls, Burley, Pocatello, and Idaho Falls, Idaho, where we visited the temple grounds.

Just before reaching this "temple by the river," we passed through Shelley, a small farming community. On entering the town, I said to Corraine "We had an Argentine missionary from this town. His name is Wendell K. Young—and there he is!" A pickup truck had just stopped in front of a store and Wendell got out. We had a nice visit with him before continuing. We also stopped at Sugar City, Idaho, and visited with the father of Grant Thomas, another former Argentine missionary. I remembered that he was the manager of the cooperative store in that town.

We spent several days in Yellowstone Park. I wasted the usual amount of film by standing too close to Old Faithful. We saw the bears and were happy they didn't attack us while we were sleeping, although we could hear them as they raided the garbage cans.

We, of course, had all four of our children with us: Barbara Lynn (16), Argina (12), Frederick G. (7), and Nancy Lou (5). Nancy made friends with a chipmunk and I have some good pictures of it eating from her hands.

We left Yellowstone late and drove to Jackson Hole. What a beautiful view the Tetons made across the flat gray lake just before sundown. I thought this the most beautiful sight in the United States and regretted spending so much time in Yellowstone.

We decided to spend the night in Jackson Hole and found an adequate campground. I opened the trunk of the car and started to get our gear out. Just then a huge cloud of the most vociferous, hungriest mosquitoes I had seen or heard since my oxteam trip to the Indians in Formosa, Northern Argentina, found us. I slammed the trunk shut, yelled to everyone to get into the car, and drove on. Some time later we found a chuck wagon serving meals to tourists. The food was excellent and, before sleeping that night, we thoroughly enjoyed the dinner, with only a few mosquitoes in attendance.

The Presidency's busy schedule. We finally reached Salt Lake City on Saturday, July 19. I called my sister, Naoma W. Seaich, from our motel. "Where in the world have you been?" she asked. "Brother Murdock has been looking for you for the last ten days and wants you to call him day or night." We were originally scheduled to sail from New Orleans about the first week in August, but it seemed our plans had changed. I called Brother Murdock and he asked me to come to his office first thing Monday morning. There were still no passenger ships in operation; they were all being reconverted from troop transports. We were now scheduled to leave New York on a freighter at an earlier date, but there would still be time for us to participate in the celebration and leave about the twenty-eighth.

On Monday, July 21, we went to the Church offices to see President McKay as had been requested. He was the busiest man in Utah. He excused himself from a meeting only long enough to ask if we could wait until after the twenty-fourth to discuss the new mission. We said, of course, that would be fine, and he suggested that we come to see him on the twenty-fifth.

Our former Argentine missionaries had planned an outing at Lagoon for Tuesday afternoon. That morning, I received an urgent call from Elder Murdock. He told me that our ship's departure date had been advanced again, and that we would have to leave for New York the next day to catch the freighter.

Corraine and I went to the Church office building in the morning and asked to see President McKay. Claire Middlemiss, his secretary, said it was impossible to see him because he was in an important meeting. We explained our problem, so she took us to the door of the meeting room, went in, and in a few moments President McKay came out. He didn't appear to be too happy about the interruption. I apologized for the inconvenience, and explained the urgency of Brother Murdock's call and said that we had to leave for Uruguay the next evening and it would be nice to be set apart for the mission before leaving. "But you must be! You have to be set apart. Now it's a question of when we can do it. Oh my, what a busy day."

He asked whether it would be convenient for us to return at five o'clock that afternoon, and we assured him that we would come at any time he suggested. We then went to Lagoon and had a very enjoyable time meeting with our former missionaries and their families. At the appointed hour we were back at Church headquarters. President McKay was just leaving the Church office building through the front door. He said that a caravan of cars, decorated to look like the ox teams and wagons that had left Nauvoo to follow the Mormon trail, was just arriving, and he had to go to the reviewing stand to receive it. He asked that we watch the stand, and when he left, to come back to his office with him. This we did.

It was our privilege to spend about thirty minutes visiting with and receiving instructions from President McKay; then he was joined by President Clark. President George Albert Smith came in for a moment to ask a question. He was dressed in a Boy Scout uniform and was on his way to attend a Scout function. He extended his love to us, wished us well and left. The two counselors in the First Presidency then set us apart:

July 22, 1947

Blessing upon the head of Frederick Salem Williams by Presidents J. Reuben Clark, Jr. and David O. McKay, Counselors in the First Presidency, President Clark being voice, setting him apart to preside over the Uruguayan Mission.

Brother Frederick Salem Williams, in the name of the Lord Jesus Christ and by virtue of the Priesthood which we hold, we lay our hands upon your head and set you apart to preside over the Uruguayan Mission. This is a new mission, as you know, which we are just now establishing. On the manner in which the mission is begun will depend to no small extent the future growth of the mission, and the influence which it will yield in that country. You have served in that area. You know the people and the officials. Our Heavenly Father, we pray that thou wilt make available to Brother Williams all that he has learned—the language, the manners and customs, prejudices, beliefs and all persons when he has heretofore served there. Bring all things to his memory that would be useful to him in spreading thy gospel.

We say unto you, Brother Williams, be humble, patient, charitable to the people, to their beliefs; and be kind and exercise likewise all these qualities toward the missionaries who will be sent to aid you in your great work. We ask our Heavenly Father to lead you to those who will be able to help you in establishing the mission, in finding a place to live, in finding your headquarters, and in securing anything and everything that may be necessary for you to have successfully to open this mission.

We pray that our Heavenly Father will give you increased insight into the beliefs of the people, that you may know how to approach them in order that you may carry to them in a convincing manner the message which you have to impart.

We bless you with the spirit of discernment, that you may know those who seek the truth and understand them and that likewise you may know those, if any, who would seek to lay a trap for you and to delay or perhaps defeat your work. We pray that the Lord will bless you with every blessing that it is necessary that you should have to meet these situations.

We bless you with the spirit of fatherhood toward the people and toward the elders.

We bless you with fluency in the language; and if you need further knowledge thereof, that that will come to you easily. You have had great experiences in the past, and we ask our Heavenly Father to increase these to you and to make available to you the wisdom that should come from those experiences.

We ask our Heavenly Father to give you health and strength. We pray that He will bless you in your traveling, both in going to your mission, while you are on your mission, and in your return.

We bless you with every blessing which it is necessary that you should have to fulfill this mission, and say again be humble, prayerful and longsuffering and fill your heart only with the desire to do the work of the Lord. Shut out all other interests that might detract you and draw you away so that your whole thought and effort may be focused upon that one purpose.

We seal these blessings upon you and every other blessing which it is necessary that you should have in order that you may perform this mission, in the name of the Lord Jesus Christ and through your faithfulness, even so, Amen.

Approved: s/ J. Reuben Clark, Jr.

July 22, 1947

A blessing upon the head of Sister Corraine Smith Williams by Presidents J. Reuben Clark, Jr. and David O. McKay, Counselors in the First Presidency, President McKay being voice, setting her apart as a missionary and to labor with her husband in the Uruguayan Mission.

Dear Sister Corraine Smith Williams, esteemed handmaiden of the Lord, by virtue of the Holy Priesthood and the authority in us vested we, servants of the Lord, unitedly lay our hands upon your head and set you apart as a missionary of the Church of Jesus Christ of Latter-day Saints to labor with your husband in the Uruguayan Mission.

Once again the responsibility has come to you and your husband to represent the Lord in a foreign field. It is a great honor and an expression of the confidence that the servants of the Lord have in you both. It is also a manifestation that the Lord has approved of your efforts in the past. May you have the assurance now that He will go with you as you accept this, another call, to be an ambassador of truth. We bless you that you may go in peace and travel in safety whether by land or by sea or by air. May you feel the Lord's divine protection and know that He will be with you always as long as your feet are firmly planted in the pathway of duty.

We bless you that you may approach this new responsibility with humility, with thanksgiving and with gratitude, and as you face duties that carry you before the public, we bless you that the man-fearing spirit may leave you. It comes to us all; but by relying on the Lord and having confidence in His nearness and in His guidance, that spirit may be overcome. And we bless you that you may overcome it, particularly when you face audiences and begin to bear your testimony of the restoration of the gospel of Jesus Christ. May the spirit of the Lord prompt what you say and especially inspire your thoughts.

Your special mission, as your husband's, is to bear witness that the Lord and His Son Jesus Christ appeared to the Prophet Joseph Smith and restored the authority of the priesthood, authorized men to represent Him to establish His Church here among mankind, never more to be thrown down nor given to another people. May the testimony of the truth of this restoration burn in your bosom and be indeed more effective, if that be possible, in the future than it has in the past; that those into whose company you may be thrown may feel the radiation of that testimony and be convinced that you have something which the world in general does not possess.

We bless you with health, Sister Williams, and with strength sufficient to carry the responsibilities of this new assignment. Be wise in your labors, take proper care of your health. The Lord desires you to enjoy health, to live and to be able to perform every duty that awaits you. To that end listen to the whisperings of the still, small voice to which guidance you are entitled, and you will know how far to go, what restraints to put upon yourself, in order that you may conserve the strength which is yours and which you will need.

We bless you with discernment, with discretion, with charity for those whom you meet and with a sincere desire to help the people unto whom you are now sent, and as those people sense your sincerity and your willingness to serve them and your willingness to lose yourself, as it were, for the sake of others, it will impress them even more than what you say, and they will realize that there are people in the world who are willing to serve mankind and to lose themselves in that service.

We bless you that you may have increased ability as a mother and as a wife to take care of your home and yet perform the added duties and labors that come to you as the wife of the president of this mission.

We set you apart to guide the affairs of the women, to preside over the Relief Society and young ladies association. When they come to you for advice, we bless you with wisdom and sympathy that you may give to them that which they need in order to encourage them and to strengthen them in the faith.

We bless you that you will indeed be a mother to the missionaries who are sent there. They too will need your motherly care and guidance. They will need your instruction and encouragement. They are filled with doubt sometimes. May you get close to them and be a source of strength to those young men who will now be sent to represent the Lord in that mission.

These blessings with others that you have in your heart that you feel will be needful and helpful to you in learning the language, in speaking it, in having increased ability to speak fluently and to the comfort and encouragement and satisfaction of your audiences always—all these we seal upon you through your faithfulness in the name of the Lord Jesus Christ, Amen.

Approved: David O. McKay

It was late afternoon on Wednesday, July 23, 1947, by the time we packed our car and departed Salt Lake City. Mona and a few others went with us as far as the "This is the Place" monument, which was covered over with sheets to be unveiled the following day. We said our goodbyes and were off. Leaving like this meant that we would miss the big day of the celebration.

We expected to drive only a few hours and then check into a motel, but soon realized the futility of this plan after finding only no vacancy signs on all the motels between Salt Lake City and Laramie, Wyoming. It was morning when we reached Laramie, so we continued driving all day and spent the night in Nebraska. We tried to spell each other off, but it only afforded us catnaps.

We followed the Lincoln Highway to Chicago, driving as far each day as possible. We got a chance to drive on the Pennsylvania Turnpike, the first time I had seen such a highway. While in Pennsylvania we took a wrong turn and followed the Susquehanna River several miles toward the place where the Aaronic Priesthood had been restored before we realized our error. However, time did not permit us to continue to this hallowed spot.

We arrived in New York City late Sunday evening, July 27, four days after leaving Salt Lake City; we claimed our reservations at the McAlpin Hotel (Broadway at 34th Street) and delivered our car to the bellhop for storage, in preparation for its shipment to Uruguay.

Monday morning we contacted our former Argentine missionary, R. Glen Brewer, who was to handle the customs brokerage on our equipment and supplies. We also saw the agents for our ship, who advised us that it was being loaded and would leave whenever that operation was completed, with only a three-hour notice given. We should, therefore, call the agent's office every three hours unless we were at a location where we could be reached by telephone.

After taking care of all details pursuant to our sailing, we relaxed and enjoyed New York: Radio City Music Hall, the top of the Empire State building; seeing *"Oklahoma!"* on stage. We also visited the Statue of Liberty and rode the ferry; and we kept in constant touch with the steamship agency.

When it became apparent that there would be a delay, we also tried to visit the Hill Cumorah.

After all, we had a new car and, apparently, time on our hands. The agents wouldn't hear of it and assured us the ship would leave without us. So near, and yet so far from Palmyra.

On Thursday, July 31, we were notified that the ship was still being loaded, but that it was in Philadelphia and would not be returning to New York. It would sail from Philadelphia at six p.m. on August 1, and we would need to transfer all our baggage and equipment to that city. Between trunks, boxes and cases this was quite a job: seventeen altogether.

We left New York by train a little before noon on August 1, and upon arriving in Philadelphia went immediately to the port to find our ship. We were dismayed at its size. The S.S. *California Express*, a refrigerator ship of Norwegian registry and crew, had a miniscule three thousand-ton capacity.

We left our suitcases in the three staterooms assigned to us, hired a taxi and went to see what we could of Philadelphia. Our Negro driver had been stationed at Fort Huachuca, Arizona, while in the service, and when he learned that we were from Arizona, exerted himself to make our visit memorable and informative. We enjoyed seeing Independence Hall, the Betsy Ross house, and other historical places.

We returned to port at five p.m. in time for the six o'clock sailing, but were surprised and not a little concerned to see our ship leaning heavily against the dock. We made our way up the gangplank and inched along sideways through the companionway toward our cabins. The ship was listing at a thirty-degree angle, and we had to keep our hands against the lower wall of the companionway to remain upright. The staterooms were a mess. Our trunks had all fallen over; suitcases, boxes and other loose gear all rested against the walls of the cabins in a jumble.

We asked the crew the cause of this unseemly position for an ocean-going ship, and were told that the fuel tanks on one side of the ship were empty and somehow it had lost its balance, but that it would shortly be righted. It would not be ready to sail that evening, however. We seemed to be playing the Army's favorite game: hurry up, then wait.

While in Philadelphia I bought the evening paper and was grieved and disappointed to read that my friend, the recently-inaugurated President of Uruguay, Tomás Berreta, had died in Montevideo of cancer that day. I had planned to call on him upon arriving in Uruguay.

We spent an uncomfortable night trying to sleep and had to place pillows against the bunk railings to keep from rolling to the floor. The following day the ship was righted to some extent and we sailed at seven p.m. on August 2, 1947, with the ship listing only fifteen degrees.

The twelve passengers and crew sat sideways at the tables in the dining room; each had to brace his feet so he would not slide off his chair. It was strange to see dishes slowly sliding off the table; we had to maintain constant vigilance. Our list continued for almost a week, until we reached Trinidad where the ship was fueled to capacity, whereupon it righted itself completely and thereafter remained on an even keel.

Trinidad was our only stop between Philadelphia and Buenos Aires. We were carrying a shipment of seed potatoes for the Argentine government and it was urgent that they arrive in time for the spring planting. The ship traveled at full speed the entire trip.

The crew was very friendly. All spoke English, and they did what they could to make us comfortable, with one exception. The faucet in our stateroom broke and we couldn't turn off the cold water. We reported it immediately but it took the crew twenty-four hours to fix it. In the meantime it depleted the ship's fresh water supply so badly that we could only shower in sea water for the balance of the trip.

The passengers had the run of the ship, but it was dangerous to go on deck. The ship was so small and the deck so close to the sea that whenever we went outside we invariably received a seawater shower from the waves washing over the deck.

We also encountered some rough weather and high seas. It soon became too rough for me and I took to my bunk to keep from getting seasick. I read in my bunk for two days and missed the captain's dinner. I knew what would have happened had I remained on my feet: I would have made my contribution to the dinner. All of the passengers were present at the captain's dinner to begin with, except me; but one by one they excused themselves before finishing dinner; only Barbara and the captain completed the meal.

I was never too fond of fish, even the kind I liked most. On this ship we were served fish I had never even heard of; fish cooked in every conceivable manner, from caviar to you-name-it. It was served for all meals, but thankfully other foods were also offered.

On Monday, August 25, we entered the harbor at Buenos Aires. This in itself was an achievement. The harbor was clogged with ships, some of which had been waiting for more than ninety days to unload. The post-War flow of goods was arriving from many countries and each ship had to wait its turn to be unloaded. However, we were carrying a priority cargo. and a still-unloaded freighter was pulled from the dock to permit us to tie up.

We went to the Continental Hotel, called President and Sister W. Ernest Young of the Argentine Mission, and tried to adjust our sea legs to the solid earth once more. The Youngs came to visit us at our hotel. Alice Banks called her parents in Montevideo and made arrangements to fly there the next morning.

On Wednesday we attended a district meeting with the missionaries of the Argentine Mission. It was good to get back into this atmosphere. Then and in subsequent meetings, President Young pledged every support possible to help us get started in Uruguay. Many elders expressed their desire to come and help us, each wanting to be first in a new mission.

Friday evening, the 29th, we sailed for Montevideo on the *General Artigas*, one of the night boats of the Dodero Company, and arrived in Montevideo at seven a.m.

NOTES

Chapter I

1. J. Reuben Clark, Jr., was named by President Herbert Hoover to be Ambassador of the United States of America to México where he served from October 3, 1930, until March 3, 1933. Just over a month after he resigned, he was sustained as Second Counselor in the First Presidency of the Church. But his service on behalf of the United States Government was not at an end. President Franklin D. Roosevelt appointed him to several committees and named him the United States delegate to the Seventh International Conference of American States at Montevideo, Uruguay. It was while traveling in that capacity that he visited with the Saints across the river in Argentina. See David H. Yarn, Jr., "Biograhical Sketch of J. Reuben Clark, Jr.," Vol. 13, *BYU Studies* (Spring 1973), p. 241.

The MS. "History of the South American Missions 1925-1935," on file with the Historical Department of The Church of Jesus Christ Latter-day Saints, records that on December 28, 1933, "President J. Reuben Clark of the First Presidency arrived at Buenos Aires on the S.S. *Southern Cross*, coming from Montevideo, capital of Uruguay, where he had been laboring as a United States delegate to the Pan-American Conference. The following day, in the morning, he had a conversation with Elder Reinhold Stoof concerning the conditions of the Mission. During the evening of the same day President Clark spoke in a special meeting in the Liniers hall before 60 present. He encouraged the saints to live according to the commandments of the Lord that they might receive the promised blessings. His sermon, given in English, was translated into Spanish by Elder Marden D. Kimball. After the meeting President Clark shook hands with all present. On the following day the missionaries met in the room of President Clark in the City Hotel and embarked on the S.S. *Southern Cross* at noon for Rio de Janeiro."

2. J. Reuben Clark, Jr., had been sustained as a member of the Council of the Twelve and also as First Counselor in the First Presidency at the October, 1934 General Conference, following the death of Anthon W. Ivins. David O. McKay was sustained as Second Counselor at the same time. See Report of the 150th Semi-Annual *Conference* of the Church of Jesus Christ of Latter-day Saints, October 5, 6, 7, 1934, p.1.

3. Unfortunately, I do not have a copy in my possession and am relying on my memory.

4. Telegram in possession of Frederick S. Williams.

5. *Church News* section of the *Deseret News*, Vol. 6, No. 20, May 17, 1947.

6. Letter to the First Presidency dated from South Gate, California, May 27, 1947, a copy of which is in my personal files.

Place where South American Mission was dedicated. *(l.to r.):* Reinhold Stoof, Ella Stoof, Melvin J. Ballard, Rey L. Pratt, J. Vernon Sharp. Photo by Waldo I. Stoddard.

Elders Melvin J. Ballard and Rey L. Pratt. Buenos Aires, 1926.

Reinhold and Ella Stoof at Salt Lake Temple, about May, 1926.

Frederick S. Williams. 1928.

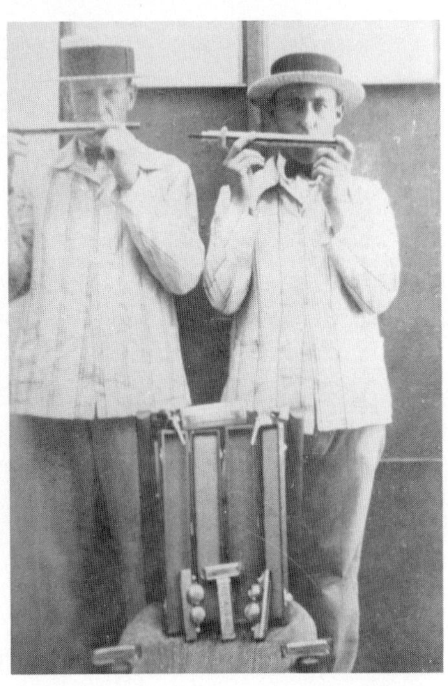

Elders Frederick S. Williams and Paul W. Davis. 1927.

South American Mission Force, August 1927. *Seated (l. to r.):* I. Russell Spencer, Frederick S. Williams, Douglas B. Merrill, Paul W. Davis, Lewis E. Christian, Waldo I. Stoddard. *Standing (l. to r.):* Ella Stoof, Pres. Reinhold Stoof, Jewel C. Jensen, Heber C. Clegg, William F. Heinz.

Entire membership of the Church at baptism of first Latin member, Eladia Sifuentes, 15 June, 1926. *(l. to r.):* Eladia Sifuentes, Ana Kullick, María Bieberstorf *(holding baby),* Ernst Bieberstorf, Domingo Quici, Emilia Gianfelice, Pres. R. Stoof, Elizabeth Plassman, Nicolás Lafrata *(son of Sis. Gianfelice),* Rogelia Morales, Elder Wlado I. Stoddard, William Friedricks, Emile Hoppe. *Children standing in line (l. to r.):* Meta Bieberstorf, Juanita Gianfelice, Antonio Gianfelice, G. Emil Hoppe. Photo taken by Elder J. Vernon Sharp.

President Stoof visiting Chaco Indians, May 1927. Indian chief, second from left. This was the first attempt to proselyte among the Lamanites in the South American Mission. Photo by Waldo I. Stoddard.

The W. Ernest Young Family. *(l. to r):* Carl, Amy, Cecile, W. Ernest and Walter.

The Frederick S. Williams Family, 1942. *(l. to r.):* Barbara L., Frederick S., Frederick G., Corraine S. with baby Nancy L., and Argina.

Presidents of the three Spanish language missions of the Church, at El Paso, Texas, July 1938, with Elder Melvin J. Ballard in front of the first chapel built for the Spanish-speaking people in the United States. *(l. to r):* Elder Ballard, President and Sister Lorenzo Anderson (Mexico), President and Sister Orlando C. Williams (Spanish-American, at El Paso), President and Sister Frederick S. Williams (Argentina).

First all-member Presidency of Liniers Branch: Donato Gianfelice, 1st Counselor, Pedro Cedolín, President, Alfonso Guillamón, 2nd Counselor.

Fermín Barjollo, from Rosario.

Argault Family with President Williams in Neuquén.

Relief Society Bazaar, Liniers Chapel, 1939.

Casa Rosada, in Plaza de Mayo, in late 1920. The building is the "White House" of Argentina.

Sports — Newspaper coverage of *"Los Mormones."*

"Hill Billy Boys" Orchestra. *Front row (l. to r.):* Dale Gardner, Phil Davis, Gerald McQuarrie, saxophones; Robert Sorensen, accordion; Grant Thomas, piano. *Back row (l. to r.):* Donald Brown, drums; Hugo Jenkins, trumpet.

Liniers chapel, the first constructed in South America by the Church. Dedicated April 9, 1939.

Dedication of Liniers chapel, April 9, 1939. *(l. to r.):* Donato Gianfelice *(seated). Standing:* Roland Kaiser, Elder Marden Duke, Elder Harold Brown, Elder Darrel Taylor, President Frederick S. Williams, Elder Ernest Wilkins, Elder Rolf Larson, Elder Ben R. Allen, Sister Williams, Elder James Jesperson, Elder J. Donal Earl. *Seated:* Teresa Brandi.

The sinking of the German battleship *Graf Spee,* outside of Montevideo harbor, mid-December, 1939. The ship was scuttled by order of its captain.

Mission Team in 1st Division of Argentine Basket Ball Federation, 1939. *(l. to r.) Front Row:* Ben Allen, J. Donal Earl, Ivan Hatch, Samuel Borén, Max Willis. *Back Row:* Pres. Frederick S. Williams (Coach), Riley Goodfellow, Rolf L. Larson, Dale Bergeson, Dwight Dana, Juan Borén.

National Champions, 1st Division Argentine Base Ball League, 1939. *(l. to r.) First Row:* Pres. Frederick S. Williams, Richard J. McBride, Max Willis, Dwight Dana, J. Donal Earl. *Back Row:* Dale Bergeson, James Jesperson, John H. Meyers, Jesse Smith, Ben Allen, Ivan Hatch, Marion Vance, Rolf L. Larson.

Liniers chapel. Congregation present at dedication service, April 9, 1939.

Mothers and Daughters banquet. Liniers chapel. 1940.

Argentine Mission Office Staff. *(l. to r.) Standing:* Eurídice Turano, Elder Wayne Fronk, Greta Shimkat. *Seated:* Elders Grant Thomas and Kay Schwendiman.

Missionary Force of the Argentine Mission, October 1938.

(l. to r.) 1st row: Samuel J. Skousen, Roy A. Watson, Clyde M. Edmonds, Pershing L. Farnsworth, Richard McBride, Ernest J. Wilkins, O. Clement Williams. *2nd row:* Boyd Cheney, Argina Williams, Corraine S. Williams, Pres. Frederick S. Williams, La Prile B. Mitchell, Edgar B. Mitchell, Ivan E. Hatch, Barbara Williams. *3rd row:* Reed J. Chalk, Gerald O. Lynn, Paul Lloyd, Ben E. Clark, Lyman S. Shreeve, James A. Petrie, Jr., Dale Bergeson, Robert T. Standing, A. Marden Duke, L. Peirce Brady, Marion I. Vance, Morris E. Nelson, Orson H. Asay, Jesse B. Smith, Verden E. Bettilyon, Claude W. Stuart, Oren E. Moffett, J. Donal Earl. *4th row:* James A. Mortensen, Ben R. Allen, Rulon J. Holman, Willard I. Skousen, H. Darrell Taylor, Jesse L. Allen, Don H. Smith, Alma V. Whipple, James A. Jesperson, Max L. Willis, Harold Brown, Rulon M. Moon, Lavon H. Flake, Karl R. Fenn, Rolf L. Larson, Junius L. Payne, George Brinton, Henry R. Lunt.

Left: Arrival in Montevideo of Elder and Mrs. Stephen L. Richards, and President and Mrs. Frederick S. Williams from Buenos Aires on night boat.
Above: Dr. Gerritt de Jong, Jr., Corraine S. Williams, Carma de Jong and President Frederick S. Williams in front of the Uruguayan Mission Home, 1948.

The Williams Trio at the *Alianza Cultural,* in Montevideo, c. 1950. *(l. to r.):* Barbara, Corraine S., Argina.

Frederick S. and Corraine S. Williams, with Sister Leanore and Pres. Harold Brown, of the Argentine Mission. Buenos Aires, 1949.

Dedication of land for construction of first health center, 24 February 1945, in Montevideo. Speaking, Luis Mattiauda, Minister of Public Health. Present was Dr. Juan José Amézaga, President of Uruguay, U.S. Ambassador William Dawson, Dr. Fabini, Mayor of Montevideo, A. J. Kranaskas, acting chief of the U.S. Field party, Frederick S. Williams, Business Manager, Institute of Inter-American Affairs.

First Mission Home of the Uruguayan Mission owned by the Church. Brito del Pino 1525, Montevideo.

Queens of the first *Green and Gold Ball,* at the *Centro Yugoeslavo.* 1948.

Sister Juana Gianfelice *(left),* from Argentina, taking Eduarda Argault's place as she was released as a missionary. 1949.

Arrival to Buenos Aires of the Barkers to assume the Mission presidency, July 27, 1942. *(l. to r.):* Sister Kate M. and President James L. Barker, Sister Corraine S. and President Frederick S. Williams.

First Uruguayan Mission Presidency. *(l. to r.) Standing:* Wilford M. Farnsworth, 1st Counselor; Bryon Palmer, Secretary. *Seated:* Frederick S. Williams, President; Dr. Junius Gibbons, 2nd Counselor. Organized November 1, 1950.

The Williams Family. *(l. to r.):* Corraine S., with Mary Corraine, Frederick S., Frederick G., Nancy Lou, Argina, Barbara Lynn. Montevideo, March 1950.

Reducto Branch Elders *(l. to r.):* Dene Ogden, Donald B. Cox, Stewart D. Burton, Juan D. Sciorra.

La Comercial Branch Elders *(l. to r.):* J. Fred Bushnell, Arvil A. Harris, Russell W. Janson, Thaddeus E. Shoemaker, Galen A. Bigler.

Malvín Branch Elders *(l. to r.):* William N. Jones, Melvin Brady, Terry C. Smith, Kay W. Young, L. Cecil Millet, Gerald Nielsen.

Arroyo Seco Branch *(l. to r.):* John W. Cook, Preston J. Bushman, Arthur Smith, Lee O. Squire, Robert N. Nelson, Franklin D. Richards, Jr.

Uruguayan Mission Choir members at Mission Home, prior to taking bus for a singing engagement.

Group baptism at the "terreno" baptismal font in Montevideo.

First Uruguayan convert baptisms *(l. to r.)*: President Williams, María Esther Rodríguez, Avelino Rodríguez, Diber Preciozi, Elder Preston Bushman, Jr.

First chapel in Isla Patrulla, Uruguay. Elders Elwin T Christensen and L. Cecil Millet.

Lady Missionary Force, February 1951. *(l. to r.)*: Mersel Day, María Aguilera, Velora Gaugh, Kathryn Hacket, Yolanda Vinci, La Von Evans.

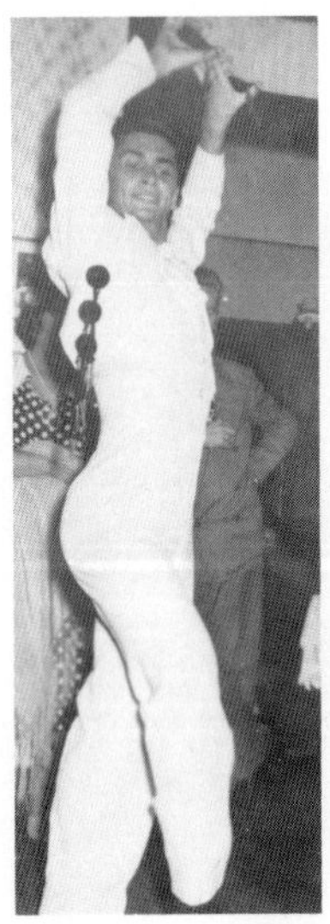

Elder Roy Fitzell dancing *"Malagueña."*

First Uruguayan Mission Quartet. *(l. to r.)*: Glen L. Slight, Vernon L. Melander, Maughan W. McMurdie (accompanist), Dallas Keller, Wayne R. Cardon.

Missionary conference of all Uruguayan missionaries (December 1947), assembled on roof of Mission Home.

Uruguayan Mission Choir. *(l. to r.) Front Row:* Jim Gibbons, Perla Fazio, Unidentified Member, Edith Pokorny, Diber Preciozi, Blanca Nieves, Argina Williams, Barbara L. Williams, Corraine S. Williams, Marta Canals, Sonia Aulisso, Renée Ramírez, Elsa Nieves, Susana Orsan, Unidentified Member, Frederick G. Williams. *Second Row:* President Frederick S. Williams, Preston J. Bushman, Wilford M. Hale, Robert L. Marsh, Norval C. Jesperson, Max H. Garrett, Russell W. Janson, Alton Sorensen, Jr., James R. Dale, Glenn Slight. *Third Row:* Wayne R. Cardon, Keith J. Chapman, Oscar Nieves, Dallas Keller, Maughan W. McMurdie, Vernon L. Melander, Jewel F. Bushnell, B. LaMar Williams, Unidentified Member.

Missionaries, visitors, friends and investigators gathering in front of first meeting place, Mayor Bullo Street No. 157, for Clara Krish's baptism. January 13, 1951.

Clara Krish, first baptism after the work officially opened in Asunción, Paraguay.

Mission Trio at radio station in Asunción, Paraguay, June 1950. Elder Glen Slight, Sister Corrain S. Williams, and Elder Dallas Keller, with Elder Maughan McMurdie at the piano.

Section of the basketball stadium in São Paulo, when the University of Utah Basket Ball Team toured Brazil in 1949.

Elders Roland Minson and Harold Christensen holding Brazilian Flag at BYU game, 1950.

Arrival of the BYU Basket Ball Team in São Paulo Airport, June 10, 1950.

Missionary Octet singing the American and Brazilian National Anthems prior to basketball game. They also entertained during half-time rest period. *(l. to r.) Front Row*: Elder Harry Maxwell, Elder Orlin Johnson, Elder Winegar, Elder Warren Anderson, Elder Lloyd Stevens. *Back Row:* Elder Richard Fowles, Elder Raymond Maxwell, Elder Henry Goldsmith.

President Rulon S. Howells with first group of missionaries in the Brazilian Mission, taken in Joinville, Santa Catarina, May 1935. *(l. to r.) Front Row:* Elder Paul Stohl, Pres. Rulon S. Howells, Elders Emil Schindley and Merlin Palmer, all from Salt Lake City, Utah. *Back Row:* Elder Melvin Cannon (Salt Lake City, Utah), Elder Patterson (Arizona), Elder Reed Bayles (Blanding, Utah), Elder Harlan Smith (Idaho Falls, Idaho), and Elder Henry Hunger (Salt Lake City).

Brazilian Mission missionary conference, directed by President and Sister Rulon S. Howells and held in May, 1950, in São Paulo.

President and Sister J. Alder Bowers of the Brazilian Mission, after visit to Argentina. Pres. and Sister Williams bidding them farewell.

First Mission Home purchased in Brazil. Rua Itapeva 378, São Paulo.

BYU Basket Ball Team that toured Brazil in 1950.

First presidency of the Lima Branch, July 1956. *(l. to r.)*: Frederick G. Williams, Clerk, Stanley A. Moore, 1st Counselor, Frederick S. Williams, President, Col. Charles H. Shaw, 2nd Counselor.

Mel Hutchins demonstrating his ability.

President Rulon S. Howells, Sister Mary P. Howells with daughters L. Marian and R. Dorothy. Brazil, 1952.

Elder and Sister Spencer W. Kimball's arrival for first visit to Cuzco, Perú, with Pres. and Sis. Arthur Jensen, of the Uruguayan Mission, and Bro. and Sis. Frederick S. Williams. 1958.

16-inch, 2 1/2 lbs. gold Tumi from the Peruvian National Museum. Photograph by Elder Milton R. Hunter, of the First Council of Seventy.

Dedication of the Toquepala chapel, Southern Perú, 1958. *(l. to r.):* President and Sister Arthur Jensen, Elder and Sister Spencer W. Kimball, Brother and Sister Frederick S. Williams.

Original chapel of the Lima, Perú Branch (1210 Avenida Orrantia, San Isidro), purchased in 1956; now Mission Home of the Lima South Mission. Photo by Charles H. Shaw.

Lima Branch Sunday School, early 1957. *Adults:* Sis. Leighton, Shaw girl, Nancy Shaw, Beatrice Shaw, Nancy L. Williams, Loriol Allred, Edna Moore, Elder Paul R. Gardner, Frederick S. Williams, Elder Dee A. Hall, Stanley Moore, Elder Monte McLaws, Elder Sheryl plowman, Henry Leighton (pilot baptized by Frederick S. Williams the same day as Mary Williams). *Children:* — Leighton, Mary Williams, unidentified child, — Allred, — Allred, — Allred, Richard Moore, — Moore, Diane Moore, "Pichuca" Moore. Photo by Charles H. Shaw.

CHAPTER II

URUGUAY: THE FAVORABLE RELATIONSHIP BETWEEN CHURCH AND STATE

I FELL IN LOVE with Uruguay on my first visit in 1927. The people were open and friendly and they seemed to be genuinely happy. However, not until I had lived and worked there in government service and learned a little about its history and culture, did I know what made the difference.

What is today Uruguay, known traditionally as *La Banda Oriental* (the East Bank of the River), remained free of Spanish domination for almost two hundred years after the initial establishment of Buenos Aires in 1535. This was due in part to the fierce Charrúa Indians living there, who defended their coasts from any and all intruders, something the first explorers, under Juan Díaz de Solís, learned to their sorrow. After discovering the estuary of the River Plate in 1516, they decided to capture some of the Uruguayan Indians and take them back to Spain. The landing party was ambushed and all except one man was killed. That man, severely wounded, was kept a prisoner and in later years served as an interpreter for later would-be colonists who tried to deal with the Charrúa, Chana and Guaraní Indians.

The Portuguese established the first white settlement in Uruguay in 1680 directly across the river from Buenos Aires and called it Colonia. Spain, wishing to check Portuguese expansion, determined to establish its own settlement downriver, and in 1726 founded Montevideo. For the next hundred years, Uruguay served as a battle zone between Spain and Portugal with first one claiming the territory and then the other. In 1777 Spanish troops attacked Colonia and drove the Portuguese out of Uruguay. In 1806 and again in 1807 Montevideo was invaded and captured by the English and then used as a base of operations agaist Spanish forces in Argentina. The British were defeated in Argentina and then withdrew from Uruguay.

Occupying an area the size of Kansas, by 1810 Uruguay had a population of fewer than 40,000, nearly half were living in Montevideo with the rest scattered in small villages throughout the country. The fighting had developed a sense of their own political identity: they were not Spanish, they were not Portuguese, they weren't Argentine. The revolution that would ultimately free them from Spain began with "El Grito de Asencio" on February 28, 1811. An army of more than one hundred gauchos from Uruguay defeated the Spanish forces under José Maldonado on the shores of the Soriano wash. Most of the defeated soldiers joined the patriots after the battle. Eventually, the most powerful and most popular gaucho leader, José Gervacio Artigas, was named commander in chief of the Uruguayan forces. By 1820 he had nearly driven the Spanish out when Portuguese troops from Brazil invaded, defeating the Spanish and Uruguayan armies, and driving Artigas and thousands of his followers into exile in Paraguay. Men, women, children, with their slaves, Indians, horses, and cattle, abandoned their homes and their possessions and with great difficulty made their way across the Uruguay River into Paraguay. When Brazil became independent of Portugal, Uruguay remained a part of Brazil, but the exiled Uruguayans joined the United Provinces of the South and their combined armies defeated the Brazilians in 1825. Not wishing to remain subject to Argentina, they declared themselves an independent nation in 1828. It became a reality because England facilitated its creation and guaranteed its sovereignty as a buffer nation between Argentina and Brazil. It took a long time, however, to form a cohesive country. For the next hundred years there was rivalry between two political parties, the Colorados (Reds) and Blancos (Whites). Their differences resulted in many civil wars.

The modern, enlightened period of Uruguayan history began with the election of José Batlle y Ordóñez in 1903. He envisioned a true democracy patterned after the Swiss government. He was re-elected in 1911 and served until 1915. During his second term he sponsored legislation separating church from state. He, and many like him, were unhappy with the politics of the Roman Catholic Church which, according to the constitution of 1830, was designated the country's official church. Unfortunately, the church did not confine its activities to religious matters but dominated politics, even as it had before Uruguay became a nation. It had always supported the imperial power of Spain and was against the independence of all the Spanish-American nations in their struggle to become free. Over the years, it had become the largest landowner in Uruguay. It controlled the cemeteries and would only permit the burial of "approved" people.

A case in point involved the burial of a Freemason who had advocated the separation of church and state. Upon this man's death, the Church forbade his burial in Montevideo. Embalming did not exist and the law stated that the deceased had to be buried within twenty-four hours. His body was taken to several cemeteries outside of Montevideo, but word was always sent ahead to prohibit his interment. Finally, those who were escorting the body stated their intention to take him to a nearby city, but instead, went elsewhere and buried him before the ecclesiastical authorities could notify the cemetery of his coming.

When he learned of this, President Batlle y Ordóñez was furious. Under his sponsorship laws were soon enacted that limited the power of the church. All connection with the government was severed, its property was confiscated, and cemeteries were placed under civil control. Even the names of religious holidays were changed and remain changed to this day. Officially, Christmas is called Children's Day; Holy Week appears on the calendars as Tourist Week. The Day of the Dead is The Day of the Beaches, and so on. The official government newspaper (of the Colorado party), *El Día*, began writing the name of deity with small letters, and still does.

Eventually, much of the church's property was returned to it, but it became just another church in that country with no special privileges. It became popular to call oneself an atheist as a sign of protest against the excesses of the Catholic Church. President Batlle y Ordóñez himself may have started the trend, for he had said "If Catholicism is religion, then I'm an atheist." Years later, our missionaries found many people who still adopted that stance. While tracting the missionaries were often met at the door with: "No thank you; we're atheists, thank God." Thousands of those self-proclaimed "atheists" are now members of our Church.

In February 1947, when Elder Stephen L. Richards of the Council of the Twelve visited our new mission, I asked an *El Día* reporter (with whom I had worked my first time in Uruguay) to help publicize the visit. He readily agreed and started making notes. Finally, he asked what Elder Richards' occupation was. When I explained that he was one of the General Authorities of our Church, the reporter laid his pencil down and said he couldn't do anything for me. He explained, "If he were a carpenter, a painter or a bricklayer I would be happy to write an article and give him all the publicity he wants, but since he is a religious man, Batlle y Ordóñez would turn over in his grave if I wrote about him." There were other newspapers, of course, that were not opposed to printing religious news.

The major Catholic newspaper of Montevideo had a running battle with *El Día*. The religious paper would make a claim, and the next day *El Día* would refute it. I subscribed to *El Día*, not only for the international and national news but to keep abreast of the contest. I remember one such exchange; the Catholic paper had stated that the Catholic Church had not been against the independence movement in Uruguay, and to support its position, stated that Larrañaga, a Catholic priest, was the secretary of the committee for independence. *El Día* answered, with Dr. Celedonio Nin y Silva writing the rebuttal. Dr. Nin y Silva said the church was a little forgetful concerning its history. He admitted that Larrañaga was a priest, but pointed out that he acted more as patriot than as priest. He also chided the Catholic paper for not mentioning that Larrañaga had been excommunicated for his participation in the independence movement, and that a reward had been offered for his capture. Dr. Nin y Silva went on to discuss the "fanciful" history the Church was wont to publish as fact; one instance was an "eyewitness" account of Pope Pius IX's entrance into heaven:

> *Pius IX entered Paradise immediately after his death, and was received there with exceptional honors. The Virgin Mary, who owed him the definition of the Immaculate Conception, personally gave him a crown as a reward for what he had done for her during his time on earth. Probably St. Anne also gave him another precious gift, since she owed him no less appreciation, since she became purified from the original sin through the Dogma of 1854; but we don't know exactly what that gift was. To the contrary, it is positive that St. Joseph went out to meet Pius IX, and cordially extended his hand and thanked him for having named him Protector and Patron Saint of the Church. A hymn of welcome was sung by the inhabitants of that celestial realm, St. Peter giving the pitch by blowing on his key.*[1]

Dr. Nin y Silva finished his article by saying: "This is the kind of history the Catholic Church likes."

Without realizing it, the Catholic Church was a positive force in helping us establish the work in many cities of Uruguay. Whenever we were ready to open a new branch, we would widely advertise the first meeting. Almost invariably, the local priests would begin to warn their congregations against us and urge them not to attend, saying the Latter-day Saint Church was evil and its missionaries were wicked. In many instances local people had received our handbills inviting them to attend, but had discarded them with no intention of going until they heard the priests condemn us, and then out of curiosity came to hear what we had to say. The details surrounding a special program held in Durazno were reported by me to the First Presidency in a letter dated August 27, 1949:

> *On the 5th of August our mission through its chorus and special numbers presented a two hour musical program in the city of Durazno which was attended by more than 700 people. The movie theater in which it was presented was filled to capacity.*

We owe a debt of gratitude to the Catholic church of Durazno for their help. They had paid announcements read over the radio telling their members they could not attend our program. The radio announcer, a friend of ours, followed the paid announcement with one of his own, urging the people to attend. He gave two of our announcements free for every one of the paid announcements he read.

They also printed handbills and passed them out from door to door and at the entrance of the theater, advising the people not to attend. The young Catholics who were giving them out at the theater finally became so curious that they tore up the handbills and went in themselves. The Catholic priest rode up and down the street on his bicycle to see who went in.

He created so much interest in the concert that more than 1,000 would have attended had there been room for that number. The local newspaper pointed out how "ridiculous" the Catholics had made themselves by "trying with all the means at their command to keep people away from the cultural program presented by the young North Americans who have been working among us for the past year."

We have noticed that in every town where the Catholic Church has actively worked against us, we have had the most success. We feel honored to have them talk against us on the radio, dedicate masses to us, or to write articles against us in their papers.

Their approach is always the same. They prohibit their members from accepting or reading our tracts; they must not talk with the missionaries or enter our locales. They use the same tactics as they did during the dark ages when they could enforce their will.

The Uruguayans are far too educated to accept such nonsense. They can't be told what to do or what not to do. They are free people living in a democracy in which the Catholic Church has no official voice, and such high-handed methods only create interest and curiosity enough to find out why their Church does not want them to come in contact with the missionaries. We appreciate their collaboration.[2]

One investigator was a close friend of some priests. He told me their reaction to the rapid expansion of the Uruguayan Mission. He said they told him we had used very good psychology by opening in so many cities all at once. "They hit Montevideo like an atomic bomb and spread all over," he reported them as saying. The investigator told me what the priests' intentions were to thwart our work. I am sure he also told his friends what I said we would or would not do. As far as I know, he was never baptized into our Church. He did, however, seem to serve a good purpose.

Let me reiterate the favorable situation the Uruguayans enjoyed with the separation of church and state by comparing the plight of the Argentines and Paraguayans. In Argentina, the Catholic Church controlled the charitable organizations and in the smaller cities, the hospitals as well. When the priests learned which people were investigating the Church and attending our meetings, they would apply pressure against them: sometimes they would be denied medical attention; in other cases, husbands or sons were fired from their jobs: such was the power of the clergy. We found the same situation in Asunción, Paraguay. Our branch started out with many investigators who enthusiastically attended the meetings, filling the chapel to overflowing. Soon the priests organized a religious procession each Sunday, which coincided with our meeting time. Throngs of Catholic faithful gathered behind wood and plaster Virgins to march along Avenida Mariscal López, the main street, just a block from our chapel. The first Sunday's march didn't seem to have the desired effect so thereafter the procession made a right turn on our street and marched in front of the chapel during our meeting. Their chants were so loud that we couldn't continue our service and had to pause while they slowly made their way down the street. After making the detour past our door, the procession returned to the main street. To further hinder our work they sent spies to see who was attending our meetings and wrote down their names. The priests would then go to those homes and with veiled and not so veiled threats urge the people not to return to our meetings. Many, through fear of losing their jobs or of not receiving medical attention, stopped coming.

These depressing actions created a negative spirit among many of the Argentines and Paraguayans. They weren't as open and happy as the Uruguayans who were free to say and do whatever they wanted. I am confident that the different mood found in Uruguay was the result of true freedom of religion; it was a joy to work there.

NOTES

Chapter II

1. The above "history" was taken from his own book *Historia Política de los Papas Desde La Revolución Francesa a Nuestros Días,* Part I, (Montevideo: Editorial Independencia, 1943), p. 92. Footnote.

2. A copy of the letter is in my possession. On September 9, 1949, I was gratified to receive a letter from the First Presidency in which they told me they had read the letter to the Council of the Twelve:

". . . in order that they might hear of the success that is accompanying your activities and of the boomerang which was turned upon the Catholic Church officials who tried to keep people away from your meetings. The Brethren of course were interested and gratified at the success which has attended your efforts. Their prayers are that the Lord will continue to be with you, as we are sure he has been in the past and will be in the future if the elders continue faithful in their work.

. . . .

(signed) Faithfully yours,
Geo. Albert Smith
J. Reuben Clark, Jr.
David O. McKay
The First Presidency"

CHAPTER III

A NEW FIELD: STARTING FROM SCRATCH

URUGUAY BEGAN as an independent mission and, except for a brief period during World War II, never came under the jurisdiction of any other. During the War, I was set apart as President of the Montevideo Branch, organized June 25, 1944, at the direction of the Argentine Mission President. The branch had been organized to fill the needs of a few Latter-day Saint members, most of whom were Americans working for the U.S. Government, it was not as a proselyting assignment, although we did try to interest our friends and associates and usually did have a few non-members present at some of our activities.[1] We knew that as soon as the War was over, the branch would be disbanded because of lack of personnel. However, a year and half after leaving Montevideo, we were privileged to return and open the Uruguayan Mission.

We arrived in Montevideo on Saturday, August 30, 1947, with seventeen trunks and cases of supplies and equipment for the new mission, including a camera and other items we were fortunate to be able to take with us out of Buenos Aires, equipment which the Argentine government ordinarily prohibited from leaving the country.[2] I was surprised to see that the entire customs area was filled to overflowing with huge, precariously-piled stacks of boxes and crates. When we left Uruguay eighteen months before, the customs area had been bare. Now the fruits of the post-War buying spree had become apparent.

The customs agent began opening our boxes. We had been told that this would be a lengthy ordeal because all the contents had to be removed and examined. I happened to be carrying a *carnet* with me, an identification document with my picture on it issued to me some years before by the Uruguayan Ministry of Health. Although a representative of the United States, as a *carnet* holder I had special privileges and in fact was considered an official of the Uruguayan government. I showed it to the offical and asked him if it were still valid. *"Ya lo creo. ¿Cuáles son sus bultos?"* was his reply. (You bet it is. Which containers belong to you?) He refastened the lid on the box he had started to inspect and proceeded to stamp "Inspected" on it and all the others. In less than fifteen minutes our possessions were on a truck and we were on our way to the Florida Hotel at the corner of Mercedes and Florida streets.

Finding a mission home the first day. We knew that local banks, which were open on Saturday mornings, acted as housing rental agents. Corraine and I went to several banks to check the housing lists for possible mission home locations; we knew the city and the preferred locations. We also knew from experience how important the location of the mission headquarters can be. We noted a few possible sites (the post-War housing shortage had also hit Uruguay) and hired a taxi. We rejected the houses in the older section of town without even stopping and drove towards the *rambla* (ocean front) and then to the area near the U.S. Embassy. There, close to a lovely park, *Parque de los Aliados* (Park of the Allies) and the National Sports Stadium, stood an unfinished two-story home at 1525 and 1527 Brito del Pino, ideal for a mission home and office. Workmen were just finishing the second story. A recently opened *Organización de Alimentos* grocery store occupied one-quarter of the ground floor. Both of us felt we should get the home; we saw no point in looking further. Its location was excellent, near Avenida Rivera, one of Montevideo's main arteries; public transportation extended to Pocitos beach or to the center of town. There was also bus service right across the street.

The workmen informed us that the spacious house, which belonged to a judge of the Superior Court who lived in Paysandú, would be completed in ten days. We also learned that he was staying with his mother in Montevideo until the house was ready. We visited him immediately. His honor, Judge Evangelista Pérez de Castillo, was surprised that we had already seen the house; he had only informed the bank of its availability the night before. He explained that he had commissioned the house because he anticipated a transfer to Montevideo. When the expected change did not occur, he had been forced to rent the house. He agreed to lease it to us for two years. Because of the late hour it was impossible to close the agreement that day, but Judge Pérez de Castillo promised to call the Banco de Crédito Monday morning to advise them to lease the home to us.

The next day, Sunday, August 31, 1947, ten persons attended the first meeting of the new Uruguayan Mission in our room at the Florida Hotel. They were our family, Frederick S. Williams, Corraine S. Williams, Barbara Lynn Williams, Argina Williams, Frederick G. Williams, and Nancy Lou Williams; Colonel Samuel J. Skousen, our former Argentine missionary, now U.S. Air Attaché in Asunción, Paraguay currently in Montevideo on business; Jeanne Seguin de Argault and her daughter Eduarda Argault, both members who, along with another daughter now in Canada, had met with us in the original Montevideo branch; and Marlene Velázquez, a non-member dentist friend of several years who had also attended the earlier branch.

The meeting was conducted like a testimony meeting, each member stating his love for the gospel and happiness in being in Uruguay for the purpose of opening it up to the work of the Lord. We looked forward to thousands joining the Church. From the Uruguayan mission history comes this paragraph:

> *All expressed the conviction that it would be a fruitful field, and that there were thousands of people in this free land who would accept the Gospel. A prayer was offered in which the help of the Lord was requested to guide the destinies of a new mission, and that He would touch the hearts of the Uruguayan people and make them receptive to the Restored Gospel. The dedication of the South American countries for the preaching of the Gospel by Elder Melvin J. Ballard on December 25, 1925, in Buenos Aires, was referred to, and all expressed their joy at being present when active missionary work was to begin in this new field of labor.*[3]

Uruguayan senator aids Church. Monday, September 1, 1947, we signed for the new mission home and received the key, but still lacked the final lease papers. That evening, Corraine and I went to the *Trocadero* movie theater on Avenida 18 de Julio. We sat upstairs in our favorite area. At intermission we were delighted to find that next to us was our lawyer friend whom we had intended to contact the next day about handling the Mission's legal affairs. Dr. Conrado H. Hughes, who had worked with our field party with the Institute, was one of the most influential lawyers and senators of Uruguay. He not only agreed to see to all legal aspects of establishing the mission, but had the document granting me power of attorney to act for the Church translated, legalized and registered at no cost to me or the Church. He told me that any church-owned property used for religious purposes was constitutionally tax-exempt. He also expressed his feelings about the Church entering Uruguay, which I quoted in a letter to the First Presidency:

> *I'm very happy to see your church come down here and work for the improvement of moral conditions among us, although I do not agree with all of your doctrines. I am a Catholic, although not a very good one. You can count on my help for anything I can do for you.*[4]

The same letter contained a description of our new mission home:

> *The day that we arrived we went house hunting and found an ideal house for a Mission Home and office. It consists of a living room, dining room, large modern kitchen (a novelty in these countries), a foyer, four bedrooms and three bathrooms on the second floor. The first floor is composed of hall (intended for some business or store) which we use as offices, lots of storage space, two bedrooms for missionaries, two bathrooms and a garage. There is steam heat upstairs, a connecting stairway from the living quarters to the office, and a small plot of land in the rear for a garden. If we were to build a Mission Home and office it couldn't be more ideal.*
>
> *When one takes into consideration that there is almost as great a scarcity of houses in Montevideo as there is in the states, we feel that we are very fortunate indeed. This house was listed for rent the day that we arrived and we went to it first. We later checked all other rentals and have not found anything suitable. We feel we were guided to it.*[5]

I have mentioned that Alice Banks had been my secretary when I was with the Institute of Inter-American Affairs. Through her I came to know her father, Cirilo Banks, very well. Using his personal influence as the manager of the foreign exchange department of the *Banco Comercial,* he was able to secure the early release of our car; it and some additional mission supplies cleared customs three days after we reached Montevideo. After seeing hundreds of automobiles in the customs area, some of which had been there for months, I was grateful that strings had been pulled on our behalf. Some minor repairs had to be effected, e.g., installation of a new battery and repair of holes that had been punched in the gas tank. My Uruguayan driver's license was still valid.

Other crates, containing our kitchen range, refrigerator, typewriters, books and forms for the mission office, linens, dishes and our kitchen table set, arrived in New York too late to ship with us. We were advised they would come at a later date.

Before leaving Salt Lake City, I had asked the Church to transfer five thousand dollars to my bank account in Montevideo. I found only $2,500 had been sent; it wouldn't last very long. I immediately wired for an additional five thousand dollars, which arrived promptly. Prices had risen at least forty percent in less than two years.

I purchased some office equipment and set about making arrangements to finish the mission home. I visited the Sierra Hermanos Electric Company which I had patronized previously. The two brothers had always been very friendly and greeted me like a long lost brother. I selected light fixtures for the mission home and asked how soon they could be installed. They explained that all the electricians had honored a strike which had paralyzed the industry for the past ninety days. No settlement was in sight. As a personal favor, however, they offered to install the light fixtures themselves; they hadn't done this kind of work in years. They worked at odd hours to install the fixtures, switches and plugs. They also offered to guarantee our rent payments to the bank. The *Banco de Crédito* had demanded a deposit of 4,500 pesos (about $2,300 or ten months' rent) as guarantee before it would sign the lease agreement. Ultimately it accepted a little over half that amount, with the Sierra brothers as co-signers. I wrote the First Presidency:

> *I have a little over $1,000.00 in the bank now, and $1,361.00 deposited in the Banco de Crédito as a guarantee for the rental of the house. Nearly all rentals are handled by the banks in Uruguay and they are very careful to protect the owner's interests. The owner gave us the key to the house on September 1st, but it took us until the 23rd to come to an agreement with the bank as to the amount of the deposit they required. They normally require a deposit equal to the amount of ten months rent on a two year contract, but they finally consented to let a friend sign as a guarantor if I would deposit the equivalent of six months rent. This I had to do to secure the house. This money earns a three percent interest but cannot be touched until the expiration of the contract. I tried every way to avoid tying up this much money, but was unable to do so. The Mission Home rental is $130.00 per month and the office $100.00.*[6]

Thanks to the Sierras, we did not have all our money tied up in the deposit.

I reported our other expenditures including the purchase of a dining room set at an auction, 170 pesos below the starting bid price of seven hundred, acquired before the auction began. The owner was the wife of the Cuban minister whose sons had played on a softball team I had organized a few years before:

> *I was able to make several excellent buys from an auction house where I was well known. They sold me furniture, in some cases a hundred dollars cheaper than the base they were going to put on it at the time of the auction. They sold us a dining room set consisting of a large table, six chairs, a china closet, and two dish cupboards, all made of oak and in excellent condition for 530 pesos.*

I learned later the wood was mahogany.

The dark side of the adventure, or six-month campout at the mission home. By September 9, 1947, our new home was barely livable and we moved in. Montevideo was bitterly cold.

We bought three small electric heaters for the three finished bedrooms; we hoped they would also help dry out the plaster. We also purchased bedroom furniture for the three rooms. Because we expected our linens and other domestics to clear customs imminently, we purchased only blankets. They were woven by the famous Compomar y Soulas S.A. woolen mills whose trademark was TEO (*"Tiempo es Oro"* or Time is Money). I quote my wife:

We were so conscious of the money we spent that belonged to the Church. We had to buy blankets, wool blankets; the process they use is the English process and so their wool blankets are soft, they are not rough and scratchy at all like some of ours made in the States. So we just slept in the blankets rather than buy sheets. We did this actually until President and Sister Richards came, when, for their sakes, we felt like we had to buy some sheets. But we were months getting our things out of the "aduana." Then we found that much of it had been stolen, lovely linen tablecloths and napkins and so forth.[7]

The kitchen contained a fuel oil stove. The house was heated with coke. We bought a few pots and pans, flatware, plates, glasses, etc. to carry us until we received our supplies. We also bought a small old fashioned ice box, a small table and six kitchen chairs; this was all we had to sit on.

The spot-heat from our three heaters felt very good, but it didn't last. A fuse burned out and we were left in the dark and cold. We bought a fuse and a candle, but soon realized we should have bought many more candles (and fuses). The fuse was replaced, and soon burned out again. We discovered that the wiring had been done rather poorly and was inadequate to carry all the current we used. Over the next several days the Sierra brothers came again and again to help us try to get light and heat. Finally, after struggling with the problem for a month, I had them replace all the conduits with a heavier grade. Until then our nightly ritual consisted of plugging in the heaters to warm the bedrooms and, after waiting briefly until the lights and heaters went out, climbing into bed and covering up with warm blankets.

It took many months to make our new mission home comfortable and efficient. Natural gas had not been piped into our home, and the oil burning kitchen stove did not work properly. We replaced it three times; Corraine had quite a time cooking on a stove that wouldn't function. We felt blessed indeed when natural gas was finally connected to the mission home. By June 1948 we were able to install our own stove.

A permanent colony of cockroaches was another irritation. They seemed to be everywhere in the kitchen, which was strange for a new house. At first we assumed they came in from the outside; we had found some gaping holes where the wall had not been built flush to the doorway lintel, and had the workmen correct that. However, it wasn't until two years later when we changed the heating system from coke to fuel oil that we found the cockroaches' home. I quote Corraine:

We had other problems with the mission home; we were moving in to a new place that hadn't even been completed, yet we found it was alive with cockroaches. Oh! I just couldn't imagine where they could come from . . . how they could get there. And we worked at trying to get rid of them for I don't know how long, and finally, when we were able to get the gas, and the water tank was taken out that had been heated by a wood stove, we found that the packing they had used around the tank for insulation was garbage—bread crusts, cigarette butts, dirty rags, food—oh! And it was just a nest of cockroaches. They had put that in a new house! Ah. We were sick. But we were so grateful when we got the gas, that meant we could have our showers and tubs with hot water in the bathrooms. It was a relief.[8]

Getting the fuel-oil system installed took considerable daring on my part. I requested the system in a letter to the First Presidency dated May 13, 1949. They categorically denied the proposal in a letter dated May 31, 1949, suggesting other means be found to heat the home. I mustered as much courage as I could and on June 14 wrote the strongest letter I dared, asking humbly, but with thorough documentation, that the First Presidency reconsider on grounds that other systems were not feasible. Uruguay was switching away from costly imported English coke; kerosene was foul smelling and dangerous, and the cost of electricity prohibitive. I also explained that it was too cold to go without heat, especially for a newborn baby:

> *We went without heat in the Argentine Mission for 4 years to the detriment of the health of the children. American specialists have told us that our son, born in Argentina, will suffer from a nose ailment all of his life that they attribute to the cold, humid winters he spent in Buenos Aires without the benefit of heat. We have a six months old baby that we would like to protect from the same risk. If we were all adults we could get by without heat.*

The First Presidency reconsidered our request and on August 12, 1949, authorized the installation of the new system:

> *Attention has been given to a second recommendation, submitted in your letter of June 14, 1949, that authorization be given for installation of an oil-burning unit and tank for heating the Uruguayan Mission Home, this installation to replace the present coke-burning system. Upon the basis of your recommendations, the Committee on Expenditures has authorized the installation as requested. We understand from your previous letter that the cost of this installation is $850.*

We camped out in the mission home for three long months until our supplies cleared customs on January 16, 1948. We received a refrigerator (good-bye, ice box), a washing machine, a range and cooking utensils, sheets, pillows, towels, report forms and office equipment, and six kitchen chairs. The matching Formica top kitchen table was sent by mistake to the Finnish Mission where I learned it was gratefully received. Unfortunately some table linens were stolen from customs, as well as a typewriter and some smaller office items. The thefts plus our unintended gift to the Finnish Mission dampened our joy. In addition, the "complete kitchen set" left something to be desired. My wife described the whole tragi-comedy in her oral history:

> *Frederick G. Williams: We were talking about the difficulty in getting some of the things out of the "aduana" that you sent down. Now were these things you had bought for the mission home in the United States, or were these your own?*
>
> *Corraine S. Williams: That's a laugh. (Laughter.) Knowing some of the difficulties we'd had in the Argentine Mission, we went to see Bishop Afflick who was in charge of the Church Purchasing Department and asked for specific things. Now one was a electric mixer, and they said, "Sorry, but we can't furnish you with that. We're not allowed to let missions have a mixer." And I said, "Well, I had*

spent hours beating mayonnaise by hand while in Argentina, because that's the only way you can make it, and you can't buy mixers." I felt like a mission home of all places should have an electric mixer, but we were refused that.

I asked for other specific things. I started naming the things I knew I couldn't get for my kitchen down there, and Bishop Afflick said, "Well, why don't we just send you a complete kitchen?" And I said, "Well, that would be marvelous." He said, "We'll just make up an order of everything you need for the kitchen and send it down." Well, I don't know who made up the order, but when it arrived, we had big lids for which there were no kettles; we had kettles for which there were no lids; we had cookie sheets that were so long no oven in Uruguay could have held them; we even had a coffee pot sent. I just couldn't believe what they sent to us. I really couldn't. I don't understand it to this day. I don't know who had the job of choosing, but it must have been just turned over to someone that didn't really know what the Church was all about; but that's what we received. And I was heartsick; I could have just sat down and cried, because I would have gone out on my own and bought certain things with our own money rather than be without and get along with makeshift the way we had to do.

FGW: Did you get your electric mixer?

CSW: We did through the Farnsworths. After he left the mission, he got a job with the National City Bank, and then he and Ella were married and they were coming back down. His boss said that they would pay all their expenses, whatever their needs, living in a hotel or what not, until they got their home and so forth, and he said, "Well, we'll probably be staying at the mission home, but we will still pay." We told him "No, we don't want you to pay." They were very dear to us. He said "Well, what we can do is buy you an electric mixer." And we said "Well, we'd love that. That would just be beautiful." So this is what happened.

FGW: That was at least two and a half, maybe three years later, then.

CWS: Oh, yes.

FGW: And you didn't have one before then?

CSW: No.

FGW: What about the furnishings and the sheets and things: were these also bought by the Church for the home?

CSW: Yes, the Church bought those. I had nothing to do with the purchase of them. I just specified more or less what we'd need. But they sent some beautiful sheets—Pepperell—more expensive than I would have purchased if I had been doing the buying.

Fred asked for a certain amount of money, I'm not going to quote it because I don't recall, and we were sent about half that amount. So we went to second-

hand stores to buy furniture. What could you do? You have a limited amount of money; you have to make it go, to cover everything. So we bought second-hand furniture for the bedrooms and cheap rugs for the floors.

We did buy a very nice living room set; we decided since we had had in the Argentine Mission the old couch that Brother Ballard bought second-hand when he went down there in 1925 (laughter) and we were actually ashamed of it when people would visit the mission home, we decided we would have a nice set for the Uruguayan mission home. Now you may not recall what it was like, but it was a beautiful living room set, overstuffed. But that was about the only new thing we had, plus the lamps and what not that . . . well, all the furnishings and tables in that room. It wasn't a large room, remember.

When Brother and Sister Richards came, they said, "Well, if you'd paid more for such-and-such it would be better." They couldn't understand that we had to buy with what money we had, what we were allotted; and it was through them, I'm sure, that we later received a good set of silver—not sterling, of course—silver plate, and some other nice things that they saw we needed. But you see we'd been down there [in South America] many years with no one seeing the need, and it just isn't that well understood by the time it gets to Salt Lake City, just what your problems are.

FGW: Did Brother and Sister Richards allow you to buy some other furniture, after they'd been there?

CSW: No. We didn't as I recall. We did get some better beds, but I don't think they were new at that. I do remember that when they came to stay at the mission home on their way down, they were there one night, or (I don't know whether it was more than one night), but we had put them up in our room because it had a private bath. There was no other door out of that bathroom. And that was my only spot for privacy. When I was ill, even the missionaries would come and knock on my door: "Sister Williams, what'll I do about so-and-so?" And so when I wanted to get away from the world, I would go in that bathroom and shut the door, and nobody could get to me. (Laughter.) My only salvation.

FGW: Now did you do all of the furnishing, or did Dad help you to pick things out?

CSW: Oh, yes. We went together; we did all of this together.

FGW: You bought a piano?

CSW: Yes. That's something else that probably wasn't approved, but we'd had the same experience in the Argentine Mission—it wasn't allotted for in the Argentine Mission, but President Young went ahead and got one because they felt it was so necessary. Well, we felt that it definitely was. The mission home was the only place we had for choir practice, for rehearsals, for some of our meetings, our firesides; I mean we just felt that that was a very necessary part of our mission home. So we found a nice piano, and I was very glad that we had. Our children needed it, you know that.[9]

Operating a new mission. While anxiously awaiting our first missionaries, I wrote the First Presidency with an estimate of the money needed to set up and operate the mission through the end of that Church fiscal year, November 30, 1947.

I carefully itemized everything: furnishings and equipment for the mission home and office ($1,800), operating expenses for two months (nine hundred dollars), printing of eight different tracts, ten thousand copies of each (eight hundred dollars), purchase of copies of the Book of Mormon and hymn books ($250), contingency funds (one thousand dollars) something of an innovation, but through hard experience in Argentina we knew to be absolutely essential, the cost for renting and equipping five halls or *locales* for meetings and as missionary residences ($5,300), plus miscellaneous items. The total, a staggering $10,035. We did not yet have a single missionary, but expected twenty-five by the end of the year. I closed the letter by asking that the Brethren "see fit to send as many as one hundred missionaries to this mission, or more:"

> *There are so many places for them to work and we can keep them busy. This is virgin territory and I'm sure there are many good people who will listen to the message of the restored Gospel.*[10]

In reply, the First Presidency expressed genuine pleasure with our efforts to date, and in fact eventually approved our budget request, but not without first asking for clarification on a few items. Since mail came by ship, the delay added confusion to an already frustrating system of communication. I know the First Presidency frequently felt I acted too independently on matters they had not had an opportunity to discuss. However, as mission president, I felt I was empowered to act, and often on-the-spot decisions had to be made; we simply could not wait a month or more for mail to make the round trip. Some correspondence became lost (even some with checks). Frequently up to three letters crossed paths and we ended up responding to information that had already been updated or was too old to be relevant. My original budget request of October 8, 1947, is a case in point. The Brethren's letter asking clarification was dated October 23:

> *However, before further remittances are made, we desire to reconsider your request in the light of your reply to the questions set forth in the preceding paragraphs.*

Their letter ended with a much appreciated vote of confidence:

> *We are happy to note the energy and enthusiasm you display in getting under way the spreading of the Gospel in Uruguay, and we are confident that vast good will be accomplished through your efforts and those of the missionaries laboring under your direction.*

Their second letter, of October 31, called attention to a minor word change in their previous letter:

> *Please refer to letter of October 23 from this office in answer to your[s] of October regarding the above subject [Operation Expense]. I am authorized to call your attention to the fact that the fifth paragraph of this letter should be changed to read, . . .*

and the clarification followed. I made the requested clarifications in a letter dated November 5:

> *This will acknowledge receipt of your favor of October 23rd, which was in answer of my letter of the 8th of October relative to operational expenses for this mission for this fiscal year.*
>
> . . . .
>
> *Referring to paragraph 5 of page 1, the $1800 is in addition to the amounts already spent for the purpose of furnishing the Mission Home and the office. This amount, however, can be reduced by $300 since Sister Williams has used the curtains and drapes she brought from our home in the states. By remaking them herself, and buying a small amount of material she has been able to effect this saving. We still have one bedroom to furnish; extra beds for missionaries; mattresses, blankets, wardrobes, chests of drawers, floor lamps and other items to secure for the Mission Home.*

I then clarified the expenditures for the office, which included $150 earmarked for automobile insurance and automobile club dues for which we had paid personally:

> *It is cheaper to join the club and have their experts take care of the legal aspects of having the car admitted to the country than to pay someone else to do it. They do this free and we get many other services and advantages by joining.*

With respect to the tracts, I explained that the missionaries would engage primarily in tracting during the first year since few of them spoke any Spanish; I proposed to "blanket the country with the inexpensive tracts so that our Church will be known." I argued that if we contacted enough people the law of averages would bring them into our meetings. I answered their other queries in similar fashion.

A letter acknowledging my clarifications was not sent until December 31, so by the time I received official approval, three months had passed since the original budget request. Of course, the period I had requested it for had long since passed:

> *We are also pleased to receive the information regarding your mission finances and your explanation of certain operating expenses.*
>
> *. . . In conformity with the approval given by the Church Committee on Expenditures, the sum of $4,535, as requested in your letter of November 5, was transmitted to the National City Bank with instructions to transmit same to you as follows: $2500 immediately (as requested in your cablegram of December 7), $535 the first week thereafter and $500 each succeeding week until the total is paid over to you. This is according to the transmittal procedure outlined in your letter of October 8.*
>
> *We are confident that with the funds so provided, the program as outlined in your letters of October 8 and November 5 can be financed adequately; and*

we feel sure that every effort will be made to conserve these funds for the most effective use thereof in furthering the work of the Lord in that locality.

Sincerely your brethren,

George Albert Smith
J. Reuben Clark, Jr.
David O. McKay

As noted above, I sometimes had to cable for money when answers to my letter requests seemed to be delayed and expenses had to be met.

Typically, I exchanged parallel and overlapping letters with the Brethren, and it was sometimes difficult to keep all the information straight. In the intervening three months, for example, in addition to my two operational budget letters (October 8 and November 5), and their three (October 23 and 31, and December 31), I wrote six letters that touched on other matters (October 15 and 20, November 10 and 19, and December 11 and 16) and had received four in return (October 28, November 4, and December 10 and 11).

Sometimes authorization would be so delayed that we missed opportunities, such as the purchase of a hall in Paysandú. I wrote the First Presidency on January 3, 1950, alerting them that our lease was about to expire and that renewal was unlikely. Lease renewal, if possible, would be at a higher price. I suggested instead that we buy a home to use for a hall, and that we had an option until February 1 to buy a very good one for six thousand dollars. The First Presidency cabled and wrote their authorization to purchase the house on February 3; but it had already been sold. I wrote on February 24, 1950, informing them of the sale and that we had renegotiated our lease on the old home with a sixty percent increase in rent.

As noted, we received permission to furnish the *locales*, the homes or apartments that served as combination chapel and missionary residences. Furnishing them was a departure from the system first established when I was a missionary in the South American Mission and later developed in the Argentine Mission. That system required each missionary to purchase necessary furnishings such as beds and bedding, tables, *Primus* stoves, and dishes. Upon transfer, each missionary sold his "kit" to the incoming elder, and purchased the kit of the missionary he was replacing at his new location. When I left the mission, there weren't any missionaries to sell to, so I donated my kit to the mission. When I returned to Argentina as Mission President nine years later, I found missionaries selling as their own the things I had donated. Though we tried to avoid it, sometimes missionaries tried to sell their goods for a profit, and many disputes ensued. In Uruguay, we instituted a new system; each *local* was furnished with a uniform list of supplies available to the missionaries:

1 kerosene stove with oven
6 each knives, forks, and dishes, plus cooking utensils
1 kitchen table
1 kitchen cupboard
4 single beds and mattresses
2 wardrobes (Uruguayan houses had no built-in closets)
4 small tables for desks
1 medicine cabinet

30 cane bottom chairs
1 pulpit
1 small portable organ
Necessary light fixtures (never furnished with a house)

Two woolen blankets were also furnished for each bed; the missionaries were expected to furnish their own sheets.

Uniform pulpits and benches made by local carpenters for each branch replaced the proposed cane bottom chairs. Each missionary was charged five dollars monthly rent and, since he didn't have any interest in branch furnishings (other than his personal belongings), even mid-month transfers imposed no difficulties on him or the mission. Of course, the missionaries purchased their own food and paid their percentage of the public utilities for each *local.*

As the only person authorized to represent the mission, I signed all rental contracts. At first, the Church was unknown in Uruguay, but I was known from my work for the United States and Uruguayan Governments during the War, so contracts were made in my name. Later, upon contract renewal the Church's name was substituted for mine.

After deciding to establish a new branch (many times dependent on the availability of a *local*), we sought a home with a living room large enough for a small chapel and rooms for classes and bedrooms for the missionaries. Sometimes the bedrooms also served as classrooms: the missionaries' bedrooms, at least on Sundays, were commendably tidy. Sometimes a small store front with living quarters in the rear served as a *local.* In every case, we secured the best accommodations available, and in general were very fortunate in Uruguay because, in some cases, we found new premises to lease.

However, our *locales* had no uniformity. Some were ground floor, some second floor. One had a glass-enclosed patio. One was unique: the best location in a small country town, it had a sod-covered roof supported in the center by a post. Its mud walls were whitewashed both inside and out; the missionaries poured the cement floor.

Organs and organists. Uruguay was still suffering the effects of disrupted trade caused by the War. Importation of manufactured goods had not yet resumed, so many things were in short supply or completely unavailable. Among them were new pianos and organs. Since music is vital to our worship service, I daily watched the newspaper ads and frequently visited music and furniture stores to purchase whatever second-hand organs were available. I found some very good ones, but never two of the same size, shape or quality. They were all pump, portable organs, both small and large. I think we had almost every kind ever manufactured. One particularly small and beautiful but very delicate portable provided both music and hilarity in the Universitaria Branch. The organist, Elder Glenn Slight, was very tall, and when he pumped his knees rose over the top of the organ in a "V," while the bellows puffed out nearly to the floor, first one side, then the other. The scene reminded us of a large, ungainly bird attempting its first take-off. We had to avoid watching the organist so that we could concentrate on the music. Eventually, new pump organs began to arrive from Italy and thereafter became standard in each branch.

As new branches were opened, we began more and more to bless the parents who had insisted their sons take piano lessons in their youth. Many missionaries could, with a little practice, play a hymn. Some played very well. Others, no matter how they tried, could not produce a recognizable facsimile, but their efforts were appreciated. Sometimes it took two elders;* each playing one hand. It was a constant struggle to provide competent musicians for each branch. In answer to how some of the early organists were chosen, I explained to one bemused church-service listener: "Each new group of missionaries is ushered into the living room of the mission home. Those who can correctly identify the piano from among the other furnishings get the job." My teenage daughters Barbara and Argina both served as branch organists throughout their stay in the mission: Barbara in Arroyo Seco Branch and Gina in La Comercial. The organ in La Comercial had a habit of "walking away" as it was pumped, requiring great agility and timing on Gina's part to pull it back or move the chair closer, according to the amount of time she had between verses, without missing a beat. In the beginning they learned a new hymn for each meeting—the first was "God Speed the Right"—until they enlarged their repertoire. Often, they both played at two Sacrament meetings each Sunday. My young son Fred also took his turn as Primary organist in Malvín in the absence of a more experienced organist. Little by little we began to find proficient players among the investigators and newly baptized members (such as Oscar Nieves and Armando Young), as well as among the missionaries (most notably, Maughan McMurdie) which added immeasurably to the success of the meetings. I even wrote the First Presidency requesting the transfer of a piano-playing elder from Argentina to our mission (March 18, 1948), and it was granted.

Soon after the mission was established, Dr. Gerrit de Jong, Jr., of Brigham Young University, and his daughter Carma visited us from Brazil where he was serving as a United States cultural representative. We took them with us to Sacrament meeting at the Malvín Branch, but arrived a little late. The congregation had already begun singing the opening hymn, *a capella*. Silently, he took his seat at the organ and in mid-verse started playing the hymn's accompaniment in the precise key in which they were singing it, and without opening the hymnal. Dr. de Jong, a concert pianist, was the first dean of the Brigham Young University College of Fine Arts.

The missionaries come. On October 10, 1947, Corraine and I went to Buenos Aires to attend the Semiannual Conference of the Argentine Mission. President and Sister W. Ernest Young were very gracious in helping to get our mission established. They lent us copies of the Book of Mormon, hymnbooks, lesson books and in countless other ways gave us their support. They also offered to let the Uruguayan Mission share in their official publication, *El Mensajero Deseret*; we accepted, and from then on it also became our mission's magazine. As co-editors, he and I alternated writing the monthly editorial.

We returned from Argentina October 14 with Elder Charles Curtis Janson and Elder Juan Sciorra. Elder Janson, my nephew from Phoenix, Arizona, had been serving in the Argentine Mission. With the consent of President Young, and with the approval of the First Presidency, he was reassigned to Uruguay to help begin the work, thus becoming the first elder of the new mission. His companion, Elder Sciorra, from the Haedo Branch near Buenos Aires, was called to serve a short-term mission. They resided temporarily at the mission home and began tracting in the immediate neighborhood. One of the first tracts we printed had a photograph on the cover showing the two missionaries talking with a woman at her front door; the woman was my wife and the house was the mission home.

On October 24, 1947, the first group of missionaries arrived from New Orleans aboard the S.S. *George Leonard*; they were Elders Wilford M. Farnsworth (Colonia Dublán, Mexico), William N. Jones (Burbank, California), and Preston J. Bushman (Snowflake, Arizona); we now had sufficient missionaries to begin work in earnest. Elder Farnsworth was named mission secretary the next day and began putting the books and reports in order. The others, under my direction, searched for a building that was large enough to hold meetings and adequately serve their housing needs.

The first such building was rented October 28; it was located on Avenida Italia 3590 in the Tenth Judicial District of Montevideo called Malvín. Elder Janson was appointed branch president and installed along with Elders Sciorra, Bushman and Jones; they began tracting near the chapel. The first Sunday School and Sacrament meetings were held on Sunday, November 9; a Primary was started on the November 12.

Within weeks of the opening of the first branch, larger groups of missionaries began arriving, sometimes only days apart. Elder E. Dene Ogden arrived in Montevideo from Buenos Aires on December 1. He had gone directly there from Brownsville, Texas, on the S.S. *Brazil.* On the same day, the S.S. *Tulane Victory* brought six more: Elders Donald B. Cox, Gerald L. Nielson, Robert N. Nelson, E. Keith Dexter, Terry C. Smith and Lee O. Squire. The following day, December 2, eleven more missionaries arrived, having sailed from Vancouver, B.C., around South America through the Straits of Magellan, aboard the S.S. *Clearwater Victory*: W. Janson (brother to Charles C. Janson), Thaddeus E. Shoemaker, John W. Cook, L. Cecil Millett, Jewel F. Bushnell, Franklin D. Richards, Jr., Galen A. Bigler, Melvin Brady, Kay W. Young, Arvil A. Harris and Stewart D. Burton. On December 10, Elder Arthur F. Smith, who, because of illness, had been removed from the S.S. *Clearwater Victory* at Punta Arenas, Chile, reached Montevideo. We now had twenty-four missionaries, only three of whom spoke Spanish (the Language Training Mission wouldn't be established until the early 1960's); therefore it was encumbent upon me to see that all of them learned the language as soon as possible. We assigned the elders to four branches within the city of Montevideo: Malvín, Arroyo Seco, Reducto, and Villa Muñoz (later changed to La Comercial). I'd go around each morning and give a Spanish lesson at each branch, then the missionaries would go out and distribute tracts door to door. A day or two later some of them would come up to me after the Spanish lesson and say: "I want you to come visit a certain family." We'd go there and invariably the person would say something like this:

> *Would you please tell me what this is all about? These young men came to my door, knocked, and gave me these tracts and pamphlets. I didn't understand them, but their faces were so imploring and they are so sincere, I couldn't turn them down. Who are they? What is this about? They don't seem to want money for the Church.*

A lot of those people came into the Church.

Since nearly all the first missionaries arrived within days of each other, there was a potential problem in determining who would be chosen senior for each pair of companions. I joked once that there was no problem at all: the first fifty percent to walk down the gangplank would be the seniors, because they were the eager beavers.

Elder Stephen L. Richards told me later that it was his suggestion that a good number of missionaries be sent down close together to get the mission started at once. This influx necessitated the transfer of the more experienced missionaries (in other words, those who had been there a week or two longer); these became the new senior companions and they would go out to open up new areas in their halting but sincere Spanish. The moves came so fast and frequently that it sometimes got ridiculous. From some of the investigators I received a petition, the essence of which was this:

We respectfully request that you not transfer the missionaries. We're just barely learning to pronounce their names; why do you have to move them? Leave them here a little longer.

I mentioned that Elder Arthur F. Smith had taken sick and was removed from his ship. A fellow passenger with the eleven elders aboard the *Clearwater Victory*, he was stricken with appendicitis while the ship was sailing through the Straits of Magellan. In critical condition, sick and alone, without money and unable to speak Spanish, he was befriended by a kindly North American oil man and his wife who went out of their way to care for him and pay his bills. I quote from the Uruguayan Mission History:

There were no medical facilities on the ship, and as his condition took a turn for the worse, the captain gave orders for the ship to return to the city of Punta Arenas, Chile. Elder Smith was removed from the ship alone in an uncontious [sic] condition. The Chilean authorities would not permit any of the elders to go ashore with him, as none of them had visas for Chile. The captain of the ship advised the missionaries to keep all of his money and clothes as they probably would be stolen. He told them that the American Consul would take care of his medical expenses for the time being and the Church could reimburse the consul later on.

It turned out that there was no American Consul in Punta Arenas, the closest one being in Santiago, 1500 miles away, nor did the Moore-McCormick Steamship Company have an agent there. In addition, no one had bothered to notify the Church of Elder Smith's circumstance, neither the authorities in Salt Lake City, nor in Argentina or Uruguay. The first I heard of it was President Young's call to me from Buenos Aires to ask me for information; when the eleven missionaries arrived in Argentina they immediately asked President Young for word of Elder Smith. Not knowing whether he was alive or dead, I quickly sent the following cable, with the address in Spanish:

Arthur Smith, Sick Passenger taken from the ship Clearwater Victory—Punta Arenas, Chile—

Cable me Quickmere Montevideo where and how you are what you need. Contact Max Witt friend of mine who was Harbormaster four years ago. If you need me will come for you by plane. Love from all. Frederick S. Williams.

We were relieved to receive his reply the following day, dated December 2:

Received telegram. I am doing fine. Will be in Buenos Aires coming Friday. Arthur F. Smith.

I quote again from the Mission History:

When Elder Smith was taken from the ship on the 23rd of November, the port medical officer took him directly to the hospital and had him operated on. A North American, Mr. W. L. Morrison, living in the Cosmos Hotel, Punta Arenas, heard of this young fellow-countryman being in the hospital and went to visit *him. Upon finding out that Elder Smith was without funds, he very graciously paid the hospital and doctor bills, and when he was able to leave the hospital took him to his hotel where he and his wife took care of him. Mr. Morrison also purchased an airplane ticket for Elder Smith to Buenos Aires. In all he paid bills totaling $246.00 (U.S. Dollars). He also contacted the American Consul in Santiago, Chile. The consulate advised the Church in Salt Lake City, sending a duplicate copy of their letter to the American Consul in Montevideo which was delivered personally to President Williams the latter part of December. Elder Franklin J. Murdock sent a draft for $250 to the American Consul in Santiago to be forwarded to Mr. Morrison.*

In the meantime, I had sent a personal check in the amount of $246.00 directly to Mr. Morrison, together with a letter of appreciation for his most generous and selfless actions. Eventually the double (and even triple) payment was resolved and he sent me the following letter, dated January 31, 1948:

Dear Sir:

I am in receipt of your letters of Dec. 10, 1947, and January 13, 1948. A few days after I had wired for you to stop payment on the first check it came thru. I would not have wired you but was afraid the check might have fallen into the wrong hands and knew a cancellation would protect you. However, I burned the check as per your instructions in the second letter and have entered the later check for payment.

In this letter I am enclosing a statement with the sustaining receipts and the cancelled memorandum signed by Arthur Smith so you and he will have a full and final statement of the transaction.

In this mail I am sending a letter to the American Consul in Santiago notifying him that I'm returning to him, for return to Mr. Murdock, the money held here in the bank.

I am glad to accept the thanks of you and Mr. Smith for such small service as I was able to render but I am well repaid for being able to help one who is, I am sure, a very sincere and deserving young man.

With best wishes for the success of your Mission and for you and your group, I am,

Yours truly,

/s/ W.L. Morrison

The final entry on this episode, recorded in the Mission History, sums up our feelings on the matter:

Elder Smith was administered to before leaving the ship at Punta Arenas and we feel that the Lord was mindful of the administration and not only healed him, but raised up friends for this servant who was in a strange land, unable to speak or understand the language.

Incidentally, Elder Smith had been a Marine during the War. He was on the *Missouri* when the Japanese surrendered; a brother had been killed in the War. He had become a pretty good poker player in the service, and en route to Uruguay upset his companions by insisting on playing to all hours of the night with the crew. Perhaps the Lord used this problem to focus his thinking. He was a very humble young man when he arrived in Montevideo. It also sobered his companions. He became an excellent and dedicated missionary.

We had arrived in Uruguay August 30, 1947. In the remaining four months of that year we had secured a wonderful mission home and office, received twenty-four missionaries, and established four branches of the Church. Many friends had been raised up to aid us. Our meetings were well-attended and there were prospects for many baptisms. On December 21 a special Christmas program was held at the mission home at which forty-seven investigators were present. Later, on Christmas Eve and Christmas Day, the missionaries joined with our family to celebrate the birth of our Savior. The final entry for 1947 in the Mission History attests to our gratitude for blessings received, and anticipation of great progress, while disclosing some of the details of our hectic schedules:

We are all appreciative of our blessings and happy to be laboring in this new mission. Spanish classes are held daily with the missionaries and a weekly meeting of all of the missionaries is convened at the mission home. Here the missionaries learn about the Gospel. Sunday Schools are held in 4 branches each Sunday morning. Two meetings in which the Gospel is preached are held at 5:00 p.m. each Sunday and two at 7:30 p.m. President Williams teaches a Sunday School class and speaks at two meetings each Sunday.

We appreciate what has been done in 1947 and look forward to a glorious year in 1948. We are grateful for the help and cooperation of all of the General Authorities in Salt Lake City, and to all who have helped the Uruguayan Mission in any way.

NOTES

Chapter III

1. See the author's projected Volume V of "The History of My Life" (1942-1947) for a more detailed account of the branch's activities. See also MS History of The Uruguayan Mission, Historical Department, Church of Jesus Christ of Latter-day Saints.

2. See author's letter to the First Presidency, October 8, 1947, a copy of which is in my personal files.

3. History of the Uruguayan Mission, p. 4.

4. Letter dated October 8, 1947, a copy of which is in my personal files.

5. *Ibid.*

6. *Ibid.*

7. Oral history interview with Corraine S. Williams conducted June 13, 1975 by Frederick G. Williams.

8. Oral history interview.

9. Oral history interview. Many of the supplies came at our suggestion. Shortly after our call to serve as Mission Presidents, I had contacted Church headquarters hoping to talk to President McKay on the opening of the mission. At the suggestion of Brother Murdoch, I wrote up certain recommendations regarding supplies for the new mission and mailed them to the First Presidency on May 27, 1947. In the letter I went into detail listing what items were indispensable, which could be purchased there, which would be better bought in the States. Much of what I recommended was honored, including an automobile, washing machine, refrigerator, gas range, but no mixer. Copy of the letter in my possession.

10. Letter dated October 8, 1947.

CHAPTER IV

THE VISIT OF ELDER STEPHEN L. RICHARDS

WHILE IN Salt Lake City preparing to leave for Uruguay to open the mission, I took occasion to invite the Brethren to visit the South American missions, so that they might know the conditions first hand. No General Authority had visited since the opening of the work in 1925. I remember President McKay, whose son had served under us in the Argentine mission, remarking, "It would be wonderful if one could be spared; we'll see what can be done."

Even before the receipt of a single elder to our mission, I renewed my request for a visitor, writing directly to President McKay:

> *Sister Williams and I would like to repeat our invitation to you to visit South American missions, and if it were possible, for you and Sister McKay to spend Christmas with us in Montevideo.*

I felt very strongly about the impact such a visit could have on the progress of the Lord's work, and proposed the itinerary, extolling the virtue of traveling at spring time:

> *Your visit to these missions would be one of the finest investments in missionary work that could possibly be made. The ease of air travel now makes it possible to visit the three missions without having to spend too much time in transit. Buenos Aires is now only twenty hours from Miami, and you could fly either from there to Buenos Aires, tour the mission and then come to Montevideo, and from here to Brazil, or visit Brazil first, then to Montevideo and on to Buenos Aires.*
>
> *It is now spring and the best time of the year for such a visit. It is lovely. If you were to come later, it might be better to visit Brazil first, before it becomes too hot, then spend Christmas with us and after the first of the year visit Argentina. Montevideo has the finest climate of any of the cities in South America and your visit here would be most enjoyable.*

I next proposed that the three mission presidents could meet together and that the practice should be continued annually:

> *Should it meet with your approval we would be happy to invite President and Sister Rex, and President and Sister Young to spend Christmas with us.*

We all feel it would be wonderful to have an annual Mission President's conference which would give us a spiritual up-lift that we miss by not attending the conferences in Salt Lake City.

I renewed my plea that he come, and closed by suggesting that the Brethren too could profit by visiting the missions personally:

Please excuse my presuming that you might come. But, President McKay, we need a visit so very much. It will mean so much to the Saints, the missionaries, the presidents and to our investigators. It will also be a very pleasant eye-opener to the General Authority who makes the visit, and will give the Church a better understanding of the problems and the opportunities that exist in South America.

Won't you please come and visit us? You could take a fifteen-day rest from Rio de Janeiro to New York or New Orleans on a ship after touring the missions. Your trip would supply you with a great deal of material for an April Conference talk.[1]

President McKay responded to my overture in a warmly worded letter dated October 28, 1947, which seemed to hold out the promise of a visit, even though it would not be as soon as we requested:

This will acknowledge the receipt of your kind letter of October 20, 1947, repeating your cordial invitation to me to visit the missions of South America during the last two months of 1947.

Such a trip would be most delightful and to me very informative. My son Robert has been urging me to take it ever since he returned from his Mission. In this other returned missionaries have joined him.

Of this I am convinced, that one of the Presidency should visit these missions in the very near future. We should then be in the position to render clearer judgement regarding the matters that come before us from time to time.

We have the matter under consideration, but prospects for a visit this year are very dim.

I also took the occasion to write a lengthy letter to Elder Spencer W. Kimball in which I expressed my conviction that the "future missionary field is in South America" and of my hope that a General Authority would be sent: "What the South American missions need more than anything else is the visit of one or more of the General Authorities." I ended my plea with, "Won't you please come and see?"[2]

Feeling so keenly the need of closer ties with the Brethren, it was with pure joy that we received word from Stephen L. Richards that he had "been appointed by the First Presidency to visit the South American missions" and was scheduled to leave New York City by ship January 15, 1948.[3] I immediately sat down to respond to his requests and made a number of suggestions relative to travel, what things he and his wife should bring and not bring (getting cameras through customs "is more trouble than they are worth"), what letters of introduction would be helpful, etc., and ended the two-page letter by stating our appreciation that after twenty years of waiting, the South American Saints "would have the privilege of hearing an Apostle of the Lord."[4]

On February 2, 1948, Elder and Sister Stephen L. Richards arrived in Montevideo aboard the S.S. *Argentina* en route to Buenos Aires. Sister Williams and I, together with most of the missionary force, met the ship and welcomed our distinguished visitors and five new elders for our mission. We took them to the mission home and later toured in Montevideo before taking them to their ship; they were scheduled to visit the Argentine Mission first. After touring that mission for almost a month, Brother Richards was scheduled to visit ours for a week. On February 26, 1948, pursuant to a telephone invitation from him, Corraine and I traveled to Buenos Aires to return with him and Sister Richards on the boat.

Elder Richards held a conference with President Young and me, and later that evening the three couples attended a farewell in Brother and Sister Richards' honor before they boarded the S.S. *General Alvear*, one of the night boats that crossed between Argentina and Uruguay. The ships sailed each evening at ten and arrived at seven the following morning.

That night before going to bed, Brother Richards expressed his concern about clearing customs. I told him there would be no problems and no delays getting into Uruguay. He told me, however, that they had arrived in Buenos Aires from Montevideo at seven in the morning and it was two o'clock in the afternoon before they had cleared customs, and the ordeal had exhausted him even before his tour of the mission started. As I recall, President Richards was still recovering from a recent heart attack and wasn't feeling very strong. In fact, in his initial letter to us he indicated as much:

> *We do not wish to incur excessive expense and yet the brethren desire us to have lodging and service which will be adequate to the needs of people of our age. Neither of us is in the most robust health and we have to be a little careful.*[5]

Visiting the far-flung branches of the Argentine mission by car had also taken its toll. Thus, it was with a great deal of trepidation that he anticipated our arrival in Uruguay; he feared a repeat of the delays going through customs. I assured him that there would be no problems.

The next morning, to add to his concern, we learned that another ship had arrived a few minutes before ours; we had to dock quite a distance from the customs house itself. As we were leaving the ship, Harold Brown, who was working for the American Embassy in Montevideo, met us with his camera to take pictures of Elder and Sister Richards and Sister Williams and me. In fact, all the missionaries were at the dock to welcome our party. The photo session delayed us even more, and Brother Richards urged us on with statements like: "Look, let's go, let's get through customs." I again reassured him, and told him that in all likelihood our bags were already in the car. "Oh," he said, "it can't be." We walked up to customs and, sure enough, his bags had already been cleared and were out in the mission car, awaiting our arrival. He couldn't believe it. Once again, my friends in the inspection department had allowed our baggage to go through without delay. Elder Richards was very relieved and grateful.

It was Saturday, February 28, 1948. The morning newspaper, *La Mañana*, published a lengthy and favorable article. The front page read: "One of the Twelve Apostles of the Mormon Church will arrive today in our city.—Mr. Stephen L. Richards, Attorney and Banker.

Story on page four." Inside, the story read (the original was in Spanish; I copy the English translation taken from the Mission History):

ONE OF THE TWELVE APOSTLES OF THE MORMON CHURCH WILL ARRIVE TODAY IN OUR CITY

. . . .

MR. STEPHEN L. RICHARDS, ATTORNEY AND BANKER

. . . .

The President of the Uruguayan Mission makes some interesting statements.

Today, Dr. Stephen L. Richards, one of the twelve people who exercises the calling of the Twelve Apostles of the Mormon Religion, arrives on board the S.S. "General Alvear." To be able to give to our readers some information about his personality and about the object of his trip, we interviewed Mr. Frederick Williams, President of the Uruguayan Mission of the Church of Jesus Christ of the Latter-day Saints, more commonly known by the name of Mormon Church.

. . . .

Mr. Williams courteously answered our questions and made among others, the following statements.

WHO ARE THE MORMONS?

The Church of Jesus Christ of the Latter-day Saints is the name of the Church, but it is more commonly known under the name of Mormons. This nickname was given us because of the sacred book that we have which is called the Book of Mormon, which we accept together with the Bible as sacred scripture.

The Church was organized in the year 1830 with six members. At the present time, its membership is about one million. In the year 1847, because of the religious persecution in the states of Missouri and Ohio, the Church emigrated to the Rocky Mountains, at that time an unknown desert region. The largest number of members of our Church reside in the following states: Utah, Idaho, California, Arizona, Wyoming, Colorado, Nevada, Washington and Oregon; although there are many in every state of the Union, with large numbers in Illinois, New York and Washington, D.C.

Quite a number of Senators and Representatives in Washington have been members of the Church. At the present time there are two Mormon Senators and five representatives. The first Counselor to the President of the Church was Ambassador of the United States to Mexico. He came to Montevideo as one of the delegates sent by President Roosevelt to the Foreign Ministers' Conference held in the year 1932. His name is J. Reuben Clark, Jr.

.A President elected by the Twelve Apostles presides over the Church. He chooses two Counselors. These 15 men are the principal authorities at the head of the Church.

THE PERSONALITY OF STEPHEN L. RICHARDS

Stephen L. Richards, attorney and bank director, exercises the calling of one of the Twelve Apostles. He is travelling to visit the Missions of our Church in South America. He has been in Argentina for nearly one month, where the Church established a mission in the year 1925. That Mission now has 93 missionaries and about one thousand members.

He will be in Uruguay for one week before going to Brazil where he expects to remain for two weeks. The Brazilian mission has many members.

The Uruguayan Mission was established the 1st of September of 1947, although a number of Mormons lived in Uruguay before that time.

Mr. Williams was the Business Manager of the Interamerican Cooperative Public Health Service when it was established. There were other members here in the course of the Military service working in the Naval Attache's office of our government.

THE CHURCH IN URUGUAY

At the present time, there are 38 missionaries in Uruguay. Nearly all of them have been in the armed service of our country. We do not like war, but when it comes, we support our government all that we can. The headquarters of our Mission is on Brito del Pino street. The Mission Home was recently purchased by the Church. There are four branches in Montevideo and one in Treinta y Tres, Mercedes and Paysandú. Upon the arrival of other missionaries, we will open branches in other departments [states].

We believe in a healthful life and we enjoy sports. We hope to soon organize a basketball and baseball team.

The missionaries pay their own expenses while in the mission field. The length of their mission is two and one half years, after which they return to their homes in North America, to be replaced by others. There are nearly five thousand throughout the world. The missionaries do their own cooking and housekeeping. They are nearly all young men between 20 and 30 years of age.

THEY ARE NOT POLYGAMISTS

The practice of polygamy ended in the year of 1890. Since that date, any member that advocates this practice has been excommunicated by the Church. We believe that we must obey the laws of the country in which we live. When the Supreme Court sustained the law making polygamy illegal (May 1890), the Church ended this practice. This belief was accepted before that date (since 1843) as a commandment of God. Only three percent of all the members of the Church ever practiced polygamy.

Saturday was leisurely spent; Elder Richards met with mission officials to discuss his schedule and then we visited points of interest in and near Montevideo. Samuel J. Skousen, U.S. Air Attaché in Asunción, Paraguay, flew into Montevideo for the day with his wife Beth, also present were Jean Larson, wife of Rolf Larson, our former Argentine missionary employed by the U.S. Government in Rio de Janeiro, and Sister Larson's mother. Brother Richards had had a strenuous three weeks in Argentina and said he would like to take it easy and rest as much as possible while still being of service to us. This was fine with us: ours was a new mission with no significant problems; we had lots of enthusiastic young missionaries, but not a single member in the entire country.

On Sunday, February 29, 1948, Brother and Sister Richards visited the Sunday Schools of the Malvín, Arroyo Seco and La Comercial branches. He spoke in each one, giving advice and bearing his testimony. That evening, instead of Sacrament meeting (with no members to take the sacrament they were really preaching meetings anyway), we held a combined branch meeting of the Capital District at the YMCA auditorium. Investigators as well as some especially invited guests came from all over Montevideo. The Mission History records:

> *A mixed chorus furnished special music and Oscar Nieves played two piano solos. Apostle Richards spoke at some length explaining the practical aspects of Mormonism.*
>
> *His words were well received by the people in attendance, amounting to 145 investigators. The concluding speaker was President Williams, who also acted as interpreter for Brother Richards throughout the day. At the close of the meeting almost all of the investigators and friends came and shook hands with Brother Richards, expressing their great pleasure in meeting him and for his splendid message. They requested that he return soon to visit them again.*
>
> *This public meeting was a great success. We appreciate the courtesy of the Y.M.C.A. in permitting us the use of their hall free of charge.*[6]

After Sunday School Elder Richards asked how the people lived. "What do they do on Sunday?" I said, "If you want to see the people, then we'll have to go to the beach; that's where they are." He said "Then we'll go to the beach." And we drove along the *rambla* or ocean front, I think as far as Carrasco. Uruguay's beautiful beaches are jam-packed on Sundays.

On Monday, March 1, we held a meeting with all the Capital District and Treinta y Tres missionaries. The highlight of the all-day meeting was Brother Richards' testimony and instructions. First, each missionary bore his testimony and expressed his feelings concerning the Lord's work. The majority were military veterans and expressed joy in the service of the Lord, which brings life, rather than in the military, which had so recently brought death. One quite new elder stood up to say "I don't know if I have a testimony or not, but I've come on this mission to see if I can get one." When Brother Richards rose to speak, he rather severely castigated the elder, saying he should not be on a mission if he didn't have a testimony. I remember seeing my son Fred—who was quite young at the time—looking pained at the way Elder Richards dealt with this young missionary, a particular friend of Fred's. At the close of his remarks, however, Brother Richards apologized to the elder, explaining that he had admonished him to make a point.

Because of his exhaustion after his visit in Argentina, Elder Richards had asked that we not schedule any event without first checking with him. His only really strenuous day had been the day of the elders' meeting, so he felt rested well enough to travel a little. I recommended that we visit Mercedes and stay overnight; it wasn't too far from Montevideo and the roads were almost all paved. He agreed.

On Tuesday, March 2, 1948, after attending a luncheon as guests of the Montevideo Rotary Club, Elder Richards and I and our wives as well as Elder Keith Dexter, began our trip to Mercedes in the mission car. Near the end of the paved road we were overtaken by tremendous wind and rain, a typical Uruguayan storm. The rain was so dense it was impossible to see any distance and we slowly felt our way along. I noticed a poor rain-drenched woman standing by the side of the road, trying to get a ride. I stopped and invited her into the front seat with me and my wife. It was a mistake; that she was soaking wet was bad enough, but she had evidently been cooking in small, unventilated quarters and smelled of burnt meat and smoke; it was not very pleasant. Then Brother Richards remarked: "The Brethren advise us not to pick up anyone." I was embarrassed and more than a little uncomfortable until we dropped her off.

We finally arrived in Mercedes, on the beautiful Río Hun, and went directly to the Brisas del Hun Hotel, where comfortable quarters had been reserved. After resting and eating, we began an elders meeting at 10:00 p.m. with the four missionaries assigned to Mercedes and the four assigned to Paysandú at the Mercedes *local.* Work had just begun in Mercedes; as yet no Sunday School or other meetings had been held.

Elder Richards' instruction was most edifying, as were the sweet testimonies borne at that meeting as the spirit of the Lord poured out upon all present.

We said good-bye to the missionaries the following day and returned to Montevideo. We lunched in Colonia Suiza at the exquisite Nirvana Hotel, a beautiful resort show place. Corraine and I had spent a weekend there some years before. The Richards enjoyed it very much. In fact, the whole trip was most pleasant, and we especially delighted in the beautiful rolling hills of the Uruguayan countryside known as *"la tierra purpúrea,"* or the purple land, because of the purple sheen of the spring flowers.

That evening at the mission home, Brother and Sister Richards related some of their experiences, especially those associated with the dedication of various temples. She would encourage him: "Stephen, tell the one about . . ." and he would tell another experience. Then he would say: "Irene, now you tell them about," and she'd begin a story. Some were serious, others instructive or spiritual; still others were humorous, and we had many good laughs. We especially enjoyed their anecdotes about the lives of the General Authorities. I had always thought Brother Richards possessed one of the most orderly and serious minds among the Brethren. After a week with them, I also saw what warm and genuine people they were; each possessed a keen sense of humor and enjoyed life and all its beauties. In every respect they were wonderful human beings as well as committed servants of the Lord.

On Thursday, March 4, we shopped downtown. I purchased a very beautiful pigskin wallet for Brother Richards which he thought was the finest he had ever seen. After my release as mission president three and a half years later, I bought another wallet for him and gave it to him personally when I returned to Salt Lake City. As I presented it, he pulled out his old one and said "This is the finest wallet I ever had. It's kind of worn now, so I sure do appreciate getting this new one." I suppose he used it until his death.

Later, we took Brother and Sister Richards to dinner at a famous restaurant named Moroni's. I asked Brother Richards whether he liked steak, and he said he did, so we ordered a chateaubriand for him. We knew it would really impress him. When the steak was brought in on a large platter and placed in front of him he said "I can't believe it. There is no such thing!" The meat hung over the sides of the platter and each serving was as large as a Sunday roast. It was very delicious, and he ate every bite of it.

That evening most of the missionaries from the Capital District visited with the Richardses at the mission home. The missionaries sat on the floor and listened to his counsel and to the very interesting stories both he and Sister Richards told.

I had asked Brother Richards whether he would be willing to speak before the American Association of Montevideo and he replied he would enjoy doing so, so I called the program chairman and arrangements were made for Brother Richards to address the Association. The meeting was scheduled for noon, Friday, March 5, at the Nogaro Hotel. His address was entitled "Knowledge is power, not wisdom;" it was a beautiful talk and was very well received:

> *Those in attendance at the luncheon expressed many complimentary remarks about Elder Richards' address, "Knowledge is power, not Wisdom". They commented upon the practicability of the Mormon theology and Brother Richards' speaking ability. President Williams, Elder Farnsworth and Harold Brown were also in attendance at the luncheon.*[7]

Friday evening the Richards, Williams and Browns attended a reception at the American Embassy hosted by Ambassador Briggs. Before leaving the mission home Brother Harold Brown, who worked at the Embassy, alerted Elder Richards that "Probably the only thing they will be serving tonight besides scotch and bourbon will be Coca-Cola." He then asked: "Would you be averse to drinking Coca-Cola?" Elder Richards answered: "No, I would not." Harold asked: "Has the Church ever taken a stand against Coca-Cola?" and Elder Richards answered: "No, it has not." And sure enough, that night only hard liquor and Coca-Cola were served. When the waiter offered a tray of drinks, Brother Richards served glasses of Coke to Corraine, Leonore Brown, Sister Richards, me, Harold Brown, and finally to himself, and we all drank them. We met many people that night, officials of the U.S. Government as well as members of the American community, some of whom had heard Elder Richards speak at luncheon. It was a most enjoyable evening.

Of course, Corraine and I had been closely connected with the American Association for several years; some of the faces had changed, but the activities remained the same. Corraine had also belonged to the Women's Club and together we had worked at the USO, talking with the lonesome boys, taking them shopping, etc. We also had enjoyed dancing. When we were set apart to preside over the mission, Corraine took occasion to ask President McKay about continuing our connection with the American Association and with dancing. From her oral history:

> *I asked President McKay when he interviewed us—he spent I guess 30 minutes or more just talking about our mission and whatnot—and I said, "President McKay, we have many friends in Uruguay and we've danced with them and so forth. Should we go on with this association and dance while we are on our mission?" He said "No, no, I don't think so." We hadn't danced in the Argentine Mission; I think we led the Grand March or something like that once when we'd have our Gold and Green Balls, that kind of thing. But we never did dance.*

I really didn't want to because our missionaries couldn't, and I didn't want them to get any feelings of wanting something like that. But President McKay said, "No. I don't think anyone loves to dance more than I do, but I don't do it.'[8]

With Elder Richards' visit, the subject of the American community came up again. He wanted to know if we were involved, and we said no, although Harold and Leonore Brown were, of course. I quote again from Corraine's oral history:

I told him that I had belonged to the Women's Club when I was there before and was active in the organization, and I said, "Do you think it would be well for me to join again or not?" Having received a "No" on the question of dancing from President McKay, I really didn't know what he might say. He said: "By all means, identify yourself with that organization." So I did; I joined again. This was an added thing, they met once a month. Of course, I used to think, "Oh my, what a far cry from Relief Society, their attitudes and the things they'd argue about." And they said: "We are not a charitable organization, and we don't approve of giving money for this, that and the other," and you know. But some of their events were very nice, and one thing I recall that endeared that organization to me was the fact that when we arrived there on our Government job I was ill. I thought maybe I was getting flu or something; I became ill on the way—not really ill, but as time went on, the first few days in Uruguay I was very ill; and it turned out that I had typhoid fever, and I spent five weeks in the hospital. Well, I didn't know a soul, but the Ambassador's wife came to visit me, the First Secretary's wife came to visit me, and every so often I had visits from different members of the Women's Club and I really appreciated that. I was in the hospital for Christmas and the Ambassador's wife sent the children all gifts, and so did the First Secretary's wife. When I tried to thank them and talk to the Ambassador's wife about it she said, "Well, I didn't really know what to do. I thought once of having the children come over to the Embassy for Christmas, and then I thought that wouldn't really seem like home or Christmas to them." So she didn't, but I appreciated this and so I felt close to this group, and there were some very nice women in it. I enjoyed them. And it so happened that later on our missionaries were invited to participate on a panel and our singing groups were invited to sing for different occasions. . . . We sang for the celebration of the Fourth of July and so forth; we had McMurdie and Keller and different ones that could sing solos, and our group singing, and it was very well accepted, very well received. I felt that Brother Richards' advice was good and I think it paid off.[9]

After the reception with the Ambassador, we returned to the mission home where the Richardses made final preparations for their departure later that night. A large group of both members and investigators escorted them aboard the S.S. *Uruguay* which was to take them to Santos, Brazil.

The next day, March 6, 1948, I wrote the First Presidency notifying them of Elder and Sister Richards' departure and gave a brief report of their stay:

Brother and Sister Stephen L. Richards left Montevideo at midnight last night for Brazil, on the S.S. Uruguay.

They had been with us for one week and we are most grateful for even these few days. Brother Richards' words of counsel and advice left us better prepared to carry on our activities. Sister Richards' humor and wit were enjoyed by us all. We shall always treasure the memory of this short visit.

They were quite tired after having been on a strenuous tour of the Argentine Mission, but I believe they were quite rested before leaving Montevideo.

Elder Richards talked at the American Association luncheon yesterday and his talk was well received. Last night we were all invited to a reception at the American Embassy, going from there to the ship. I feel sure that his visit here will be of great worth in the furthering of our work in Uruguay. He made an excellent impresssion of our investigators and our friends.

We are very grateful that they were permitted to visit this mission.[10]

We learned subsequently that their visit in Brazil was as hectic, if not more so, as their visit in Argentina had been. The only automobile the Brazilian Mission had was a jeep that had been purchased and donated to the mission by three of our former Argentine missionaries who were then living in Rio de Janeiro. The President took the Richardses on an extended trip through the countryside (more unpaved roads) and it was apparently so rough that he almost fainted. They took him to a hotel and had a doctor look at him; the rest of the trip was cancelled. Some good may have come from the experience: I'm told the Brazilian Mission got a new automobile shortly thereafter.

I wrote Brother Richards on his return on the States, thanking him for the visit and reporting the progress made since his departure. Of particular note was the well-attended baptismal service of our son Fred, the first baptism performed in the mission. Soon many would follow, as is evidenced in the letter that follows:

It is our hope that you and Sister Richards are now fully recovered from your arduous tour of the three South American Missions and that all of your loved ones were well upon your return.

Your visit has done us a great deal of good and the work has progressed steadily and rapidly since you were here. In many of our meetings the missionaries and some of the investigators must remain standing as all available benches are occupied. This is the way we like to see it. There were 72 people present when our son Freddy was baptized and since then some eight people have asked for baptism. Come Spring we hope to have a large baptism service and really get the Mission started off right.

. . . .

Since your departure from Montevideo, we have opened one local *in the capital city, one in Salto, and have missionaries in Durazno and Florida looking for* locales. *The Lord has blessed us greatly and the work is progressing more rapidly than I thought possible. The missionaries are all in good health and spirit and working diligently to acquire a knowledge of the language.*

Last week we added Mutual to our list of activities and had an attendance of 96 investigators in four branches. It keeps us all busy preparing lessons for our organizations because we can adapt only a few of the lessons that we have been reviewing from the Church to the needs of our investigators...

. . . .

We are very grateful for the visit you and Sister Richards had with us and we want you to know that we learned a good deal and appreciate very much the advice and counsel that you gave us. Our investigators and friends were well impressed with what you did and said and our missionaries were very happy to have received your counsel.[11]

I believe Apostle Richards' visit had a tremendously beneficial effect; here was a General Authority who had seen our situation first-hand; had met the people, could appreciate the cultural and social norms under which we had to operate, and could therefore be an advocate in the leading councils of the Church, especially after his call to the First Presidency three years later. His visit certainly set the tone for our mission and I believe was responsible for its rapid growth and development.

NOTES

Chapter IV

1. Copy of the letter is in my possession.

2. Letter dated December 4, 1947, a copy of which is in my possession.

3. Letter dated December 10, 1947.

4. I wrote him December 16, 1947, and he responded December 23, 1947; a copy of my letter and the original from him are both in my possession.

5. Letter of Stephen L. Richards to Frederick S. Williams, December 10, 1947.

6. Uruguayan Mission History, p. 6.

7. Uruguayan Mission History, p. 7.

8. Oral history interview with Corraine S. Williams conducted by Frederick G. Williams, June 13, 1975, pp. 17-18.

9. Oral history interview with Corraine S. Williams, pp. 18-19.

10. Letter to the First Presidency dated March 6, 1948, copy in my possession.

11. Letter to Stephen L. Richards dated April 19, 1948, a copy of which is in my possession.

CHAPTER V

BRANCHES ESTABLISHED AND QUICKLY BEAR FRUIT

AN AIR OF positive expectancy constantly surrounded our work, a sense that things would move quickly, that progress was sure and that our labors would be crowned with success. Everything we did reflected confidence, whether establishing branches when there were no missionaries, or organizing auxiliaries when there were no members. We worked hard, we planned big, we expected success, and we were not disappointed.

I have explained before why, as the newly-called presidents of the mission, we felt very confident. I have also suggested that the use of music to interest people (rather than competitive sports) was a factor and that timing as well as the character of the Uruguayan people made them amenable to our message. In addition, the Apostle's visit just as the work got underway and a corps of dedicated, hard-working missionaries who, because they spoke no Spanish initially had to exercise faith and rely on the Lord more than usual, enabled the Spirit to be manifest in greater abundance. We were also blessed with strong members from the States such as the Harold Browns and later the Wilford M. Farnsworths in Uruguay[1] and the Samuel J. Skousens in Paraguay who could give leadership. We greatly appreciated the continuing support given us by the Argentine Mission. Not only did President Young and his missionaries help us make a strong beginning with their basketball team and musical program,[2] but members of the mission presidency such as L. Pierce Brady and especially Argentine members such as Samuel Borén would visit periodically to speak to the Uruguayans.[3] The Argentines acted as role models for our investigators.

The sister missionaries were also a positive force in the success of the new mission. I called Sister Eduarda Argault on a mission January 7, 1948;[4] from the beginning, the Uruguayan Mission was graced by sister missionaries, each of whom was a tremendous asset. Sister Argault's first companion was my daughter Argina, who served with her for two months,[5] until the arrival of Elza J. Vogler from Río Cuarto, Argentina. Sister Vogler had been set apart in Buenos Aires by Elder Richards, and arrived in Uruguay March 4, 1948. Sisters Argault and Vogler were the first to tract in the Pocitos area and there found some excellent contacts, among them the Canals family. The father, Jacobo Canals, worked at Radio Espectador,[6] and through him we were able to present radio programs which were heard throughout Uruguay and as far south as Chubut in Southern Argentina. The station received many cards and letters from the Welsh people living there, thanking us for the lovely music.

At the conclusion of her one year mission, Sister Argault was replaced by Sister Juana Gianfelice of Buenos Aires, Argentina.[7] Both she and Sister Vogler served until October 7, 1949. Their success, especially in Universitaria and Reducto, prompted me to request that other sister missionaries be sent from the States. I wrote to the First Presidency:

The excellent work performed by the two Argentine lady missionaries, and the way they have been accepted leads me to believe that this would be a fertile field for lady missionaries from the States. If you care to send them this far from home, we would be pleased to receive two or four of them.

Because I had no secretarial help at the office, and we needed musicians desperately, I lobbied for these skills:

If they were selected for special abilities, such as stenography or musical talents, it would help us to no end. We need a stenographer and an accompanist very much.[8]

The first sister missionaries sent were La Von Evans and Mersel M. Day who arrived February 12, 1950. Like the elder missionaries, they spoke no Spanish, so they worked out of the mission home. Neither had secretarial or musical skills; however, they helped enormously in auxiliary organizations. Sister Evans was tall and a home economics major; Sister Day was short with a lightning wit and a talent with words.

Sister Kathryn Hackett arrived December 4, 1950, and Sister Velora Gough on February 11, 1951. Both were stenographers (what supreme pleasure!) and both were musical as well. With their arrival, Sisters Evans and Day were assigned to Arroyo Seco Branch where they became companions to the first Uruguayans called to serve full-time missions: Sister Yolanda Vinci from Salto Branch, and Sister María Aguilera from La Floresta Branch. During our four years, nine full-time sister missionaries served; three were called from Uruguay (two were recent converts); two from Argentina and four from the States.

Uruguay is divided into nineteen geographical departments, most of whose capital cities share the same name. By the end of 1947 we had organized four branches, all in Montevideo. As more missionaries arrived from the States, we were able to open up new areas. During 1948, we organized ten additional branches, two more in Montevideo and seven in the interior. By "organized," I mean the date a hall was leased and missionaries began to proselyte in the area. Usually four, but sometimes only two missionaries would be sent to commence the work. Some type of Sunday meeting would be held within a month or so of their arrival.

The first branch established in the interior was in Treinta y Tres, on January 22, 1948 (a large home on Basilio Arroyo, 331). While I worked for the government, we had constructed a health center in that city, and I knew many influential people there who helped us secure the home, one which many parties were attempting to get as it was the only available one of that size and condition. After the Treinta y Tres branch, two more branches were established in western Uruguay, Mercedes and Paysandú. The following table lists chronologically the branches established in 1948 and, when available, the first meeting date and the number of investigators present (figures from mission history).

BRANCHES ORGANIZED IN 1948

Branch/City	Date Organized	First Meeting	Investigators
Treinta y Tres	22 Jan 1948	Not Available	
Mercedes	16 Feb 1948	14 Mar 1948	14

BRANCHES ORGANIZED IN 1948 (Continued)

Paysandú	18 Feb 1948	28 Mar 1948	19
La Floresta (Montevideo)	13 Mar 1948	28 Mar 1948	22
Durazno	22 Apr 1948	Not Available	
Salto	24 Apr 1948	Not Available	
La Florida	27 Apr 1948	13 Jun 1948	24
Pocitos (Montevideo)	16 May 1948	6 Jun 1948	22
Melo	1 Oct 1948	7 Nov 1948	167
Rocha	4 Oct 1948	28 Nov 1948	49

We found that the relatively large number of investigators attending first branch meetings was not an uncommon phenomenon, nor did the investigator attendance fall off during subsequent meetings. For example, when I visited Mercedes and spoke for the first time there on April 5, 1948, thirty-two investigators attended. The attendance at Melo made it unique. Elders arrived in Melo on July 27, but they had not been able to locate a suitable building for two months. At the first service on November 7, there were 167 investigators inside, including the Brazilian Consul and his wife, and an equal or larger number stood outside trying to hear through the open doors and windows. Both the new mission secretary, Elder John W. Cook, and I spoke. Two investigators played organ solos and a missionary quartet sang. After the meeting, an older woman approached me with these words: "President Williams, I believe every word you said tonight and I'm ready to be baptized." I told her that was wonderful and quickly arranged for the missionaries to teach her.[9]

The success that attended us in our initial meetings continued and attendance increased in each of the fourteen branches operating through 1948, our first complete year. It was not uncommon to have fifty or sixty investigators out to meetings regularly, and all this commenced by missionaries who spoke no Spanish and were generally isolated from one another except for a companion and one other pair of elders. But Uruguay was ready for the gospel, her people seemed to hunger for the things we could teach them, and they were patient and understanding of our shortcomings.[10]

One of the most incredible yet thoroughly satisfying results of our proselyting program (which consisted almost solely of tracting) was that among the large numbers of investigators attracted by our message the majority received testimonies and were committed to the gospel. They lived its teachings and participated in the full program, as far as we would allow them. In fact, we called many of them to leadership positions in the auxiliaries (MIA, Primary, Sunday School) and even as branch officers. La Comercial placed its Mutual entirely in the hands of investigators:

> *On June 30th (1948), the MIA was reorganized in the La Comercial Branch. The missionaries stepped down and appointed the following officers from among the investigators: President, Oscar Nieves; Counselors, Tito Spinelli and Diver Preciozzi; Secretary, Gladys Méndez; Treasurer, Mirta Gómes; Mensajero Deseret representative, Renée Ramírez... The investigators are helping us out by giving talks, bearing their testimonies and bringing new people to church. They go from meeting to meeting, visiting other branches at odd hours.*[11]

The Arroyo Seco Branch reorganization was even more far-reaching as investigators were called as officers in each auxiliary and even as secretary to the branch president:

14th [August, 1948]: A Branch party was held in honor of the officers of the various organizations of the Arroyo Seco Branch. Some eighty people were present to join with these officers: Branch President, Elder Melvin Brady; Branch Secretary, Nelly Rodríguez; Mensajero Deseret correspondent, Elida Alvarez.

Sunday School: Elder Dale Payne, Superintendent; Elsa Ghiringhelli and Miguel Perillo, Counselors; Lorely Sollesel, Secretary.

MIA: Elder Glen Slight, President, with Matilda Ferrari and Rubén Labastie, Counselors; Mirtha Fernández, Secretary.

Primary: Marie Fernández, President; Gladys Ceforelle and Margarita Pérez, Counselors; Jorge Fernández, Secretary.

The Malvín branch followed suit on August 28, 1948, and placed the Sunday School and Primary entirely in the hands of non-members, and likewise called an investigator as Branch Secretary:

The Malvín Branch honored its officers with a party Saturday night. A very large crowd was present (104). The branch officers are as follows:

Branch President: Elder Stewart K. Burton; Ana María García, Secretary.

Sunday School: Avelino Rodríguez, Superintendent; Rosa Leytes and Libio Fornica, Counselors; Ana María García, Secretary.

MIA: Elder John O. Whitaker, President; Ana María García and Teobaldo Gravetto, Counselors; Zulma Gonda, Secretary.

Primary: Nelly Telerraqui, President; María E. Rodríguez and Hilda Racagno, Counselors.

Investigators spoke in Church regularly and at mission-wide conferences; they performed in roadshows and concerts, conducted meetings, played musical instruments, sang in choirs, traveled to other branches to speak, even tracted with the missionaries; not one was yet a member of the Church. We didn't concentrate on baptisms; however, we were teaching the elders Spanish, teaching investigators gospel fundamentals, and establishing bases throughout the country. We knew that the baptisms would follow, because faithful investigators came week after week and month after month to the meetings and behaved as members.

We wanted to baptize them, of course, and it wasn't too long before we overcame our hesitation to perform that ordinance. I'm sure our reluctance stemmed from never having seen people baptized, either in Argentina or even in the United States, after only a relatively short acquaintance with the gospel. Once baptisms began, however, they never stopped.

First baptisms. When our son Fred turned eight the opportunity arose to teach the ordinance of baptism by example, and we made the most of it. We invited the entire mission and on April 3, 1948, seventy-two investigators listened to a talk on baptism by Harold Brown and witnessed the baptismal ceremony I performed on Frederick G. Williams in the Arroyo de Carrasco. Soon after, Freddy admonished others to follow his example. I'll never forget the opening of one of his sacrament meeting talks: "Jesús se bautizó. Los misioneros se bautizaron. Yo me bauticé. Y sé que todos *Uds.* se van a bautizar . . . Espero." (Jesus was baptized. The missionaries were baptized. I was baptized. And I know all of you are going to be baptized . . . I hope.)

The first convert baptism was performed in Asunción, Paraguay on August 21, 1948, when Samuel J. Skousen, Air Attaché of the United States Embassy, and President of the Asunción Branch, baptized Carlos Alberto Rodríguez. Authorization had been obtained previously from the First Presidency to officiate in this ordinance (Mission History, July 8, 1948).

Investigators began requesting baptism, and I reported to Elder Stephen L. Richards that "come Spring we hope to have a large baptism service and really get the Mission started off right" (letter dated April 19, 1948). Special classes to prepare those contemplating baptism began in October, and the first Uruguayan converts were baptized November 4. The Mission History records:

> *The 4th was a historical day for the Uruguayan Mission. Representing the first citizens of this country to accept the message of the Restored Gospel, Avelino Juan Rodríguez, his wife, María Esther Rizzo de Rodríguez, and Diber Alba Preciozzi entered the waters of baptism. The ordinance was performed in the Arroyo Carrasco at a point not far from the mouth of the stream. It was a beautiful summer day, ideal for the baptisms. Before the actual baptisms took place, a meeting was conducted on the sandy shores of the stream by President Williams. The group consisting of the three candidates, some members of their families and various missionaries, enjoyed a wonderful spirit and some very sincere testimonies were born. After the meeting, the first to enter the water was Brother Rodríguez, being baptized by President Frederick S. Williams. Sister Preciozzi followed and was baptized by Elder Preston J. Bushman, after which Sister Rodríguez was baptized by President Williams.*

The Rodríguezes lived in quarters behind the ODA store below the mission home. We had fellowshipped them for some time and he had even accompanied me on interior trips where he would speak in Sacrament meeting with me. Sister Preciozzi was from the La Comercial branch, and had been serving as a counselor in the MIA. The Rodríguezes attended Malvín where Brother Rodríguez had served as Sunday School superintendent, and she as a counselor in the Primary Presidency.

Two days later, five were baptized in Treinta y Tres[12] (Elia Magallanes de Riano, Delia Magallanes, Mabel Dora Ramos, Gabriela Amabilia Hoz and Nemecio Francisco Riano). This brought convert baptisms during November to a total of eight.

Four baptismal services were held in December. Two baptisms in Durazno (Clara Silva, María Celia Barcelona), one in Mercedes (Berta Burger de Dalmas), and thirty-four in Montevideo. The largest service was held for the Capital district at Carrasco on December 8, 1948, for twenty-eight baptisms (candidates from Arroyo Seco, La Comercial, Pocitos and Malvín). Over two hundred investigators participated in a picnic in the morning and in the afternoon witnessed the service:

> *A large crowd of people gathered on the shore to view the baptisms and some were heard to remark on the similitude of our baptism to that practiced by Christ. A number of investigators stated their desires of being baptized in the near future.*[13]

During 1949, eight new branches were established,[14] all but one in the interior:

BRANCHES ORGANIZED IN 1949

Branch/City	Date Organized	First Meeting	Investigators
Universitaria (Montevideo)	6 Jan 1949	23 Jan 1949	95
Tacuarembó	12 Mar 1949	27 Mar 1949	27
Minas	15 Mar 1949	10 Apr 1949	180
Santa Lucía	31 May 1949	12 Jun 1949	43
Maldonado	19 Aug 1949	2 Oct 1949	100
Isla Patrulla	22 Aug 1949	2 Dec 1949	100
Rivera	6 Oct 1949	2 Dec 1949	24
Trinidad	9 Nov 1949	Not Available	

The most interesting branch was Isla Patrulla. In the heart of Uruguay's *gaucho* country, it is no island but a small village surrounded by ranches. I had two purposes in mind when I opened this area to the gospel. First, a very good convert family baptized in Treinta y Tres lived on a nearby ranch. Second, the Catholic Church had been spreading adverse propaganda about the Mormon Church, being interested only in people in the larger cities, and having no interest in people who lived in the back country. I wanted to care for our new members' spiritual needs, and took up the challenge to see what could be done among the country people.

On April 8, 1949, Elders Loyal Cecil Millet, Charles C. Janson, Wilford M. Farnsworth and I went by car to Isla Patrulla. We performed two baptisms, visited several families, and were served a delicious *asado*. Cottage meetings were held at the Roviras' and at other ranches; we traveled on horseback.

On August 22, 1949, I rented a large sod-roofed, dirt-floored house. It was as good as most of the other dwellings, besides being the only one available. A post buried in the ground supported the center ridge pole that supported the roof. Elders Millet and Edwin T. Christiansen were assigned to Isla Patrulla. The mission supplied cement and the elders the man power to lay a cement floor in the hall of the local, the only cement floor in the village. The missionaries wore boots and bombachas (the *gaucho* baggy pants) as did everyone else. Barefoot urchins came to make friends and watch the elders work. One said: "I feel sorry for you." "Why?" asked the elder. "Because you have to wear boots all day. Don't your feet hurt you?"

For transportation we bought a two-wheeled cart and a gray horse soon named "Fiddlebomb." (Incidentally, while I lived in Perú I received a request from the Uruguayan Mission to sign a release for the cart, which had been purchased in my name. It was sold in 1958.)

On December 2, 1949, we held the first meeting. One hundred people crowded into our hall and a few stood outside. Many of the people wore knives in their belts. Others had pistols. This Sunday was no different from other days, as far as they were concerned. José Gervasio Artigas Martínez, a good friend and investigator and the foreman of a large ranch, led the singing for us, his spurs jingling as he beat the time with his foot.[15]

After the meeting I met the Justice of the Peace, the highest ranking official in the village. During our long conversation, he told me that he had been worried about the meeting because he didn't know how the people would respond. He stood at the door to be ready to put down any disturbance that might occur. He was amazed at the people's conduct, and after the first few minutes knew that the meeting would go well. He complimented us on our messages and activities and said he was greatly impressed with the missionaries and their hard work.

We visited the Isla Patrulla elders regularly to see what progress was being made. On one hot summer day I spoke in one of the meetings. There was no cross ventilation and the room was very warm. I suppose my sermon was too long, but for some reason, the elder seated nearest the open doorway fell asleep. As I spoke, I was startled to see the horned head and shoulders of a cow come through the door and stop about a foot from the sleeping elder. Perhaps the cow's breath awoke him, but he opened his eyes, looked directly into the cow's eyes and leaped away from his bench. The cow ambled away; the elder remained attentive the balance of the meeting. Because of the scarcity of Spanish-speaking elders, I was accustomed to giving forty-five minute talks. Perhaps I should have paid more attention to the suggestion of my seven-year old daughter, Nancy, who, after one of the meetings, said, "Daddy, you talk too long."

I attended a large baptismal service in Isla Patrulla. Artigas Martínez, the gaucho foreman, and I rode out looking for water deep enough for the baptisms. It had recently rained and the arroyos were full of pools of water. We found one that was sufficiently deep, but it contained a recently drowned cow. Artigas roped the cow and pulled the dead animal out; the pool became our baptismal font.

The power of prayer. Like the others, the Salto Branch held great promise for numerous baptisms. Elder Thaddeus E. Shoemaker, branch president, and Elders Glenn E. Manning, B. Lyle Schofield and Robert E. Clayton worked diligently from April of 1948, and found many investigators. Supervising elders visited regularly to lend a hand, and I visited Salto four times during the year. Surprisingly, in spite of our efforts none of the investigators expressed a desire to be baptized even though the work was advancing so rapidly in all the other branches of the mission.

Finally, the first baptisms were set for March 26, 1949, and we prepared to attend a series of weekend baptismal services and other meetings in Mercedes, Paysandú, Tacuarembó, as well as Salto. Sisters Vogler and Gianfelice accompanied Corraine and me. Elder Shoemaker, since transferred to another branch, also came. We arrived in Salto in a downpour the night of March 25. Rain had fallen continuously over the whole of western Uruguay for a week; it didn't look like it would let up in the near future.

Sixty people—the baptismal candidates and their families and friends—met at the church on Saturday morning. Some were understandably hesitant to go through with the ordinance because of the rain. Because there was no other facility, we were forced to use the swollen Uruguay River for the baptisms, and of course there were no dressing rooms or shelters for the relatives and friends. I assured them that the baptisms could be carried out, and after a prayer in the chapel, we stuffed as many people as we could into cars and made our cautious way through the downpour to the river. From where we parked, about thirty yards away, it was impossible to see the flood-swollen stream through the heavy rain.

I signaled the others to remain in their cars and started to walk to the river's edge, but before I had gone twenty feet I was completely soaked, even with my raincoat.

At the river bank I removed my hat and talked to the Lord. I told him of his servants' labors, and of the problems we had experienced incidental to these first baptisms. I mentioned that I had been called by his prophet to open the work in this nation, that these would be the first fruits of many to be gathered in this part of Uruguay, and that the hands of prophets had been laid upon my head giving me the authority to succeed. I felt that what I was about to do was in accordance with the sixty-first section of the Doctrine and Covenants: "Wherefore, let him do as the Spirit of the Living God commanded him, whether upon the land or upon the waters . . ." and I felt "that this power had been given by his spirit . . ." Feeling serene and confident, in the name of the Lord Jesus Christ, and in the authority of the Holy Melchizedek Priesthood which I held, I rebuked the weather and commanded the rain to hold off until the baptisms had been performed.

Never in my life have I felt such a sweet and humble spirit within myself. Four presidents of the Church have laid their hands upon my head, as well as nine other General Authorities (seven were apostles) to ordain and set me apart for positions of responsibility, and I have felt the Spirit of the Lord at those times, but never to the same extent as during the rainstorm. Neither before nor after had my "bosom burned within me" to the same degree that it did then. I felt all was right in the world and that nothing could stop the Lord's work from going forward. Never before had I felt so humble. When I returned to the cars, the rain had ceased. The lady candidates dressed behind blankets held by their female friends, while the elders did the same some distance away. We performed six baptisms that day, and, after the participants changed into dry clothes, we returned to the cars. The rain resumed almost instantly. The downpour didn't cease until after our return to Montevideo two days later.

My sacred experience that day remained a secret between the Lord and me for twenty-five years, when I was constrained to tell my wife, who had witnessed the occurrence.

NOTES

Chapter V

1. The successful establishment of the Uruguayan Mission is due to the dedicated endeavors of a hundred and sixteen missionaries and their enthusiasm for the work of the Lord. However, special acknowledgment is due to two individuals who, because of their training and knowledge of the Spanish language, were able to help at the particular time when the newly arrived missionaries were still struggling with the language.

In the first group of elder from the States came Wilford M. Farnsworth, a recent graduate in business from Brigham Young University. Born and raised in the Mormon colonies in Mexico, he had learned Spanish in his youth. Having served as an ensign in the United States Navy he was a little older and more experienced than the others. He was called as the first mission secretary and it was he who organized the books that kept track of the financial and historical aspects of the mission. His quick mind and excellent accounting ability were very helpful to the new mission. Upon his release, he returned to the States where he married Ella Hull, who had completed a mission in Hawaii, and took a job with City Bank of New York. We were delighted when they were assigned to Montevideo, where they arrived July 17, 1950.

On February 12, 1948, just five months after the opening of the mission, Harold and Leanore Brown arrived in Uruguay, where he was assigned to the United States Embassy as Vice-Consul. Both proved a great blessing to the struggling new mission. Both spoke fluent Spanish, Harold speaks it better than any Anglo I have ever known. Before their arrival, Elder Farnsworth, Corraine and I would speak at the four branches in Montevideo, alternating the hours of the meetings so that we could participate in all. With the arrival of the Browns, my load became lighter. We divided the meetings among us, instead of having to give three different discourses every Sunday. The Browns were also a tremendous help musically; it was good to feel their support in the new mission. We had to write and print our own tracts and lessons. At the beginning of the Mutual year, Corraine, Leanore, Harold, Wilford and I each wrote six MIA lessons which served for the whole year.

On December 24, 1848, Harold and Leanore received a call to preside over the Argentine Mission. Their departure was keenly felt by all of us, but the Argentine Mission gained immeasurably. During the following two and a half year, the two missions cooperated for the benefit of both.

2. Held at the Alizanza Cultural Uruguaya-Norteamericana, January 17, 1948; the event attracted 300 people to the musical program and 1500 to the game. On Sunday, the 18th, 250 people attended the Conference in the Teatro Ateneo.

3. Brady came with the mission group in January, and with his family on May 15, 1948. Borén brought a group with him from La Plata in January 1948. The Mission History reads: "On Saturday the 24th, Brother and Sister Samuel Borén, Oscar Lavista, Hugo Salvioli, Mrs. Rolf Salvioli and Elsa Paco, members of the La Plata Branch of the Argentine Mission, arrived in Montevideo to spend a few days at the Mission Home. They visited and spoke in four branches on Sunday the 25th. Their testimonies were well received by the Uruguayan investigators . . . Elder Borén is a former Argentine Missionary and Branch President of the La Plata Branch. A native Argentine, he is at present president of the district where he lives."

4. Eduarda Argault, together with her sister Renée and mother Juana, had come to Uruguay from Argentina to escape an oppressive and dangerous home situation. Originally from France, the women had saved up the money for their move to Canada and eventually the United States at the time of her call to serve a mission. Exercising great faith in the Lord, she postponed the trip to accept the call and used the money for the trip to finance her mission. Cf. Part Two, Chapter VIII.

5. Gina was only 13, but very mature for her age. She loved to tract and gloried in the missionary activities. One elder said of her in a missionary testimony meeting that she "did more missionary work than any elder there." She continued to do missionary work after this call. On one occasion, Gina was holding a series of cottage meetings with a lady investigator who wouldn't permit the elders to visit her, feeling that if the young men called on her, people would not understand and her beauty parlor business would suffer. Gina and her companion, a young member girl, never knew when the woman would be home to see them and, as likely as not, even on nights when an appointment had been set, she would have to work late at her shop. Since there was no telephone, they took a chance each time they went.

One night, we asked Gina if she wouldn't like to go to a movie with us. She indicated that she had a potential cottage meeting to teach. We offered to take the two by the investigator's home, and if she were not there, then they could both go to the show with us. Gina agreed; it had been a long time since she had been to a show.

As we were getting ready to go in our car, Gina said she had decided not to go afer all, that she would prefer to go by bus with her companion. We again offered to drive them, but she said, "No, if I went with you I would wish that our investigator were not home so I could go to the show, and that wouldn't be right." The two went on the bus, but the investigator was not at home.

6. The whole Canals family eventually came into the Church: Martha first, then Walter. A son, Omar, was born in 1948, and I was asked to bless him even though his parents were not yet members. Today, Walter is a vice president of Bonneville Corporation in Salt Lake and arranged radio and television coverage of general conferences, cultural programs and BYU basket ball games in nearly all Latin American countries. Omar is a member of the general board of the Young Men's Mutual and in charge of the Spanish translation department of the Church.

7. Juana was a daughter of Donato and Emilia Gianfelice, one of the oldest and dearest member families in South America, one I had known and loved first as a young missionary. Juana's older brother, Antonio (today a patriarch), had been instrumental in introducing Elders Ballard and Pratt to his family in 1926. Cf. Part One, Chapters III and VI.

8. Letter dated May 14, 1949. I renewed my request on August 24, 1949, and was gratified to receive this acknowledgment from the First Presidency, September 8, 1949: "We shall do our best to find lady missionaries who are suitable to send to South America."

9. I was in the Melo Branch on another occasion and she sought me out again after church: "I'm still ready to be baptized," she said. Seventy-nine year old Margarita Miranda de Aguino was in the first group of baptisms held in Melo, April 9, 1949. Another baptized that day was Martin Erasmo Gorospe, who, as a Bishop of the Central Ward of Melo, visited in my home in Downey on his way to a General Conference in 1979.

10. One rather common slip in those days was to call our tracts "fallutos" (a failed person or thing) instead of "folletos." A classic slip involved a door approach by the newest of two elders who drew a blank and stood in silence before the waiting lady who had asked: "¿Que desean?" (What do you want?). His companion whispered in his ear: "Tell her who are are," which sounded to him like "Tell her, jugar," which is what he said, much to her astonishment. *Jugar* means to play.

11. Oscar Nieves, an accomplished organist, had been secretary to Sir Middleton Drake a former British Ambassador to Uruguay. He spoke excellent English and his friends were well-to-do, cultured, and powerful. He introduced us to many of them. He spoke in Church, traveled to the interior to tract with the elders, and held group meetings in his home. The Mission History records on April 2, 1948: "An investigator, Oscar Nieves, invited thirty friends to his home to meet the missionaries and to hear their message. His mother and sisters prepared sandwiches and cakes. The mission presented a missionary quartet, and Sister Williams, Barbara, and Argina sang two trios. President Williams then spoke, explaining Gospel principles. There were three lawyers, two doctors and several teachers present. The program was well received and several conversations continued ater the meeting until midnight." Oscar and his sister Blanca joined the Church.

12. From the Mission History: "Radio Station Treinta y Tres began broadcasting the notice of the opening MIA social in Treinta y Tres for the 5th of June (1948). The Catholic Church had circulated rumors that the missionaries were communists and many people would not talk to them. They went to the radio station and explained their difficulty. The owner, angry at what he had heard, broadcast the following for five consecutive days: 'Two young North Americans came to see me stating that some people were circulating the rumor that they were communists. This is not true. These two young men are here on a religious mission to teach religious truths. Both defended the freedom of the world in the last war. Each Uruguayan should go and hear what they have to say. Next Saturday they are having the opening social for their Mutual organization. You fathers and mothers should let your young people attend this meeting. Better still, go and take them with you." Fifty-five people "packed" the *local* on that opening night, with many more outside trying to get inside.

13. Uruguayan Mission History.

14. Only one other branch besides these eight was established in Uruguay during my administration (Canelones, April 2, 1951); while two were organized in Asunción, Paraguay, one in 1950, another in 1951.

15. Artigas won the mission-wide competition for *Mensajero* magazine subscriptions sold.

CHAPTER VI

MUSIC: SWEET AMBASSADOR OF THE LORD

IN ARGENTINA we had used sports to attract the people, and we accomplished our goal, but not without hard feelings. When opening the new mission in Uruguay, we decided to take a different approach. The athletic competitions in Argentina were not simply between two teams, but between Argentina and the United States, and the natives (and to some degree the elders) felt their national pride was at stake; we found we made more friends when we lost than when we won. We didn't want the same situation in Uruguay. Missionaries were permitted to participate in sports to a limited extent, but only if they became part of an established team. Rather than draw attention to our mission through sports, in Uruguay we opted for music. There is no competition with music; no one loses, everyone wins.

While in Salt Lake City before leaving for Uruguay, I asked the Brethren for their permission to use the radio to spread the gospel. I felt the opening of a new mission would be an excellent opportunity to test the efficacy of radio broadcasts to attract investigators. Corraine and I met with Gordon B. Hinckley, head of Church communications at the time, to get his reaction and suggestions to the idea. Wanting to disarm him a little, I began by saying, "I understand you are the most difficult person in the Church to deal with." He expressed surprise, but sweetly and vigorously denied the allegation. I then explained my idea, which he thought had merit and should be carried out, but he said I must clear it first with President McKay. David O. McKay encouraged us in the project, but only if we could secure free air time; he felt that the Church should not buy time. As it turned out, we were rarely permitted to preach the gospel over the Uruguayan airwaves, but we were able to present music in the Church's name. The combination of music and radio had far-reaching effects.

My ace in the hole was my wife, a soprano with a beautiful solo voice, and my two eldest daughters, Barbara and Argina. From them I had solos, duets, and, most important, an exceptionally fine trio.[1] Corraine was also the arranger (and later composer with an impressive list of credits), and she had succeeded in training the girls to perform a complex and varied repertoire of religious and secular music. We felt that if we were also blessed with musically talented missionaries, we would be set.

Corraine and the trio first performed at the opening services of each branch, beginning with Malvín, November 9, 1947, and continuing through the rest of the year, culminating with the December 21, 1947, Christmas concert held at the mission home before the missionaries, forty-one investigators, and friends. The trio sang together for about three years. When Barbara left Uruguay (April 14, 1950) to attend Brigham Young University, three successive missionaries replaced her: Glen L. Slight, B. LaMar Williams (my nephew), and Kathryn Hackett.[2]

We next formed a mission chorus. Directed by Elder Preston J. Bushman, these choirs were at first organized only for special occasions such as our 1947 Christmas concert, the visit of Elder Richards in February 1948, and the first mission-wide conference in July 1948. Regular rehearsals and continuous performances began in September 1948. Elder Glen L. Slight took over as director on January 1, 1949, when Elder Bushman was transferred to Paysandú, and over the next year and a half polished it into an outstanding performing organization. He was succeeded by Dallas Keller and later by Maughan W. McMurdie, all of them exceptionally gifted soloists and musicians.[3]

The backbone of the mission chorus was my family in the women's section (including nine-year old alto Freddy), and in the men's, all the missionaries in the Capital District who could carry a tune plus eleven-year old Jimmy Gibbons (son of Dr. and Sister Gibbons serving a mission in Uruguay). But right from the start, investigators, mostly young women who had never sung before, participated. The chorus became a missionary tool with great impact, both in terms of the friendshipping and fellowshipping opportunities it provided the non-members and members who sang in it, but in terms of its drawing power at live concerts, over the radio and in mission, district and branch conferences. The music was beautiful, masterfully performed and uplifting. The Uruguayans enjoyed music and were justly proud to find their own compatriots performing. Many previously untrained non-members (and later, members) developed into competent, and in some instances, outstanding singers who regularly performed in their home branches and on special mission programs such as roadshows, conferences, pageants, and cantatas.[4]

Soon the chorus stabilized at forty voices and rehearsed at the mission home each Thursday evening at seven-thirty. It performed two to three times a month in both secular and sacred programs all over the country (travelling by bus) and in Buenos Aires; in fact, the chorus performed anywhere the missionaries could arrange concerts. Even when the young people were out camping for a week we held choir rehearsal, attracting an appreciative audience in the process:

> *Feb. 22 (1950) President and Sister Williams with Elder Glen Slight visited the campamento and conducted chorus practice there. Passersby congregated to listen to the rehearsal and soon a whole crowd of people, offering appreciative comments about the music, had accumulated (Uruguayan Mission History).*

We were a little apprehensive at first about taking the young investigators and member women on overnight trips with a group of young North American elders. We were pleased by the response and support we received from their parents; all gave their consent and the weekend trips were all well received wherever we appeared. No disagreeable or unfortunate consequences ever occurred. Before our excursion to Argentina, the chorus received some very sage counsel from President McKay:

President Frederick S. Williams
Uruguayan Mission
Montevideo, Uruguay

Dear Brother:

The receipt of your letter February 7, 1950, is acknowledged in which you say that you have received a request from the President of the Argentine Mission for the Uruguayan mission choir to furnish the music for two sessions of the annual conference of the Argentine Mission to be held in Buenos Aires, April 9, 1950.

Our first reaction to this request was rather negative, but inasmuch as the choir already has a fund accumulated from concerts held, from which their traveling expenses will be paid, and inasmuch as the mingling of members of the two missions will inevitably result in developing a spirit of confidence and brotherhood among the members, we feel impressed to grant your request.

Needless to say, every effort should be put forth to impress the members with the responsibility which is theirs, for from the moment they leave their homes until they return, they will be looked upon as representatives of The Church of Jesus Christ of Latter-day Saints, and men and women will judge the Church not only by their actions but by their conversations. Always they should be ladies and gentlemen, whose words and actions are above reproach. Let us hope that it may be said by strangers and friends alike that the Church had given these young people a culture and refinement most admirable.

Sincerely yours,
THE FIRST PRESIDENCY
/s/ David O. McKay

The last paragraph was translated into Spanish and distributed to all members along with my own list of admonitions. The excursion was a great success, and all the choir members behaved and sang beautifully.[5]

Although there were one or two groups formed to sing in church from time to time, the mission quartet came into being only after the arrival on February 17, 1949, of bass Elder Vernon L. Melander. However, the first quartet performance recorded in the mission history took place June 5, 1949, considerably later than the debut of the other two performing groups in 1947. But the quartet quickly became a mainstay and a favorite at all the concerts and conferences sponsored by the Church. Besides Melander, members of the original quartet were Elders Wayne R. Cardon, tenor, Dallas Keller, baritone, and Glen L. Slight, second tenor.[6]

As I indicated, the missionaries had contacted the Canals family in Pocitos. Their son Walter and daughter Tita became investigators. Their father, Jacobo Canals, worked for Radio Espectador in Montevideo and through him we were invited to present special radio programs. Soon we were offered the opportunity to present a weekly fifteen-minute radio program. We thought it over, and, feeling that the Lord had had a hand in opening this door, accepted the offer. The program was broadcast live (of course), Wednesdays at 9:45 p.m. I acted as the announcer, and although I was not permitted to proselyte over the air, I always began and ended the programs by identifying the Church:

> *La Mision Uruguaya de La Iglesia de Jesucristo de Los Santos de Los Ultimos Días, se complace en presentar un programa de música por el (cuarteto or trío).*
>
> *(The Uruguayan Mission of the Church of Jesus Christ of Latter-day Saints is pleased to present a musical program by the (quartet or trio).)*

The quartet and trio alternately presented the weekly program. Both had theme songs to sign on and off the air. The quartet used "How High the Moon" (in Spanish, *"Habrá Canciones"* and the trio, "Song of the Islands," sung without words. The first regular broadcast by the quartet was on Wednesday, November 2, 1949; they sang a capella. The trio was preparing its program for November 9 (also *a capella*) when, to our surprise and great joy, a marvelous accompanist and singer arrived to begin his mission. Elder Maughan W. McMurdie was the answer to prayers to God and petitions to the First Presidency. He arrived just in time to accompany the trio on its first broadcast. The radio programs were heard throughout Uruguay and via short wave in Argentina. The station received letters of appreciation and congratulations from as far away as the Welsh colonies in Patagonia. Our program was broadcast weekly for four months; we then discontinued it because we felt we could not devote the time necessary to its preparation. From the Mission History:

> *March 1 (1950) Last November 2 a series of weekly broadcasts over radio station Espectador was started by the mission trio, composed of Barbara, Argina and Corraine S. Williams, and the mission quartet, composed of Elders Glen Slight, Dallas Keller, Vernon Melander and Wayne R. Cardon. The last broadcast in this series was given Wednesday, March 1, with a special half-hour program of music by these two groups with Elder Maughan W. McMurdie at the piano. The coming events in the mission will not permit us to spend the necessary time to prepare the programs. We can return to the air as soon as we want to, however.*

In fact, we presented our next broadcast less than a week later, on March 5, when these two groups and the chorus performed in connection with our mission-wide conference, but there were no more regular broadcasts. For three consecutive Christmases the chorus broadcast a special program, a part of which was a spoken message I prepared and read.[7] We did the same at Easter and on other occasions.

Elder Maughan W. McMurdie was already an accomplished singer and musician when he arrived November 7, 1949. He could sight read any music placed before him, and, if no music were available, but if someone could sing, hum or whistle a song for him, he could play it by ear. He sang beautifully and would often accompany himself on the piano or organ. Even though he knew the music, he felt more comfortable if the sheet music were before him. However, when he soloed he never looked at the music, and when he reached the bottom of the page, he automatically reached up and turned it over. One of the few times I remember seeing him playing from the written music was in Mercedes one hot Sunday afternoon. It was so hot that the benches and organ had been moved out into the patio for Sacrament meeting. A small breeze helped to cool the atmosphere. I happened to take my eyes off of him while he was accompanying himself. When I glanced back, he as leaning over, trying to follow the music that had blown from the organ to the ground, a few feet away. I quickly picked it up and replaced it on the organ while he continued without interrupting his song or the accompaniment.[8]

The arrival of Elder LeRoy W. Fitzell on February 12, 1950, also boosted our musical talent. He was a good singer and a professional dancer. He had performed professionally since he was eight, appearing in several movies and in many concerts.[9] His specialty was Spanish dances. The audiences went wild; he received standing ovations each time he performed, and they couldn't believe he wasn't Spanish. One man said, "Well, he must have been kidnapped from his gypsy parents when just a child." A critic told me he had seen the best Spanish dancers in the world, and none was better than Fitzell.

The combined talents of our soloists (Corraine S. Williams, Dallas Keller, Glen L. Slight and Maughan W. McMurdie), the trio and quartet, the mission chorus, and Roy Fitzell's dances as the showstoppers, provided exceptional entertainment. As the mission progressed and branches were established throughout the country, we used the musical groups to attract people to our conferences. Typically, a local club sponsored a public program in a theater on a Saturday night, with a private program for its own club members presented either before or after the public performance. The club normally furnished us with the theater for our Sunday conference session and, in addition, paid round-trip bus expenses for our forty-member chorus. The local radio station broadcast a special program put on by our group at least once (sometimes more often) during the weekend. I almost always gave a short talk to explain our program and what we were doing in Uruguay.

Newspapers also publicized these events; thus many people had an opportunity to attend church and listen to our message who otherwise would not have known about it. We also held elders meetings, baptismal services and auxiliary leadership training meetings at the same time.

In Montevideo we presented programs at high schools, in theaters, for the Boy Scouts, the YMCA, Crandon Institute (an American parochial school), and prestigious clubs like the Montevideo Rowing Club. One concert at the Rowing Club was sponsored by the wife of the President of Uruguay, Mrs. Batlle Berres. We also performed regularly for various organizations within the American community, at churches, at the U.S. Embassy and at picnics.

The whole musical group traveled to Buenos Aires, and twice without the chorus we traveled to Asunción, Paraguay, to present programs in high schools, cultural institutes, in two theaters and on two different radio stations. The President of Paraguay and many of the foreign diplomatic corps attended one or more performances. These same groups performed during our semiannual mission-wide conferences in both the cultural segment on Saturday night and the two sessions of conference on Sunday, both of which were held at the Ateneo Hall in Montevideo.

It wasn't always possible to take all the performing groups into the interior, but some of our musical talent appeared in every one of the branches several times a year. During our presidency, the chorus performed sixty-nine times (fourteen radio shows), the quartet 140 times (fifty-four radio shows), and the trio 144 times (fifty radio shows). We received reams of publicity and the good will of countless people. Many curious people who came to enjoy the music returned and investigated the gospel. Many became members. I feel the music played a very important part in making us known in Uruguay and in the establishment of the mission.

NOTES

Chapter VI

1. The trio had its origin in Venezuela while we were working for the government there in 1943. During the war years there was very little entertainment available, especially in Maracay. While washing dishes, Corraine taught the girls their parts, patiently repeating them (though frequently interrupted by prolonged giggling spells) until Barbara, 12, could carry the alto part and Argina, 8, the melody, while Corraine added the third part. Their first song was "Calm as the Night," not an easy song for beginners.

We entertained visitors from the U.S. Government in our home and the trio would sing. We received many compliments; one visitor who understood and enjoyed music suggested they make a life career of singing.

The trio increased its repertoire in Uruguay during the two years we were there working for the Institute of Inter-American Affairs and often sang in two languages. The girls' voices matured and blended beautifully with Corraine's.

2. Slight was released September 1, 1950; Williams on February 14, 1951. In addition, there were special occasions (due to illness or the girls' school schedule) when others filled in the missing voices in the trio. These included Dallas Keller, Maughan McMurdie, Velora Gough and Leanore Brown. A representative list of both the secular and sacred music sung by the trio taken from the Uruguayan Mission History includes the following: Annie Roonie, Maria Bonita, Pretty Quadroon, Garden in the Rain, Mi Paraguaya/La Uruguaya, Hawaiian War Chant, Down in the Valley, Trade Winds, Winter Wonderland, Adorar al Niño, Nostalgias Tucumanas, Anahi, The Bridge Builder, Pedimos Hoy Por Ti, Cantemos a Ti, Señor, Prayer Perfect, God is Ever Beside Me, He Shall Feed His Flock, The Green Cathedral, Oh My Father, Bless This House, I'm in Love With You, Honey.

Corraine's solos included, The Holy City; L'Amour Toujour, L'Amour; My Faith in Thee.

All the sacred, and many of the secular numbers, were translated into Spanish by Frederick S. Williams, some on the run just before they were to be performed.

3. Keller took over on September 1, 1950, and served as chorus director until his release March 27, 1951, when McMurdie took over.

At first the chorus had no regular accompanist and it often sang *a capela* (or even accompanied by Tabernacle organ records). Elder Leland Wakefield, an accomplished pianist serving in the Argentine Mission, accompanied the chorus at the first two mission conferences, and on Radio Espectador. B. LaMar Williams, however, was the choir's first regular accompanist, followed by Maughan W. McMurdie, who accompanied all the performing groups from November 1949, on the date of his arrival in the mission field. On one occasion, Nene Mendoza accompanied the chorus, and, after McMurdie began directing it, April 2, 1951,

Armando Young was the accompanist. Both these Uruguayans were accomplished pianists. Mendoza participated in many concerts both as a soloist and accompanying vocalists such as Dallas Keller as she did in their own concert which drew more than 500 people on, August 25, 1949, in Trinidad.

4. At the close of the afternoon session of mission conference, Sunday March 25, 1951, the Easter cantata "Victory" was presented in Spanish (my translation). Soloists were Juanita Gómez, soprano, Edison Fau, bass, Esther Salvetti, soprano. A trio included Edith Pokorny, soprano, Nelly Parada, contralto and Elder Wilford Hale, tenor. A bass solo was sung by Lucas Parada, accompanied by the chorus; a contralto solo was sung by Mabel Fazio, and a quartet by Elders Vernon Melander, bass, Herman Rhoton, tenor, Marta Canals, alto and Perla Fazio, soprano, completed the special numbers.

5. From the Urugauyan Mission History: "April 11, 1950, President Williams and his family returned from Buenos Aires on the morning of the eleventh, reporting that the conference in Argentina has been truly inspirational and the music of our chorus, quartette and trio was greatly appreciated there.

"Members of the choir who made the trip were: Elder Robert Marsh, Elder LaMar Williams, Elder Duane Majors, Elder Lyle Schofield, Elder James R. Dale, Elder Glenn Manning, Sister Lavon Evans, Lucas Parada, José García, Marta Canals, Sonia Aulisso, Blanca Nieves, Elsa Nieves, Edith Pokorny, Perla Fazio, Mabel Fazio, Renée Ramírez, Nelly Parada, Susana Orsan, Bermilia Preciozzi."

"The quartette was made up of Elders Glen Slight, Dallas Keller, Herman Rhoton, and Vernon Melander, the trio was made up of Corraine S. Williams and her daughters Barbara and Argina."

"Elder Glen Slight directed the chorus and Elder LeRoy Fitzell did several solo dance numbers."

One very conspicuous name missing from the record was that of Maughan W. McMurdie who regularly accompanied all these groups on the piano. Freddy Williams was there too as the History records April 6, 1950.

Among the secular and sacred pieces in the mission chorus' repertoire was: By the Bend of the River, Ol' Man River, Carry Me Back to Old Virginny, Jingle Bells, King Jesus is a Listening, El Tren del Evangelio, O Divine Redeemer, God So Loved the World, Hallelujah Chorus, A Ti Señor, Though Deepening Trials, See the Mighty Angel Flying, The Heavens Resound, The Lord's Prayer, Let the Mountains Shout for Joy, Gently Raise the Sacred Strain, I Spoke With God Last Night, The Lord Bless You and Keep You, Song of the Redeemed, Reverently and Meekly Now, Come, Come Ye Saints, Hosanna Anthem, Battle Hymn of the Republic, Victory. All of the sacred numbers were sung in Spanish, most my own translations.

6. When Elder Cardon was transferred to Paraguay, March 15, 1950, he was replaced by Elder Herman G. Rhoton. Elder Slight, released September 1, 1950, was replaced by B. LaMar Williams in both the quartet and trio, and when he left on February 14, 1951, he was replaced by Maughan W. McMurdie. With the release of Elder Dallas Keller on March 27, 1951, the quartet disbanded. Soloists among the several quartet members included Elders Slight, Keller, Melander, and McMurdie.

Among the musical numbers they performed, as recorded in the Mission History were: Chloe, With a Song in My Heart, Ol' Arks a Moverin', How High the Moon, I Don't Know Why, Strike Up the Band, Kentucky Babe, I Don't Know Anyone Lovelier Than You, Twenty-Third Psalm, Thanks Be to God, My Heart is a Silent Violin, Hear My Prayer, Firm in the Faith, Why Should I Falter, O Son of Mine, Were You There When They Crucified My Lord, and As Torrents in Summer.

7. On the first, Corraine was expecting our fifth child, Mary. When it came time to go to the hospital, I asked if I could have five more minutes to finish my Christmas radio talk. No! But Corraine was very accommodating: she had the baby, I set up a radio for her and I got to the station in time to give the talk.

8. Maughan W. McMurdie has served on the music faculties of Brigham Young University, the University of Washington and Western Illinois University, where he currently teaches opera workshop and composition. He directed the Anchorage, Alaska, symphony and chorus for three seasons. He is the composer/musical director of the Nauvoo Pageant.

Among the songs he performed, as recorded in the Mission History were: Only a Rose, Torna Sorrento, The Palms, I've Got Plenty of Nothin', and, I Walked Today Where Jesus Walked.

Piano renditions included, Saber Dance, Fire Dance, Impromptu, La Comparsa, Cakewalk.

9. After his mission, Roy Fitzell appeared in several more movies, on television (he was a regular on "Your Hit Parade") and stage. He toured the United States and Canada as one of the leads in *Plain and Fancy*, a musical comedy. For several years he was a professor of dance at the University of California, Irvine.

Among his dance routines, included in the Mission History were: Irish Washerwoman, Stepping Out With My Baby, Malagueña (with castanets), Sevilla, and Prelude to Carmen (with cape).

CHAPTER VII

THE WORK BLOSSOMS: ORGANIZING MEMBERS AND FRIENDS

SUCH WAS the interest of the investigators that right from the beginning we decided to get them together for a conference. The first one was held in July 1948, just ten months after our arrival to open the mission. Without a single baptized convert, the conference proceeded beautifully with the investigators' full participation. I invited President Young of the Argentine Mission to join with us, and he brought a group of missionaries and members to assist us. Saturday morning, July 24, 1948, was the recreation portion for the missionaries; a basketball tournament was held. Then a "union" meeting of all the auxiliary organizations was held at 1:30 p.m. at Victoria Hall, where instructions were given and ideas exchanged. That evening, a roadshow was held, each branch presenting a special number and skit. It was a very interesting three-hour occasion. It was at this activity that the trio introduced "La Uruguaya," the new mission song. I had just finished the words the night before. Four hundred people attended the proceedings.

Sunday, July 25, was cold and rainy, but in spite of the weather, a combined total of 538 people congregated in the Ateneo Conference Hall on Avenida 18 de Julio for the two sessions. Investigators sang in the chorus, spoke on the program, and played the organ prelude and postlude.

The next conference, held six months later, was even grander, as was each succeeding conference, thereafter held every six months. They were always well attended as missionaries, members and investigators looked forward to the fellowshipping and activities which always included a baptismal service and dance, as well as a radio program, sporting event, roadshow, leadership meeting, testimony and elders' report meeting, and the spiritual Sunday sessions. The flyer announcing the third conference (September 22 to 26, 1949) includes the following events, their places and scheduled times:

Thursday, 22 September 1949

Gold and Green Ball 8:30-12:00
Club Húngaro

Friday, 23 September 1949

Missionary Report meeting
Mission Home 8:00-3:30
Officers and Teachers 6:00-8:30
Club Húngaro
Movie: "It's a Wonderful Life"
Cine Roi 8:45-12:00

Saturday, 24 September 1949

Tour of the City 9:00-12:00
Picnic/Bar B.Q. 1:00-3:00 at the "Terreno"
Baptismal services 4:00 (21 were baptized)
Carrasco
Roadshow 7:30-10:00
Victoria Hall

Sunday, 25 September 1949

First Session 10:00-12:00
Ateneo Theater
Radio Broadcast 4:00-4:30
Radio Espectador
Second Session 5:00-7:00
Ateneo Theater

Monday, 26 September 1949

Basketball tournament 9:30
Club Bohemios
Continuation of Missionary Report 3:30-7:30
Mission Home

This same pattern was followed in the interior for branch and district conferences, although on a more modest scale.

Activity was the name of the game in the new Uruguayan Mission. No sooner had we concluded the first conference when we started planning for an MIA-sponsored Gold and Green Ball. Each branch was asked to select its representative princess. After these were chosen, they were invited to the Mission Home where we explained how we expected them to conduct themselves at the dance, and how we proposed to choose a queen from among them. Between our meeting and the dance held at the Yugoslavian Center, November 26, 1948, a baptismal service was held, so that by the night of the dance, one of the six princesses (Diber Preciozzi) was a real member of the Church. I quote from the mission history:

> *On the night of Friday, the 26th, the first Gold and Green Ball of the Uruguayan Mission was held in the Club, "Centro Yugoeslavo." During the past week, the hall had been beautifully decorated in the Mutual colors, gold and green, by the missionaries and various investigators. More than 300 people crowded into the club to enjoy the night's festivities. Music for dancing was offered by two orchestras, one consisting of missionaries who played typical American music, including jazz, and the other, a professional Uruguayan, played typical music of this country.*
>
> *The princesses from the various branches wore formal dresses and upon their heads a crown with the name of the branch which they represented. The princesses selected by the mutual Organizations of the branches were Ana María García, from Malvín; Matilde Ferrari, from Arroyo Seco; Diber Alba Preciozzi, La Comercial; Gladys Alanís, La Floresta; María de Carmen Boedo, Reducto;*

and Marta Haydée Canals, Pocitos. To elect a queen, each princess was allowed to take a rose from a vase, one of which contained a gold pin in the stem, denoting "queen." Sister Mará de Carmen Boedo of the Reducto branch chose the correct rose and in a picturesque coronation ceremony was made queen of the ball by President Frederick S. Williams.

A national deputy or representative of the Uruguayan Assembly from Florida was presented to me that night by his daughter, an investigator. He had come to the dance to see what kind of people the Mormons were before giving his permission for her baptism. I talked with him several times during the evening, and in parting, he expressed his amazement that some 350 young people could have such a good time without drinking. He said he wouldn't have believed it could happen. He was so impressed with the young people and the missionaries that he gladly gave his permission for his daughter's baptism.

Periodic dances were held in the same facility, and the young people joyfully participated. Our second Gold and Green Ball had princesses representing seventeen branches, with six hundred people in attendance. Uruguay is a country of clubs, which supply all the social activities for its members, but only its members. If one does not belong, the only place available for dancing are the cabarets. We therefore supplied a need for wholesome entertainment for the youth.

In addition to Priesthood, each branch had a Primary, Mutual, Sunday School, and Relief Society organized and operating, and we constantly met with the leaders to give instruction and vision to their callings. An exhausting but exhilarating series of meetings were continuously scheduled throughout Uruguay and at the mission home. We were the moving force behind the establishment of Scouting in Uruguay, and many branches had operating troops. On March 8, 1951, the Uruguayan Mission's MIA board consisted of the following officers:

Elder Richard G. Scott, President
Elder LeRoy W. Fitzell, Activity Counselor
Juan Magnone, Adviser for Special Interest Class
Elder James S. Taylor, M-Men Adviser
Elder Wilford M. Hale, Boy Scout Leader
Brother Héctor Ramos, Boy Scout Leader
Sister LaVon Evans, President
Sister Velora Gough, Activity Counselor
Corina de Mello de Magnone, Adviser for Special Interest Class
Dafne Otero, Gleaner Girl Adviser
Ella Hull Farnsworth, Gleaner Girl Adviser
Sister Kathryn Hackett, Beehive Leader

By July of 1951, we had Uruguayan members set apart and serving as counselors in four branch presidencies (although the highest office held in the Priesthood by Uruguayans was Priest in the Aaronic Priesthood): Santa Lucía, Maldonado, La Comercial and Reducto.

Leanore Brown had been the President of the Mission Primaries until the end of 1948 when she and her husband were called to preside over the Argentine Mission. Thereafter, my daughter, Barbara Lynn Williams, took over as Primary President and, of course, Corraine was over the Relief Society, so my family was very much involved in the mission leadership. We had to write our own materials for each of these auxiliaries and continued to update them through monthly columns in the *Mensajero Deseret*. Elder Jay Dale, a gifted artist, gave invaluable service in the production of the manuals.

Women, especially, were not used to having any independent identity apart from their husbands, and Relief Society offered them the first opportunity many of these women had had for personal growth and expression. The Relief Society was officially organized October 19, 1948, with some forty non-members in attendance:

> *The first meeting of the Relief Society in this mission was held in the branch of La Comercial, with women from all of the Montevideo branches in attendance. The meeting directed by President Corraine S. Williams. A very fine program was presented, consisting of a welcome and introduction to the Relief Society by Sister Williams. Musical numbers by Elders Preston J. Bushman, Elwin T. Christensen, and a trio composed of Sisters Corraine S. Williams, Barbara Williams, and Leanore Brown. Explanation of lesson material and activities for the year by Sister Elsa Vogler. Talk on the theme, "Charity Never Fails," by Sister Eddie Argault, and remarks by President Frederick S. Williams.*
>
> *After the meeting, refreshments were served and photographs were taken of the group. There were 51 in attendance, 40 of whom were investigators of the Church. The following is a list of the names of those who were present in this memorable meeting:*
>
> *Margarita Praxedes de Albornoz, Elena Bralich de Auliso, Sonia Bralich Auliso, Ethel Bouissa, Palmira E. de Bouissa, Mera Herminia de Casas, María Irma Cobas, Consuelo Marrozos de Cobas, Martha H. Canals, Jehova S. de Fassia, María A. A. de Fernández, Matilde R. Ferrari, Francisca Roldán de García, Alice Gottlieb de Kuhne, María L. Lópes de Mayo, María M. de Martínez, Amanda Piriz de Nieves, Elsa Nieves, Ana Susana Orsan, Boris Nidelko de Orsan, Victoria Pabazzo, Margarita Elina Piriz, Mermilia Manay de Preciozzi, Ang(e)lina Olivera de Masciotta, Cecilia Mayo, María Celia Beade de Méndez, Gladys Méndez, Bermilia Preciozzi, María Renée Ramírez, María Ester Rizzo de Rodríguez, Angela Trino de Rodrígues, Elia Saunches, Isidora Laporte Saunches, Elena Simón, Barbara Lynn Williams, Leanor Jesperson Brown, Corraine S. Williams.*

We found that our young Uruguayan members and investigators had never experienced much group activity, and that none of them had ever been camping. I felt it was time they were given this opportunity. I made suggestions and asked for help from the youth leaders. We found ourselves fortunate in our friends. One investigator said his relative owned several lots in Parque del Plata, a few miles east of Montevideo along the beach. The lots were covered with pine trees. He received permission for us to establish a camp there for a week.

We needed tents, and we were in no condition to buy them. One member said that the army had lent tents to groups before, so I went down to the designated office to inquire. The soldier at the desk said that in the past the army had lent tents to groups for camping purposes, but that they had been returned mildewed. His superior officer, who was in charge of these items, had given orders that they should not be lent out in the future.

I expressed my disappointment and asked if I couldn't at least speak to his superior. I handed him my personal card. He said it wouldn't do any good, but he would see if the officer would receive me. Almost immediately, the receptionist returned and asked me to enter. The officer rose from his desk and extended his hand to me and surprised me with the warmth of his greeting. He said that he recognized my name from the card and remembered that I had signed several checks in his name many years before. He reminded me that when I was with the Institute of Inter-American Affairs that the Servicio de Cooperación de Salud Pública during 1943 to 1944 had carried out a program for the vaccination of fifty thousand children in Uruguay for diphtheria. We had recruited all the help we could and the army had assigned a number of its personnel to assist. He had been one of them, and he had been paid for his time by us.

He asked what he could do for me. I explained our problem and he asked how many tents we needed. I told him our estimate and he granted our request. He also suggested a cook's tent and two more to serve as restrooms. He said there would be no charge for the use of the tents but asked only that we bring them back in good condition. The first campamento was held February 28, 1949; the second, February 20, 1950.

On February 28, 1949, several dozen young people congregated at the mission home with their own food and bedding at about five a.m. to load on trucks. My children, Barbara and Argina, were among those who participated. They played games along the beautiful beach, swam in the South Atlantic, and at night were entertained around the campfire.

The parents of these young people were very pleased with this activity and were grateful they could participate. The youth were enthralled with the activities. The only complaints we ever received were from the missionaries in charge: they were the only ones who weren't permitted to swim.

The next year we again organized the campout, but included the Boy Scout troops in the mission. The campout was followed by a youth convention, the first in the Mission, held at the *terreno* or chapel lot in Montevideo.

With the First Presidency's authorization, we purchased seventeen hundred square meters of land in April 1949, situated on Boulevard Artigas, close to Calle Joaquín Suárez. The land was behind a row of houses on the boulevard, but included the vacant lot and two homes. Later, the homes would be demolished to make the chapel more visible from Boulevard Artigas.

The *terreno* or lot became very valuable to us as an activity center. Missionaries, members and investigators spent several Saturdays cleaning it up so that it could be used for our activities. Swings and teeter-totters were constructed for the use of the young children, and a volleyball court was laid out for the older ones. We had a baptismal font dug on the property where all the baptisms were carried out in the Capital District from that time on, instead of having to go to Arroyo Carrasco. A small rustic two-room building was constructed to serve as dressing rooms. The *terreno* also served for Relief Society bazaars, Mutual parties, Priesthood conferences and more. Many wonderful activities and good times were had on this *terreno* before the construction of the first chapel in Uruguay. The architect's drawings were sent to the First Presidency on March 31, 1951, but it was completed after we left the country.

I announced the beginning of the first phase of the Welfare Program for the Uruguayan Mission in the February 1951 *Mensajero Deseret*. The first project was assigned to the Rocha Branch. Elder James McGregor gave the suggestion and made the initial contacts before his release the same month.

An investigator, and later member, Emilio Amaral, offered to give the Church permission to use 17 *cuadras* of land. We investigated the possibilities on repeated trips to Rocha in November 1950. When the agreement was consummated, Amaral and a friend, Mr. Gauthier—the man from whom the mission had purchased the Rocha *local*—lent their tractors for plowing the ground, which was sown with wheat and sunflower seeds; (the most popular cooking oil used in Uruguay and Argentina is made from sunflower seeds). The missionaries plowed the fields by night so that the men could use their tractors elsewhere during the day. Eventually, twelve hundred willow trees were planted as windbreaks around the property and several fruit-bearing trees were also planted.

The completed project was to include incubators for 350 eggs and the procurement of several beehives. A well was dug and an addition built onto the house of a nearly blind member, Domingo Pizarro, constructed to make living on the site more comfortable for him and his large family, most of whom also suffered from poor eyesight. The townspeople of Rocha became enthusiastic about the project and many came to help with the work or offered the use of tools and even trucks when these were needed to haul materials. One local official exulted: "I'm happy to see Christianity in action at last." A small house was also constructed on the land and the Rovira family was invited to come from Isla Patrulla to work on the project.

As far as I know, Mr. Gauthier and his wife, originally from the Swiss colony of Colonia Suiza, never joined the Church; they were wonderful people and treated the missionaries very well, but were satisfied with their own religion. Emilio Amaral, on the other hand, joined his wife in becoming a member of the Church. He owned the Ford Agency in Rocha. Captain August Martinsen Lien, a Norwegian fishing boat captain who was converted in Rocha, worked very hard in the welfare program before eventually returning to Norway. Many members of the Uruguayan Mission contributed one peso (a little less than a dollar) to the Welfare Fund to get it started.

From the very beginning, I had been ably assisted by excellent Mission Secretaries whom I used like counselors; they presided at meetings, conducted business, traveled to the interior branches, etc. Those who served with me were Elders Wilford M. Farnsworth (from 25 October 1947), John Wallace Cook (from 27 July 1948), Delbert H. Rock (from 16 May 1949), Byron C. Palmer (from 2 March 1950), and Lloyd C. Burnett (from 9 March 1951). As the workload increased, I felt the need to expand the leadership and asked the First Presidency for counselors. I prepared the groundwork, however, by giving a rather detailed account of our activities:

> *The Uruguayan Mission is steadily growing and shows promise for the future. We have 7 branches in Montevideo and 10 in the interior. On the 16th of this month, elders will be sent to San Carlos and Santa Lucía to look for "locals" incidental to the opening of two new branches.*
>
> *Uruguay is divided into 19 Departments (including Montevideo). We are now working in 11 Departments, and the missionaries next week will start the work in 2 more.*
>
> *The 77 missionaries now laboring in Uruguay (including the two lady Argentine missionaries) are working hard and are very enthusiastic in their work. The Lord has blessed us greatly; more and more people are attending our meetings*

and becoming investigators. We opened the branch in Minas last month with a total of 180 people in attendance. In our Salto Branch, some 70 to 80 people attend sacrament meeting each Sunday. The seats will accommodate only 60 people. The majority of our chapels are crowded.

Two weeks ago we held a fireside chat at the Mission Home for the young people of Montevideo. More than 70 were present. Next Sunday we expect 100. We very definitely need a larger hall. If we had one we could have a constant congregation of more than 200 by combining three of our branches. We trust the Church will see fit to build a recreation hall on the property that was purchased. We could use it in the very near future. It would serve as a chapel, district meeting house, and a place for missionwide conferences, as well as a gym.

We have had 54 baptisms since January 1st. Within the past six months, 103 converts have come into the Church. There are about 20 more awaiting for baptism this month, inspite of the cold weather and the fact that we perform all of the ordinances in rivers. We expect at least 150 baptisms during 1949.

The mission is growing so rapidly and there are so many activities to get started that I feel I should have more help. I am putting in 17 and 18 hours per day, and loving it, but I am unable to get as much done as I want to do, and I do not want the work to suffer because of me.

I suggest that I be permitted counselors (May 14, 1949).

No response was forthcoming, however, so things remained the same. A year later, I renewed my request: "If it be your desire, I should like to again recommend the appointment of counselors for the Uruguayan Mission President." I then indicated my choices and concluded with:

If in your judgment we have advanced to where the mission would be benefited by the designation of counselors, I would be pleased to have these two named. If not, I shall be happy to continue as before (July 14, 1950).

Action was eventually taken and approval given for counselors to be called. On November 1, 1950, Wilford M. Farnsworth, now back in Uruguay with his wife, was set apart as first counselor, and Junius M. Gibbons—a sixty-four year old retired dentist serving a mission with his wife and youngest child—as second counselor.

When the Gibbons were released, approval was obtained to call Elder Byron C. Palmer as second counselor; he was set apart March 22, 1951.

We also depended on the Elders we called as District and Branch Presidents. For the last two years, our mission was divided into seven districts:

Capital	**Eastern**	**Western**	**Central**
Malvín	*Treinta y Tres*	*Mercedes*	*Durazno*
Arroyo Seco	*Melo*	*Paysandú*	*La Florida*
Reducto	*Isla Patrulla*	*Salto*	*Trinidad*
La Comercial			
La Floresta			

Capital cont.	Southeastern	Northern	Paraguayan
Pocitos			
Universitaria	*Rocha*	*Tacuarembó*	*Deseret*
Santa Lucía	*Minas*	*Rivera*	*Ciudad Nueva*
Canelones	*Maldonado*		

At the close of my mission, we combined Pocitos and Universitaria to form the Parque Rodó Branch.

An idea of my routine for traveling can be gleaned from the following schedule:

President Williams' Schedule Feb. 18 — June 30, 1951

Sunday, February 18	Reducto
Sunday, February 25	Santa Lucía
Sunday, February 4	Universitaria
Sunday, March 11	Trinidad
Sunday, March 18	Comercial
Sunday, April 8	Durzano and Florida
Sunday, April 15	Pocitos
Friday, April 20	Isla Patrulla
Saturday, April 21	Treinta y Tres
Sunday, April 22	Treinta y Tres in the morning, Melo in the afternoon
Friday, April 27	Go to Rivera
Saturday, April 28	Elders' Meeting
Sunday, April 29	Rivera
Monday, April 30	Tacuarembó; Return home on the night train
Sunday, May 6	Arroyo Seco
Saturday, May 12	Maldonado
Sunday, May 13	Maldonado
Friday, May 18	Mercedes
Saturday, May 19	Paysandú
Sunday, May 20	Salto
Friday, May 25	Arrive at Asunción
Sunday, May 27	Asunción
Wednesday, May 30	Leave for Encarnación by train
Friday, June 1	Arrive home
Sunday, June 3	La Floresta
Sunday, June 10	Minas
Sunday, June 17	Malvín
Sunday, June 24	Rocha

A member of the Mission Presidency was assigned to visit the branch conferences that I was unable to attend.

Summing up. Two girls, cousins of the Vice President of Uruguay, became interested in the church and were baptized soon after we opened the mission. They told a relative about the Church and he in turn told the President, Luis Batlle Berres. The President asked the Vice President to investigate us and report to him.

José Brum, brother of the Vice President (and at his behest) invited all the missionaries to his ranch near Montevideo so his brother could get acquainted with us. We had a glorious day. There were horses to ride and all the *asado* and other good food we could eat. We enjoyed ourselves immensely and in return performed a program of song and dance.

Later Brum told me what he had reported to the President about us. His opinion was very favorable. The President then directed him to tell me that we were welcome. He was especially pleased with the MIA program we had for the young people of his country. Señor Brum also told me that the President liked our church better than the Catholic Church, and that we had just as much right to be there as it did. He said if we ever encountered difficulty to contact him. Since that time many of the General Authorities who have visited Uruguay have gone to the government house and have been received by the President.

In January 1963, President Hugh B. Brown of the First Presidency left Salt Lake City to tour the South American missions. He first visited various cities in Brazil, then went to Asunción, Paraguay, and continued on to Argentina. After meeting with the saints in several cities and making an official visit to the Mayor of Rosario, he and the other members of his party flew to Montevideo.

Members and non-members both welcomed him at Carrasco Airport with songs. Milton Fontana, one of the owners of a television station, interviewed President Brown. The proceedings at the airport and the interview were later seen by the Uruguayan audience in an hour-long broadcast. The official caravan with its police escort went to the municipal building where Mayor Figoli expressed his personal appreciation for the beneficial influence the church had had on the youth of his native country:

> *During the last 15 years we have been closely observing the activities of your church and we cannot but appreciate what you are doing for our people. Your youth program has contributed much in the development of our young people. We personally appreciate the visit of such a high dignitary of the Church of Jesus Christ of Latter-day Saints.*

The same escort accompanied the official party to visit the President of the Republic of Uruguay, His Excellency, Faustino Harrison, who, after welcoming President Brown, stated:

> *We are very much in accord with what you are doing here in Uruguay. We recognize the contribution of the Mormon Church in the betterment of our citizens.*

These two quotes, along with my translations of the original Spanish which appeared in the April 1963 issue of the *Liahona*, are a reaffirmation of what Vice President Brum had told me. I am grateful that they continued watching our activities closely in Uruguay and for their appreciation of the contribution made by our church to the citizens of Uruguay.

When we were released on July 31, 1951, after nearly four years, the Uruguayan Mission had a total of twenty-five organized branches: twenty-three scattered throughout Uruguay and two in Paraguay. Total convert baptisms numbered 515. During 1949 and 1950, the Uruguayan Mission baptized more than the combined totals of the Argentine and Brazilian Missions. We didn't work any harder than the missionaries in the other two missions. The difference was that the Uruguayan people were more willing to listen to the gospel at the time. We owned the mission home and seventeen hundred square meters of ground for the future construction of a chapel on Boulevard Artigas in Montivideo. We also owned a lot in Paysandú and a large lot and home in Rocha. Priesthood holders included thrity-four deacons, twenty-four teachers, thirteen priests and two elders.

After being set apart as the new presidents of the Uruguayan Mission, President McKay stated to me:

> *President Williams, it won't matter how many other presidents preside over the mission in Uruguay, you will always be known as the "Father of the Uruguayan Mission." It is rare for a man as young as you to be given the responsibility of opening up a new country. Just how old are you?*

I told him I had turned thirty-nine the previous month. The Brethren asked that the blessings of the Lord would accompany us.

After three years and ten months of dedicated and hard work by 116 missionaries, it was pleasing to receive from President McKay the commendation that the new Uruguayan mission, since its organization had progressed faster than any other mission in the Church since the establishment of the British Mission a century before. All of us who served there are very grateful to our Heavenly Father for his influence and help in preparing the field by touching the hearts of the Uruguayan people. My words to the Uruguayan Mission song seem appropriate to close this chapter.

LA URUGUAYA

Bajo el cielo azul, Banda Oriental,
Recuerdo yo, de tus encantos.
Fue donde conocí, al compás del son,
Pueblo tan amable gue le di mi corazón.

La Uruguaya, Missión querida,
Siempre en mi corazón, serás tú bien acogida;
Por ti yo canto, por ti yo ruego,
Que bendiciones tu vida siempre la colmarán.

Aunque lejos voy, no olvidaré,
De tu amor, grato recuerdo.
Por toda amistad, gracias yo daré.
Pido que recuerdes, que jamás olvidaré.

La Uruguaya, Misión querida...[bis]

Quiero yo volver, al pago de ayer,
De nuevo ver a mis amigos;
Gozar de amistad, cantos a cantar,
Predicar las nuevas en capilla y hogar,

La Uruguaya, Misión querida...[bis]

English translation

LA URUGUAYA

Under azure skies, lies Uruguay,
As I recall, land of enchantments.
It was there I met, in a joyous mood,
Such lovely people that I gave away my heart.

La Uruguaya, beloved mission,
You'll always be well-received and find a place in my heart.
Of thee I sing, for thee I pray,
That you may always be crowned with blessings your whole life through.

Although I travel far, I shall not forget,
Your special love, my fondest memories.
Your friendship and your warmth, I am grateful for,
I ask, please remember, for I never will forget.

La Uruguaya, beloved mission...[bis]

I'd like to return, to those former scenes,
And once again behold my friends.
Sharing their kindly ways, join them in singing songs,
And then preach good tidings both in chapels and in homes

La Uruguaya, beloved mission...[bis]

(Translated by FSW and FGW)

CHAPTER VIII

PARAGUAY: THE SEEDS ARE SOWN

I FIRST VISITED Paraguay during November 1939, and as far as I have been able to ascertain, I was the first member of our Church to do so. My purpose was to visit the Toba Indian tribe, located in the then *Gobernación* (reservation) of Formosa, Argentina. Elder Edgar B. Mitchell accompanied us as we arrived after a day long trip (plus an all-night delay caused by a train derailment) from Encarnación, across the Paraná River from Posadas, Argentina.

To visit Asunción at that time was to see a city of a century before. Only one new public building had been constructed since the time of President Carlos Antonio López, who was in power from 1844 to 1862. During the presidency of his son, Francisco Solano López, who succeeded him upon his death, more efforts were expended in preparation for defense and military objectives than for the construction of public buildings. After Paraguay's defeat by the "Triple Alliance" (Argentina, Brazil and Uruguay) in March 1870, the country began a period of some sixty years of revival; eighty-five percent of the men between eleven and seventy had died in the war.

Only one street was paved. The street car ran down the middle of this wide avenue named "Mariscal Francisco Solano López". The street car carried the dead to the cemetery. A flanged wheel trailer with a flat top was hitched to the rear of the street car, and the bodies reached their final resting place at the end of the regular run. If there wasn't enough room for all the passengers in the street car, the overflow crowd walked behind the corpse.

More interesting than the colonial city were the Paraguayans. I had never seen a happier, more pleasant people in my life. There were apparently no strangers in Asunción. Everyone spoke to whomever they met in the street, even to us, strange as we may have appeared, two blond North Americans wearing the typical gaucho dress of boots and *bombachas*. Our booted feet looked strange to the unshod majority. We saw a parade of the Presidential guard dressed in resplendent uniforms, marching barefoot.

We heard them singing in the houses we passed and on the street. Frankly there were more women working than men. The women brought their merchandise to the markets and sold it to other women. The more affluent rode side saddle on their donkeys, balancing a huge basket of vegetables with one hand, and shading their faces with an umbrella with the other. Sometimes they carried babies in their arms. Unembarrassed mothers breast-fed their infants in the thronged streets.

Although the houses were old, they looked beautiful amidst the many hued flowers that surrounded them; climbing roses and other plants covered many of the walls.

After the relative cold of Buenos Aires, Asunción was a delight to my soul. I fell in love with the Guaraní people and wondered how long it would be before they were permitted to hear the gospel. I hoped that the borders of the Argentine mission might be extended to include this happy people, but I never thought that I would be permitted to have a hand in its opening to the Restored Church. World War II had to run its course before this could come about. It took time for the Lord to maneuver key people to accomplish His purposes.

Samuel J. Skousen served a devoted and successful mission in Argentina, first under President W. Ernest Young and then under my direction. After his release he became a B-17 bomber pilot in the United States Air Force. He made a name for himself and his airplane in the Far East Sector of the War and was written about in newspapers and magazines. After the War, he was assigned as an Assistant Air Attaché to the American Embassy in Rio de Janeiro. When General Dwight D. Eisenhower toured South America, Sam was his pilot.

In Brazil Sam was always involved in mission activities. The Brazilian Mission was just recuperating from the effects of the War and needed all the help it could get. Three former Argentine missionaries, Samuel J. Skousen, Rolf L. Larson and L. Pierce Brady, all were working in Rio for different agencies of the United States Government. As faithful and hardworking members of the church, they contributed greatly to the mission. Together they bought and presented to the mission president the first church-owned vehicle in Brazil, a used Jeep.

Brother Skousen made contact with a Paraguayan by the name of Carlos Alberto Rodríguez and his girl friend, a Brazilian singer by the name of Mafalda Figueira. Carlos had previously known a former Argentine missionary, Eldred C. Olsen, in Asunción in 1943. They became good friends and the couple began attending church. They were married and departed for Asunción about the same time that Sam was appointed Air Attaché at the American Embassy there, in late 1946. Sam continued his friendship and he and his wife Beth were a great influence for good on their friends. He flew the Rodríguez family to Buenos Aires for one of the mission conferences and there they requested baptism. President Young wrote the First Presidency requesting permission for Brother Skousen to baptize them in Asunción. I received the authorization on July 18, 1948. It stated that the membership records should be sent to the Uruguayan Mission in Montevideo which would supervise their activities. Carlos Alberto Rodríguez was baptized by Brother Skousen in the Church of Christ's font on August 21, 1948. He became the first convert baptism of the new Uruguayan Mission.

Before his baptism the Rodríguez family accompanied the Skousens to the first Uruguayan Mission Conference on July 24 and 25. On July 26, Sam Skousen was set apart as the first branch president of Paraguay. Mafalda was baptized by Brother Skousen on January 15, 1949, after the birth of her baby.

As an individual, a friend and an official of the U.S. Government, Brother Skousen endeared himself to the Paraguayan people. He loved them and they responded. He was highly regarded for his competence and loved for his understanding of their history, traditions and problems. He spoke excellent Spanish and learned to communicate somewhat in Guaraní. His good impression on government officials helped facilitate the opening of the mission.

As a matter of historical interest, the Rodríguez home had been in their family for many generations and housed a distinguished guest for many years: José Gervasio Artigas, the father of Uruguayan independence. His last years in exile were spent at this house in the outskirts of Asunción. The "Artigas Tree" is still standing near the house. Under its shade, Artigas visited with his guests. Carlos Alberto gave me several mementos that had been kept in the house since the death of that great man.

On February 23, 1949, after a five-hour trip by hydroplane from Buenos Aires, I arrived in Asunción for the first time since my first visit ten years before. The Skousens and the Rodríguezes met me. That night Sam and I attended a Rotary Club dinner meeting. On the following night, we were guests of honor at the home of a Brazilian government official;

there we met Colonel Claudio Luis Gutiérrez, the Paraguayan Army Chief of Staff and many other officials. On the night of the twenty-sixth, Colonel Gutiérrez dined with us at the Skousens'. During the evening we heard shooting in the distance. The Chief of Staff had been very nervous all evening. When he heard the shots, he went to the door and, without saying a word, disappeared into the night. He knew that a revolution was in the making, and that he was on the wrong side. I never saw him again, but I learned that he had been placed in custody, but finally had been permitted to leave the country. He had promised to help me when the time came to establish the mission.

On Sunday, February 27, the "Mormon colony" was invited to dine with the American Ambassador, the Honorable Fletcher Warren and his wife at the official residence. Afterward they, the Frank Gilpins and I met with the Skousens in their home for a Sacrament meeting at which I spoke. Frank Gilpin was the director of the Industrial School, under the Institute of Inter-American Affairs, for which I had worked.

On February 28, I accompanied Brother Skousen to a dinner at the home of the American Army officer, Colonel Crowell. On March 1, I flew to Buenos Aires and on to Montevideo.

Colonel Skousen, his wife and children left Asunción in March 1949 for another assignment.

I received a letter, dated August 17, 1949, from Elder Spencer W. Kimball, Chairman of the Indian Relations Committee, asking how many missionaries were involved in working with the descendants of Lehi, and how many Indian converts had been baptized. I answered him on August 29, the same day I wrote the First Presidency requesting permission to open Paraguay to the gospel. I had to tell him frankly that Uruguay had no Indians as such; its population was ninety-nine percent white, with one percent a mixture of Negro and Indian blood, and we had no way of finding Indians other than by door-to-door tracting. We had two members who claimed to have Indian blood. I quote one paragraph of my letter to Elder Kimball:

> *I wrote a detailed account of my suggestions and recommendations to the First Presidency relative to the work in Asunción. If you were interested, perhaps they would permit you to read the letter, and if you feel as I do, I'm sure a word from you would greatly enhance the possibilities of opening the work in the first Lamanite Mission in South America.*

Here are some of the paragraphs from my letter of the same date to the First Presidency, given for historical reasons:

> *Both Elder Skousen and myself feel that it would be advantageous and desirable to begin missionary work in Paraguay. We feel that if the Church is to ever start there, this the best time to begin . . . Elder Skousen has always been a wonderful missionary and a devoted member of the Church. He lived and was known as a Mormon in Paraguay and has built up a good will that will be invaluable to the Church, if used. He introduced me to both government officials and business men and I was amazed to see the good will gained by him towards the Church.*
>
> *We have the contacts to facilitate the opening of the work. Brother Rodríguez, our member, is related to the President of Paraguay and is from one of the old,*

best families. We have two North American members (the Gilpins from Arizona) working for the American Government. They can help us also in making the official contacts.

The American Ambassador, Honorable Fletcher Warren, invited all of the English-speaking Mormons to lunch at the Embassy. At that time we discussed the topic of the possible opening of a branch in Asunción. He thought our missionary activities would be very successful and would like to see us start work there. He said he had worked in five countries in Central and South America and feels Paraguay would be better for us than any of the ones he knows. Among other countries he has worked in Nicaragua, Guatemala and Perú . . .

By opening the work in Paraguay the Church would have its first Lamanite Mission in South America. It has a population of approximately 1,250,000, a mixture of Spanish, Portuguese, Italian and Indian blood. There are more than 50,000 uncivilized Indians, living principally in the Gran Chaco. The balance of the Indian blood is mixed with the European people. The Paraguayans are happy, friendly, alert and intelligent.

I don't think the work will move along as fast as it has here in Uruguay at first, but I have every reason to believe that it will be successful.

I would be happy to receive your views as to the advisability and desirability of the Uruguayan Mission opening a branch in Asunción.

A letter from the First Presidency dated October 11, 1949, brought great joy to all of us in the Uruguayan Mission. In part it read:

Dear President Williams:

Your letter of August 29 was received in due course, in which you suggest that we begin missionary work in Paraguay. You call attention to the character of the Paraguayans and to the fact that they are mostly Indians of the Guarani race, which forms the basis of the Indian population of South America from northern Brazil to Argentina.

Your letter was referred to the Council of the Twelve and by them to the Missionary Committee, and was on October 6, 1949, brought before the Council of the First Presidency and Quorum of the Twelve. After discussion it was unanimously decided that you should be requested to go forward with the opening of a mission in Paraguay at Asunción, the work to be later extended after experience had been gained and when it should seem wisdom to extend the work.

The Brethren, while heartily approving the opening of missionary work there, decided that it would not be necessary at this time to establish a Paraguayan Mission but that the work should be part of the Uruguayan Mission. We trust that you will go forward in this work with care and after careful consideration, so that we shall not make any advance from which we must later retreat because reversal is detrimental to the cause of the Lord.

We and the Brethren pray that the Lord will bless you and inspire you in this mission so that His work may be expanded, and that more souls may be brought to enjoy a testimony of the Restored Gospel and the restored priesthood. With these prayers, we are

Faithfully yours,

George Albert Smith
J. Reuben Clark, Jr.
David O. McKay
The First Presidency

In my October 20, 1949, letter to the First Presidency thanking them for the privilege of opening the work in Paraguay, I stated that it would take us until the first of the year to get things in order. The receipt of a power of attorney for that country, its legalization before the Paraguayan Consul in the States, and other time-consuming matters would take that long.

At a party for the Montevideo area elders at the mission home on Christmas Eve, 1949, I announced the names of the first elders assigned to open the work in Paraguay. All of them would have liked the opportunity. Those chosen to go were Elders Wilford M. Farnsworth, Keith J. Morris, Norval Craig Jesperson and Daryl Lamar Anderson. Elder Farnsworth, as my special assistant, would accompany my wife Corraine and me by plane, and the other three would follow by riverboat.

We three traveled by night boat to Buenos Aires on January 5, 1950, and took a riverboat the next morning for Asunción. We stopped at Rosario, Paraná and Corrientes, along the great Paraná-Guazú River, and reached Asunción four days later. The Gilpins invited us to stay with them while there, and we enjoyed their hospitality.

With a note of introduction from Colonel Samuel J. Skousen in hand, Elder Farnsworth and I called on the Chief of Staff of the Paraguayan Army, General Alfredo Stroessner. He received us cordially and gave us a note of introduction to Dr. Pacífico Montero de Vargas, the minister under Secretary of State for Foreign Affairs under whom religions were regulated. I looked around his office and noted the impression Brother Skousen had made on him. He had only three pictures on his office walls: General Dwight D. Eisenhower, the President of Paraguay, and Sam Skousen. Stroessner took over the government in 1956 and has maintained it to the present. The American Embassy also provided us with a letter of introduction.

I made the appointment with Dr. Vargas, and Elder Farnsworth accompanied me again. We were received almost at once by the minister and were extended a welcome. Even before we could say what church we represented, Dr. Vargas remarked: "You are welcome. I am happy to see religious denominations come to Paraguay. Some day we are going to find the truth. My ancestors (Guaraní Indians) welcomed the Spanish when they first reached Paraguay, going down to the water's edge with musical groups. They said they had long awaited their coming."

He referred to the Spaniards who, when starved out Buenos Aires at its first founding, went up river seeking food and friendlier Indians. This happened on August 15, 1537, when Pedro de Mendoza, who headed the expedition to the Río de la Plata area, sent Juan de Salazar up river to locate Ayolas and Irala who previously had sailed up the river seeking a path to Perú and its riches.

Dr. Vargas continued:

> *My people thought that the great "White God" had returned and were anxious to be instructed. When communication had been established between the Spaniards and the Guaraní Indians, the soldiers told my ancestors about the true religion. They told about the flood. "Yes, we know about that. That happened when everyone was drowned except one family who found safety in the top of a very tall tree." They were told about the Virgin and Child. "Yes, we know about that." They gave the same answer when told about the apostles and other things pertaining to the primitive church.*
>
> *When the soldiers approached the priest to ask how they knew about these things when they were bringing Christianity and its teachings to them for the first time, the priest answered: "The Devil told them in order to deceive them."*
>
> *This was the same answer given by the priests to Cortés' and Pizarro's soldiers when they were confronted with the same traditions.*

Dr. Vargas said: "Obviously they were deceived, as we are now. Some day we hope to find the truth."

When permitted to speak, I told him the reason that his ancestors knew of those traditions was that the Savior had visited America, organized His Church, and His doctrine had been preached for hundreds of years, and that the traditions had been handed down from generation to generation to the present time. I told him that I had a book that I had brought for him that told of the Savior's visit, and one that contained the fulness of His gospel.

He received the Book of Mormon very graciously. After a lengthy visit, he told me where to present the solicitude to ask for permission to open proselyting work in Asunción.

Our power of attorney had been legalized by the Paraguayan Consul in New York City but had not been translated into Spanish. I inquired as to the official translator for the government, and was told that there was none. However, I was directed to a young man who had spent some time in New York, and told that he would be appointed the official translator. I found the young man and he undertook the translation, but I also found that his knowledge of English was very meager. I helped him with the translation, doing most of it.

I secured the necessary *papel sellado*, or stamped paper required for every official transaction not only in Paraguay, but throughout Latin America, borrowed a typewriter, requested permission to work in Asunción, as directed by my Power of Attorney, and settled down to wait. I had been told by many that it would take months for official government machinery to take its course.

The day after our interview with Dr. Vargas, he called personally to ask for twenty-five more copies of the Book of Mormon to be distributed to government officials. I didn't have that many with me, but promised to send them to him from Montevideo, which I did.

During our three weeks in Asunción, Corraine and I and Elder Farnsworth decided to fly to Iguazú Falls. This was my second visit to those world-famous falls, located where Paraguay, Brazil and Argentina meet. We flew to Foz and then crossed the river to our hotel on the Argentine side. After we returned to Asunción, we made repeated visits to the Ministry to try to expedite matters, and also visited with the Gilpins.

Leaving Elder Farnsworth with the Gilpins, Corraine and I returned to Montevideo via Buenos Aires on January 27, after finding and renting a suitable *local* for the missionaries and a large room to serve as a meeting place. It was located at Mayor Bullo 157. When living quarters were assured, I cabled Montevideo to have the above mentioned missionaries leave. They sailed January 20, 1950, together with Oscar Nieves, a Uruguayan member. Oscar went merely to accompany them to Asunción.

The four missionaries purchased the necessary furniture for their rooms, had benches and a pulpit made for the chapel, and began making friends. They weren't at liberty as yet to proselyte.

The first elders entered Paraguay on tourist visas, but Elder Keith J. Morris was able to make arrangements for them to stay as long as they desired.

Elder Farnsworth continued calling at the Ministry, and to our delight, finally received the desired permit on February 27, 1950. He discovered from members of other churches that they had been requesting similar permits for more than a year without success. He was told that we and the Catholic Church (it is covered under the Paraguayan constitution) had permanent permission to operate within Paraguay. Other religious organizations had to have their temporary permits revalidated on a monthly basis.

The mission received some unexpected help in obtaining our permit so rapidly. It was just another of those seeming coincidences that happened so often in the opening of the Uruguayan Mission, but we saw the Lord's hand in them.

While waiting for permission to begin our work the elders made themselves known at one of the sporting clubs and played basketball with the local athletes. Because they were taller than the Paraguayans they attracted a lot of attention. Two men in particular became very friendly. One was the commander of the Paraguayan River Navy. When he learned that Elder Farnsworth had served as an ensign in the United States Navy, a kinship was established. The other was the Minister of Public Works for Paraguay. He was anxious to practice his English and in their conversation it came out that he had studied at Columbia University in New York City. Elder Farnsworth had also received his midshipman training at Columbia. A bond was established between them.

When told that they were waiting for permission to begin missionary work, the Minister of Public Works offered to facilitate its authorization. He said that his uncle was the Minister of Interior, where the request for our permit to work in Paraguay had been filed.

We went with Elder Farnsworth, searched and found the petition and personally guided it through the labyrinth of offices where about twenty signatures were required for its approval. I am sure that had it not been for his intervention and help it would have taken months in the normal course of events. The Lord does work in mysterious ways. He uses people, placing them in the right place at the right time, and many times they do not know that they are furthering His work.

According to my power of attorney we had requested to work only in Asunción, but the permit covered the entire country.

Elder Farnsworth returned to Montevideo on March 28 (he was replaced by Elder Wayne Cardon) and Keith J. Morris was appointed both branch and district president. Under his spirited, enthusiastic leadership the work really began to take hold. He was blessed with a quick mind, unbounded energy and a desire to accomplish all things in the shortest possible time. Under his leadership and example many investigators were found and the nucleus of a branch began to form. Things began to go so well that the Catholic Church took note and started doing what they could to stop us. Our small branch was just a block from Avenida Mariscal López along which they held a religious procession every Sunday carrying one of their saints in the vanguard of several hundred of their faithful. For the first time as they came to the street leading to our branch, the procession made a right turn to pass in front of it. It then continued around the block and then proceeded on the main street as usual. Spies took the names of the investigators, who were then threatened with the loss of their jobs or the opportunity of receiving medical attention in the hospitals if they continued attending the Mormon services. Many dropped out, but a few continued to attend meetings and began preparing for baptism.

It was called "La Rama de Asunción" (Asunción Branch), and changed to "Deseret," on May 14, 1951, when a second branch was established called "La Rama de la Ciudad Nueva."

The first convert baptism after opening the work was Sister Klara Ans de Krisch, a very lovely lady of German descent.

President David O. McKay visited the Uruguayan Mission in January 1954. When he returned to the United States in February, I met him at the Los Angeles International Airport. After telling me somewhat of his visit to the mission he asked me how I felt about the work in Paraguay. He went on to say that the mission president suggested it be closed down because the work was going so slowly.

I told him I had every confidence that the Paraguayan people would respond, and that it would be a shame to write off all the good work that had gone into opening the country for the gospel, and that the time would come when it would prosper. I told him that I felt that the finding of even one person of the quality of Sister Klara Krisch compensated for all the effort.

President McKay responded: "I feel the same as you do, President Williams."

As this is written, I feel our efforts were vindicated. There is now a Paraguayan Mission and the first stakes have been organized. There are chapels, branches and wards in that country. Missionaries are teaching the gospel in Guaraní in the interior of the country, the language of the Church's first Lamanite mission in South America. The acorns from the slowly growing Gospel tree planted by Elder Melvin J. Ballard in Buenos Aires on Christmas Day of 1925 have fallen from the branches that now shade Paraguay. They are now sprouting and will produce the fruit of life eternally.

CHAPTER IX

PERU: THE DAWNING OF THE DAY OF THE LAMANITES (1956-1959)

NO RECORDS EXIST to show the number of Latter-day Saints who have lived at different times in Peru; however, many have contributed to the development of the country. The Cerro de Pasco copper mine was consolidated and developed by A.W. McCune, a member of the Church, who later donated his home in Salt Lake City to the Church. He brought several young Latter-day Saints to work with him in Peru. Chauncey Spilbury came as the tutor of the McCune children. Chauncey's younger brother came to work with the company and became manager, serving in this capacity for many years.

Stanley A. Moore, a former Argentine missionary, came to Peru in 1943 to work for Panagra as a radio engineer. Except for two years, he resided in Peru continuously with his wife, Edna Zaldívar, and their four children, all born in Lima, until the 1960s. They held Sunday Schools in their home during their sojourn. Other families had come and gone: John Alius, a United Press correspondent, Eugene Turley, from Phoenix, Arizona, an advertising executive, Quintin West, an agronomist serving with the world food production organization.

In February 1954, President and Sister David O. McKay and their son Robert Riggs McKay visited Lima and a special meeting was held. After the meeting President McKay discussed with the priesthood holders the possibilities of establishing a mission in Peru. President McKay planned to research Peruvian law to see if a mission could be legally established. His visit was a spiritual tonic to the members of the Church residing in Lima.

A year later Elder Mark E. Peterson and his wife visited Lima during a tour of the South American Missions. His enthusiasm and spiritual messages were greatly appreciated. During these years, only Sunday School was held regularly; some special meetings were held in Lima when distinguished visitors came. Stanley A. Moore and his family kept the spirit of the gospel alive.

On January 1, 1956, I arrived in Lima with my wife Corraine, son Frederick G., and daughters Nancy Lou and Mary, to establish a home and an import/export business in that country. I had just been released as the first President of the Los Angeles Temple Mission and Director of the Bureau of Information. We were delighted to make contact with Stanley Moore, my former missionary, and soon met together for Sunday School. He very graciously transferred the meetings to our home on Avenida La Paz 1369 in Miraflores, because he had a car and we did not at first; therefore, it was easier for them to come to our home than it was for us to go to theirs.

Soon other Latter-day Saint families began to arrive. Colonel Charles H. Shaw, U.S. Air Attaché, and his family in February; the Wells Allred family in March, a marketing specialist with the World Food Production Organization. Also during March a young lady by the name of Ana Gloria Giustra was contacted. She had attended church in New York for a few months while visiting in the United States. Other Latter-day Saint families connected with the Southern Peru Copper Mines, like the Warren Smiths, or Cerro de Pasco, and the Kay W. Footes, also came.

After a few months, I saw an opportunity for the Church to enlarge its scope and influence. On April 16, 1956, I wrote to the First Presidency telling them of our arrival and of the establishment of our home and business in Peru. I also expressed the hope that Elder Henry D. Moyle, who was scheduled to visit the South American missions in May, could organize us officially. Part of that letter reads:

> *We have here both a problem and an opportunity that I trust will merit his [Elder Moyle's] attention.*
>
> *At the present time we have this group of Latter-day Saints in Lima: 2 High Priests, 4 Elders, 1 Priest; 5 women, 4 girls from the ages of 17 to 11, plus 12 children from the age of 10 days to 9 years, or a total of 28 members. Elder Foote just arrived last week from Chile and within two months will bring his wife and 4 children which will increase our numbers to 33. Also, at San Juan, to the south of Lima, there are three additional members with a fourth arriving within the month. Two of the members will go to the states this month. Everyone else will be here for at least two years.*
>
> *Our problem is that we have no organization. We belong to no mission. Our recommends are scattered throughout the Church. The former group leader, Brother Turley, has been gone from Peru for over a year. When we arrived only a Sunday School was being held. At our suggestion we started a Sacrament Meeting, Priesthood Meeting, Primary; and, since school started April 2, I teach a seminary class each morning to my two children and to one other, with material I brought from California.*
>
> *We have found two other English-speaking people who attend our services. One is a lady from Jerusalem. The other, a young Italian girl by the name of Ana Gloria Giustra, who attended services in the state of New York before returning to her home in Lima. If we were to start Spanish cottage meetings we know of 15 people who would attend. Without an organization or authorization, we don't know just what or how much to do. We trust that Brother Moyle can help us under your direction.*
>
> *We are sure that there are other Latter-day Saints in or around Lima, but they are difficult to find. We have just casually found some of them. Could it be announced in the Church Section that if any members have friends or relatives in Peru to send us their names and addresses? They could also write that they get in touch with us. The meetings are held in our home, Avenida La Paz 1369 (Miraflores), Lima, Peru, telephone 5-6968. They can also contact Brother Stanley A. Moore, Calle Casimiro Ulloa 217 (San Antonio), Lima, Peru. He has no telephone.*

I feel that a mission could very advantageously be established in Peru. It would take time for us to get well established as the Catholic Church is very strong and would fight us with every facility at their command. There are thousands of good people who are not satisfied with what they have and I am sure that many would join the Church if they were given an opportunity.

We have a very fine Ambassador, Mr. Ellis Briggs. It was he who worked for the release of the two Elders who were imprisoned in Prague. President Richards will perhaps recall him, as we went to the Embassy to meet him while he was visiting the Uruguayan Mission.

A previous letter dated January 18, 1956, was addressed to President Frank D. Parry of the Uruguayan Mission. In the concluding paragraph, I mention this:

How could we arrange to have our little Mormon group come under the Uruguayan Mission? We should like to be affiliated in some way. We are 10 members (2 families). All returning missionaries are welcome to stay with us while in Lima.

On February the 21, 1956, President Parry answered in part:

We appreciated very much your letter of January 18 informing us of your new residency in South America. Even before your letter arrived, we heard that you were in South America through the rumors of the saints and they even have the day and the hour that you are to arrive on a visit here in Montevideo. You certainly have a host of loved ones among the saints and among the Church people here in Montevideo. They are looking forward to your visit and the opportunity to renew their friendship and acquaintanceship.

You requested in your letter information as to how you could become affiliated in some way with the Uruguayan Mission—you, your family and one other family in Lima. We have passed this information on to the First Presidency and will abide by their suggestion and decision. We are looking forward to a visit with you as soon as you make your trip through South America.

On February the 29, 1956, I wrote President Parry:

President Valentine wrote that he had received permission to add Chile to the Argentine Mission and he thought that Peru would fall under the jurisdiction of the Uruguayan Mission. I hope that this is the case. I trust that someday missionaries may be sent here. There are many of the descendants of father Lehi whom I feel would accept the message of the restored Gospel of the Savior.

On April the 17, President Frank D. Parry of the Uruguayan mission wrote me the following.

We have received communications from the First Presidency authorizing the establishment of a branch under the Uruguayan Mission at Lima, Peru. We also have received permission to send two missionaries into that city to work towards the end of establishing permanent missionary work in that country.

Brother Williams, we would like to request your assistance in endeavoring to secure permits from the proper authorities to begin missionary work. It would be desirable, if it is feasible, to contact the mayor of the city and government officials in higher positions to acquaint them with the nature of our work and its record of accomplishment in other areas. We should also determine whether or not recognition of the Church by registration or otherwise is essential and how it may be accomplished. Also we will need to secure quarters and housing for the two missionaries to be sent to your city. Brother Williams, if you could attend to these enclosed initial steps and give us some definite information immediately, we would certainly appreciate it.

On May 16, 1956, I addressed the following letter to the First Presidency:

President Parry of the Uruguayan Mission asked me to check on the legal requirements incidental to our Church's beginning missionary activities in Peru. Together with an attorney friend I went to the Ministry of Foreign Affairs and to the General Office of "Culto" (Office of Religious Activities under the Department of Justice). Upon talking to them and to other religious groups, I offer these conclusions and recommendations:

1. *The Constitution guarantees complete religious liberty, but it is not easily enjoyed because of the pressure exerted by the Catholic Church. The country of Peru is much more Catholic than is Argentina; much more militant.*

2. *Pressure will be exerted on government officials to delay action on visas for missionaries and other items that we shall require.*

3. *To get any action on a request to carry out missionary activities, we must utilize all the backing that we can.*

I suggest that you make use of the prestige of the Church with the Secretary of State in Washington, requesting that the American Ambassador in Lima be instructed to introduce Elder Henry D. Moyle to the Foreign Minister during his visit to Lima. Brother Moyle could at that time present an official application for permission to carry out our missionary program. This application can be prepared here by myself and my attorney, if you so desire, and be ready for Brother Moyle. We can accompany Elder Moyle, if he so desires. I shall be most happy to do anything that I can to see that we be permitted to have missionaries here.

. . . .

According to Brother Moyle's schedule, he will arrive in Lima on the 9th of July. The 10th of July would be a good date for him to see the Foreign Minister, as he leaves the 11th for Cuzco, returning to Lima on the 13th. He will still have the 14th for any unfinished business in Lima.

On April 17, 1956, I received the following letter from Brother Henry D. Moyle:

> *I anticipate coming to Lima on July 9th. The brethren have suggested that I go up to Cuzco, Lake Titicaca, which takes four days. If there are any preliminary arrangements to be made prior to making that trip, I should be happy to have you make them for me and to communicate with me if there is any further information I may need. My schedule calls for my presence in the Argentine Mission from the 16th of May to June 1st, the Uruguayan Mission from June 1st to June 18th and the Brazilian Mission from June 18th to July 5th, and I will be in Santiago from July 5th to July 9th. I leave for the Central American Mission on the 16th of July.*
>
> *You may feel free to arrange for any meetings of the saints or investigators you may desire during my stay in Lima, and particularly on Sunday. I especially arranged to be there on Sunday for this purpose.*
>
> *I will be happy to hear from you when I get to the South American Missions to know more definitely of the plans you have for me while I am in Lima. Sister Moyle will accompany me.*

Lima Branch Organized. Elder Henry D. Moyle and wife arrived in Lima on July 6, 1956; President Frank D. Parry and daughter Sharon had arrived the day before. We made reservations for the Moyles at the Crillon Hotel. We visited with them Friday night, picnicked Saturday, and Sunday morning held Sunday School in our home on Avenida La Paz. This was a joyous occasion, the house was completely filled with people. Our little makeshift chapel contained equally makeshift benches made of boards covered with folded blankets placed between chairs; thus six or seven people could avail themselves of the space provided by two chairs. We held classes in bedrooms and in the back yard. We had been holding Sunday School and Sacrament meeting for several months, but this was a wonderful opportunity to partake of the sacrament in the presence of an Apostle and President Parry. Twenty-seven people attended that day.

After church, we invited our guests to dinner at our home and then that night, a special meeting was held in the home of Colonel Charles Howard Shaw, the American Air Attaché, near Avenida Javier Prado at 320 Los Cedros. During the meeting, attended by thirty people, the Shaws, the Moores, the Allreds and the Williamses, together with Ana Gloria Giustra and two returning Argentine missionaries, all bore testimony of the restored gospel. A trio, my wife, son Fred and daughter Nancy, sang "The Bridge Builder." That evening, July 8, 1956, the Lima Branch was organized. Elder Moyle set me apart as Branch President, the first in Peru, with Stanley A. Moore as first counselor, Charles H. Shaw as first counselor, and my son Fred G. Williams as secretary. Apostle Moyle spoke prophetic words about the future of the work in this country and invoked the Lord's blessings on the branch and its members.

On Monday, Colonel Shaw and I, with the help of Mr. Timberlake of the U.S. Embassy, arranged for an interview for Brother Moyle and President Parry with the Minister of Justice and Religion in Charge of Foreign Affairs, General Félix Huaman. We were received very graciously and Brother Moyle, a seasoned attorney as well as General Authority, eloquently explained the purpose of our visit. I interpreted for both Brother Moyle and the Minister. The interview lasted forty-five minutes, and we left with the necessary information to gain permission to do work in Peru. When we returned to our home, Elder Moyle asked President Parry and me to get together to draft the formal petition to the Peruvian government. I got out my typewriter and started typing the document directly into Spanish. Brother Parry took one look at it and said, "You go ahead and write it out, and we'll talk later." Then he went downstairs and began reading a book. I typed out the memorandum, which Brother Parry and Brother Moyle approved. We all signed the final draft.

Elder Moyle cancelled his trip to Cuzco. He had been suffering from a heart condition, and decided that the high altitude would be detrimental to him, so they stayed in Lima until July 14. He said, "If we could find a home, I would buy it now for a chapel." But we were unable to find one while he was there.

We invited Brother and Sister Moyle for a formal dinner the first Sunday after their arrival and one other evening during the week. After a visit to a member's home, we were about to take the Moyles back to their hotel. Corraine asked me to invite the Moyles to our home for a potluck supper if I thought the invitation would not offend them. I answered her in Spanish, "The only way to find out is to ask." So she said, "Elder Moyle, would you like to take potluck supper with us, that is, take your chances on whatever we have on hand in the kitchen?" He said, "Would I? I'd be tickled to death. Why I've even been eating corn flakes in the hotel room with mineral water, I was afraid of the milk." So we turned the car around and started home. Brother Moyle asked, "Do you know of a place that has some good cheese?" I said, "Yes, there's a place that has it imported from Europe." "Well, I like cheese, let's go by and see what we can find." We stopped and he bought five or six kinds of cheeses. Once home, we sat around the table on stools and opened a couple of cans of tuna, brought out the cheese, milk and corn flakes, and had a very enjoyable meal. Brother Moyle said, "That's the best meal I have had since I left home. Everywhere I go the people try to kill me with kindness and goodness and prepare big meals; something like this is just wonderful."

Having made the formal application to do missionary work in Peru, we were anxious to have the missionaries arrive. President Parry sent us Elders Darwin Thomas and Sherl Plowman, August 3, 1956; they became the first missionaries to labor in Peru. Generally speaking, he would send missionaries who had four or five months to go to complete their missions. We had four and sometimes six missionaries working in Lima. In the beginning, our home was their headquarters; later they lived in *pensiones*.

The elders started tracting and soon people began coming to our English Sunday Schools. We started a Spanish class for them. Sacrament meetings were held in Spanish.

We began looking in earnest for a place that would serve as both headquarters and chapel, and were fortunate to find a home less than one block from where the Lima Branch had been organized. It was a beautiful three-story, Tudor style mansion just twelve years old. It was large and sumptuous: a beautiful chapel with a large yard. The price seemed right.

I wrote a letter to the First Presidency with the necessary information on the purchase of the home, and they immediately sent the purchase price, which I remember was fifty-two thousand dollars. We purchased the home and held the first meeting, a Christmas Eve party on December 24, 1956. All our English-speaking members were there, as well as several investigators. This first meeting was held on the roof, which had been appropriately finished for outdoor parties.

This building, at 1210 Avenida Orrantia in San Isidro, Lima, was the first piece of property owned by the Church in Peru. It is at present the headquarters of the Lima South Mission.

Right after the first of the year we all worked to fix up this home. The large living-dining room was adequate for a chapel, the sun porch was curtained by the Relief Society sisters to make a room for a small kindergarten children class, and the four upstairs bedrooms became classrooms. It made a wonderful home for our small Lima Branch, and so served until the organization of the Andean Mission on November 1, 1959.

Subsequently, under the authority of the First Presidency, I requested the *Personería Jurídica* for the Church in Peru. *Personería Jurídica* means the official recognition of the Church as an official entity within the confines of Peru. I secured the aid of my attorney friend, Dr. Manuel García Calderón to prepare the papers, which we presented to the proper ministry and then went time after time to see if anything had been done about it to activate it.

After many, many months, I suppose probably fourteen or fifteen, and after numerous visits to the ministry, an investigator came out to the home and said he was checking the request, and said that he wanted to know more about the Church. I took him in my car, and we went over to visit the chapel. We showed him what was there and told him just what was going on. I said:

> *There's a better way that you can find out what kind of people we are, here's our schedule of meetings, we hold Sunday School at this time, and Church at such and such a time, and Mutual on Tuesday nights, at this hour, why don't you just come. Investigators are coming all the time, and friends; you could just see what is going on. We won't be putting on a front for you, they won't know who you are.*

He said, "I think I'd just like to do that, you might be surprised to see me out there some day." As far as I know he never did come, but perhaps some other investigator from the government may have come.

A few months later I found that the recognition had been granted, and that we were legally and lawfully constituted and officially recognized to work within the national territory of Peru.

Soon after arriving in Peru, we had written to the three mission presidents in South America telling them of our whereabouts, and offering to put up missionaries if they visited Peru on their return to the United States; we got a lot of visitors. We also were visited by some General Authorities, as I have already indicated.

In 1957, we were delighted with the visit of Dr. Milton R. Hunter of the Council of Seventy. Although his PhD from Stanford was in history, Brother Hunter was an amateur archeologist and of course was always interested in things pertaining to ancient America. It was my privilege to take him around to different museums and sites in and around Lima. I made arrangements through two ministries of the Peruvian Government—it took about a week—to have the National Museum's safe opened and the contents photographed by Brother Hunter. At Pachacamac, he photographed Sister Williams and me standing in what looks to be a baptismal font, a picture which was used in Dr. Hunter's *Christ in Ancient America*, Vol. II (Salt Lake City: Deseret Book, 1959), and was subsequently printed in the large, illustrated Book of Mormon and elsewhere. We spent a very pleasant month with Brother Hunter.

On making inquiries at the National Museum on who might have private collections, several names were given us, among them Hugo Cohen. I think we visited all of them, but the Cohen collection was by far the most impressive. Right from the first time I called and spoke to Mr. Cohen on the telephone, he was most gracious to us. At the appointed hour, Brother Hunter and I appeared at their home, armed with a lot of photographic equipment.

The Cohen home is a beautiful two-story mansion; the gold collection is in a room upstairs, which in reality is a large safe filled with some four hundred pieces of Incan and pre-Incan gold, Paracas weaving, *wacos* and other items. We requested permission to take pictures of the artifacts, which was readily granted, and they let us take whatever we wanted out of the showcases, set them on the table or hold them to be photographed. I held a number of priceless works while Brother Hunter took their pictures.

He had taken over thirty-six exposures, when he said, "Fred, these won't come out. This is a new camera and my openings are not correctly set. Now what do we do?" I said I would explain the problem to the Cohens. Mr. Cohen, a man I judged to be in his early seventies said to go ahead and shoot them all over. Brother Hunter turned to me and said, "Now my batteries are weak; I'll have to go down town and get some new batteries." So I explained that problem to them. Mr. Cohen again was most gracious and told us to go ahead and leave and that we could return whenever we wished. I asked if it would be all right to return in an hour, he said that that would be fine. After obtaining the batteries and new film, we were greeted by the Cohens once more, who were just as cordial as they were before. We spent another two hours taking pictures. Many of them have appeared in Dr. Hunter's books, and in the illustrated Book of Mormon.

There was a time when the Church was considering building a visitors' center and museum at the Cohen home; and for that purpose, I traveled with Brother Milton R. Hunter, and Apostle Howard W. Hunter to Peru in 1967. It was finally determined that the Church as an institution should not get involved, but that private members would be encouraged. For a number of years I tried to interest various groups and individuals, making many trips down. Mr. Cohen had died in 1962, and his widow was anxious to place the collection in safe hands.

Among the General Authorities who have seen the collection are Milton R. Hunter, Spencer W. Kimball, Harold B. Lee, Theodore M. Tuttle, Joseph Fielding Smith, Howard W. Hunter and Gordon B. Hinckley.

Second Lima Branch organized. In two years our branch grew to such an extent that it was entirely too crowded for all the people to attend our meetings on Avenida Orrantia. So we found another place that would be adequate, on Mariátegui Street, and the First Presidency authorized the purchase of this building, and sent the money for its purchase. I don't recall the purchase price, but I believe it was somewhere around thirty thousand dollars. This I purchased in the name of the Church, the second piece of property owned by The Church of Jesus Christ of Latter-day Saints in Peru. We remodeled it, took out a wall to enlarge the living room, and then President Parry came and organized a new branch. Stanley A. Moore was made president of the Mariátegui Branch. We divided what Church property we had evenly, such as chairs and other facilities, and from that time on we had two branches in Lima. Each one grew rapidly and carried on all the activities of the Mission.

The members of each branch took delight in visiting with the others, going to the different meetings, and it made a very pleasant association between the two groups. There was no rivalry, or only friendly rivalry, but no envy or jealousy with one another.

One of our early converts was the most famous folk singer of Peru, Luis Abanto Morales. He was a radio personality and made records which sold throughout Peru. His voice could always be heard on the local radio, and it was wonderful to have him come on a Tuesday night. We'd tell him that we were going to have a little fiesta that night at Mutual, and he would come directly from the radio station, and bring with him whatever musicians there might be there at the time. One night he brought the accompanist for Ima Sumac; she was indisposed, but had planned to come; she had appeared briefly on the radio and then gone to her home.

We had some glorious times there with our fiestas and local talent. Brother Luis Abanto was very generous with his time and with the time of others that he would bring, insisting that they come and present their numbers free of charge to the Mormons.

All this time we were having problems getting permanent visas for missionaries; hence only missionaries who were practically through with their missions in Uruguay were eligible to come into Peru. In one way this was good, because for the most part they were mature missionaries, all of them speaking fluent Spanish. One of these was our nephew, David Smith.

When I applied for a visa to go to Peru, after a short visit there and after consulting an attorney who had a friend in the agency who granted visas (I made my application to the Peruvian consulate in Los Angeles), it took a little better than two months. Making application for these permanent visas for the full-time missionaries coming to Peru from Uruguay, I found that most of the elders had practically finished their missions before they were received. I presented the request in the name of the Uruguayan Mission in Lima, but we were getting nowhere. We knew that if we were going to have a fully constituted mission, we would have to get better service on visas, but this was rather difficult under the Peruvian law. It seems that the Lord prepares ways so that His purposes can be performed, and here is rather an interesting sidelight on how this particular problem was solved.

The missionaries were instrumental in baptizing a very lovely girl by the name of Elba Coloma who spoke some English and, being enthused with what the missionaries had told her about Brigham Young University, had decided to go to school in Provo. She requested admittance at the university; we sent up her papers and eventually she was accepted by the department, but the Office of Admissions had not yet sent the official letter of acceptance to her, which she needed to obtain her visa from the American Consulate. She wanted to go up a few months early to live with her uncle who lived in San Francisco and perfect her English before school started. Time went on and soon it was impossible for her to do that because no visa was forthcoming. In desperation, just a few days before classes were to start, I sent rather a nasty telegram to President Wilkinson. In it I reiterated the entire history, how she had been accepted, but still lacked the official notification from the University that she was a full-time student and therefore could not obtain a visa. I added that this was very poor public relations for the United States and especially for The Church of Jesus Christ of Latter-day Saints.

Well, the telegram got results. The next day she received a phone call from the Consul, in which he explained that they had received a cable from BYU and that she could now pick up her visa, which she did and immediately left for the United States, arriving just in time to begin the Fall 1958 term.

It so happened that Elba Coloma's uncle was the man in charge of visas for the Peruvian government, and he was very much interested in his niece. He told Elba's mother that if there were anything that he could ever do to help me—since I had been kind to go to bat for his niece—to be sure to call on him. Remembering our problems with visas, I promptly went to see him, and told him what the situation was regarding our missionaries. He said, "Leave it up to me, I'll see what I can do to help you. When you want a new visa, come and see me personally."

The most dramatic example of his help came a year later. I believe that it was the month of August 1959, when we received the word that the Andean Mission was to be organized and that J. Vernon Sharp would be the mission president. Whatever date that was, I received a cablegram from the First Presidency stating that President and Sister Sharp had left Salt Lake City for New York where they would embark on one of the Grace Line steamers for Lima, Peru, some five days hence, and would I kindly secure a permanent visa for them and have it cabled to the Peruvian consulate in New York.

I remembered back to the two months that it had taken me to get a permanent visa for Peru and the trouble we had had getting visas for the missionaries; then I remembered my friend Mr. Coloma down in the Foreign Ministry. I went down at ten o'clock when the office opened, and told him my problem and he said, "Would five o'clock be too late for this afternoon?" I said, "No, that would be wonderful." "Well, come back and see me at five." I returned at five o'clock in the afternoon and the visas were ready in the form of a cable, which I sent to the Peruvian Consulate in New York, and another copy to the First Presidency stating that the permanent visas were ready. I don't think the First Presidency ever did realize the problem that we'd had in gaining a permanent visa for anyone; they just requested that it be done, and fortunately it was done. When in Peru in August 1967, I found that Mr. Coloma had died; but he had set up the procedure and established the machinery to service the missionaries, and it has been going on ever since. Without this great service, it would have been impossible to establish the mission on the basis that it is, because it would have taken so many months to get visas, and as the Church members know, the missionaries don't know that far in advance where they are going.

Spencer W. Kimball. In the latter part of March 1959, Elder Spencer W. Kimball and his wife reached Lima as part of their South American tour. They were accompanied by President and Sister Arthur Jensen, the new president of the Uruguayan Mission. It was my privilege to show them Lima and the evidences of an ancient civilization. From the top of the Temple of the Sun at Pachamac, he stated that he thought it was larger than the one at Teotihuacán, just outside Mexico City.

The Kimballs and Jensens were guests at our home on Elder Kimball's birthday. He suggested we have some music and singing and accompanied us on the piano. He played the Mexican Hat Dance and President Jensen, remembering the days he spent in the Spanish-American Mission, did a creditable imitation.

The Jensens then excused themselves to visit with the missionaries. Corraine wondered if the Kimballs would like to go to a movie. Elder Kimball said that they would. We explained that we had recently seen an Austrian musical based on the lives of the Trapp Family which we had enjoyed very much.

We went to the theater and sat in the sparsely occupied balcony. The movie, of course, was in German. It had Spanish subtitles for the dialogue, which Corraine interpreted for Sister Kimball and I for her husband.

We held a combined meeting of the two Lima branches, and an overflow crowd enjoyed the Apostle's words. It was my privilege to interpret for Elder Kimball.

The visitors desired to visit Cuzco and Machu Picchu, and invited Corraine and me to accompany them. I took time off from my duties as general manager of the Peruvian Airline "TAPSA" and we left on an early scheduled flight on a C-46 plane. Fifteen minutes out of Lima while circling over the ocean to gain altitude, we noticed oil covering the wing and the windows of the left side of the plane. An oil line had broken, so it was necessary for the pilot to shut down that engine, and we returned to Limatambo Airport on one engine.

We had another C-46 in maintenance, so after about an hour delay we changed to it and flew uneventfully to Cuzco.

At the time, Cuzco's only airport was almost in the center of the city at 11,400 feet above sea level. Planes had to land up hill and takeoff down hill, the direction of the wind notwithstanding. It was a very short runway. I arranged to seat Elder Kimball up front on the third seat in back of the two pilots so that he could get a better view of Cuzco while landing. He seemed to enjoy that experience.

Corraine had flown with me before to Cuzco several times, usually with the same reaction, deathly sick with *soroche,* or altitude sickness. This trip was no exception. She went to bed immediately upon reaching the hotel and declined dinner. Elder Kimball was concerned and asked if she would like a blessing. She received a beautiful one and was promised to be well enough for the trip to Machu Picchu the following morning.

This visit to the "greatest tourist attraction in the Americas" was our first, too. We also thoroughly enjoyed the trip along the Urubamba Valley, held sacred by the Incas, and the great ruins themselves. However, Elder Kimball didn't enjoy Cuzco as much as he would have liked. He was grieved by the abject poverty of the Indian people living there. He remarked that he had seen poverty in Europe and in North American countries, but never had he seen it to the extent that he saw it in Cuzco.

One of the purposes of Elder Kimball's trip to Peru was the dedication of a Latter-day Saint chapel in Toquepala, southern Peru. There a gigantic copper mine had been developed by removing more than forty million tons of overburden before reaching the copper deposit. The engineer in charge was Warren Smith from Arizona, a life-long and active member of the Church. He had taken with him many employees from the colonies of northern Mexico who had worked with him in the Arizona copper mines he had managed. They and their families needed a place to worship. The company donated the building materials and they did the work of construction in their spare time and very soon they had completed a fine modern chapel.

The Kimballs and the Jensens left for Ilo to see about organizing a branch there. We were invited to the dedication, to be held the following Sunday. Brother Smith, whose daughter had lived with us in Lima while attending school, arranged for Corraine and me to fly down Saturday in the company's twin-engine plane. We flew to Ilo and from there in a single-engine plane to a short runway carved out of the side of the mountain near the mine. The chapel at that time was said to be built at the highest elevation of any in the Church, over ten thousand feet above sea level.

In preparation of the dedicatory program, Elder Kimball noted that they had no musical numbers listed. Knowing that Corraine and all her family sang, he asked if she would sing a solo. She hesitated since she hadn't brought any music with her. "We have a hymnbook," he answered. She wondered who would accompany her. "I'll accompany you," he responded, and so we had special music.

All the company officials attended the dedicatory service. The local branch president, Elder Robinson, Elder Kimball and I were the speakers. It was my privilege to interpret for Elder Kimball again.

The following day Corraine and I returned to Lima aboard the two airplanes that had taken us south. The Kimballs and the Jensens returned a few days later.

Elder Kimball's visit was long remembered. His love and compassion were evident in all of his actions. I remember one in particular. A lovely Peruvian member, Sister Williams, one of the first to be baptized, took ill and was hospitalized with cancer at the time of his visit. She requested that he administer to her.

He was willing, so we went to the hospital; however, they would let only one person into visit her at a time. I went in and anointed her, and then Elder Kimball went in and sealed the anointing in English. She died soon after, but was so happy that an apostle of the Lord would come and visit her under these circumstances. Hers was the first funeral service I conducted in Peru.

As branch president one of my concerns was giving the priesthood to some of our members. Peru has a high infusion of negro blood and one family in particular presented me with a difficult decision to make. The father was definitely Spanish, no dark blood at all. The mother was questionable and a daughter, our organist, looked definitely black. Her two younger brothers, now old enough to receive the priesthood, presented a problem.

The missionary district president who had baptized them requested that I give them the priesthood, but after seeing the sister of their mother, I just couldn't make up my mind.

The question came up in a priesthood meeting with Elder Kimball after his arrival. I told him that it had been suggested that I give them the priesthood, but that I was still undecided. In his kindly manner, he said, "President Williams, if there is any doubt in this matter, give them the benefit of the doubt." The next Sunday they were both ordained deacons.

Harold B. Lee organizes the Andean Mission. I was still living in Lima when Brother Harold B. Lee came through to organize the Andean Mission. Brother and Sister Vernon Sharp, the newly called Presidents, had arrived earlier and had then gone to Argentina to meet the Lees and accompany them to Santiago and Lima. On Sunday, November 1, 1959, it was my privilege to drive the Sharps and Lees from the hotel to the chapel. On the way, we drove down to Los Cedros and I pointed out to them Colonel Shaw's home where the first branch had been organized. I was also privileged to interpret for Brother Lee when he spoke and organized the Andean Mission. Some of his statements were quite prophetic. Later, in 1966, while in Brother Lee's office in Salt Lake City, he recalled that occasion and said, "You know, in thinking over what I said, I certainly spoke of things that were beyond my knowledge. I think that they must have been prophetic and under the inspiration of the Lord." His words focused on the great future that is in store for that particular part of the Lord's vineyard, and of the countless number of Lamanite people who would come into the Church, descendents of Father Lehi, and that the theater where much of the action found in the Book of Mormon had taken place in that region.

At this dedicatory meeting, Luis Abanto Morales sang a solo, a song for the new mission for which I had written the words and he the music. Brother Lee liked it so much that he asked him to repeat it, which he did. Brother Abanto told me in August 1967 that he had been requested to sing it a number of times on special occasions. This was the second time I had written the words to a mission song.

Canción de la Misión de Los Andes
(Música de "Santa Rosa de Lima", de Luis Abanto Morales)

La Misión de Los Andes,
La Misión amada, la recién llegada
a la América del Sud.

La Misión de Los Andes,
obra tan divina que a todos nos enseña
el amor y la virtud.

La Misión de Los Andes, te damos nuestro amor
dando gracias al Señor.

En el cielo los ángeles se ven complacidos
al ver el comienzo
de la obra del Salvador.

In December 1959, since our old chapel was now being used as the Mission Home, it was necessary to secure new property. I was instrumental in leasing for the Church the chapel on Pasoldán, a street running off of Avenida Arequipa. It was necessary for me to do this since President Sharp's power of attorney had not yet been legalized. When President Sharp's power of attorney finally arrived, I translated it, typed it on the official stationery of the Ministry of Foreign Affairs, Translation Department, and had it legalized. I had had a great deal of contact with Mr. Alborno, the head translator, who always accepted my translations. He had given me a supply of official stationery and anything that I wanted translated, I'd translate and type it up and he would just stamp it. He would still charge me the same rate as though he had done all the work himself, but at least I would get it out immediately and not have to wait three or four weeks for the translation.

Living in Peru was a wonderful experience: there the old and the new coexist in a remarkable way. My whole family worked in the Church, as though we were on a mission. Corraine was the first Relief Society President, Fred was branch secretary and president of the Mutual as well as branch organist; Nancy was branch chorister and first counselor in the Primary and second counselor in the Sunday School Presidency. They brought their friends to church and converted several of them.

When we arrived in January 1956, there was a small Latter-day Saint group that held a Sunday School in English. Within eight months, the Lima Branch was organized and missionary work begun; soon several members filled the Church; my daughter Mary was the first baptism. By the time the Andean Mission was organized on November 1, 1959—just over three years after the start of the work—there were three organized branches, each with its own building fully paid for, and approximately seven hundred members. It was a gratifying way to start a new mission, and I'm grateful I had a hand in it.

EPILOGUE:

THE OAK TREE SPREADS ITS BOUGHS

NOVEMBER 1, 1959, was a significant date in relation to the prophecy made by Elder Melvin J. Ballard at the opening of the South American Mission. On that day, five hundred members of the Church crowded into the tiny branch headquarters in Lima, Peru, to attend the dedication of the Andes Mission. Before the dedicatory prayer, Elder Harold B. Lee spoke at length concerning the origins of the South American Mission. He recalled Elder Ballard's prophecy that, at the beginning, the work would progress slowly, even as an acorn grows slowly from a seedling and eventually becomes a mature tree with "branches (that) extend over all of South America to bless its people."

Elder Lee himself became prophetic, and I, standing at his side as interpreter, felt the deep spriritual context of his word. He stated that the time would soon come when Father Lehi's children would be inspired to accept the Book of Mormon and enter the Church in great numbers. "Soon," he said, "the Pacific Coast of the Americas will become the most fertile proselyting field of the Church."

Corraine and I met with Elder Lee six months later, and during our conversation he reminded us of that November 1, 1959, meeting. He said: "President Williams, you will recall that I said things in the dedicatory service that I knew not of. I truly felt the spirit of prophecy."

Thirty-four years had passed since the dedication of the South American Mission in 1925, and three missions had been established in Argentina, Brazil and Uruguay. In 1956 Elder Henry D. Moyle established a branch in Santiago, Chile, as part of the Argentine Mission, and one in Lima, which was placed under the Uruguayan Mission. These were the only Church organizations to be established on the South American Continent in thirty-four years.

During that time the members in Argentina and Brazil had reached about four thousand each, with about three thousand in Uruguay. The Chilean and Lima branches each numbered seven hundred members. By 1959 fewer than twenty thousand members lived in all of South America; there were no stakes, modern chapels, or temples.

What has happened in the past twenty-five years on the west coast of America? According to the 1985 Church Almanac (which contains statistics to September 1984), the Church has extended its branches over the wall (see Figure 1).

Figure 1. Latin American church statistics

As can be seen in the figure, branches of that oak tree extend over the other South American countries as well.

Continuing Elder Lee's prophecy into Central America, only one mission (an off-shoot of the Mexican Mission organized in 1952) existed before 1959. Even in those troubled countries, the oak tree has spread its branches.

As of November 1959, Mexico had a total of two missions and seventeen thousand members. The first mission had been established in 1879, closed in 1889, and reopened June 8, 1901. The second was organized on June 10, 1956 and designated the Northern Mexican Mission. Only one stake, in the Mormon Colonies, had been organized. *(See table below Figure 1 for statistics on Mexico.)*

REGIONAL TOTALS • NOVEMBER 1959 to SEPTEMBER 1984

Region	Missions	Stakes	Temples	Members
West Coast	15	82	4	206,788*
East Coast	14	86	2	239,239
Total South America	29	168	6	545,952

OTHER REGIONS

Region	Missions	Stakes	Temples	Members
Central America	5	23	1	73,124
Mexico	8	76	1	238,839

**Not including approximately 1,500 members living in Chile and Peru before November 1959.*

....

California (Spanish-Speaking). In 1959 only a few small Spanish language branches existed in southern California, each with a total membership of about one hundred. Today, although there are no missions exclusively dedicated to the Hispanic peoples, all missions in California have Spanish-speaking missionaries, and baptisms among people of Latin American descent living in California exceed those of any other ethnic or language group.

The Huntington Park California West Stake, comprised of seven Spanish language wards, was organized on June 3, 1984, as the first Spanish language stake created in the United States. In addition, there are some 30 other Spanish language wards in the Los Angeles area each with a membership of over three hundred, and many branches.

The prophecy is being fulfilled: the branches of the oak tree have truly extended over all of South America and brought blessings to thousands. Elder Lee's prophecy is also being fulfilled. Since 1959, Church membership along the Pacific Shore from Chile to Mexico has grown to twice the English-speaking Church membership of California, and that membership includes many Hispanic people who were converted in Latin America before they emigrated to the United States.

PART IV

APPENDICIES

APPENDIX A

BRIEF BIOGRAPHY OF MISSION PRESIDENTS WHO SERVED IN SOUTH AMERICA FROM 1925-1950

	Called	Released
SOUTH AMERICAN MISSION		
Melvin J. Ballard	6 December 1925	15 July 1926
Reinhold Stoof	15 July 1926	14 August 1935
ARGENTINE MISSION		
W. Ernest Young	14 August 1935	31 August 1938
Frederick S. Williams	31 August 1938	1 August 1942
James L. Barker	1 August 1942	6 September 1944
W. Ernest Young	6 September 1944	22 March 1949
Harold Brown	22 March 1949	13 December 1952
BRAZILIAN MISSION		
Rulon S. Howells	25 May 1935	13 October 1938
John Alden Bowers	13 October 1938	1 June 1942
William West Seegmiller	1 June 1942	13 April 1945
Harold M. Rex	13 April 1945	28 January 1949
Rulon S. Howells	28 January 1949	6 October 1953
URUGUAYAN MISSION		
Frederick Salem Williams	30 August 1947	31 July 1951

ARGENTINE MISSION

W. Ernest Young. (1935 to 1938; 1944 to 1949)

In addition to my account here, President W. Ernest Young has published his *Diary* which contains a detailed account of both his administrations.

Walter Ernest Young was born November 22, 1887, near Manassa, Colorado. At age nine he moved with his parents to the Mormon colonies in Chihuahua, Mexico. In 1910 he served a mission in Mexico under President Rey L. Pratt; he baptized Rafael Monroy (1913) who two years later was assassinated by rebels along with a companion for not forsaking their new religion.

On June 9, 1915, he married Cecile Skousen and soon became first counselor in the Colonia Dublán Ward, Mexico. He was Bishop of the Juárez Ward for ten years beginning in 1922. He presided over the Argentine Mission twice.

Always a gifted teacher, he was the principal of the Colonia Dublán Grammar School and taught at the Juárez Stake Academy during his thirty-year teaching career. He received both a B.A. (1935) and an M.A. (1939) in Education from Brigham Young University. In 1950 he began working in the Church Translation Department and then in the Historical Department. He retired in 1970. The Youngs have three children: Amy, Walter and Carl.

What characterizes President Young's first mission in my mind is that he established the work firmly in the Spanish language, expanding proselyting activities and challenging the members to assume greater responsibilities.

When he returned in 1944 he was faced with a far different situation. He, his wife, and their nineteen-year-old son Carl were the only missionaries. This situation continued until the end of the War, except for two elders from the Mormon colonies, Fletcher Memmott and Charles Call. As Mexican citizens, they were not subject to the U.S. draft. Within two years after the end of the War, four married couples were called to serve in Argentina: Marion I. Vance, his wife Elizabeth, and three children (David, Kenneth and Susan); Lyman S. Shreeve, his wife Afton, and two children (Lyman Sidney, Jr. and Patricia); Edgar Keith Stott and wife Leona; and James O. Jensen and wife Roeine. This was the second Argentine mission for elders Vance and Shreeve.

Also in Argentina in private business was former Argentine missionary L. Pierce Brady, his wife Bea and their two children. He was counselor to President Young.

Frederick S. Williams. (1938 to 1942)

I have the distinction of being the first missionary in South America to return as mission president. I would characterize my administration in the following manner: because of the excellent work of Presidents Stoof and Young, I was able to direct a more effective mission effort. I had the member and missionary base on which to develop programs; I could call local members leadership to positions and to fill missions. Through a variety of programs we became better known than ever before. My work seemed naturally to focus on developing leadership qualities in the youth. I was the most blessed of all the early mission presidents in South America. My wife Corraine and two daughters accompanied me to the mission (Barbara L. and Argina); two children were born in Argentina (Frederick G. and Nancy L.).

I was born June 15, 1908, in Colonia Dublán, and named Frederick Salem; my parents moved to the States soon thereafter because of rebel activities. At age eighteen, I was called to serve a mission in the newly established South American Mission. On June 3, 1930, I married Corraine Smith and soon began working as court crier and interpreter to the United States District Court, Phoenix, Arizona; two years later I was named secretary to the Honorable F.C. Jacobs, U.S. District Judge.

In 1938 I was called to preside over the Argentine Mission; in 1947 I presided over the newly organized Uruguayan Mission, which also included Paraguay. Our fifth and last child, Mary, was born in Uruguay. Between these two Church assignments I was the Business Manager for the Institute of Inter-American Affairs, Division of Health and Sanitation, an agency of the U.S. government, first in Venezuela and later in Uruguay.

In 1955 I was called to preside over the newly created Los Angeles Temple Mission, and appointed first Director of the Bureau of Information. Business took my family and me to Lima, Peru, in 1956, where I was General Manager of TAPSA, a Peruvian airline. I became the first branch president of the Church on the western coast of South America, and aided in the establishment of the Andes Mission in 1959.

I served for ten years in the South Los Angeles Stake Presidency (1961 to 1971), and since 1973 have been a Patriarch, not only in my stake, but to the Spanish- and Portuguese-speaking members of the Church who come properly recommended. For three years (1972 to 1975) I was also a counselor to President Paul of the California Los Angeles Mission.

By 1975, I had published more than 170 articles in my column, "Americalogical Corner," in the California *Intermountain News*; and thirty-six in a monthly column entitled "To Argentina with Love" in *ALAS*. I made my living teaching English as a Second Language to adults in three school districts.

James L. Barker. (1942 to 1944)

President Barker's mission was characterized by a pall as the war ground proselyting almost to a standstill—the last missionaries had returned home. Under those circumstances it was difficult to keep all the members active, and a number fell away. It became his duty to prune away the dead branches and to train the active members with leadership capability. He did well; the members responded by carrying out the full Church program on their own.

James Louis Barker was already a well-known figure in Church and international educational circles when he assumed leadership of the mission. He was born July 27, 1880, at North Ogden, Utah, and obtained his B.A. from the University of Utah at age nineteen. He served a mission in Switzerland from 1901 to 1904. On May 30, 1906, he married Kate Montgomery. For the better part of the next decade the Barkers lived in Europe while he attended the Sorbonne in Paris and the University of Neuchâtel in Switzerland, where he received his "License de Lettres."

During his long academic career he served as head of the Modern Language Department of the Brigham Young University, President of Weber College in Ogden, and head of the Modern Language Department of the University of Utah; the last post he held for twenty-eight years. He was a renowned phonetician, a member of both the Linguistic Society of France and the Modern Language Society of America, and was decorated by the French Government.

He was also a member of the General Board of the Deseret Sunday School Union for many years and a gifted writer of Priesthood and Sunday School manuals. He later published one of the classic studies in Mormondom in two volumes: *Protesters of Christendom, Apostasy from the Divine Church,* and *The Restoration of the Divine Church.* His collection of over fifteen hundred special books was donated to the BYU Library following his death, May 29, 1958.

President Barker spoke flawless French and was fluent in German, Italian and Spanish. However, he always spoke Castilian Spanish which was quite different from the Spanish of the Argentine *porteños* and the Uruguayans of Montevideo.

Kate Barker had served for several years as a counselor to Amy Brown Lyman in the Relief Society General Presidency. The Barkers were called to preside over the French Mission in 1946.

The last year of the Barker administration coincided with our first year in Uruguay, where I worked for the Institute of Inter-American Affairs. Corraine and I attended the Argentine Mission conferences and became well acquainted with President and Sister Barker. They also visited us in Montevideo. On one visit (June 25, 1944) he organized the Montevideo branch under the Argentine Mission. I was the first branch president.[1] We also became well acquainted with James L. Barker, Jr., who worked in Montevideo.

Harold Brown. (1949 to 1952)

President Brown was born June 3, 1917, at Duncan, Arizona. He attended school at Juárez Academy, Mexico, and served a mission to Argentina from 1937 to 1940.

As mission president he served during some of the difficult Perón years; the missionaries were harassed by the police and he was even arrested and placed in jail. I have known Harold since he was a young man working for our construction company in Tucson. Later I became his mission president, and still later he married my niece, Leanore Jesperson. We have always felt close. Before his call as president, he and Leanore had been living in Montevideo where he was assigned to the United States Consulate; we were serving as Mission Presidents in Uruguay, and we very much enjoyed their spirit and support. The Lord has found him to be a faithful, willing servant and he has responded to a number of important callings. In addition to being Mission President in Argentina, he was called to be the first President of the Mexico City Stake (1961 to 1972); he was a Regional Representative of the Twelve Apostles (called 1972) and Leonore was a member of the Relief Society General Board starting in 1967. They were called as the first presidents of the Mexico City Temple.

Harold combines a brilliant mind with a deep-rooted faith. He attended both the University of Mexico and Harvard, where he received his M.A. He nearly received his doctorate, but he interrupted his studies a number of times to accept calls from the Church.

It was particularly satisfying to line up Harold and Bill Farnsworth to speak in sacrament meeting before I delivered the closing address. Bill would get the congregation's attention, Harold would call them to repentance, and I could be the nice guy.

BRAZILIAN MISSION

My connection with the Brazilian Mission over the years has been indirect, but I would like to include my impressions of the men who presided over that land—all of whom, save one, I knew personally and had dealings with in the course of my own administrations, either in Argentina or Uruguay.

Rulon S. Howells. (1935 to 1938; 1949 to 1953)

My first contact with President Howells was significant in its own small way. Just before we left Salt Lake City for Buenos Aires in July 1938, his mother asked us to take him a tube of his favorite shaving cream, which he was unable to buy in Brazil. She said he would meet our ship at Santos to pick up the shaving cream.

Our ship docked at Santos for several hours, but no one met us, so I decided to mail it to him. I put the tube (now wrapped for mailing) under my coat and started for the post office. An alert guard stopped me at the foot of the gangplank but allowed me to proceed when I showed him the package.

Shortly after reaching Buenos Aires we received a letter from President Howells thanking us for the shaving cream and apologizing for not meeting the boat. Something had come up and he had been unable to travel to Santos on that day. He was released just two months later, after serving more than three years.

In every sense, he was the father of the Brazilian Mission, serving as its first President. Up to that time, all the work had been carried on in Southern Brazil under the South American Mission. He established his headquarters in São Paulo, and organized and expanded the mission to embrace the entire country.

My next contact with him was in Salt Lake City in July 1947, while we were preparing to open the Uruguayan Mission. He was director of a state-wide publicity commission. My sister, Lucy W. Brossard, worked as his secretary, and we had a pleasant reunion with him.

Two years later, he was called as Brazilian Mission President a second time; we corresponded regularly concerning mission matters. On April 18, 1951, he and his wife Mary visited us in Montevideo. From there, we accompanied them to Buenos Aires where, together with President Harold Brown of the Argentine Mission, we held the first regional Mission Presidents' Conference in South America. We exchanged valuable insights into missionary work and mission problems. Such conferences later became, and still are, routine.

Rulon Stanley Howells was born in Salt Lake City, Utah, on May 25, 1902. He served a mission to Germany from 1922 to 1925, and on August 26, 1931, married Mary Pierce, a gifted soprano.

In 1935 Brother Howells graduated from University of Utah law school and was called to preside over the opening of the Brazilian Mission. In 1939 he was appointed Executive Secretary of the Utah Democratic Committee and also ordained a Bishop of the South Eighteenth Ward, Ensign Stake. In 1940 he became the Assistant Attorney General of the State of Utah. He has since held a number of important posts in state government, including Commissioner of Publicity and Industrial Development (1946 to 1949).

Brother Howells is a successful author of five books including *His Many Mansions* and *The Mormon Story*. When I approached him about helping to write this history, he promptly and graciously responded with a sizable typewritten manuscript covering both of his administrations. His narrative follows as Appendix C.

When the new Brazilian Mission was organized (May 25, 1935—President Howells' birthday), the following seven missionaries were laboring in three districts. The combined district membership was 113:

Joinville District (80 members):
- Joseph Herbert Henry Hunger
- Paul Stoll

Santa Catarina District (30 members)
- Phillip Guy Patterson
- David H. Smith

Porto Alegre District (3 members)
- Emil A. Schindler (soon released; his second mission)
- Melvin C. Cannon (Tracy Y. Cannon's son)
- Reed Bayles

Elder Merlin C. Palmer accompanied the Howells to the mission field. Another thirty members were scattered throughout different cities of the South. The total mission membership was 143. Of those, 107 had been baptized during President Stoof's administration; the rest were either members who had emigrated from Europe (e.g., the eight-member Lippelt family, and Max Zapf) or were children of record. The 143 members included sixty-four women, forty-four men and thirty-five children.[2] Among the forty-four men were four priests (including Max Richard Zapf, ordained June 20, 1932, and Wilhlem Ramsdorf, ordained June 18, 1930), four teachers[3] (including Georg Franz Lippelt, ordained August 1, 1930; Carlos Stark, ordained June 18, 1933; and Richard Siedschlag, ordained November 29, 1933), and seven deacons (Oskar Otto, ordained May 26, 1932; Robert Richard Zapf, ordained February 26, 1933; Rudi Arthur Zapf, ordained March 2, 1933; Richard Schulz, ordained December 3, 1933; Oscar Siedschlag, ordained December 3, 1933; Alvin Heinrich Barsch, ordained July 15, 1934 and Karl Buechli, ordained July 15, 1934).

President Howells' narrative mentions that he directed the translation of the Book of Mormon into Portuguese. Two groups were engaged in the project, one headed by Mário Pedroso (a non-member) in São Paulo, and the other by Daniel Shupe in Rio de Janeiro. Gordon Irving of the Church Historical Department interviewed Brother Shupe on February 22, 1973, as part of the Oral History Program. Brother Shupe went into detail regarding the process and the length of time (two years) it took to complete his translation. He also accorded a large measure of the success of the translation to his first wife, Agda Soares Vieira, and mother-in-law (both of whom were non-members) for their part in editing the manuscript into acceptable Portuguese. But he pointed out that at times he had to insist on his interpretation, which was prompted by the Spirit:

> *One time . . . a certain word that they wanted to put down, I knew . . . was wrong, [it] gave the wrong meaning and I prayed about it and slept through the night. The next day it came out clear which one I should use. That really happened several times (p. 42).*

Additional information on the subject is contained in the oral history interview of President Howells, also on file at the Church Historical Department. Although the translation was essentially complete, the Book of Mormon was published on March 15, 1940, under the direction of President Bowers. (see below).

President Howells also directed the translation and the publication of the Doctrine and Covenants (1950) and the Pearl of Great Price (1952), as well as the translation and compilation of the first Portuguese hymnal (1951). He truly laid a strong foundation.

John Alden Bowers. (1938 to 1942)

J. Alden Bowers replaced President Howells shortly after I became Argentine Mission President. He and his wife Amelia (married September 24, 1926) were active members in Ogden, where he served in the stake MIA presidency. Born in Marysvale, Utah, on November 22, 1903, he received a B.S. from the University of Utah in 1925 and filled a mission in Germany from 1926 to 1929.

We corresponded concerning mission problems from time to time but did not meet until 1939 (we were not authorized to leave our individual mission territories). President Bowers wrote that he was planning to tour the southern part of his mission, and I had business in Paraguay, so we agreed to meet on October 19 in Uruguaiana, a Brazilian city just across the Uruguay River from Paso de los Libres, Argentina. My traveling companion, Elder Edgar B. Mitchell, and I crossed the river and spent two enjoyable days discussing areas of interest to the two missions.

On April 27, 1941, the Bowers unexpectedly visited us in Buenos Aires. We organized an *asado* in their honor, and they both spoke at a Sacrament meeting in the Liniers chapel.

President Bowers was released June 1, 1942, after three and one-half years. He was a reserve artillery captain in the United States Army, and war had broken out. He went almost directly to Europe after returning to the United States. He told me later that he never expected to come back.

I gathered from released Brazilian missionaries en route home through our mission that he placed emphasis on making friends for the Church throughout Brazil rather than building up existing branches. His administration saw a general shift toward Portuguese and away from German.

William W. Seegmiller. (1942 to 1945)
President Seegmiller replaced J. Alden Bowers. I never met him, although we corresponded.

William West Seegmiller was born October 16, 1876, in St. George, Utah. He filled a mission to Germany from 1899 to 1902. He was called as Bishop of the Kanab Ward from 1905 to 1910, when George F. Richards called him Kanab Stake President, a position he held for fifteen years. In 1937 he was called as President of the Western States Mission where he served until July 1941. When called to preside in Brazil he became the first mission president to fly to his field of labor, due to the threat of submarine warfare.

This mission was not a happy time for President Seegmiller and his wife, Ada; they served merely as caretakers. Their few missionaries were all soon to be released. All were worried about returning home and going to war. One released elder came to Buenos Aires where he was determined to stay until the war was over. His mother enlisted my aid and between us we persuaded him to return home.

A few missionaries remained in Brazil to take jobs after their release. During the next few years they became almost entirely inactive in the Church, greatly aggravating President Seegmiller's problems.

Eventually he was left without missionaries and his only help came from three former Argentine missionaries who were working for the U.S. Government in Brazil: Rolf L. Larson, L. Pierce Brady, and Samuel J. Skousen. All three had served under me in Argentina.

Rolf served as mission secretary in Rio de Janeiro, where he lived. President Seegmiller telephoned him every evening from São Paulo with that day's events so Rolf could keep the mission books current.

These three kept the spirit of the mission alive. They tried unsuccessfully to regain the interest of former Brazilian missionaries. Some of the latter moved and did not, or would not, give their new addresses. They didn't want to be bothered.

In an August 23, 1973, oral interview L. Pierce Brady's widow Bea disclosed that a number of returned Argentine missionaries living in Rio de Janeiro met for Church during the war, but no native Brazilian members. She and Pierce were called as local missionaries, and during their three-year stay succeeded in converting three people from the diplomatic corps. One diplomatic corps acquaintance, although not a member, proved to be a blessing for our missionaries in Europe:

> *Pierce and I were in a position—well, we couldn't afford a whole lot —but we invited several guests to our home one night for dinner. Included among our guests was Walter J. Donnely, who later became Ambassador of the United States in Czechoslovakia. It was through this one experience—I thrill every time I talk about it, because we became quite close friends with the Donnelys. We had a certain rapport with these people. There were many things that constituted our close friendship. But they were at the dinner table with some other people we had—there were eight of us at the table. They commented, "Oh, you're from Utah. You must be members of The Church of Jesus Christ of Latter-day Saints?" We said, "Yes, we are." And Mormonism took over our conversation that night.*

The Donnelys were particularly interested and so consequently, later, when they had this tight rein on people going through the Iron Curtain as a result of World War II, it was Walter J. Donnely who was the instrument in getting our missionaries out from behind the Iron Curtain.[4]

By the end of 1943 all but one missionary had returned to the United States, and he departed in January, accompanied by Wan, the Seegmillers' son:

Our hearts are heavy today because when Elder Platt and our youngest son leave Rio de Janeiro next Saturday we shall be very lonely. They are both going home to report to their local draft boards for military service. (Letter quoted in "History of the Brazilian Mission," Church Historical Department.)

Having no missionaries meant the end of active proselyting and the closing of all but a few branches. One branch able to continue the full Church program was that of Campinas, in the interior of São Paulo. It was the first area allocated for Portuguese mission work, and also the first branch organized completely with local brethren, November 14, 1943.

President Seegmiller's feelings during this trying time are vividly explored in excerpts from fifteen letters he wrote to his son Sailor and his wife Bonnie between May 8, 1942, and March 22, 1945 (on file at the Church Historical Department).

May 8, 1942 — *From: WWS*
To: Sailor

The mission has been officially transferred and President and Sister Bowers are on their way home . . .

The home we are renting here is larger than we need but it is not very modern. Wan is starting to the American School tomorrow. We have started to take lessons in Portuguese from one of the missionarys [sic] . . . We are returning the missionarys [sic] home as fast as possible to report to their draft boards. It is hard, however, to get space on the clipper and this is the only means we have for transportation.

August 4, 1942 — *From: WWS*
To: Sailor

Wan is still getting along very well in school and is learning the Portuguese language rapidly . . .

Private automobiles have been taken off the streets and highways in Brazil on account of gasoline shortage. The street cars and busses are so crowded that transportation is rather difficult. The cost of living has increased very greatly since we came here . . . .

It would be wonderful if the war would close and you and Bonnie would be able to come by boat and visit us in Brazil before we are released. I expect we are all hoping for an early victory notwithstanding the fact that the evidence seems to be that there is still a very hard struggle ahead of us. Tough as it is, I feel confident that victory will be ours. Without victory to our armies the outlook would be very discouraging.

August 23, 1942 — *From: Wan Seegmiller*
To: Sailor

Between this paragraph and the preceding one I have been down to see the show "Hellzapoppin". When we stepped out of the theater we heard a cheer rise from a crowd up the street. We investigated to find out that the first notices had been posted saying that Brazil was in the war, the newspapers are not even out yet. There has been a lot of indignation among the Brazilians since there were five Brazilian ships sunk the other night, it was just a matter of time.

November 2, 1942 — *From: WWS*
To: Sailor

The missionaries are going home regularly and no more are coming to Brazil. It will not be long until Mother, Wan and I will be here alone without missionaries. This is not a very happy prospect and we wonder just how we shall get along.

January 12, 1943 — *From: WWS*
To: Sailor and Bonnie

More than half of the missionaries who were in Brazil when we came have returned home. We have thirty-two left. Four will be leaving in April and ten in May. The last will be released in November.

February 19, 1943 — *From: WWS*
To: Sailor

We left Salt Lake City on the 27th of this month. It will be a year since we said good-bye to all of you . . .

March 31, 1943 — *From: WWS*
To: Sailor

Wan is now seventeen years old. I hope that the war will be over before he is of military age but if not, he is willing to serve and we are willing that he should. I want my boys, all of them, to be loyal, courageous American citizens. I would be ashamed of my own son if he were not willing to defend our country.

September 27, 1943 *From: WWS*
To: Sailor

We have only eight missionaries left and they will all be in the United States to report to their respective local draft boards within the next three months . . .

October 22, 1943 *From: WWS*
To: Sailor

Seven of our missionaries are booked to return home on the 23rd of November. This leaves Elder Platt the Secretary. He will return in January, and then, we shall be here without other missionaries.

November 12, 1943 *From: WWS*
To: Sailor

Wan's graduation exercises will be held on the 17th of this month. I guess you have read President Roosevelt's proclamation of October 26, 1943, providing for the selective service registration of all American male citizens of military age in foreign countries.

December 15, 1943 *From: WWS*
To: Sailor and Bonnie

We have just been reading in the Brazilian newspapers that this country will soon have an army overseas fighting side by side with our North American soldiers. We are proud to have Brazil as our friend and ally. We are always treated kindly.

December 28, 1943 *From: WWS*
To: Bonnie

All of our missionaries are home now excepting Elder Platt. Wan holds the office of Elder and does regular missionary work.

January 28, 1944 *From: WWS*
To: Sailor and Bonnie

Wan left Rio at 6:30 a.m. on January 22. He should arrive in Miami about 4:00.

He has been doing missionary work here for some time. He is an Elder and baptized a very fine man and a splendid woman the last Sunday he spent in São Paulo. Wan has a good knowledge of the Portuguese language. He speaks it better than any missionary whom I have known here.

October 17th, 1944 — *From: WWS*
To: Sailor

You state that the girl who writes my letters does a very neat job. I am sure that she appreciates your compliment. She is here now writing letters for me. Her name is Lucy Mac-Knight. Her parents were born in Brazil but their parents were North Americans. They came to this country soon after the Civil War with a company of pioneers who settled in the interior some distance Northwest of this city. Their posterity is large now but they are fast becoming Brazilian. A good many of them speak, read and write English. The one who is writing this letter has no Brazilian blood in her but she has not been to the United States. We know a good many of these early American colonists. They are a sturdy class of people and wherever we find them they are our friends. . .[5]

Mother and I have already voted and returned our ballots to Salt Lake City. The day we voted we were told that we were the first North Americans to vote absentee ballots at the time in São Paulo.

March 22, 1945 — *From: WWS*
To: Sailor

I expect that Bonnie has told you that we have been released. Our successor will arrive here about the 21st of April. We shall leave for home about the 7th of May and hope to be in Salt Lake City for mother's birthday.

Harold M. Rex. (1945 to 1949)

Born in Randolph, Utah, July 24, 1915, Harold Morgan Rex, after completing a mission in Brazil (1936 to 1938), returned to the States where he worked in Washington for two and a half years and then signed on as Business Manager for the Institute of Inter-American Affairs and was sent to Rio de Janeiro.

In December 1944 he returned to Randolph, and two months later was sent to Brazil to succeed President Seegmiller. It was during his presidency at the close of the War that the work began to be pushed seriously in Portuguese. In January 1948 he began *A Gaivota* (The Seagull, later changed to *A Liahona*), the mission magazine patterned after our *Mensajero Deseret.* He also called the first Brazilian member to serve a full-time mission, Alfredo Lima Vaz (1946) from Campinas.

President Rex was the first Brazilian president to have an automobile: a jeep. Although uncomfortable, it was a superior means of getting around. Rolf Larson, Pierce Brady and Samuel Skousen bought it used and gave it to the mission when they left. Inadvertently, the jeep became the principal reason for its own replacement with a modern, comfortable car. As I indicated, when Stephen L. Richards and his wife visited the mission in 1948 they were taken to visit an interior branch in the jeep. The ride was too much for him. He was recuperating from a heart attack, and they were forced to stop to obtain medical help. Soon after his return to Salt Lake City, authorization came to purchase a new car.

A graduate of George Washington University and the University of Utah, President Rex returned to work with the U.S. Government and then spent some time in La Paz. He was later transferred to Colombia, where he helped secure government permission to begin missionary work in Bolivia, his former post of duty.

On several of my trips to Peru in the late sixties and early seventies, I met with Harold and his wife Diana in Lima. They married October 14, 1940, have five children. He was with a U.S. Government agency called International Development in Perú and served as counselor in the Andeș Mission and later in the Lima Stake Presidency (1970). They have since left Perú.

NOTES

Appendix A

1. The Uruguayan Mission History records: "On June 25, 1944, under the direction of President James L. Barker, of the Argentine Mission, the Montevideo Branch was organized as a part of that mission, with the following officers:

Frederick S. Williams, President
James V. Graves, 1st Counselor
James L. Barker, Jr., 2nd Counselor
Eldon R. Johnston, Branch Secretary
R. Glen Brewer, MIA President
Eldon R. Johnston, Sunday School Superintendent
Corraine S. Williams, President of the Primary
Barbara Lynn Williams, Secretary of the Primary

"During the year 1944, regular Priesthood meetings Sunday Schools, Sacrament meetings, Mutuals and Primary meetings were held, ward teachers were appointed and regular visits made."

2. All the foregoing figures were compiled from a variety of sources including the, South American Mission History, South American Baptism Report, Brazilian Mission Correspondence File (1933-1940) and assorted other Brazilian Mission files containing reports, all of which are found at the Church Historical Department.

3. I was not able to find a record of who the other priests were in the South American Mission History. It may be that the record of the ordinances may have simply been ommited, or perhaps the brethren were already priests when they came over from Germany, and therefore their ordinations would not be included in the Mission History. A fourth teacher, Rudolf Busch was ordained June 25, 1933.

4. Interview conducted by Frederick G. Williams.

5. At the close of the Civil War, an estimated 10,000 ex-Confederates sought homes in Latin America, principally in Mexico and Brazil. They were attracted to Brazil by the generous terms offered by Emperor Dom Pedro II and by the fact that they could hold slaves; the abolition of slavery did not come in Brazil until 1888. Although a number of colonizing sites were established, all but one failed, and within five years most were back in the States. One colony did succeed chiefly because the members decided to get out and work the land and learn the language. Established near Campinas at Americana, it was composed of some 800 members, whose descendants, down to the fourth generation, continue to speak Southern English, as well as their native Portuguese.

Suprisingly, this small but hearty group has made two significant contributions to their adopted homeland: schools and the establishment of protestant faiths. Of interest is the fact that fully one-half of the descendants of Rev. Elijah Quillin (who introduced the Baptist faith to Brazil) are now members of the L.D.S. Church. Converted in Brazil, most of them now reside in California. See California *Intermountain News* (March 1, and 22, and April 5, 1973).

APPENDIX B

THE FIRST FOURTEEN MISSIONARIES

I'D LIKE to tell briefly about the missionaries who preceded me and those with whom I worked.

James Vernon Sharp (20), Salt Lake City, Utah. Arrived March 6, 1926, departed June 10, 1927.

I've already mentioned that Elder Sharp and Elder Stoddard arrived with President and Sister Stoof. Vern was an outstanding missionary. He arrived with a full knowledge of the Spanish language and two years of missionary experience in the Mexican Mission. He loved people and thoroughly enjoyed what he did. He had a great sense of humor and enjoyed playing tricks on people. He was known to the German people as the prankster. For example, we had to be careful when getting off street cars and buses with Elder Sharp behind us. He would suddenly put his hand over the hand of his victim and pin him to the handrail so that his feet dangled in the air.

He told us that Elders Ballard and Pratt had eaten bread and milk for supper every night, which Vern thoroughly disliked. When we served him bread and milk he would fill the bowl with milk, break up the bread and literally throw the pieces into the milk, splashing the liquid on the table. He'd remark, "I don't think we should have to thank the Lord for this kind of food; I'm sure he knows we are grateful for bread and milk."

During the eight days that he was in the mission after my arrival, he asked us to buy and prepare fresh ears of corn, which he was very fond of. It was never served in the mission home where he was living. President Stoof (and I have heard it said of other Germans) did not eat corn; *that* cereal was for horses, not for humans.

Elder Sharp left Buenos Aires on March 10, 1927. He and Elders Merrel and Christian traveled by train to Tucuman for a brief stop and then continued to Jujuy where he and the other two elders established what they hoped would be a prosperous branch near the Bolivian border. He continued to La Paz on April 25, investigating conditions there until June 4 in order to make a report to the First Presidency concerning the advisability of opening a mission in Bolivia. He crossed Lake Titicaca by steamship, visited Cuzco and Machu Picchu, Arequipa and Mollendo, and took a boat home.

He maintained an avid interest in the South American missions and was most cooperative in getting little things that would help the work and make life more pleasant for the missionaries and the mission presidents. On November 1, 1959, he became the first President of the Andes Mission, headquartered in Lima, Peru.

Waldo I Stoddard (21), Baker, Oregon. Arrived June 6, 1926, departed July 2, 1928.

Elder Stoddard came to the South American Mission directly from Oregon State University where, as a senior, he had been student body president. Although rather short, he was an outstanding basketball player. He played guard on the team that won the Pacific Coast Conference championship.

His outstanding abilities in many fields had been recognized before his call to Argentina. He along with two others had been chosen to tour the Orient for a YMCA program. His family was in the lumber business and he spent his summers working in the family business. He was well off financially, which on more than one occasion was a blessing to the mission.

I have never seen anyone who could concentrate so keenly on the subject at hand. When studying he was oblivious to all extraneous activity. We could speak to him, but he would not hear. When he completed the lesson he had completely mastered it and would then turn to something else.

He learned Spanish very quickly and spoke it well. He also played the organ and, with the President's permission, took weekly lessons in music theory. Because of his efficiency he could carry on outside activities and still be a better missionary than the rest of us.

He was a most delightful companion and the one who exerted the most influence on the formative months of my mission. He owned a portable typewriter and was always gracious in lending it to those of us who didn't have one. He also had brought a tuxedo with him, which he used on one occasion; his formal presentation at the YMCA.

He brought a letter of recommendation to the director of the YMCA in Buenos Aires and hoped to help the Church public relations. The director was extremely pleased to meet him until he asked Brother Stoddard what he was doing in Buenos Aires. When he was told that Elder Stoddard was a Mormon missionary, his attitude changed immediately. "That is the trouble with you missionaries. We try to win them from Catholicism and you come along and get them all mixed up with different contending religions." That was the end of the friendly visit.

Elder Stoddard had a most pleasing personality and a radiant smile with beautiful white teeth. Local people had a hard time pronouncing our names, so they coined nicknames for each of us. They called him *"el de los dientes,"* the one with the teeth. (Williams was hard to them; since the Spanish alphabet does not contain the letter "W" I was called by my first name, *"Hermano Federico,"* Brother Frederick).

Elders Stoddard, Clegg and I played first division basketball for the Olimpia Basketball Club. The American and Argentine styles of play were so different that it was good to have three of us to play together. We lost the championship playoff because we literally ran out of gas. We didn't have time to practice and only played twice a week. They simply ran us to death in the last game. Both of my companions were much better players than I with years' more experience, but I surely enjoyed playing with them.

Bathing became a problem in the cold, rainy winter months in Buenos Aires. Our facilities were meager: our bathrooms consisted of a stool set on ceramic tile, a cold shower and a wash basin. There was no way to heat the water. We enjoyed the cold shower during the summertime, but when we tried to keep warm during the damp winter days, wearing heavy underwear, sweaters, a heavy suit, an overcoat and a scarf around the neck (we dressed the same way indoors or out, except we substituted a bathrobe for the overcoat) it wasn't much fun to undress and take an ice cold shower. As a preliminary ritual we ran around the patio until our bodies were warm, dashed into the cold water, gasped for breath, soaped, rinsed and shivered, grabbed a towel and tried to get dry, and then ran around the patio until our blood thawed enough to permit us to dress again.

The prospect of a complimentary hot shower in Buenos Aires on a cold day overcame our reluctance to pay a small monthly fee to participate in YMCA activities: calisthenics, basketball, volleyball, swimming. How we gloried in our two hot showers each week! We felt warm for almost as long as it took us to travel home on the subway and street car. It surely beat one cold shower a week. Elders Stoddard and Clegg also played tennis at the Vélez-Sarsfield Tennis Club, which also had hot showers. It was considered prestigious for Americans to play there; a fair enough exchange.

Lewis E. Christian (24), St. George, Utah. Arrived December 22, 1926, departed December 26, 1928.

Elder Christian arrived in Buenos Aires with Heber M. Clegg, I. Russell Spencer, Preston E. Ashton and Jewel C. Jensen; they were the first to arrive after President Stoof and his party. He was a very serious and dedicated missionary, a few years our senior. He had worked as a plasterer in Los Angeles. He studiously devoted himself to the work, but found the language came slowly. He exerted a good influence both on missionaries and the members. However, he had no time for levity; missionary work was a serious business.

I. Russell Spencer (21), Centerville, Utah. Arrived December 22, 1926, departed May 3, 1928.

Elder Spencer was a sincere, devoted young man but he rarely felt well enough to tract or leave the *local.* One day, October 19, 1927, he became so ill that we called a doctor who rushed him to the hospital for treatment of a ruptured appendix. For several days he hovered between life and death. Through our faith and prayers we felt that he was permitted to return to his missionary activities, although he never really felt well and ultimately was released to return home.

Preston E. Ashton (20), Salt Lake City, Utah. Arrived December 22, 1926, departed February 14, 1927.

Elder Ashton had been released before I arrived in the mission, so I never met him. He became ill almost immediately after he arrived in Argentina and was promptly released to return home. His companions always spoke highly of "Pete." He would have made an excellent missionary.

Heber M. Clegg (19), Salt Lake City, Utah. Arrived December 22, 1926, departed December 26, 1928.

Elder Clegg and I were close friends and companions. He was known by the members and investigators as *"El Rubio"* (the blond one). He suffered from hay fever and sneezed constantly. He was a good basketball player and the best tennis player of any of the missionaries. He was also engaged and wrote his fiancée almost every day. We always kidded him about his correspondence, but he continued to write her anyway. We took it upon ourselves to create a few problems for him and wrote his fiancée telling her that he was "seeing Esta" every day, creating out of "Spanglish" a fictitious name from the time-honored custom of the daily siesta. Marge became perturbed and wrote demanding an explanation. It took Heber several months to clear up the situation. It took a long time in those days to clear up anything. The mail took thirty days one way; after sixty days, if you hadn't made a carbon copy, it was more than probable you didn't remember the question, so the answer didn't make any sense.

Jewel C. Jensen (19), Bear River, Utah. Arrived December 22, 1926, departed February 27, 1928.

Elder Jensen was a tall, good looking, pleasant young man. He had been working in the fields on his father's farm one day when his bishop came to interview him for his mission. During the course of the interview he and his bishop lit up cigarettes and smoked while talking. We other missionaries suspected that he continued to smoke from time to time while a missionary. He also was released early because of his health.

I and three other missionaries arrived in Buenos Aires March 2, 1927. The other three were Paul W. Davis, William F. Heinz, and Douglas B. Merrel. During the weeks we were together in the mission home and en route to Argentina, I became well acquainted with my three companions.

Douglas B. Merrel (27), Duncan, Arizona. Arrived March 2, 1927, departed May 3, 1928.

Elder Merrel was older than most missionaries and seemed to me to be in his late thirties, although he was only twenty-seven. He was married and had left his wife and four children to answer a call from the Church.

Brother Merrel spoke excellent Spanish—by far the best we had in the mission at that time—and was the natural choice to head the Spanish work in our mission beginning on November 3, 1927.

In Villa Ballester he and I were companions, and I was always delighted to be with him. He had a nice singing voice and even invited me to sing a duet with him. We sang in church once. I can't remember ever being asked to sing again. So much for my voice.

Every night Elder Merrel wrote to his wife, whom he missed very much. He was homesick to such an extent that I believe it caused him to be physically ill.

Despite his excellent knowledge of the gospel and great fluency in Spanish, he was not an imposing speaker. Shy and timid, he could not bring himself to look at his audience, but talked down to his folded hands before him. Person to person he made a good impression, but congregations soon lost interest in what he was saying and looked at his hands—which he clasped and unclasped constantly—to see why they were so interesting to him.

His health grew progressively worse and the First Presidency decided to send him to a dry climate in the States. After a brief reunion with his family, he finished his labors in the Mexican Mission.

William Fred Heinz (19), Rexburg, Idaho. Arrived March 2, 1927, departed April 7, 1929.

Elder Heinz's father, an immigrant from Germany, owned a potato farm in Idaho. Fred had learned German from his parents, but never studied it. His German, naturally, was mixed with English words. If he became angry at something he would burst out in German words, which I was later told were cuss words that shouldn't be used in polite society. As I knew no German, I didn't know whether that was true.

He was very cheerful and very easy to get along with; I enjoyed his company on our long sea voyage. On reaching Buenos Aires, he began working with the German members under President Stoof, and our only contact was at our missionary meetings.

He went to Brazil with President Stoof and Elder Schindler to start missionary work on September 12, 1928, and remained there the rest of his mission.

Paul W. Davis (19), Phoenix, Arizona. Arrived March 2, 1927, departed September 8, 1927.

Elder Davis and I were pals in Phoenix before our mission call. He had worked a lot with local Mexicans and could communicate very well in their language.

When we received our mission calls within a few days of each other we became inseparable. We double dated, blessed the sacrament together at meetings, and had a joint farewell. We took the same train to Salt Lake City and shared a double bed in the hotel while attending the Mission Home. He stayed with me at my sister's home the week before we left for Salt Lake City. In New York we shared the same hotel room and were cabin mates on the S.S. *Western World*.

In Buenos Aires we shared the same double bed at our apartment until he was transferred to Dock Sud. We both played harmonica and performed many duets, both for our own enjoyment and for Church programs.

Paul rarely expressed his feelings and it was difficult to know what he was thinking. While we were together he worked hard as a missionary and at his study of Spanish. He progressed much more rapidly than I in that respect, because of his head start. After some time, I noticed that he never expressed any great enthusiasm for the missionary work, but I had no idea that he might be unhappy in this calling.

While living in Villa Ballester I was greatly surprised to receive a letter from him stating that he was be sailing September 8, 1927; he didn't like the work and was going home. Of course my companion and I went to see him off and tried to find out why he wanted to leave. He said only that he felt he was wasting his time and wanted to go home.

I received a letter from him from New York. It said he had work as a restaurant dish washer and that he had been in Yankee Stadium when Babe Ruth had hit two home runs. He had saved almost enough money to purchase a train ticket for the West and would be going as soon as he could. That was about the last time I heard from my erstwhile pal and companion.[1]

Frederick S. Williams (18), Phoenix Arizona. Arrived March 2, 1927, departed June 15, 1929.

I was the youngest missionary, but I served the longest of any of my companions, including those who preceded me; I received special permission from the First Presidency to remain beyond the usual two-year mission.

Harry P. Brundage (26), Ray, Arizona. Arrived October 9, 1927, departed December 28, 1929.

After Paul W. Davis' departure I was the only missionary from Arizona, so I was delighted to meet an elder from my state among the new arrivals. Harry was considerably older and somewhat set in his ways, but he was a delightful companion. He had worked in mining camps for a number of years with Spanish-American personnel, and picked up a large vocabulary of "Tex-Mex," which he felt was the same as Spanish. In fact, he felt he spoke better Spanish than the Argentines. If he had a weakness as a missionary, it was his lack of interest in studying Spanish. He never did learn to speak it correctly, although he was fluent in his own way.

We became very close. From early December 1928 until late May 1929, we were the only Spanish-speaking missionaries on the South American Continent. We shared a *local,* cooked, prayed, studied, traveled and preached together. We never had any problems; we got along beautifully. My only complaint concerns the length of his talks in meetings—an unusual objection, I'm sure—his were always too short. That meant I had to speak longer to take up the allotted time.

Emil A.J. Schindler (23), Germany and Salt Lake City, Utah. Arrived October 9, 1927, departed July 20, 1930.

Elder Schindler had resided in Salt Lake City for a few years after emigrating from Germany. President Stoof had known him previously, and thought very highly of him. I am sure that he had written to Salt Lake City and asked that he be called to South America to help begin the German work in Brazil.

I didn't get too well acquainted with him in Argentina, as he was there for just a few months and devoted all his time to the German people. He was a serious individual, somewhat older than I, but I liked him very much and missed him when he was transferred to Brazil.

On my release, I decided to visit him in Joinville where he had been laboring alone for over two months. I spent several days with him in Brazil. I found that he had a delightful sense of humor and was an excellent host. In the few months he and Elder Heinz had worked in Joinville, they had interested quite a number of people in the gospel and had made many friends. Elder Schindler must be considered the father of the German Brazilian Mission. President Stoof laid the groundwork in that country, but Elder Schindler did the actual work and performed the first baptisms. He returned to serve a second mission in Southern Brazil from February 18, 1932 to August 1, 1935.

John B. Gardner (22), Salt Lake City, Utah. Arrived April 26,1929, departed July 16, 1931.

Elder Gardner arrived only seven weeks before my release, but I was delighted with him and his spirit. He began studying Spanish and was always prepared in the daily classes that I directed. His Spanish study didn't last very long, however, for soon after my departure, he was transferred to Brazil to be a companion to Elder Schindler.

Victor J. Wheeler (20), Ogden, Utah. Arrived April 26, 1929,departed October 25, 1931.

Elder Wheeler arrived with John Gardner, and I spent seven delightful weeks with him. A serious, dedicated missionary, he began at once to prepare himself for the work at hand.

During his mission he became a great help to President Stoof and completed an excellent mission among the Spanish-speaking members of the South American Mission.

Sinking of the S.S. *Vestris*. Our little band of missionaries, thousands of miles to the south of Zion, welcomed any news from the States. Because ordinary transportation was so slow, the "latest" news was always at least thirty days old, except, of course, the cabled bulletins in the local newspapers.

President Stoof received some exciting news in the mail: two new elders had been called to our mission. They were scheduled to sail from New York on November 10, 1928, on the S.S. *Vestris*.

Parents and friends of the missionaries in the field had asked the two elders, David H. Huish, from Arizona, and Keith W. Burt, from Canada, to bring clothing and gifts to us elders who were so far away. I was to receive a new overcoat to see me through the next winter. My sister Naoma wrote that she was sending clothing, a Christmas gift and fruitcake. The other elders also had received news of expected gifts.

Our joyous anticipation of new companions, gifts and clothing was shortlived, however. The first news of impending tragedy came to our attention while we were in Buenos Aires on mission business. We heard newsboys in the streets shouting "extra, extra." Scanning the headlines we saw that the *Vestris* was sinking. We purchased a paper and read that it was foundering in a storm.

During the next few days we anxiously awaited further news about the two elders. When the final accounting was given, Elder Huish had been rescued, but Elder Burt perished, going down with the ship on November 12. Elder Huish never came to South America. He was reassigned to the British Mission.

The *Improvement Era* carried an article written by Elder Huish, "The Sinking of the *Vestris*."[2] I later received additional details from a surviving crewman while we were both traveling on the S.S. *Vandyke*, a sister ship to the ill-fated *Vestris*.

My roommate (you could hardly call the third class quarters on the *Vandyke* a stateroom) was Fred Hansen, the carpenter on the *Vestris*. He was the only one who took photographs during its sinking. He was just returning from the official inquest in London when I met him. Lamport and Holt, the owners, did not have direct sailings between the United States and England, so he had been sent to Buenos Aires and was now going from Buenos Aires to New York. It was a happy coincidence for me.

The newspapers had criticized the *Vestris* crew, because many of them had been saved while many passengers drowned. Hansen placed the blame on panic and greed among the passengers. When orders were given to abandon ship, many passengers remained in the unlaunched lifeboats on the upper side of the listing ship. The crew members jumped into the freezing water and were later picked up by the lifeboats that had been launched. Hansen himself jumped into the water in just his trousers and undershirt. The passengers who stayed in the unlaunched boats sank with the ship.

Other passengers were too occupied with saving their belongings to think of their own safety. Hansen said he saw women on deck clothed in layers of dresses and heavy woolen coats, with fur coats over the cloth coats. Some women had tied several pairs of shoes together around their necks. When they jumped into the water they sank as though they were carrying lead.

My brother-in-law, John T. Seaich, facetiously gave my sister credit for sinking the ship. He said it was the fruitcake she has sent me.

Experience in the Temple. After my mission, Elder Melvin J. Ballard related an interesting epilogue concerning Elder Burt, told to him by President Wood of the Cardston Temple.

Keith Burt was from Cardston, Canada. His father was the only other member of his family to join the Church. The loss of this son, given to the Lord for a two-year mission, grieved the father greatly, and he would not be comforted. He couldn't understand how a servant of the Lord could lose his life while en route to a mission field where he would devote his effort to Him.

Brother Burt worked in the Cardston Temple and he often prayed to the Lord while in the Temple asking for an answer to his problem. One day his son appeared to him in the Temple. I paraphrase what he said, as retold to me by Elder Melvin J. Ballard:

> *Father, why aren't you consoled? Why are you worrying so much about me? I am very happy and I am doing a greater work than I could have accomplished in the South American Mission. I am taking the gospel to our forefathers, to your parents, and to our grandparents, so they, too, can hear the gospel. You have worried about my body being consumed in the depths of the sea. Don't worry about it. I shall have it in the resurrection. Be at peace; I am engaged in the Lord's work.*

NOTES

Appendix B

1. During September 1970, I ran across his name in the obituary section of the California *Intermountain News* (September 17, 1970), p. 7.

2. *Improvement Era,* Vol. 32 (January 1929), pp. 185-188.

APPENDIX C

THE BEGINNINGS OF THE BRAZILIAN MISSION
by Rulon S. Howells

IN FEBRUARY of 1935 President Heber J. Grant called Rulon S. Howells to be the first President of the newly created Brazilian Mission. All of South America had been one mission prior to this time, with work chiefly carried on in Argentina and some in Southern Brazil.

President Howells had just graduated from the University of Utah Law School prior to his leaving for Brazil. No place or city was designated as the headquarters of the new mission by the First Presidency but was left up to President Howells to pick the city he thought best.

President Howells, with his wife Mary Peirce Howells, and their two-year-old daughter, Marian, left for Brazil in April of that year. They journeyed to New Orleans, where they were joined by Merlin Palmer who had been called to labor as a missionary in the new mission. The Brazilian Consul in New Orleans refused to grant them a Brazilian visa as missionaries, but finally did give them a "tourist" visa with the privilege of renewing it in six months.

It took the Delta Line ship, *Del Sul,* thirteen days to reach Rio de Janeiro, and they were met there by Daniel J. Shupe, formerly from Ogden, Utah, who had filled a mission previously in France and had been sent down to Rio as a U.S. Embassy employee. He was at that time employed by a Rio newspaper, having left the Embassy.

Brother Shupe, who had married a Brazilian girl in Rio, was a great help to President Howells. Although neither Mrs. Shupe nor any member of her family were members of the Church, they nevertheless made a great contribution to the early beginnings of the Church in Brazil by helping Brother Shupe make the first translation of the Book of Mormon into the Portuguese language at the request of President Howells.

After President Howells traveled extensively around the most populated sections of Brazil, he chose São Paulo as headquarters of the new Brazilian Mission. The official opening of the mission was recorded as May 25, 1935.

President McKay, many years later, after he had been to South America for the first time, made the remark that he often wondered why São Paulo was chosen as mission headquarters instead of beautiful Rio de Janeiro, then the capital city of the country, but after he had visited Brazil he said, "Now I know why São Paulo was chosen."

In 1935 São Paulo's population was about 950,000 while Rio's was over one and a half million. São Paulo's, as of 1970, is over five million and Rio's about two and a half million, and the nation's capital was changed to Brasília, 700 miles northeast of Rio.

A house was leased on Avenida Turmalina No. 83 where both the mission home and mission office were located for the next three years to 1938. Inasmuch as there was no literature of the church translated nor printed in the Portuguese language at the time, it was decided to carry on the work in the German language which President Howells spoke, having fulfilled a previous mission in Germany from 1922 to 1925. Church literature was ordered from the

Swiss-German Mission. At the time it was estimated that about one and one half million German-speaking people were in Brazil. Missionaries, during the first three years, all learned German.

Work changed from German to Portuguese; Book of Mormon translated. Later German language tracts and pamphlets were printed in Brazil and before President Howells was released, Portuguese tracts were also printed and 3,000 copies of the Book of Mormon, in the Portuguese language, were also being printed.

Mr. Mário Pedroso, an acquaintance of President Howells whom he met in a book store in São Paulo, became very friendly. He spoke English very well and at President Howells' request undertook to make a translation of the Book of Mormon from the English into the Portuguese language. He had the help of his friends and finally completed the work.

Through Mr. Pedroso, the acquaintance of a retired newspaper editor was made and he was engaged to compare the "Shupe" translation from Rio de Janeiro and the "Pedroso" translation from São Paulo with the English and determine the best Portuguese expressions with the English meaning.

Neither the translators in Rio nor the ones in São Paulo knew of each other's work before it was completed. It was the final draft that was taken to a large printing establishment and a contract was made for a Portuguese edition of 3,000 copies. This was the first printing of the Book of Mormon in the Portuguese language.

President Howells assigned the first missionaries, exclusively in the Portuguese language, in April 1938. The first two missionaries assigned were Grant LeRoy Brooks and Melvin Harold Morris. They were assigned to Campinas to take up their labors.

It was realized for some time previously that the Portuguese language, understood by nearly all Brazilians, would be the only language used and that German, with a few exceptions, would be discontinued as far as the church work was concerned.

Previous to the opening of the Brazilian Mission, the following missionaries had been assigned to work among the German-speaking people of Southern Brazil by President Reinhold Stoof of the South American Mission, headquarters in Buenos Aires, Argentina, and had already returned to their homes in the States: William Fred Heinz, Emil Anton J. Schindler, John B. Gardner, Wendell Cyrus Vawdery, Gerhardt Otto G. Drechsel, Ludwig Schmidt, David John Ballstaedt, Jack Cowan Cannon, Herbert Lee Berry, Joseph Reed Burgener, Sydney Rex Cluff, and Peter Loscher.

The missionary work was then only done in Southern Brazil where there was a concentration of German-speaking people and it was also the closest area to the South American Mission headquarters in Buenos Aires, Argentina.

Missionaries in Southern Brazil (Porto Alegre, Joinville, Ipomeia) at the time of President Howells' arrival were: Emil Anton J. Schindler, his second mission to Brazil, Phillip Guy Patterson, Reed Ellwood Bayles, Melvin Croxall Cannon, David Harlin Smith, Joseph Herbert H. Hunder, and Paul Stoll.

The first chapel of the church in Brazil was constructed in the city of Joinville, State of Santa Catarina, in about 1932 when this area was still a part of the South American Mission.

In this area are many German-speaking Europeans, some in the second generation from Europe. Some emigrated from Germany and German-speaking sections of Europe within the previous twenty-five years.

Missionaries had been laboring, in addition to the Joinville area, in Ipomeia, the western highlands of the State of Santa Catarina, and in the large city of Porto Alegre in the State of Rio Grande do Sul which borders on the country of Uruguay.

President Reinhold Stoof, of the then South American Mission, had been so involved in the work in Buenos Aires, Argentina, that he hadn't visited the missionaries laboring in Southern Brazil for over six months.

Many German-speaking people were found in and around the city of São Paulo, where the new mission headquarters was located, and as fast as missionaries arrived, the suburbs of São Paulo were opened to missionary work. Later, as the missionary force increased sufficiently, Curitiba, Blumenau, Novo Hamburgo and Jaraguá were opened.

Missionaries hide from mob. In the small city of Jaraguá, State of Santa Catarina, Elders Harold Rex, Paul Mertlich, and Henry Hunder were having success in holding English classes. They had also organized a Sunday School which was growing very fast and drew attention of many of the local citizens. It was decided to attract an even larger group to an illustrated lecture. The rented hall was being prepared prior to the lecture when a runner came in and told the missionaries that there was a mob coming down the street being led by a local Priest and that they were headed for the "Mormon" illustrated lecture to stop the missionaries from misleading the people. The missionaries saw the mob approaching and picked up their equipment and hurried away with the mobsters throwing stones at them. They were able to hide in a banana grove until the mob dispersed. The Elders went into Joinville later in the evening where they stayed with the Elders there. They later returned to Jaraguá and were very well received by their friends and acquaintances. The work progressed and a branch was established there.

Travel throughout Southern Brazil was, in those years, by narrow gauge railroad trains pulled by a wood burning Baldwin locomotive. The tracks usually followed the winding rivers and often, on warm days and evenings, passengers would leave the car windows open to get a little fresh air and the wood sparks would fly in and burn holes in their clothes. This would happen to the missionaries unless they watched very closely. It took three days and two nights by the Sorocabana Railroad to go from São Paulo to Porto Alegre. As air traveled developed, the same distance could be traveled by airplane in four hours.

After a period of ten years, President and Sister Howells were again called to preside over the Brazilian Mission and left, with their two daughters, Marian and Dorothy, in January 1949 on the Moore-McCormack Steamship Line from New York. They were met in Santos by President and Sister Harold Rex. President Rex was formerly a missionary under President Howells during the first mission period ten years before.

In February 1949, while en route to Brazil, President Howells, with his family, spent several days in Washington, D.C., and while there, with the help of the Utah Congressional delegation, received a U.S. State Department introduction to the Brazilian Ambassador to the United States, the Honorable Maurício Nabuco.

After a very friendly visit with him, he consented to write a personal letter of introduction to four of the Governors of the four principal states of Brazil where missionary work might be undertaken (State of São Paulo, Governor Ademar de Barros; State of Minas Gerais, Governor Milton Soares de Campos; State of Rio Grande do Sul, Governor Walter Jobim; State of Paraná, Governor Moisés Lupion). He also wrote a letter to the editor of Rio's leading newspaper, Senhor Paulo Bettencourt.

President Howells took these letters with him, and Governor Ademar de Barros and Senhor Paulo Bettencourt were of great help in getting tax exemptions for the Church and also in registering us as a Church. They were also helpful in the purchase of the first Mission Home in São Paulo, saving us over $3,000.00 in taxes.

In such a Catholic-dominated country as Brazil, it was quite significant to get a little status for our then infant organization.

Publications: Doctrine and Covenants, Pearl of Great Price. During the second mission of President and Sister Howells (1949-1954), The Doctrine and Covenants [1950] and The Pearl of Great Price [1952] were translated and printed in the Portuguese language; also the first song book with musical notes was published in Portuguese [1951].

In having tracts and pamphlets printed, both in German and Portuguese, President Howells hired an artist to illustrate the different subjects discussed in the tracts. These tracts, up to that time, even in the English version, contained only the printed word, with the exception of "Joseph Smith Tells His Own Story" which had a picture of the Prophet Joseph Smith on the cover. The illustrations throughout the tracts and pamphlets helped the Brazilians to better understand the message they contained.

In another attempt to help the Brazilians understand that we were not just representing a Protestant Church, a chart was prepared showing how the Protestants broke away from the Roman Catholic Church, differentiating our origin direct from Heaven. The Brazilians commented that for the first time, with the aid of this chart, the missionaries were able to explain our position much more easily and see that we were truly the Restored Church and not just another Protestant branch.

Brazilians are great music lovers, so when an area or city was opened or assigned, missionaries would schedule a "concert" for Sister Howells and play up her singing in the famous Tabernacle Choir. Between songs, President Howells and the missionaries would explain principles of the Gospel and pass out literature. This usually attracted many people who would not have attended a strictly religious meeting.

In November 1949, the first American lady missionaries assigned to any mission in South or Central America came to Brazil. They were Sister Deon Crane of Herriman, Utah, and Sister Rhea Horton of Los Angeles, California. In the minds of many in the mission, including President Howells and counselors, there was much anxiety as to the effectiveness of lady missionaries working among Latins. The Sisters, however, proved very effective and many others followed.

In April 1949 permission was received from the First Presidency to purchase a Mission Home. President Harold Rex had been looking for an appropriate home to buy previous to President Howells' arrival. After further looking around the São Paulo area, President Howells decided that the one President Rex had chosen was the most appropriate and an agreement was made to purchase the first Mission Home in Brazil for $41,000.00 at Rua Itapeva 378 in São Paulo. It was near the Avenida Paulista in a choice residential section. Rolf Larsen of Rio de Janeiro, a counselor to President Howells, helped close the deal.

Welfare. After moving into the new home the welfare program was stressed and the storage of wheat was started. To encourage the heavy coffee-drinking people (the Brazilian economy is based on coffee) so that they could join the Church, arrangements were made with the Seventh-Day Adventist Church in Santo Amaro (a suburb of São Paulo) to exchange a "barley coffee," which they made out of grains, for molasses, which was shipped in from Joinville. It was illegal to sell a coffee substitute, but by trade or barter we could stay within the law without excess costs.

To attract attention and get people to listen to our message, two color films were brought down to Brazil by President Howells: "The Land of the Crimson Cliffs" (Southeastern Utah) and "The Valley of Triumph" (Pioneers entering Salt Lake City Valley and the development of Utah). The Mormon Tabernacle Choir was shown in rehearsal and concert with sound. These films were shown in many places and made lasting impressions on those that viewed them. Many contacts were obtained. Two Elders were assigned to tour the mission with these films.

Elders John H. Whitaker and Cleo Jordan explained the film showings:

Eight Thousand See Film
and Hear Story of Mormonism in
Brazil

São Paulo, Brazil

A new phase of missionary work has been tried here in Brazil. We think that it has been a great success so far and that as time goes on it can even become better. We all agree that street meetings are fine, but when you have something extra to attract attention of a crowd and hold it, it really does help. This little something extra here in Brazil is a film on Utah called "The Valley of Triumph." We have this fine picture translated into the Portuguese language and it really draws a big crowd. It gives the missionaries a good chance to explain the story of the restoration of the Gospel to the people.

Our program usually starts with a short talk from a very talented Brazilian, Cleo Jordan, a local missionary from Porto Alegre, Rio Grande do Sul, in which he tells the people, by way of a loud speaker, that there are going to be some films shown in the public square, or the sports club, or wherever it might be, and he invites all that can hear him to attend. People come running from all directions, and by the time we are usually ready to put on the first film, a short film that has been put out for the U.S. State Department on public health called, "How Insects Transmit Disease," we have well over a hundred people. When the film short ends and the film "The Valley of Triumph" is ready to be shown a really large crowd has gathered and the missionaries have a good chance to tell the teachings of the Church to the people.

All the missionaries in the Branch, both full-time and local, are with us and they keep busy handing out tracts about the Book of Mormon and The Truth Restored by a Modern Miracle. Each night we have given out on the average of five hundred tracts, and we have sold copies of the Book of Mormon and Doctrine and Covenants.

At times our transportation hasn't been the best. We have some three hundred pounds of material that goes with us, and the cab drivers won't always give way and let us go in their cars. We have traveled in everything from a streamlined train to a mule cart, but we have always reached our destination.

The people here in Brazil are very receptive to our message, and they seem to take special interest in it when we can tie in the story of the way the early Mormon Pioneers were driven from their homes and crossed the plains to reach their promised land. When we show "The Valley of Triumph" to them and show that the valley has "blossomed like a rose," it seems to make it much easier to open their doors to the voices of the missionaries and they all seem more than willing to receive our message.

We believe this film is one of the best visual aids we have and always a sure way to get a fine audience to listen to our story. The color in the film always brings ahs and sighs, and because we show it on a special beaded screen, we get the best results in brilliant colors.

In just twenty days we were privileged to show our films and tell our story to over eight thousand people, and we are sure that each and every one of them left the showings with a better feeling toward the Church and the missionaries than they had when they arrived.

Elders John H. Whitaker
and Cleo Jordan

President Rulon S. Howells was elected President of the São Paulo Graded School Parent Teachers Association for the year 1950-1951. This school was supported by the large U.S. American Colony living in São Paulo. Two daughters of President and Sister Howells were attending the school at the time.

U of U and BYU basketball teams. In 1951, The Corinthian Sport Club, the largest in membership in Brazil, with headquarters in São Paulo, was celebrating its 50th anniversary. Just previously the Saturday Evening Post had very colorful pictures and articles on the University of Utah "Cinderella" basketball team that had won the National title in New York City. Armed with copies of the "Post" and other pictures, Elder Jack Bowen headed a missionary committee to promote the Corinthian Club to sponsor bringing the "U" team to Brazil to play the best Brazilian basketball teams. They finally accepted and sixteen persons, including President A. Ray Olpin of the University, Vadal Peterson, coach, and the University of Utah "Cinderella" basketball team were flown down to Brazil, all expenses paid by the Corinthian Club, for a three week engagement.

Games were scheduled in cities where missionaries were working. Pictures and printed stories about Utah, the Mormon settlement of the West, the LDS Church sports program, etc., were flown down and given to the local Brazilian newspapers and magazines. Often full page spreads were devoted to our Church. There was so much favorable publicity that when local ministers and priests started to talk against Mormonism, it had little effect.

The next year arrangements were made for the Syrian Sports Club of Brazil to sponsor the BYU basketball team on a trip to Brazil. More favorable publicity was obtained. The fine sportsmanlike conduct of the players drew cheers from the onlookers. In one game played in São Paulo over 10,000 people watched the game.

The BYU basketball team would come out on the floor before the game started with their warm-up suits which had the word "MORMONS" in big six-inch letters on the front. The letters had been cut out in contrasting color to the suits and were sewn on the warm-up jerseys by the YWCA members and friends. You could hear whispers around the audience asking who are they representing as "Mormons," and what does the name mean? Missionaries and members had been scattered throughout the audience and at the onlookers' height of curiosity, would pass out tracts explaining who the "Mormons" were.

Many times during a game, when a Brazilian player would trip and fall on the floor during a game, a University of Utah or BYU player would go over to help him up extending a "helping hand." At first the player thought this was an unfriendly gesture but as soon as the Samaritan act was understood the audience would stand and applaud. The Brazilians were not used to seeing this type of sportsmanship. Usually Latin American teams would try more to "cripple" the opposing team and appear disinterested when an opposing player would fall or be tripped unavoidably or otherwise.

Most Brazilians apparently had never seen a basketball "dunked" but when big Mel Hutchings of the BYU team would jump high enough to drop the ball in the basket, the audiences would gasp and applaud. On one occasion, the day after the first game, the Brazilians, all of whom were much smaller than Mel Hutchings, had the baskets raised so Hutchings and a couple of others of the BYU team who had practiced the dunking play, could not have it so easy to do. The new unaccustomed height, however, was also more difficult for the Brazilian players to shoot at, so from then on they were put at the regular height in spite of the "Mormon dunker's" threat.

During the half-time a missionary sextet sang six to eight numbers. This also was new for the Brazilians. They had never had any entertainment between halves before and they really enjoyed it.

Missionaries were able to use this very helpful publicity to make friends among all classes and we believe a good foundation was laid also for future work of the Church in Brazil.

In 1952 a Book of Mormon campaign was initiated. For 64 missionaries to sell 2,072 books in 23 days is a record to really be proud of. Missionaries in Brazil came together during the week of March 17th to celebrate the event. Just preceding the big annual conference, they had sold (not loaned), 1,788 copies of the Book of Mormon and 284 Doctrine and Covenants, all in the Portuguese language.

The four most successful pairs of Elders sold a total of 959 books during the 23 days, or an average of over ten books per day per pair for the whole period.

Elders Travis Haws, Idaho Falls, Idaho, and Orson White, Los Angeles, California, related that one day they sold 14 copies of Doctrine and Covenants to 14 different people without one refusal.

The lady missionaries were likewise very successful: Sister Hermine Eckersley, Payson, Utah, and Sister Yolanda Rodrigues, a local missionary filling a full-time mission from Santos, Brazil, sold 90 copies of the Book of Mormon during the month preceding the conference.

APPENDIX D

RECORD OF BAPTISMS IN THE SOUTH AMERICAN MISSION 1925-1935

THE NAMES were compiled from the Mission History and from the yearly Mission statistical report, both of which are found at the Church History Department of The Church of Jesus Christ of Latter-day Saints, Salt Lake City, Utah. In some instances names that appeared in one were overlooked in the other; hence it is the combination of both records that gives us the most accurate list possible. Members coming from other areas or who were baptized outside of the Mission's jurisdiction do not appear.

Name	Gender	Branch	Date
ADMINISTRATION OF APOSTLE MELVIN J. BALLARD (1925-1926)			
1925			
Kullick, Anna (Bierbersdorf)	F	Buenos Aires	12 Dec
Biebersdorf, Ernst	M	Buenos Aires	12 Dec
Kullick, Jacob	M	Buenos Aires	12 Dec
Biebersdorf, Mariz	F	Buenos Aires	12 Dec
Kullick, Herta	F	Buenos Aires	12 Dec
Plassman, Elisa	F	Buenos Aires	12 Dec
Total: 6	Males: 2 Females: 4	Argentina: 6	
1926			
Sifuentes, Eladia	F	Buenos Aires	15 Jun
ADMINISTRATION OF PRESIDENT REINHOLD STOOF (1926-1935)			
Gianfelice, Donato Angelo	M	Buenos Aires	22 Aug
Gianfelice, Emilia Notaro de	F	Buenos Aires	22 Aug
Lafratta, Nicolás	M	Buenos Aires	22 Aug
Quici, Domenico	M	Buenos Aires	22 Aug
Total: 5	Males: 3 Females: 2	Argentina: 5	

Name	Gender	Branch	Date
1927			
González, Isabel Flores de	F	Buenos Aires	6 Mar
González, Dominga Aurora	F	Buenos Aires	6 Mar
González, Libertad Isabel	F	Buenos Aires	6 Mar
González, Germinal Manuel	M	Buenos Aires	6 Mar
González, Ideal Francisco	M	Buenos Aires	6 Mar
González, Tito Livio	M	Buenos Aires	6 Mar
González, Delia	F	Buenos Aires	19 Mar
Sánchez, Josefa Alonzo Hernandes de	F	Buenos Aires	12 Nov
Schultis, Leo	M	Buenos Aires	13 Nov
Schultis, Maria Margarete Schwarz	F	Buenos Aires	13 Nov
Ohmar, Isidora Sánchez Alonzo de	F	Buenos Aires	26 Nov
Sánchez, Dora Castro	F	Buenos Aires	26 Nov
Total: 12	Males: 4 Females: 8	Argentina: 12	
1928			
Boggan, Mary Palmer	F	Buenos Aires	30 Jan
Plassman, Ferdinand Erwin	M	Buenos Aires	14 Feb
Alvarez, Jose Olmo	M	Buenos Aires	31 Mar
Alvarez, Catalina Jiménez	F	Buenos Aires	31 Mar
Alvarez, José Jiménez	M	Buenos Aires	31 Mar
Alvarez, Rosa Jiménez	F	Buenos Aires	31 Mar
Alvarez, Ana Jiménez	F	Buenos Aires	31 Mar
Alvarez, Horacio Jiménez	M	Buenos Aires	31 Mar
Kurz, Friedrich	M	Buenos Aires	8 Apr
Kurz, Sofia Mindum	F	Buenos Aires	8 Apr
Ballweg, Amalie Gertrud	F	Buenos Aires	13 May
Wesemberg, Albert Karl Wilhelm	M	Buenos Aires	10 Jun
Wesemberg, Ernestine Pavione Karoline (Hartel)	F	Buenos Aires	10 Jun
Notaro Luigi	M	Buenos Aires	29 Jun
Notaro, Marianatonia Govine de	F	Buenos Aires	29 Jun
Gianfelice, Antonio	M	Buenos Aires	29 Jun
Farimiera, Joaquim	M	Buenos Aires	27 Oct
Farimiera, María Concepción Peña de	F	Buenos Aires	27 Oct
San Isidro, Rogelia Serafina González de	F	Buenos Aires	8 Dec
Martínez, Ramón Luis	M	Buenos Aires	15 Dec
Martínez, Damiana Natividad Pérez de	F	Buenos Aires	15 Dec
Martínez, María Juana	F	Buenos Aires	15 Dec
Martínez, Teresa Felisa	F	Buenos Aires	15 Dec
Martínez, Aurora Antonia	F	Buenos Aires	15 Dec
Martínez, Lorenzo	M	Buenos Aires	15 Dec
Schultix, Irene Margarete	F	Buenos Aires	15 Dec
Total: 26	Males: 11 Females: 15	Argentina: 26	

Name	Gender	Branch	Date
1929			
Ruiz, José	M	Buenos Aires	20 Jan
Jaraguiones, Zéfera Alepidote de	F	Buenos Aires	28 Jan
Jaraguiones, Leonidas	M	Buenos Aires	28 Jan
Jaraguiones, Juan	M	Buenos Aires	28 Jan
Seiz, Heinrich	M	Buenos Aires	24 Mar
Gabriel, Margarete Anna Kriess de	F	Buenos Aires	1 Apr
Sell, Bertha J.A. Just	F	Joinville, Brazil	14 Apr
Sell, Theodoro	M	Joinville, Brazil	14 Apr
Sell, Alice	F	Joinville, Brazil	14 Apr
Sell, Siegfried	M	Joinville, Brazil	14 Apr
Sell, Adele	F	Joinville, Brazil	14 Apr
Zanardini, Dora	F	Buenos Aires	3 Jun
Zanardini, Adela	F	Buenos Aires	3 Jun
Total: 13	Males: 6 Females: 7	Argentina: 8 Brazil: 5	
1930			
Otto, Karl	M	Joinville, Brazil	9 Jan
Otto, Martha Johanna	F	Joinville, Brazil	9 Jan
Otto, Hedwig	F	Joinville, Brazil	9 Jan
Otto, Wally	F	Joinville, Brazil	9 Jan
Otto, Ilse	F	Joinville, Brazil	9 Jan
Buechli, Margarete Charlotte	F	Joinville, Brazil	9 Jan
Mueller, Anna Emilie Hedwig	F	Joinville, Brazil	12 Jan
Mueller, Egon Wilhelm	M	Joinville, Brazil	12 Jan
Mueller, Helga Amanda Paula	F	Joinville, Brazil	12 Jan
Mueller, Helene Ulrike	F	Joinville, Brazil	12 Jan
Mueller, Erna Carolina	F	Joinville, Brazil	12 Jan
Mueller, Adolf	M	Joinville, Brazil	19 Jan
Zimperz, Margareta Valerie	F	Vélez Sarsfield, Argentina	28 Jan
Papp, Irma	F	Vélez Sarsfield, Argentina	2 Feb
Mueller, Irma Martha Marie	F	Joinville, Brazil	2 Mar
Mueller, Elsa Adele Anna	F	Joinville, Brazil	2 Mar
Mueller, Waldemar	M	Joinville, Brazil	2 Mar
Gabriel, Wilhelm Karl August	M	Vélez Sarsfield, Argentina	3 Mar
Friedrichs, Wilhelm	M	Vélez Sarsfield, Argentina	8 Mar
Kullick, Jakob, Jr.	M	Vélez Sarsfield, Argentina	8 Mar
Escudero, Carmen Montes, Iglesias de	F	Vélez Sarsfield, Argentina	16 Mar

Name	Gender	Branch	Date
1930 (Continued)			
Escudero, Isabel Carmen	F	Vélez Sarsfield, Argentina	16 Mar
Otto, Oskar	M	Joinville, Brazil	15 Jun
David, Karl	M	Joinville, Brazil	28 Jun
David, Alwine	F	Joinville, Brazil	28 Jun
David, Waltraud	F	Joinville, Brazil	28 Jun
Sell, Ferdinand Karl Theodor	M	Joinville, Brazil	20 Jul
Buchli, Karl Hermann	M	Joinville, Brazil	20 Jul
Siedschlag, Helene Bertha Rosa	F	Joinville, Brazil	3 Sep
Siedschlag, Erna Agosta	F	Joinville, Brazil	3 Sep
Siedschlag, Adele Wilhelmine	F	Joinville, Brazil	3 Sep
Siedschlag, Auguste Wilhelmine Teresa	F	Joinville, Brazil	3 Sep
Schultz, Erna Rosa	F	Joinville, Brazil	3 Sep
Siedschlag, Olga Helene	F	Joinville, Brazil	3 Sep
Briesemeister, Annita Helene	F	Joinville, Brazil	3 Sep
Ricciardi, Pedro Maria Alfonso	M	Vélez Sarsfield, Argentina	2 Nov
Thieme, Maria Therese (Scholz)	F	Vélez Sarsfield, Argentina	23 Nov
Mueller, Lydia Annita Olga	F	Joinville, Brazil	No date
Total: 38	Males: 12 Females: 26	Argentina: 9 Brazil: 29	
1931			
Zapf, Rudi Arthur	M	Colonia Muller, Brazil	3 Feb
Zapf, Robert Richard	M	Colonia Muller, Brazil	3 Feb
Gutiérrez, Julio Cesar	M	Buenos Aires	10 Apr
Briesemeister, Gustav Robert	M	Joinville, Brazil	27 Aug
Briesemeister, Rosa Teresa Amalie (Siedschlag)	F	Joinville, Brazil	27 Aug
Briesemeister, Genni Helene	F	Joinville, Brazil	27 Aug
Briesemeister, Rosa Erna	F	Joinville, Brazil	27 Aug
Schultz, Anna Marie Wilhelmina (Siedschlag)	F	Joinville, Brazil	27 Aug
Schultz, Richard Friedrich Wilhelm	M	Joinville, Brazil	27 Aug
Schultz, Annita Teresa Rosa	F	Joinville, Brazil	27 Aug
Schultz, Genni	F	Joinville, Brazil	27 Aug
Siedschlag, Helene Bertha Carolina (Nehls)	F	Joinville, Brazil	27 Aug
Siedschlag, Oscar Luis	M	Joinville, Brazil	27 Aug
Siedschlag, Wilhelm Lauro	M	Joinville, Brazil	27 Aug

Name	Gender	Branch	Date
1931 (Continued)			
Siedschlag, Euclides Erwin	M	Joinville, Brazil	27 Aug
Biebersdorf, Meta Maria	F	Buenos Aires	11 Oct
Zanardini, Ernesto	M	Buenos Aires	11 Oct
Zanardini, Roberto	M	Buenos Aires	11 Oct
Zanardini, Saturnina Barranco de	F	Buenos Aires	11 Oct
Zanardini, Jose Manuel	M	Buenos Aires	11 Oct
Meda, Carmen Alicia	F	Buenos Aires	11 Oct
Gianfelice, Juana de Dios	F	Buenos Aires	4 Dec
Almirall, Ramon	M	Buenos Aires	6 Dec
Almirall, Teresa Rmengol de	F	Buenos Aires	6 Dec
Calderón, Marcelina Guinaldo de	F	Buenos Aires	6 Dec
Calderón, Pilar Josefina	F	Buenos Aires	6 Dec
Calderón, Eleodora	F	Buenos Aires	6 Dec
Fischer, Berta Auguste Wilhelmine (Meiran)	F	Buenos Aires	25 Dec
Total: 28	Males: 12 Females: 16	Argentina: 14 Brazil: 14	
1932			
Sanchez, Delia Carmen	F	Buenos Aires	8 Jan
Caminos, Juan José	M	Rosario, Arg.	6 Feb
Caminos, María Lucher de	F	Rosario, Arg.	6 Feb
Arias, María Catalina Paz de	F	Rosario, Arg.	6 Feb
Arias, Ramona Benita	F	Rosario, Arg.	6 Feb
Zimperz, Wilhelmine Hedwig Obst de	F	Buenos Aires	9 Mar
Bauer, Elisabeth Kunze de	F	Rio Preto, Brazil	27 Apr
Sell, Eugene	M	Joinville, Brazil	15 May
Buchli, Gertrud	F	Joinville, Brazil	15 May
Siedschlag, Rudolf Richard	M	Joinville, Brazil	24 May
Siedschlag, Paula Ida Steuernagel de	F	Joinville, Brazil	24 May
Siedschlag, Wilhelm Hermann	M	Joinville, Brazil	24 May
Siedschlag, Alfred	M	Joinville, Brazil	24 May
Siedschlag, Paula Theresa	F	Joinville, Brazil	24 May
Jaraguiones, Jorge	M	Buenos Aires	12 Jun
Hoppe, Gerhard Emil	M	Buenos Aires	12 Jun
Busch, Rudolf August	M	Joinville, Brazil	9 Jul
Busch, Hedwig	F	Joinville, Brazil	9 Jul
Guinaldo, Inés Curto de	F	Buenos Aires	17 Jul
Stark, Wilhelm Heinrich Carl	M	Joinville, Brazil	14 Aug
Krumm, Michael	M	Buenos Aires	25 Aug
Busch, Emil Otto	M	Buenos Aires	17 Sep
Busch, Helmut Otto Bruno	M	Buenos Aires	17 Sep
Schroder, Ida Brier	F	Joinville, Brazil	7 Oct
Schroder, Olga	F	Joinville, Brazil	7 Oct

Name	Gender	Branch	Date
1932 (Continued)			
Schroder, Elvira Isolda Anita	F	Joinville, Brazil	7 Oct
Schroder, Erna	F	Joinville, Brazil	7 Oct
Schroder, Elly	F	Joinville, Brazil	7 Oct
Schroder, Hertha	F	Joinville, Brazil	7 Oct
Behling, Hermann August Karl Eduard	M	Joinville, Brazil	7 Oct
Behling, Philipine Cristine Caroline (Lucht)	F	Joinville, Brazil	7 Oct
Behling, Alfons Ferdinand Rudolf	M	Joinville, Brazil	7 Oct
Behling, Rudolf Karl Otto	M	Joinville, Brazil	7 Oct
Ramsdorf, Wilhelm	M	Joinville, Brazil	7 Oct
Ramsdorf, Elsa Alwine Wilhelmine (Briesemeister)	F	Joinville, Brazil	7 Oct
Steuernagel, Frieda Rosa Briesemeister	F	Joinville, Brazil	7 Oct
Steuernagel, Emil Richard Paul	M	Joinville, Brazil	7 Oct
Sell, Anita	F	Joinville, Brazil	7 Oct
Beicke (?), Erna Johanna Wilhemine (Behling de)	F	Joinville, Brazil	7 Oct
Arias, Aurora Suárez de	F	Buenos Aires	23 Oct
Arias, Pilar	F	Buenos Aires	23 Oct
Zanardini, Ricardo	M	Buenos Aires	23 Oct
Barraza, Dominga Britos de	F	Rosario, Arg.	25 Nov
Costantini, Luis	M	Buenos Aires	27 Nov
Total: 44	Males: 19 Females: 25	Argentina: 17 Brazil: 27	
1933			
Hack, Robert	M	Rio Preto, Brazil	29 Jan
Papp, Mariá Teresa Schmidt de	F	Buenos Aires	11 Feb
Papp, Juan Koloman	M	Buenos Aires	11 Feb
Papp, Sofía	F	Buenos Aires	11 Feb
González, Floreal Aroldo	M	Buenos Aires	11 Feb
Arias, Aurora	F	Buenos Aires	11 Feb
Petruzzelli, Onofrio	M	Buenos Aires	11 Feb
Hidlgo, Luisa	F	Buenos Aires	4 Mar
Fernández, José	M	Buenos Aires	4 Mar
Blind, Heinrich	M	Rio Preto, Brazil	7 Apr
Bauer, Gotthilf	M	Rio Preto, Brazil	7 Apr
Kirsteirn, Karl Gottlieb	M	Rio Preto, Brazil	7 Apr
Zapf, Lydia Linders	F	Rio Preto, Brazil	21 Apr
Zapf, Walter	M	Rio Preto, Brazil	21 Apr
Zappa, Blanca Candia	F	Rosario, Arg.	20 May
Cedolín, Pedro Antonio	M	Buenos Aires	27 Aug
Cedolín, Pedro	M	Buenos Aires	27 Aug
Cedolín, María Magdalena Del Toso de	F	Buenos Aires	27 Aug

Name	Gender	Branch	Date
1933 (Continued)			
Cedolín, Maria	F	Buenos Aires	27 Aug
Barsch, Alvin Heinrich Nicklaus	M	Joinville, Brazil	28 Aug
Barsch, Martha Toni Merz	F	Joinville, Brazil	28 Aug
Barsch, Dora	F	Joinville, Brazil	28 Aug
Pallotta, Miguel	M	Buenos Aires	24 Sep
Pallotta, Angelina Ferretti de	F	Buenos Aires	24 Sep
Pallotta, Juan	M	Buenos Aires	24 Sep
Ziemer, Alfred August Ernst	M	Joinville, Brazil	6 Oct
Richter, Amalie (Wagner)	F	Joinville, Brazil	6 Oct
Behling, Margarete Adele Erika	F	Joinville, Brazil	6 Oct
Muller, Ilse Bertha Antonie	F	Joinville, Brazil	6 Oct
Stark, Martha Gertrud	F	Joinville, Brazil	13 Oct
Kiess, Wilhelm Hermann	M	Rio Preto, Brazil	27 Oct
Clava, Isaac Isaiah	M	Buenos Aires	17 Dec
Kreil, Paul Karl Ewald	M	Porto Alegre, Brazil	23 Dec
Kreil, Anna Luice (Reminek)	F	Porto Alegre, Brazil	23 Dec
Kreil, Rudolf Paul	M	Porto Alegre, Brazil	23 Dec
Total: 37	Males: 20 Females: 17	Argentina: 19 Brazil: 18	
1934			
Errero, Clotilde Alcala de	F	Buenos Aires	10 Feb
Meda, Carmen Languini de	F	Buenos Aires	10 Feb
Fernández, Elena Vidal de	F	Buenos Aires	10 Feb
Wollenweber, Martin	M	Jaraguá, Brazil	19 Mar
Wollenweber, Anna	F	Jaraguá, Brazil	19 Mar
Wiest, Franziska (Kiermayer)	F	Jaraguá, Brazil	19 Mar
Kiermayer, Gertrud	F	Jaraguá, Brazil	19 Mar
Clava, Josefina Betorrelli de	F	Buenos Aires	24 Mar
Schimkat, Ludwig Ernst	M	Buenos Aires	1 Apr
Mai, Joseph Xaver Paul	M	Buenos Aires	5 Apr
Mai, Henriette Katharina (Stickelmann)	F	Buenos Aires	5 Apr
Biebersdorf, Edith Elisabeth	F	Buenos Aires	5 Apr
Travaglianti, Carmen Caruso	F	Buenos Aires	19 May
Imbrociano, Carolina Travaglianti de	F	Buenos Aires	19 May
Imbrociano, Nunzio	M	Buenos Aires	1 Jul
Travaglianti, José	M	Buenos Aires	1 Jul
Iglesias, Cristina García	F	Buenos Aires	7 Jul
Anazan, Pilar Lucia Iglesias	F	Buenos Aires	7 Jul
Ponce, Cristina Ercilia	F	Buenos Aires	7 Jul

Name	Gender	Branch	Date
1934 (Continued)			
Toth, Johanna Kaintz	F	Buenos Aires	20 Sep
Santana, Francisco	M	Buenos Aires	10 Nov
Santana, Amelia Piscicelli	F	Buenos Aires	10 Nov
Santana, Elsa Celia	F	Buenos Airs	10 Nov
Barsch, Edeltraud	F	Joinville, Brazil	18 Nov
Muller, Erika	F	Joinville, Brazil	18 Nov
Kirstein, Agnes Auguste Maria (Hoppe)	F	Joinville, Brazil	2 Dec
Bauer, Erich Wilhelm Friedrich	M	Joinville, Brazil	2 Dec
Boren, Mariano Ferrando	M	Buenos Aires	25 Dec
Bochema, Salvador	M	Buenos Aires	25 Dec
Sciorra, Santiago	M	Buenos Aires	25 Dec
Sciorra, Victoria Sciorra de	F	Buenos Aires	25 Dec
Sciorra, Juan	M	Buenos Aires	25 Dec
Caserta, Vincente	M	Buenos Aires	25 Dec
Caserta, Francisca Moino de	F	Buenos Aires	25 Dec
Romero, Graciana Bigot de	F	Buenos Aires	25 Dec
Romero, Alberto Nestor	M	Buenos Aires	25 Dec
Total: 36	Males: 13	Argentina: 28	
	Females: 23	Brazil: 8	
1935			
Carrizo, María Haydee	F	Buenos Aires	No date
Romero, Angélica Maria	F	Buenos Aires	26 Jan
Núñez, Martina Otero de	F	Buenos Aires	26 Jan
Busse, Elisabeth Wilhelmine Anna	F	São Paulo, Brazil	3 Feb
Guinaldo, Cirilo	M	Buenos Aires	9 Feb
Biebersdorf, Ernesto	M	Buenos Aires	10 Feb
Friedrichs, Magdalena	F	Buenos Aires	10 Feb
Stoof, Melvin	M	Buenos Aires	10 Feb
Bond, Ursula María Fadanelli de	F	Buenos Aires	24 Feb
Zanardini, Amelia	F	Buenos Aires	24 Feb
Lacrouts, María Rosa Regueira de	F	Buenos Aires	19 Mar
Lacrouts, Ruben Ernesto	M	Buenos Aires	19 Mar
Mario, Odorifero Gaudenzia de	F	Buenos Aires	21 Mar
Pagani, María Peirauo	F	Buenos Aires	4 Apr
Carrizo, Juana Rosa	F	Buenos Aires	4 Apr
Sánchez, Adela Nieto de	F	Buenos Aires	26 Apr
Sánchez, Genoveva Martin	F	Buenos Aires	26 Apr
Cicenni, Enriqueta Adele Schinelli	F	Buenos Aires	No date
López, María de la Purificación de	F	Buenos Aires	13 May
López, María Teresa	F	Buenos Aires	13 May
Brazilian Mission is divided from South American Mission, 25 May 1935			
Pereyra, Angela Mericia Zabala de	F	Buenos Aires	1 Jun
Pereyra, Hector Jonatan	M	Buenos Aires	1 Jun

Name	Gender	Branch	Date
1935 (Continued)			
Pereyra, Amado Ruben	M	Buenos Aires	1 Jun
Pereyra, Ercilio Leonidas	M	Buenos Aires	1 Jun
Pereyra, Nehemias Juan	M	Buenos Aires	1 Jun
Gianfelice, Sara	F	Buenos Aires	1 Jun
Call, Antonia María	F	Buenos Aires	6 Jul
Sciorra, Maria	F	Buenos Aires	6 Jul
Sciorra, Eva	F	Buenos Aires	6 Jul
Sciorra, Victoria	F	Buenos Aires	6 Jul
Valente, Quintina Sciorra de	F	Buenos Aires	6 Jul
Pagani, Amanda Amalia	F	Buenos Aires	6 Jul
Gorges, Katharina Elsa	F	Buenos Aires	8 Aug

Argentine Mission replaces the South American Mission; President Stoof Departs, 22 August 1935

Total: 23 Males: 8 Argentina: 32
Females: 25 Brazil: 1

278 Total Baptisms in South American Mission, December 1925 August 1935:

Males: 102 Argentina: 176
Females: 176 Brazil: 102

Baptisms Argentine Mission

Name	Gender	Branch	Date
1935 (Continued)			
Call, Martha Maria	F	Buenos Aires	28 Sep
Call, Elena	F	Buenos Aires	28 Sep
Call, Hector	M	Buenos Aires	28 Sep
Herrera, Maria Carmen	F	Buenos Aires	12 Oct
Notaro, Maria Angela	F	Buenos Aires	12 Oct
Caruso, Nicolas	M	Buenos Aires	12 Oct
Arias, Josefina	F	Buenos Aires	12 Oct
Friedrichs, Anna	F	Buenos Aires	26 Oct
Jindeo, Javiete (sp) Quintero (sp)	M	Buenos Aires	No date
Gorges, Rosa Schnabel	F	Buenos Aires	21 Nov
Turano, Eurídice	F	Buenos Aires	25 Nov
Picolo, Rosa Peirauo de	F	Buenos Aires	25 Nov
Alvarez, Rosina González de	F	Haedo	7 Dec
Alvarez, Pura Josefina	F	Haedo	7 Dec
Alvarez, Angela	F	Haedo	7 Dec
Alvarez, Andrés	M	Haedo	7 Dec
Sequín, Carmen	F	Liniers	14 Dec
Estévez, María Leonora	F	Liniers	14 Dec
Alvarez, Pedro	M	Haedo	21 Dec
Alvarez, María	F	Haedo	21 Dec
Alvarez, Rosa	F	Haedo	21 Dec
Alvarez, Pedro José	M	Haedo	21 Dec

22 Total Baptisms in New Argentine Mission, Last Quarter 1935

APPENDIX E

MISSIONARIES WHO SERVED IN THE FOUR SOUTH AMERICAN MISSIONS 1925-1950

Name	Priesthood/ Gender	Age	From
SOUTH AMERICAN MISSION 1925-1935*			
1925			
Ballard, Melvin J. (Mission President)	Apostle	52	Utah
Wells, Rulon S.	Seventy	72	Utah
Pratt, Rey L.	Seventy	58	Utah
1926			
Stoof, Karl Bruno Reinhold (Mission President)	Elder	39	Utah
Stoof, Martha Frida Ella (Hirte)	Female	25	Utah
Stoddard, Waldo Izatt	Elder	21	Oregon
Sharp, James Vernon	Elder	20	Utah
Christian, Lewis Earl	Elder	24	Utah
Spencer, Isaac Russell	Elder	21	Utah
Ashton, Preston Eugene	Elder	20	Utah
Clegg, Heber Milton	Elder	19	Utah
Jensen, Jewel Carlyle	Elder	19	Utah
1927			
Davis, Paul W.	Elder	19	Arizona
Heinz, William Fred	Elder	19	Idaho
Williams, Frederick Salem	Elder	18	Arizona
Merrel, Douglas Burdell	Elder	27	New Mexico
Schindler, Emil Anton Joseph	Seventy	23	Utah
Brundage, Harry Pierce	Elder	26	Arizona

**Compiled from South American Mission Records B7143R; General Mission Record of Missionaries Leaving Salt Lake City CR/301/22; Financial, Statistical and Departure of Missionaries CR/301, all courtesy of the Historical Department of The Church of Jesus Christ of Latter-day Saints.*

SOUTH AMERICAN MISSION (CONTINUED)

Name	Priesthood/ Gender	Age	From
1929			
Gardner, John B.	Elder	22	Utah
Wheeler, Victor J.	Elder	20	Utah
Woodbury, Melvin Lambert	Elder	21	Utah
Bagley, Elwin E.	Elder	19	California
Bluth, Lothaire E.	Elder	19	Mexico
Spencer, Adrian G.	Elder	19	Wyoming
Vawdrey, Wendell Cyrus	Elder	19	Utah
Drechsel, Gerhardt Otto Guido	Elder	20	Utah
1930			
Schmidt, Ludwig	Elder	27	Illinois
Walker, Clive Stevenson	Seventy	25	Utah
Ballstaedt, David John	Elder	25	Utah
Jones, Thomas Wynne	Elder	24	Idaho
Cannon, Jack Cowan	Elder	22	Utah
Laird, Norman Harris	Elder	19	Idaho
Peterson, Niels Marcus	Elder	19	Utah
1931			
Berry, Herbert Lee	Elder	19	Arizona
Kimball, Marden David	Elder	19	Arizona
Burbidge, Grant Milton	Elder	19	Utah
Burgener, Joseph Reed	Seventy	23	Utah
Cluff, Sidney Rex	Seventy	21	Utah
Loscher, Johann Peter	Elder	26	Utah
Durham, Eugene Richards	Seventy	25	Utah
Franz, Walter Berthold	Elder	19	Utah
1932			
Borgquist, Parley Paul	Elder	19	Utah
Schindler, Emil Anton Joseph**	Seventy	27	Utah
1933			
Patterson, Phillip Guy	Elder	19	Arizona
Bayles, Reed Ellwood	Seventy	20	Utah
Cannon, Melvin Croxall	Seventy	20	Utah
Fox, George Wallace	Seventy	20	Utah
Tremelling, Louis	Elder	20	Idaho

**Second Mission

Name	Priesthood/ Gender	Age	From
1934			
Larsen, Clyde V.	Seventy	25	Utah
Zollinger, Floyde Aikele	Elder	26	Utah
Hunder, Joseph Herbert Henry	Seventy	21	Utah
Smith, David Harlin	Elder	19	Idaho
Stoll, Paul	Seventy	30	Utah
Smith, Justin Mack	Elder	24	Utah
Lofthouse, Vernal Frederick	Seventy	29	Idaho
Steel, Marion Roy	Seventy	24	Idaho

MISSIONARIES WHO SERVED IN ARGENTINE MISSION 1935-1950*

*Compiled from Missionary Record Argentine B7143R and B7144R; General Mission Record of Missionaries Leaving Salt Lake City CR/301/22; Financial, Statistical and Departure of Missionaries from Argentina CR/301, all courtesy of the Historical Department of The Church of Jesus Christ of Latter-day Saints.

Name	Priesthood/ Gender	Age	From
1935			
Ostendorf, August George Martin	Elder	29	New York
Cummings, Julian W.	Elder	19	Utah
Valentine, Lee Benson	Seventy	23	Utah
Rowe, Grant Browning	Seventy	23	Utah
Young, W. Ernest (Mission President)	High Priest	47	México
Young, Cecile Skousen	Female	46	Mexico
Armstrong, Vaughn William	Elder	19	Utah
Smith, Verle Gardner	Elder	24	California
Holland, Ross W.	Elder	19	Idaho
Alleman, William Max	Elder	20	Utah
Maurer, Harry DeWitt	Seventy	27	Utah
Beus, Jay Richard	Seventy	19	Utah
1936			
Clark, Ben E.	Elder	21	Utah
Murphy, Thomas Franklin	Seventy	22	Idaho
Anderson, Jerald Arthur	Elder	19	Idaho
Hollbrook, Jay Russon	Seventy	20	Utah
Chalk, Reed J.	Seventy	26	California
Payne, Junius Lothair	Seventy	21	New Mex
Cheney, Boyd C.	Elder	20	Utah
Flake, Lavon H.	Elder	23	Arizona
Holman, Rulon J.	Seventy	23	Idaho
Brady, Lee Pierce	Elder	20	Utah

Argentine Mission (Continued)

Name	Priesthood/ Gender	Age	From
1936 (Continued)			
Skousen, Willard Ivan	Elder	23	Arizona
Lamoreaux, David Tenney	Elder	21	Arizona
Shreeve, Lyman Sidney	Seventy	20	Arizona
Nelson, Morris Edmond	Seventy	19	Arizona
Smith, Don Hyrum	Elder	19	New York
Jesperson, James Avril	Elder	22	Arizona
Lunt, Henry Rudd	Elder	21	New Mex
Lynn, Gerald Orvel	Elder	21	Wyoming
Petrie, James Andrew, Jr.	Elder	21	Arizona
Mortensen, James Anton, Jr.	Seventy	22	Arizona
Stuart, Claude William	Seventy	20	Idaho
1937			
Duke, Addison Marden	Seventy	23	Idaho
Allen, Ben Rich	Elder	20	Arizona
Fenn, Karl Rogers	Elder	20	Arizona
Vance, Marion Isacc	Elder	20	Arizona
Smith, Jesse Byron	Elder	20	Wyoming
Allen, Jesse Lawrence	Elder	20	Idaho
Brown, Harold	Elder	20	Arizona
Quist, Homer Brown	HP	27	Idaho
Hatch, Ivan Eugene	Elder	21	California
Moon, Rulon Merlin	Elder	22	Utah
Larson, Rolf Lamport	Seventy	21	Arizona
Taylor, Harvey Darrel	Elder	20	Arizona
Brinton, George Alden	Elder	19	Utah
Earl, Joseph Donal	Seventy	24	Washington D.C.
Williams, Orlando Clement, Jr.	Elder	19	Arizona
Skousen, Samuel James	Elder	20	Arizona
Willis, Max Lynn	Elder	21	Arizona
Standing, Robert Thorpe	Elder	20	Utah
1938			
Bergeson, Dale Allen	Elder	24	Utah
Edmonds, Clyde Midgley	Elder	20	Utah
Moffett, Oren E.	Seventy	20	Utah
Whipple, Alma Virgil	Elder	20	Arizona
McBride, Richard J.	Elder	26	Arizona
Asay, Orson Harris	Seventy	22	Wyoming
Watson, Leroy Alfred	Elder	20	Arizona
Farnsworth, Pershing Lamar	Seventy	20	Arizona
Bettilyon, Verden Elliott	Seventy	19	Utah

Argentine Mission (Continued)

Name	Priesthood/ Gender	Age	From
1938 (Continued)			
Wilkins, Ernest J.	Elder	19	Arizona
Williams, Frederick Salem (Mission President)	HP	30	Arizona
Williams, Corraine Smith	Female	29	Arizona
Lloyd, Paul	Seventy	23	Utah
Mitchell, Edgar Bentley	HP	52	Utah
Mitchell, LaPrile Barber	Female	50	Utah
Tippetts, Marion Eugene**	Seventy	25	Wyoming
Meyers, John Henry	Seventy	20	Idaho
Wheeler, Byron Coulam	Elder	20	Utah
Dana, Isaac Dwight	Elder	21	Arizona
Fitzgerald, Earl Moss	Elder	21	California
Young, Wendell K.	Elder	20	Idaho
Goodfellow, Riley W.	Elder	21	Utah
Taylor, Dan Nielson	Elder	21	Idaho
1939			
Knight, Donald Anderson**	Elder	23	Utah
Bowers, Leslie Marvin	Seventy	23	California
Palmer, Asael Delbert	Seventy	20	Canada
Costantini, Luis	Elder	66	Argentina
Borén, Samuel	Elder	23	Argentina
Brown, Donald L.	Seventy	21	Utah
Huish, Billy Hugo	Elder	20	Arizona
Madsen, Russell J.	Seventy	22	Utah
Pugmire, F. Richard	Elder	21	California
Tolman, Charles Freeman	Seventy	21	Wyoming
Parisi, Salvador	Elder	25	Argentina
Anderson, Keith Phillips	Seventy	20	Utah
Barton, James Richards	Seventy	22	New Mex
Brewerton, Denton Young	Seventy	21	California
Christensen, Dale M.	Seventy	19	Idaho
Edward, John Alexander	Elder	20	Utah
Haley, John Jarvies	Elder	19	Utah
Janson, Lawrence Alma	Elder	20	Texas
Knowlton, Clark Shumway	Seventy	25	Utah
McCullough, Leland Stanford	Elder	19	Utah
Fatheringham, Billie Forrest	Elder	20	Utah
Quealy, Jay Ambros, Jr.	Seventy	22	California
Sorensen, Robert Glissmeyer	Elder	21	Utah

** First served in Brazil

Argentine Mission (Continued)

Name	Priesthood/ Gender	Age	From
1940			
Antoniette, Roberto Pedro	Elder	22	Argentina
Alvarez, Pedro José	Elder	18	Argentina
Burton, Jack	Elder	22	Utah
Jones, Evan	Elder	23	Utah
McCune, Keith Noble	Elder	20	Utah
Banks, Berry Frederick	Elder	20	Utah
Beck, Rex Eugene	Seventy	20	Idaho
Cooley, Edward Jensen	Seventy	19	Maryland
Gunnell, Ruel Jay	Seventy	20	Utah
Davis, Phil Erwin	Seventy	19	Arizona
Ellsworth, William Vaughn	Seventy	20	Arizona
Geslison, Clarence Mathew	Seventy	20	Utah
Radcliffe, Bruce McRae	Seventy	20	Utah
Reed, Junius Joseph	Elder	21	Arizona
Russell, Gardner Hale	Elder	20	Ohio
Sowards, George N.	Seventy	21	Colorado
Adams, Melvin Bigelow	Elder	21	California
Barker, James Louis, Jr.	Elder	20	Utah
Moore, Stanley Alan	Seventy	22	Utah
Smith, George Reynolds	Elder	19	Utah
Amundsen, Eugene Knight	Elder	20	Utah
Middleton, Charles Franklin, Jr.	Seventy	20	California
Scoville, Frank Joseph	Elder	21	Utah
Copen, Floyd Martin, Jr.	Elder	19	Nevada
Jones, Joseph Earl	Seventy	22	Utah
Smith, Joseph Marion	Elder	20	Utah
1941			
Fronk, John Wayne	Seventy	21	Utah
Matthews, Milton Paul	Seventy	21	Utah
Mortensen, Richard H.	Elder	20	Utah
Barton, Sylvester Lorenzo	Seventy	22	Utah
Brewer, Raymond Glen	Seventy	20	California
Christopherson, Robert Guthrie	Seventy	20	California
Dowdle, Harold Lowe	Seventy	21	Idaho
Farr, Norman Ernest	Elder	23	Arizona
Gardner, Dale La Von	Elder	20	California
Gibby, Wendell Albert	Seventy	26	Utah
Halgren, Leon Aldous	Elder	23	California
Harris, Delbert Junior	Elder	21	Utah
Olsen, Eldred Carlyle	Seventy	21	Utah
Jenkins, Ostler Hugo	Elder	20	California
Kerr, George Russell	Elder	22	California

Name	Priesthood/ Gender	Age	From
1941 (Continued)			
Christensen, Gerald Norman	Elder	22	Utah
Christensen, Neil H.	Seventy	20	California
Durrant, William Stanford	Elder	20	Utah
Hughes, Donald Charles	Seventy	20	Utah
Huish, Jack Lamar	Elder	20	Arizona
McKay, Robert Riggs	Seventy	20	Utah
Richey, Rolla Dean	Seventy	20	Arizona
Sessions, Rex	Elder	21	California
Schwendiman, Kay Austin	Seventy	20	Utah
Wale, William Nibley	Elder	20	Utah
Brown, Kendell Erwin	Elder	21	Arizona
McQuarrie, Gerald Hill	Seventy	20	California
Millett, Maurice Robert	Seventy	20	Arizona
Thomas, Grant Ricks	Seventy	20	Idaho
Ellsworth, Eugene	Elder	20	Arizona
Walker, Leon Randmall	Seventy	23	Nevada
Burt, Stanley Andrew	Elder	20	California
Decker, Charles Adams	Elder	18	Utah
Evans, Sears Joseph	Elder	20	Utah
Lunt, Owen Raynal	Seventy	20	Texas
McCarrey, Rulon Squires	Seventy	29	Utah
Pratt, McKay Larsen	Elder	24	California
1942			
Gianfelice, Antonio	Elder	21	Argentina
La Vista, Oscar	Elder	26	Argentina
Barker, James Louis (Mission President)	HP	62	Utah
Barker, Kate Olive Montgomery	Female	61	Utah
1944			
Young, Walter Ernest (Mission President)	HP	57	Mexico
Young, Cecile Skousen	Female	55	Mexico
Young, Joseph Carl	Elder	19	Mexico
Memmott, Fletcher Stowell	Elder	20	Mexico
Call, Charles Harvey	Elder	19	Mexico

Argentine Mission (Continued)

Name	Priesthood/ Gender	Age	From
1945			
Vance, Marion Isaac**	HP	29	Arizona
Vance, Elizabeth DeWitt	Female	26	Arizona
1946			
Shreeve, Lyman Sidney**	HP	31	Arizona
Shreeve, Afton Kartchner	Female	30	Arizona
Marble, Glen Bert	Seventy	21	Idaho
Stott, Edgar Keith	Elder	27	Virginia
Larsen, Gordon Peter	Seventy	23	Utah
Barker, Dell John	Elder	21	Utah
Brammer, Joseph Smith	Seventy	21	Utah
Cluff, Marvin William	Elder	37	Arizona
Carrier, James Charles, Jr.	Seventy	23	California
Oliver, Allen Barnes	Seventy	21	Utah
Yeaman, Sterling Elwin	Seventy	23	California
Davis, Lynn Hamilton	Elder	24	Utah
Hawkins, Jesse Nathanial	Seventy	25	Colorado
Thompson, Keith Fredrick	Elder	21	Utah
Gorton, Henry Clay	Seventy	23	Idaho
Stott, Sterling Stewart	Seventy	22	California
Young, Ronal Theo	Elder	21	Nevada
Hall, Wendell Herbert	Elder	23	Utah
Williams, Owen Blair	Elder	21	Utah
Rigby, Robert Glen	Elder	21	Utah
Black, Harvey Bischoff	Elder	20	Utah
1947			
Wood, Robert William	Elder	21	Utah
Fitzpatrick, Joseph Alan	Seventy	24	Colorado
Hall, Donald Ray	Elder	23	Utah
Haymore, Lester Demarcus	Seventy	23	Utah
Pace, Lorin Nelson	Seventy	22	Utah
Mortensen, Benjamin Franklin	Elder	19	Arizona
Jensen, James Orval	Elder	25	California
Jensen, Minnie Roeine Seamons	Female	23	California
Taylor, Arden Eugene	Elder	27	Utah
Sloan, George Greer	Seventy	24	Arizona
Stott, Leona Pearl H.	Female	27	Virginia
Cole, Carl Robert	Elder	21	Arizona
Anderson, Kent	Elder	20	Idaho
Bangerter, Blauer Lorenzo	Seventy	24	Utah
Brimley, Dale Bradford	Elder	21	Arizona
Bruce, Wallace Thompson	Elder	21	Utah

**Second Mission

Argentine Mission (Continued)

Name	Priesthood/ Gender	Age	From
1947 (Continued)			
Curtis, Brandt B.	Elder	23	Texas
Glade, Harvey Smith	Elder	20	Utah
Jones, Leland Ross	Elder	21	Arizona
Layton, Robert Lynn	Elder	22	Utah
Richards, Lee Gill	Elder	22	Utah
Webb, Robert Arthur	Elder	24	Utah
Barnes, Ralph Raymond	Elder	20	Utah
Hansen, Clyde Wayne	Elder	25	Utah
Latimer, Louis Wallace	Elder	21	Utah
Thomsen, Blaine Clarkson	Elder	20	California
Caroll, Ernest LeRoi, Jr.	Elder	22	Utah
Clark, Richard Ray	Seventy	24	Idaho
Stoddard, Ellwyn Reed	Seventy	20	Utah
Wall, John Ray	Seventy	24	Utah
Jones, Marriner LaRue	Elder	20	Mexico
Romney, Maxel	Elder	22	Mexico
Aston, Lloyd Ray	Elder	21	Utah
Walker, Keith Russell	Seventy	23	Utah
Weight, Kenneth Edward, Jr.	Elder	22	Utah
Yancey, Harold C.		21	Idaho
Cameron, Eugene Grant	Elder	20	Arizona
Fish, Joseph Albert	Elder	21	Arizona
Janson, Charles Curtis	Elder	21	Arizona
Ogden, Rulon Clyde	Elder	23	California
Watson, Robert Conrad	Seventy	21	California
Bramwell, Ernest Craig	Elder	21	Utah
Chamberlain, Cloyd Royal	Elder	21	Utah
Schofield, Keith Bailey	Elder	24	California
Taylor, Dale H.	Elder	21	Utah
Porritt, Budge T.	Elder	21	Idaho
Bowman, Harold Israel	Elder	20	Utah
Hepworth, Jasper David	Seventy	23	Utah
Richardson, Edwin James	Elder	22	New Mexico
Roberts, Louis Clark	Seventy	21	Utah
Smith, Milton Edmund	Elder	20	Utah
Terry, Rex Nelson Mattice	Elder	22	Utah
Wilkes, William LeRoy, Jr.	Elder	24	Oregon
Crosby, John Harris	Elder	21	Arizona
Rich, Parley Lanoon	Seventy	23	California
Smith, David Funk	Elder	20	California
Williams, Fenton Lyle, Jr.	Elder	20	California
Marsh, Howard John	Elder	23	California
Moody, Gordon Bishop	Seventy	21	Utah

Argentine Mission (Continued)

Name	Priesthood/ Gender	Age	From
1947 (Continued)			
Lee, Thomas Wilford	Seventy	21	Utah
Cannon, Russell Anderson	Elder	19	California
Bennett, Bryant Boyd	Elder	19	California
Jones, Lawrence Aaron	Seventy	22	Utah
Costantini, Enriqueta Jacobo Molenmaker de	Female	70	Argentina
Costantini, Luis**	Elder	74	Argentina
Brown, William Robert	Elder	20	California
Wakefield, Leland Kimball	Elder	24	Massachusetts
Jensen, Richard Ernest	Elder	21	Utah
Winsor, Kenneth William	Elder	19	Utah
Gray, Dean William	Seventy	21	Utah
McIntyre, Benjamin Layton	Elder	26	California
Johnson, Lyle Arthur	Elder	21	California
Herrin, Carroll West	Elder	18	California
Reese, Lowell Grant	Elder	21	Utah
Dalton, Gerald Jenkins	Elder	22	Utah
Wilson, Marion Lyman	Elder	22	Washington
1948			
Eldredge, Edgar Ellis	Elder	21	Idaho
Townsend, Clarence Martin	Elder	23	Wyoming
Phelps, Ira Joaquin, Jr.	Elder	22	Utah
Asay, David Harris	Elder	23	Wyoming
Schuck, Roy Kenneth	Seventy	21	Utah
Hale, Robert Lloyd	Seventy	22	Utah
Pace, Thomas Glen	Elder	20	Utah
Crookston, James Albert	Elder	20	Arizona
Bradshaw, Rodney Owens	Elder	23	Arizona
Morgan, Carl Emerson	Seventy	25	Utah
Goodge, Joseph Lee	Elder	21	Colorado
Clark, David Gleave	Seventy	21	Utah
Andrus, Paul Burch	Seventy	23	Utah
Williams, Dwayne A.	Elder	20	Arizona
Anderson, William Edward	Elder	20	California

***Second Mission

Argentine Mission (Continued)

Name	Priesthood/ Gender	Age	From
1949			
Bramwell, Stanley Kent	Elder	20	Utah
Chase, Fred Dunn	Elder	20	Idaho
Hawkins, Ralph Leslie	Elder	25	Colorado
Whitworth, Raymond Francis	Seventy	21	Idaho
Asay, Robert Dix	Elder	22	Wyoming
Dorff, Reginald Ray	Elder	21	Michigan
Knowlden, George Stanton	Elder	20	Utah
Tangren, Loras Burke	Elder	19	Colorado
Robinson, Raymond Morgan	Elder	21	Utah
Hartley, Leonard Lamar	Seventy	21	Idaho
Slade, James Wilford	Elder	21	Colorado
Finch, Curtis Oliver	Seventy	23	California
Brown, Harold (Mission President)	Seventy	31	Mexico
Brown, Leanor Jesperson	Female	31	Mexico
Grimes, Don Marston	Elder	19	Idaho
Bowers, Richard Sanders	Elder	19	Utah
Tyler, Vernon Lynn	Elder	20	California
Rosen, Harold Earl	Elder	20	Utah
Alma, John Burgoyne	Elder	20	Utah
Cannon, Mark Wilcox	Elder	21	Utah
Allen, Eugene Robinson	Elder	20	Arizona
Stephens, Keith Thomas	Seventy	26	Utah
Patterson, Ellsworth Arthur	Elder	20	Arizona
Stevens, Fred Merlin	Elder	20	Idaho
Smith, Kermit H.	Elder	23	Oregon
Wells, Robert Earl	Elder	22	Nevada
Murdock, Paul Bingham	Elder	20	California
Wilden, Fontella	Elder	33	Colorado
Brady, Elvas Lionel, Jr.	Elder	21	Utah
Stone, Ronald Verl	Elder	22	California
Clark, Calvin Edward	Elder	20	Utah
Haws, John Keith	Elder	20	Utah
Waite, Golden J.	Elder	20	Utah
Collier, Wendell	Elder	20	Utah
1950			
Oguegy, Luis Ernesto	Elder	22	Argentina
Avila, Juan Carlos	Elder	22	Argentina
Allred, Byron Harvey	Elder	21	Idaho
Brown, Marvin Earl	Elder	21	Arizona
McMahon, Francis Dean	Elder	23	California
Tucker, Owen Keith	Elder	21	Arizona

Argentine Mission (Continued)

Name	Priesthood/ Gender	Age	From
1950 (Continued)			
Jones, La Var Allred	Elder	20	Arizona
Merryweather, Keith Bullock	Elder	23	Utah
Murdock, Vernon LeRoy	Elder	22	Utah
Neff, Amos Barr	Elder	21	Utah
Mazzuchi, Roy	Elder	19	New Mexico
Johnson, Dean Moroni	Elder	20	Arizona
Bradshaw, Merlin Elmer	Elder	20	California
Fausett, Grant Clayton	Elder	20	Utah
Price, Thomas Daniel	Elder	26	California
Maughan, Scott Jarvis	Elder	21	California
Excell, John Harold	Elder	22	Utah
Wilson, Paul Mauritz	Elder	23	California
Worthen, Robert Kay	Elder	21	Utah
Butterfield, Franklin Herman	Elder	24	Utah
Reese, Robert Arthur	Elder	22	California
Larkin, Glen Garn	Elder	22	Utah
Silotti, Donald Victor	Elder	20	Utah
Coray, Herman Carlson	HP	54	Utah
Gibson, Franklin Kay	Elder	20	Arizona
Jenkins, Jack Edwin	Elder	24	Utah
Whipple, Melvin Reed	Elder	23	Nevada
Gandola, Roberto Hercules	Elder	22	Argentina
Judkins, Newell Kay	Elder	20	Utah
Larsen, Arnold Clarence	Elder	20	Utah
Loveridge, Gary Joseph	Elder	20	Utah
Brown, Catherine Scott	Female	64	Arizona
Pace, James Byrum	Elder	20	Utah
Park, Ivan John	Elder	20	Utah
Foy, Norman Thomas	Elder	20	Utah
Johnson, William Ray	Elder	21	Utah
Killian, James Frank	Elder	19	Utah
Dimter, Lauren Wilfred Hanley	Elder	20	California
Coons, Dix Scott	Elder	20	Arizona
Judd, Floyd Fuller	Elder	20	Arizona
Hymas, Scott Simpson	Elder	20	Idaho
Fielding, Leslie Delray	Elder	19	Idaho
Flitton, Dee W.	Elder	20	Utah
Gillmore, Clinton Harold	Elder	21	California
McLane, Dale Banks	Elder	20	Utah
Zaugg, Waldo Stringham	Elder	20	Oregon
Montgomery, Earl Rex	Elder	20	Utah

MISSIONARIES WHO SERVED IN THE BRAZILIAN MISSION 1935-1950

Compiled from Brazilian Mission Records; Financial and Statistical and Departing Missionaries CR/301, General Missionary Record from Salt Lake City CR/301.22. After 1941, the record of missionaries was taken not from the Brazilian Misson records (which would include any local missionaries), but from the General Missionary Record kept on departing missionaries from Salt Lake City. Hence, any local missionaries called from 1942 to 1950 would not be reflected.

Name	Priesthood/ Gender	Age	From
1935			
Howells, Rulon Stanley (Mission President)	Seventy	33	Utah
Howells, Mary Peirce	Female	30	Utah
Palmer, Merlin Clyde	Elder	23	Idaho
Woodruff, Paul Alma	Seventy	28	Idaho
Rueckert, Harold	Seventy	21	Utah
Smart, Jay Andrew	Seventy	21	Utah
Rudd, Samuel Charles	Elder	18	Utah
Jensen, Milo Andrew	Elder	23	Utah
Kearsley, Irvin Horace	Elder	20	Idaho
Taylor, Vern Gordon	Elder	19	Utah
1936			
Grant, Davis Barton	Elder	20	California
Taylor, George Hal	Elder	20	Utah
Kennard, Leonidas H.	Elder	22	Utah
Wride, Leon Denzil	Seventy	21	Utah
Glauser, Frederick	Seventy	26	Utah
Myler, Esbee Orin	Elder	20	Utah
Rex, Harold Morgan	Seventy	20	Utah
Tippetts, Marion Eugene	Seventy	21	Wyoming
Tippets, Heber Arnold	Seventy	22	Wyoming
Mertlich, Matthias Paul	Seventy	22	Utah
Keate, Earl Norman	Seventy	22	Utah
Cragun, Calvin Gail	Elder	19	California
Knight, Donald Anderson	Elder	20	Utah
Rose, Roger Marion	Elder	19	Minnesota
Muirbrook, Elmer Charles	Seventy	21	California
Burhley, Louis Ernest	Elder	19	Utah
Stevenson, Heber John Richards	Seventy	20	Utah
Zenger, Ray Henry	Seventy	26	Utah

Brazilian Mission (Continued)

Name	Priesthood/ Gender	Age	From
1937			
Reynolds, Leonard La Del	Elder	19	Utah
Butler, Edwin Marsh	Seventy	24	Utah
English, Fred Oliver	Seventy	22	Utah
Lunt, Edward Arcel	Elder	20	New Mexico
Alder, Seth Leon	Seventy	22	Utah
Halladay, Robert Eugene	Elder	20	Utah
Edwards, Luther A.	Seventy	22	Utah
Barton, Harmon Albert	Seventy	23	Utah
Cutler, Robert Keith	Seventy	20	California
Jones, Ralph Harvard	Seventy	19	Utah
Grismore, Richard Glen	Elder	20	Utah
Madsen, Reed Robbins	Seventy	21	Idaho
Gardner, Lucius Levier, Jr.	Seventy	21	Arizona
Imlay, James Edwin	Elder	19	Utah
1938			
Palmer, Parley Eldon	Elder	23	Canada
Hymas, Max Willis	Elder	20	Idaho
Beck, Wayne M.	Elder	21	Utah
Robinson, Howard Whitmore	Seventy	20	Utah
Brooks, Grant LeRoy	Elder	19	Utah
Morris, Melvin Harold	Seventy	21	Utah
Warner, Glen T.	Elder	19	Utah
Faust, Augustus Finlinson	Seventy	19	Utah
Ballstaedt, Emmanuel Heber	Seventy	31	Utah
Erskine, Archibald McFarlane	Elder	20	Utah
Williams, Paul DeLoss	Elder	20	Idaho
Bowers, John Alden (Mission President)	HP	35	Utah
Bowers, Amelia Pettit Wright	Female	37	Utah
Arnold, Orson Pratt	Elder	21	California
Allen, Max Jones	Elder	24	Utah
Conrad, Robert James	Elder	22	Nevada
Cromar, Warren Lynn	Elder	21	Utah
Johnson, Winferd H.	Elder	21	Utah
McDonald, Jack Alex	Elder	21	Utah
Pickett, Theron J.	Elder	20	Idaho
Angerbauer, George James	Elder	20	Idaho
Hymas, Mirl Blake	Elder	20	Idaho
Bybee, Ferrel Wellington	Seventy	22	Utah
Crane, Ray Henry	Elder	20	Utah
Merrell, Paul Rees	Elder	20	Utah
Taylor, Howard Roger	Elder	20	Utah
Turner, J. Willmore	Elder	20	Utah

Name	Priesthood/ Gender	Age	From
1939			
Orme, Jesse Milton	Seventy	22	Idaho
Beck, Edward Creer	Seventy	20	Utah
Shirts, Max LeRoy	Seventy	21	Utah
Bangerter, William Grant	Seventy	20	Utah
Davis, James Douglas	Elder	21	Utah
Christianson, Woodrow Owen	Seventy	26	Utah
Pia, LeRoy Quinten	Elder	20	Utah
Call, Wayne Ephraim	Elder	20	Utah
Yeaman, Cleo Van Noy	Elder	20	Idaho
McKean, Franklin Lane, Jr.	Seventy	20	Utah
Stevenson, Joseph Victor	Elder	19	Utah
Edmunds, David Garth	Elder	21	Utah
Gunn, Ralph Charles	Elder	29	Utah
Freeman, Frank Bott	Seventy	25	Utah
Christensen, Ross Taylor	Seventy	21	Idaho
Jones, Keith Self	Seventy	19	Utah
Faust, James Esdras	Seventy	19	Utah
Phillips, Richard Verne	Seventy	27	Utah
Nelson, Warren Richard	Seventy	27	Utah
Neerings, Theodore John	Elder	20	Utah
Stoddard, Richard Howell	Elder	19	Oregon
Holbrook, Brigham Garn	Elder	22	Utah
Lillywhite, Joel Penrose	Elder	20	Utah
Johnson, Wayne Henrichsen	Seventy	24	Utah
Nixon, Norton Dean	Seventy	23	Utah
Tittensor, Jack Russel	Elder	19	Wyoming
Hicken, Lloyd Rulon	Elder	21	Utah
Bird, Heber Reid	Elder	21	Utah
Naylor, Lawrence W.	Elder	19	Utah
Benson, Theodore Nelson	Seventy	20	Utah
1940			
Blechert, Fredrick Otto, Jr.	Seventy	20	Utah
Sorenson, Lynn Andrew	Seventy	20	Utah
Taylor, Lester P.	Seventy	20	Utah
Stanger, Richard Frank	Elder	21	Idaho
Coltrin, Ira Hugh, Jr.	Seventy	20	Idaho
Briggs, George Barlow	Elder	20	Utah
Asper, James Emerson	Seventy	19	Utah
Miner, Harold Paul	Seventy	22	Utah
Blaser, Glenn Frank	Seventy	20	Utah
Sorensen, Asael Taylor	Elder	22	Idaho

Brazilian Mission (Continued)

Name	Priesthood/ Gender	Age	From
1940 (Continued)			
Johnson, Hal Roscoe	Seventy	20	Idaho
Holt, Joseph S.	Elder	24	Arizona
Doyle, George Gregory III	Elder	19	Arizona
Bradshaw, Floyd D.	Seventy	20	Utah
Kruger, Alma Edmund	Seventy	20	Utah
Tucker, Melvin LeRoy	Seventy	20	Idaho
Packer, Ellis Reed	Seventy	20	Utah
Farr, Lionel M.	Seventy	20	Washington, D.C.
Farr, Harmon E.	Elder	29	California
Bell, Cornelius Charles	Seventy	20	Utah
Harrison, Daniel Bird	Seventy	23	Utah
Koch, John Roy	Seventy	20	Utah
Plewe, David Herman	Seventy	20	Utah
Gardner, Spencer Delos	Seventy	19	Michigan
Forsyth, J. LeGrand	Elder	21	Utah
Erickson, Joseph Glen	Elder	20	Utah
Drechsel, LeRoy Alfred	Elder	20	Utah
Zollinger, Arthur Carl	Seventy	23	Utah
Rich, John Perry	Elder	20	Utah
Porter, Warren Child	Seventy	20	Idaho
Peterson, Reed Lawrence	Seventy	19	Idaho
Olsen, Don J.	Elder	20	Utah
Judd, David Stoddard	Elder	19	Utah
Fisher, Grant A.	Seventy	21	Utah
Johnson, Sheldon Chris	Elder	20	Utah
Duckworth, Raymond B.	Seventy	20	Utah
Austin, Joseph Ray	Elder	20	Utah
Ashworth, Don Ferrin	Seventy	19	Utah
1941			
Duffin, C. Harlow	Elder	21	Utah
Call, Willard B.	Seventy	21	Utah
Boss, Kenneth Rulon	Seventy	23	Utah
Werrett, Gerald P.	Seventy	20	Utah
Silver, LeGrande C.	Elder	22	Utah
Rice, Sargent Grant	Elder	24	Idaho
Platt, Benjamin Richard	Elder	20	Utah
Hunt, Jay Byron	Seventy	20	Utah
Harmon, Paul Lewis	Seventy	21	Utah
Haacke, Rulon B.	Elder	21	Utah
Gibson, M. Carl	Seventy	21	Nevada
Thatcher, Clifton L.	Seventy	19	Utah
Anderson, Lee Reeder	Seventy	21	Utah

Brazilian Mission (Continued)

Name	Priesthood/ Gender	Age	From
1941 (Continued)			
Scott, Robert R.	Seventy	21	Utah
Paulsen, Finn B.	Elder	21	Utah
Andrus, J. Quentin	Elder	21	Utah
Morris, James E.	Seventy	28	Utah
Nelson, Joseph M.	Seventy	20	Utah
Wilson, Dee H.	Seventy	20	Utah
Garrick, Max Carleton	Seventy	20	Utah
Guest, Calvin Warren	Elder	20	Utah
Horne, Gail Bond	Elder	20	Arizona
Madsen, Albert Acomb	Elder	20	Utah
Perschon, Joseph Arthur	Elder	20	Utah
Poetschlag, Harry Ernest	Elder	21	New York
Badger, Briant Garr	Elder	23	Utah
Darger, Stanford Parley	Elder	21	Utah
Haws, Don Porfirio	Elder	20	Arizona
1942			
Seegmiller, William West (Mission President)	HP	66	Utah
Seegmiller, Ada Pratt	Female	61	Utah
1945			
Rex, Harold Morgan (Mission President)	HP	29	Utah
Rex, Diana Haycock	Female	28	Utah
Mertlich, Mathias Paul	HP	22	Not Available
Mertlich, Ruth Evelyn Evans	Female	18	Not Available
1946			
Vaz, Alfredo Lima	Elder		Brazil
Baron, Cecil John	Elder	24	Not Available
Tucker, Grant Cartis	Elder	24	Not Available
Wilson, Warren Joseph	Elder	20	Not Available
Gold, Donald Franklin	Elder	21	Not Available
McCulley, Jessie Lewis	Elder	21	Not Available
Thomas, Bynon David	Seventy	25	Not Available
Bowles, George Hancock	Elder	22	Not Available
Nielsen, Thayle Hansen	Elder	27	Not Available
Turner, Charles Elmo	Elder	22	Not Available
Beck, Evelyn Williams Moon	Female	25	Not Available
Beck, Wayne Moore**	Seventy	29	Not Available
Bailey, Dale S.	Elder	21	Not Available
Jensen, Franklin Ross	Elder	22	Not Available
Maas, Arnold Edgar	Elder	29	Not Available
Smith, Joseph Raymond	Elder	25	Not Available
Wilson, Walter Teddy	Elder	22	Not Available

** Second Mission

Brazilian Mission (Continued)

Name	Priesthood/ Gender	Age	From
1946 (Continued)			
Alius, Johannes Alfred	Elder	21	Not Available
Bowen, Jack Arthur	Elder	22	Not Available
Fowles, Jay Revere	Elder	22	Not Available
Pinegar, Wallace Lynn	Seventy	20	Not Available
Sellers, Richard Kent	Elder	20	Not Available
1947			
Pool, Robert Frame III	Elder	26	Not Available
Clark, Dean Angus	Elder	20	Not Available
Lewis, Joseph William	Elder	21	Not Available
Johnson, Carlotte Renne	Female	20	Not Available
Johnson, Floyd A.	Elder	21	Not Available
Nielson, Marecel L.	Elder	21	Not Available
Walker, Sanford Smith	Elder	20	Not Available
Worsley, Merrill Eugene	Elder	20	Not Available
Bloomquist, Milton Ray	Elder	21	Not Available
Boehm, Walter John	Elder	20	Not Available
Gibson, Robert Emerson	Elder	20	Not Available
Hilton, John Levi	Elder	20	Not Available
Maxwell, Harry John	Elder	22	Not Available
Maxwell, Raymond Wolf	Elder	20	Not Available
Smith, La Verne Emery	Elder	24	Not Available
Tew, Blaine Orson	Elder	20	Not Available
Heath, Joseph Mitchell	Elder	21	Not Available
Jolley, Weldon Bosen	Elder	21	Not Available
Tyler, Kent Brown	Elder	21	Not Available
Lloyd, Harries Ashton	Elder	20	Not Available
Dellenback, Frederick Herman	Elder	20	California
Anderson, Warren Le Grande	Seventy	22	Not Available
Barwick, James Henry, Jr.	Elder	24	Not Available
Benson, Leonard Daniel	Elder	22	Not Available
Boyce, Richard Pender	Elder	19	Not Available
Faust, Rex Finlinson	Elder	24	Not Available
Larson, Daniel Birch	Elder	21	Not Available
Ludwig, Herbert Richard	Seventy	23	Not Available
Stringham, Henry Dunyon	Elder	22	Not Available
Sorensen, Stanford Peter	Elder	23	Not Available

Brazilian Mission (Continued)

Name	Priesthood/ Gender	Age	From
1948			
Kunzler, Hyrum Grant	Seventy	21	Not Available
Little, Gerald Lee	Elder	22	Not Available
Polatis, Lowell Tanner	Elder	21	Not Available
Viehweg, Ross Gordon	Elder	20	Not Available
Boehm, Rolf Johannes	Elder	24	Not Available
Wride, Marion	Elder	20	Not Available
Lee, Boyd Harmon	Elder	21	Not Available
Munck, Albert Juan	Elder	20	Not Available
Hess, Gerald Lawrence	Elder	22	Not Available
Stoll, Rowland Paul	Seventy	21	Not Available
1949			
Jackson, Weston Brice	Elder	21	Not Available
Stoker, Wayde Clark	Elder	20	Not Available
Whitaker, John Hawkley	Elder	20	Not Available
Howells, Mary Peirce	Female	45	Utah
Howells, Rulon Stanley (Mission President)	HP	47	Utah
Crane, Deon May	Female	21	Utah
Horton, Rhea Lucile	Female	32	California
Bushman, Dean Nelson	Elder	20	Not Available
Martin, Elmo Roylance	Elder	25	Not Available
Houston, Joseph Stanley	Elder	20	Not Available
Holden, Joseph Wesley	Elder	24	Not Available
McBride, Kenneth Leon	Elder	21	Not Available
Stevens, Lloyd Jay	Elder	20	Not Available
Taggart, Scott Hinckley	Elder	22	Not Available
Brown, Jack Albert	Elder	20	Not Available
Moon, Clarence Irwin	Elder	20	Not Available
Sant, La Monte	Elder	20	Not Available
Snow, Vernon La Vard	Elder	22	Not Available
Cotant, Richard Kent	Elder	20	Not Available
Leavitt, Lawrence Junior	Elder	21	Not Available
Williamson, Reo L.	Elder	22	Not Available
Goldsmith, Henry Lloyd	Elder	20	Not Available
Slade, Curtis William	Elder	23	Not Available
Smith, Elwyn Lugene	Elder	20	Not Available
Taylor, Stanley Kay	Elder	19	Not Available

Brazilian Mission (Continued)

Name	Priesthood/ Gender	Age	From
1950			
Isfeld, Victor Leo	Elder	21	Not Available
Jorgenson, Glenn A.	Seventy	21	Not Available
Morris, Herbert Newel	Elder	23	Not Available
Rees, John Verl	Elder	24	Not Available
Crawley, James	Elder	21	Not Available
Fowles, Richard Mathews	Elder	20	Not Available
Jensen, Thomas Fenton	Elder	20	Not Available
Thomas, Edward Murray	Elder	28	Not Available
Gledhill, Roy J.	Elder	20	Not Available
Johnson, Louis Orlin, Jr.	Elder	22	Not Available
Lapray, Lyle Edward	Elder	21	Not Available
Young, Dean Arthur	Elder	20	Not Available
Hardcastle, Blaine Hyrum	Elder	20	Not Available
Olsen, Farrel John Jr.	Elder	21	Not Available
Wilcox, Paul Hawkes	Seventy	21	Not Available
Winegar, Wendell Dean	Elder	25	Not Available
Nilsson, Bruce Ray	Elder	27	Not Available
Wood, Herman Kimball	Elder	20	Not Available
Crandall, Horace Dean	Elder	19	Not Available
Lyman, Donald Robinson	Elder	20	Not Available
McClellan, Roy Alvin	Elder	20	Not Available
Ridge, John William	Elder	21	Not Available
Bentley, Craig Burlington	Elder	20	Not Available
Haws, Travis Glenn	Elder	20	Idaho
Momberger, Glenn Lee	Elder	20	Not Available
Taylor, Con Lloyd	Elder	19	Not Available
Anderson, Calvin Reed	Elder	20	Not Available
Fawson, Arlo Dean	Elder	20	Not Available
Nield, De Loyd Minor	Elder	20	Not Available
Waldron, Frederick Glen	Elder	20	Not Available
Miller, George Cottam, Jr.	Elder	20	Not Available
Packer, Doyle Winward	Elder	20	Not Available
Wilson, David Harvey	Elder	21	Not Available
Johnson, Duane Kay	Elder	20	Not Available
McDonald, Ralph George	Elder	20	Not Available
Rasmussen, Rulon Eugen	Elder	20	Not Available
Rhees, Delbert Earl	Elder	20	Not Available
Soderberg, James Rupert	Elder	20	Not Available

MISSIONARIES WHO SERVED IN URUGUAYAN MISSION 1947 - 1950

Compiled from General Mission Record of Missionaries Leaving Salt Lake City Cr/301/22; Uruguayan Mission History. Both courtesy of the Historical Department of The Church of Jesus Christ of Latter-day Saints.

Name	Priesthood/ Gender	Age	From
1947			
Williams, Frederick Salem (Mission President)	HP	39	California
Williams, Corraine Smith	Female	38	California
Janson, Charles Curtis**	Elder	21	Arizona
Sciorra, Juan D.	Elder	Not Available	Argentina
Farnsworth, Wilford Martindale	Elder	24	Mexico
Bushman, Preston J., Jr.	Elder	25	Utah
Jones, William Nathaniel	Elder	21	California
Millett, Loyal Cecil	Elder	19	California
Ogden, Elmer Dene	Elder	20	California
Cox, Donald Burns	Seventy	28	Utah
Dexter, Edward Keith	Elder	25	Utah
Nelson, Robert Naylor	Elder	19	California
Nielson, Gerald LaMar	Elder	20	Utah
Smith, Terry Creager	Elder	20	California
Squire, Lee Oliver	Elder	20	Utah
Janson, Russell Williams	Elder	19	Arizona
Shoemaker, Thaddeus Eugene	Elder	21	Pennsylvania
Richards, Franklin Dewey, Jr.	Elder	20	Maryland
Cook, John Wallace	Elder	21	Idaho
Bushnell, Jewel Fred	Elder	19	Utah
Bigler, Galen Albert	Elder	22	Arizona
Brady, Melvin	Elder	20	Utah
Burton, Stewart Dawson	Elder	19	Utah
Harris, Arvil A.	Elder	20	Utah
Young, Kay Wright	Elder	19	Utah
Smith, Arthur Flint	Elder	19	Idaho

**Served first in Argentina.

Uruguayan Mission (Continued)

Name	Priesthood/ Gender	Age	From
1948			
Argault, Eduarda	Female		Uruguay
Allen, Kenneth Donald	Elder	23	Idaho
Goddard, James Hovey	Seventy	23	Utah
Hurst, Justin Fred	Elder	24	Utah
Schofield, B. Lyle	Elder	22	Idaho
Whitaker, John Orson	Elder	21	Washington
Allen, James Vincent	Elder	20	Idaho
Buttle, Lester Gerald	Elder	20	Utah
Cardon, Wayne Roundy	Elder	21	Utah
Clayton, Robert Earl	Elder	22	Indiana
Hansen, Willard Alton, Jr.	Elder	20	Utah
Howard, Kenneth M.	Elder	21	Idaho
Jacobson, Marvin Le Roy	Elder	20	California
Manning, Glenn Erickson	Elder	24	Utah
Vogler, Elza Juana	Female	Not Available	Argentina
Larsen, Gordon P.**	Seventy	23	Utah
Tyler, Delmar Dean	Elder	22	California
Allen, Gerald Gordon	Elder	20	Utah
Cardon, Joseph Wayne	Elder	33	Texas
Haight, J. Golden	Elder	33	Utah
Koch, Robert Bates	Elder	24	Utah
Marsh, Robert Lee	Elder	26	Utah
Payne, Harold Dale	Elder	21	California
Rock, Delbert H.	Elder	21	California
Slight, Glenn Le Roy	Elder	Not Available	Utah
Stevens, Robert Van	Elder	Not Available	Utah
Bolton, Douglas Earl	Elder	26	Utah
Christensen, Elwin Thorwald	Elder	31	Colorado
Soelberg, Kenneth Burnell	Elder	23	Utah
Wilson, Don Byron	Elder	19	Utah
Dale, James Roger	Elder	21	Utah
Farr, Melvin Miller	Elder	20	Washington, D.C.
Keller, Dallas	Elder	21	Idaho
Morris, Keith J.	Elder	19	Arizona
McGregor, James Young	Elder	19	California
Smith, Gerald Edwin	Elder	20	California
Thomas, John Alfred	Elder	20	Idaho
Wakefield, Sherril Dean	Elder	20	Utah
Williams, Buel La Mar	Elder	21	Arizona
Kresser, Delbert Eugene	Elder	20	Utah
Rhoton, Herman Gardner	Elder	22	Arizona

** Served first in Agentina

Uruguayan Mission (Continued)

Name	Priesthood/ Gender	Age	From
1948 (Continued)			
Sorensen, Alton Harry, Jr.	Elder	19	Utah
Ellsworth, Lloyd Reed	Elder	20	Arizona
Finlinson, Bryce R.	Elder	21	Utah
Marchant, Norman Tippets	Elder	26	Wyoming
Murray, Edward Hubert, Jr.	Elder	23	Florida
1949			
Gianfelice, Juana	Female	23	Argentina
McBride, Paul Don Farell	Elder	21	California
Melander, Vernon Lloyd	Elder	21	Idaho
McArthur, Jacob Earl	Elder	23	Wyoming
Palmer, Byron Cazier	Elder	23	Canada
Gibbons, Edith Mildred Roberts	Female	52	Arizona
Gibbons, Junius	HP	62	Arizona
Berge, John Stark	Elder	22	California
Chapman, Keith Johnson	Elder	21	Utah
Major, Joseph Duane	Elder	20	California
Shumway, Theodore Wallace	Elder	20	California
Anderson, Daryl La Mar	Elder	21	California
Hale, Wilford M.	Elder	20	Idaho
Rigby, Wendell Dean	Elder	22	Utah
Evans, Gordon Robbins	Elder	19	Utah
Graham, Robert William	Seventy	21	Idaho
White, Ellsworth Dovell	Elder	20	California
Taylor, Kenneth William	Elder	20	California
Ralph, Horace Lowell	Elder	20	Utah
Brewerton, Teddy Eugene	Elder	24	Canada
Jesperson, Norval Craig	Elder	20	Arizona
Robison, Roland Grover, Jr.	Elder	20	Utah
Wahlquist, Charles Austin	Seventy	22	Utah
Garrett, Max Harold	Elder	19	Utah
Francis, Howard R.	Elder	20	Utah
Haynie, Paul Jr.	Elder	20	Arizona
McMurdie, Maughan Wadsworth	Elder	21	Utah
Nicolayson, Sheldon Lauried	Elder	19	California
Biggs, Robert Darrel	Elder	20	Arizona
Jennings, Richard Brenton	Elder	19	Utah
Nixon, George Sterling	Elder	20	Utah

Uruguayan Mission (Continued)

Name	Priesthood/ Gender	Age	From
1950			
Jackson, Louis Ramon	Elder	21	California
Heywood, Jared Yates	Elder	21	Arizona
Fitzell, Le Roy Waldo, Jr.	Elder	21	California
Horner, Robert Messenger	Elder	21	Idaho
Evans, La Von	Female	24	Arizona
Day, Mersel Miriam	Female	22	Idaho
Baker, Alfred Henry, Jr.	Elder	22	Arizona
Burnett, Lloyd Calvin	Elder	24	Florida
Stevens, Jack Melvin	Elder	20	Utah
Lund, Roland William	Elder	23	California
Coleman, Norman Kenny	Elder	20	Arizona
Jones, La Voy Teeples	Elder	20	Utah
Selin, Delbert Ferrin	Elder	21	Utah
Rogers, Dwayne Stailey	Elder	22	Arizona
Phelps, Richard Lau	Elder	20	California
Petersen, Almon Lee	Elder	20	Utah
Skinner, Rulon Dean	Elder	19	Arizona
Taylor, James Scott	Elder	20	Utah
Bond, Paul Robert	Elder	20	Maryland
Marshall, Edward Gibbs	Elder	20	Nevada
Alford, Kenneth James	Elder	20	Utah
Smith, Clifford Wayne	Elder	22	Idaho
Gygi, Wayne Vance	Elder	21	Utah
Glissmeyer, Carl Howard	Elder	20	Utah
Homer, John Theurer	Elder	19	Idaho
Phelps, Ray Eugene	Elder	22	Nevada
West, Emerson Roy	Elder	20	Utah
Forsyth, Ward R.	Elder	20	Utah
Clark, Earl Gerber	Elder	19	California
Hollingworth, John Armond	Elder	20	Utah
Moon, Joseph Howard	Elder	20	Idaho
Maughan, Walter Leon	Elder	20	Utah
Pass, Neel Jay	Elder	20	Utah
Petersen, Charles Gerard	Elder	21	Oregon
Sullivan, Harold Lloyd	Elder	22	California
Hackett, Kathryn	Female	23	California
Lundberg, Endfred Jon	Elder	20	California
Scott, Richard Gordon	Elder	22	Washington, D.C.
Josephson, John Cannon	Elder	20	Utah
Hunsaker, Quintin	Elder	20	Oregon
Cahill, Jeremiah Patrick	Elder	20	Utah
Nilsson, Bruce Ray**	Elder	27	Utah

**Served first in Brazil

Uruguayan Mission (Continued)

Technically the list should conclude with 1950; but since our mission continued through July of 1951, it seems appropriate to include the names of those missionaries who began their missions under us.

Name	Priesthood/ Gender	Age	From
1951			
Aguilera, Maria Theresa	Female	Not Available	Uruguay
Vinci, Isidora Yolanda	Female	Not Available	Uruguay
Bennett, Robert L.	Elder	21	Not Available
Elliott, La Don D.	Elder	21	Not Available
Gough, Velora Eva	Female	33	California
Maughan, Roy Hyrum	Elder	21	Not Available
Silver, Edward Moralee	Elder	20	Not Available
Berrett, Frank Edward	Elder	20	Not Available
Christiansen, Richard O.	Elder	20	Not Available
Osmond, George Eugene	Elder	20	Not Available
Allen, Ben Rich	Elder	35	Arizona
Allen, Lois Palmer	Female	33	Arizona
Cardon, Melvin Jonhson	Elder	20	Not Available
Decker, Rey Melvin	Elder	20	Not Available
Hale, Gerald Ardell	Elder	20	Not Available
Parke, Val Kent	Elder	21	Not Available